The Legal Legacy of the Reformation

The growing interest in the relationship between religion and law is, in the case of Christianity, often viewed in monolithic terms. Moreover, the debate is often seen in terms of the relationship of Christianity to the state along with discussions about, for example, religious freedom. Christianity is often seen as responding to claims made on it by the state and by the growth of secularism.

This book takes a different approach. First, it makes the claim that Christianity has something of value to say about various pressing issues which are of direct relevance to contemporary society. Amongst these are the place of human rights and that of individual claims of conscience. Second, it does not regard Christianity as a monolithic whole but takes as its starting point the sundering of Christendom at the Reformation, which, it claims, led in many cases to divergent patterns of thought between Catholics and Protestants about law and its place in society. However, as this book shows, in many cases, Catholic and Protestant thinking on areas such as natural law is not as divergent as it is often thought.

Five hundred years after the Reformation, the work presents a reflection on the roots of Catholic and Protestant thinking on law and its place in society. It will be of interest to canon lawyers as well as academics and students of law and religion.

John Duddington is the editor of *Law and Justice: The Christian Law Review* and a former head of the Law School at Worcester College of Technology.

Law and Religion

The practice of religion by individuals and groups, the rise of religious diversity and the fear of religious extremism raise profound questions for the interaction between law and religion in society. The regulatory systems involved, the religion laws of secular government (national and international) and the religious laws of faith communities are valuable tools for our understanding of the dynamics of mutual accommodation and the analysis and resolution of issues in such areas as religious freedom; discrimination; the autonomy of religious organisations; doctrine, worship and religious symbols; the property and finances of religion; religion, education and public institutions; and religion, marriage and children. In this series, scholars at the forefront of law and religion contribute to the debates in this area. The books in the series are analytical, with a key target audience of scholars and practitioners, including lawyers, religious leaders and others with an interest in this rapidly developing discipline.

Titles in this series include:

Legal Thought and Eastern Orthodox Christianity
The Addresses of Ecumenical Patriarch Bartholomew I
Edited by Norman Doe and Aetios Nikiforos

The Legal Legacy of the Reformation
Catholic and Protestant Approaches to Law
Edited by John Duddington

For more information about this series, please visit: www.routledge.com/Law-and-Religion/book-series/LAWRELIG

The Legal Legacy of the Reformation

Catholic and Protestant Approaches to Law

Edited by John Duddington

Routledge
Taylor & Francis Group
LONDON AND NEW YORK

First published 2025

by Routledge
4 Park Square, Milton Park, Abingdon, Oxon OX14 4RN

and by Routledge
605 Third Avenue, New York, NY 10158

Routledge is an imprint of the Taylor & Francis Group, an informa business

British Library Cataloguing-in-Publication Data
A catalogue record for this book is available from the British Library

ISBN: 978-0-367-20908-7 (hbk)
ISBN: 978-1-032-91279-0 (pbk)
ISBN: 978-0-429-26411-5 (ebk)

DOI: 10.4324/9780429264115

Typeset in Galliard
by Apex CoVantage, LLC

To Anne, Mary and Christopher and also to Walter in memoriam.

Contents

Contributors

Fr. Luke Beckett OSB is a canon lawyer based at Ampleforth Abbey, Yorkshire.

Rev. Dr. Stephen Coleman is Assistant Director at the Centre for Law and Religion in the School of Law and Politics at the University of Cardiff, and an honorary research fellow at St Stephen's House, Oxford.

Dr. Helen Costigane is a lecturer in canon law and a canonical consultant.

Frank Cranmer is an honorary research fellow at the Centre for Law and Religion at the University of Cardiff, and a fellow of St Chad's College at the University of Durham.

Fr. Richard Deadman is a canon lawyer and vicar of St Matthew's Church, Newcastle upon Tyne.

Professor Norman Doe is Director of the Centre for Law and Religion and Professor of Law at the School of Law and Politics, University of Cardiff.

Dr. John Duddington is the editor of *Law and Justice: The Christian Law Review*, a former head of the Law School at Worcester College of Technology and editor of this volume.

Rev. Paul Goodliff is a Baptist theologian, former General Secretary of Churches Together in England and now an associate research fellow and Visiting Tutor in Christian Doctrine and Tutor in Pastoral Supervision at Spurgeon's College.

Dr. Richard Hedlund is a senior lecturer at the Law School, University of Lincoln.

Professor R.H. Helmholz is the Ruth Wyatt Rosenson Professor of Law at the University of Chicago.

Professor David McIlroy is Global Distinguished Professor of Law at the University of Notre Dame (USA) in England and Visiting Professor in Banking Law at Queen Mary University of London.

Professor Russell Sandberg is Professor of Law at the School of Law and Politics, Cardiff University.

Professor Mathias Schmoeckel is Director of the Institute for German and Rhenish Legal History and Civil Law, and the Rhenish Institute for Notarial Law, and is Professor of German and Rhenish Legal History at the Rheinische Friedrich-Wilhelms-Universität, Bonn.

Acknowledgements

The genesis of this book lies in a conference which I, as editor of *Law and Justice: The Christian Law Review*, organised in 2017 to mark the 500th anniversary of the start of the Reformation.[1] At this conference, a number of those whose contributions appear in this volume gave papers, including Prof. Richard Helmholtz, Dr. Helen Costigane, Rev. Paul Goodliff and Prof. David McIlroy. Following the success of the conference it occurred to me that a more permanent memorial of the 500th anniversary might be in order and the result is this book. All of those just mentioned kindly agreed to turn what they had said into chapters. My thanks go to them and also to those others whom I approached and who so willingly agreed to contribute, in particular, Prof. Norman Doe, with whom I had two stimulating meetings at which we discussed how the book might take shape. Although I, as editor, take responsibility for everything in this book, it owes much to Norman's inspiration and continuing scholarly and indeed personal friendship extending now over many years.

It has, once again, been a real pleasure to work with Routledge, to whom those of us who write in this area are so greatly indebted for their interest in publishing scholarship in the area of law and religion, and especially Alison Kirk, Senior Commissioning Editor, and Anna Gallagher, Editorial Assistant for Law.

As ever with all my books my unceasing thanks go also to the members of my family to whom this book is dedicated: my wife Anne, for her wonderful support, loyalty and technical expertise, now extending over very many years without which my books would never begin to be written; my daughter Mary, for her seemingly faultless proofreading and sense of fun which keeps me going; and my son Christopher, for just being himself. Lastly, I cannot forget my late father Walter Duddington, to whom I owe both my own faith and thus my interest in religious matters and also my interest in the law. I hope that his son's work will survive the ever-kindly yet critical and vigilant eye which I am sure he still exercises.

John Duddington

1 I am aware that some may dispute that this was indeed the 500th anniversary but it is the accepted date.

Preface

A book with the title *The Legal Legacy of the Reformation: Catholic and Protestant Approaches to Law* may, to some, require justification. Surely the Reformation was above all a religious movement and not a legal one? Whilst this is undoubtedly true, it is also true that the Reformation had profound legal consequences. As Norman Doe remarks in his introductory chapter '*A Comparative Account of Protestant and Catholic Approaches to Church Law*': 'theology may shape law and law may realise theological propositions in norms of conduct and behaviour; and church laws should conform to the law of God, as revealed in Holy Scripture and by the Holy Spirit'. Thus, this book does not look both ways, at both law and theology, but as it were with one single bifocal lens, seeking to bring within one vision both the theology of the Reformation and its effect on both the nature of law and its actual content.

This topic has, of course, been examined before, but in slightly different ways. John Witte's study *Law and Protestantism: The Legal Teachings of the Lutheran Reformation*[2] is a classic survey which is now the standard work in this area and illuminates not only Lutheran legal teachings but much else besides. It has proved inspirational in the editing of this book. No less valuable are the two volumes of Harold Berman *Law and Revolution I: The Formation of the Western Legal Tradition*[3] and *Law and Revolution II: The Impact of the Protestant Reformations on the Western Legal Tradition*.[4] Another resource has been the collection of essays in *Law and Religion: The Legal Teachings of the Protestant and Catholic Reformations*,[5] which assesses the similarities and differences between the legal writings of the Catholic and Protestant reformers of the early modern period. Specific areas have also been subject to scholarly investigation, such as in *Canon Law in Protestant Lands*.[6]

2 CUP 2002.
3 Harvard University Press 1990.
4 Harvard University Press 2003.
5 Edited by Wim Decock, Jordan J Ballor, Michael Germann and L Waelkens, *Law and Religion: The Legal Teachings of the Protestant and Catholic Reformations* (Vandenhoeck & Ruprecht 2014).
6 Edited by RH Helmholz, *Canon Law in Protestant Lands* (Duncker & Humblot 1992).

Where this book seeks to break new ground is in its examination in one volume of both the more theoretical issues such as natural law and the place of conscience and, then, especially in the last section, the impact of the Reformation on particular areas such as marriage law, education law and criminal law as well as the important topic of human rights. Canon law is given special treatment by Professor Helmholtz in Chapter 3, as well as in other chapters, and the effect of the Reformation on church-state relationships is a continuing theme.

If the book has a message then it is this: 500 years after it occurred the sundering of Christendom at the Reformation still resonates in the law but equally the Reformation was not an isolated event. It was the product of forces in society that were present before Martin Luther nailed his theses to the church door at Wittenberg and to this extent the Reformation did not create change in all cases but instead recognised new forces at work in society and at times accelerated changes which, had the Reformation not occurred, might well have come about anyway. It is the task of this book to sift through all these developments and, it is hoped, to shed new light on them.

John Duddington

Part One

Church Law and the Reformation

The connecting thread of the chapters in this part is church law and how, if at all, it was affected by the Reformation. In Chapter 1 Norman Doe gives an overview of Protestant and Catholic approaches to church law and, from a contemporary perspective, argues that the *Statement of Principles of Christian Law* (2016) shows profound similarities between the juridical understandings of the nature and objects of the churches, both Protestant and Catholic. In Chapter 2 Frank Cranmer explores how both ecclesiastical and secular law were shaped by the Reformations not only in England but also in Scotland. He notes that the breach was more profound in Scotland than in England, but even here some of the basic principles of Western canon law persisted. Then, in Chapter 3, R.H. Helmholz examines the persistence of mediaeval canon law after the Reformation and argues that the commonly held view that the Reformation brought with it a rejection of the medieval canon law is in fact wrong. Instead, much the larger part of medieval canon law remained in force in both Protestant and Catholic lands.

DOI: 10.4324/9780429264115-1

1 A Comparative Account of Protestant and Catholic Approaches to Church Law

Law in the Life of the Visible Church

Norman Doe

Introduction

This chapter compares the contemporary approaches of the Protestant and Catholic traditions to law and their use of regulatory instruments to facilitate and order the lives of their churches as these have emerged as a result of the Reformation of the sixteenth century and beyond.[1] What follows studies the canon law of the Latin (or Roman) Catholic Church and the regulatory instruments of the following broadly Protestant ecclesial traditions: Anglican, Lutheran, Reformed, Presbyterian, Congregational and Baptist. For each tradition, laws regulate a wide range of matters in the institutional lives of churches, including ministry and government, doctrine and worship, rites of passage, property and relations with the state. What follows examines a selection of these matters, namely: the nature and objects of a church; the sources, forms, effects and purposes of its laws; the faithful; ordained ministers; church governance; and doctrine and worship. These laws are examined here in the wider context of what the Catholic and Protestant churches share juridically in the form of the *Statement of Principles of Christian Law* issued in Rome in 2016 by an ecumenical panel of jurists and theologians and which was launched at the 11th Assembly of the World Council of Churches, in Germany, in 2022.[2]

The Nature and Objects of a Church

Whereas the Latin Church is organised on a global basis, within the Protestant traditions, each church is generally ordered on a national, regional or local

1 That Protestant churches are today prolific legislators is perhaps ironic in light of Martin Luther famously protesting against Rome by burning the books of papal canon law in 1520 at Wittenburg. However, this chapter does not deal with the rich history of Protestant church laws, for which, see e.g. J Witte, Jr. *Law and Protestantism; The Legal Teachings of the Lutheran Reformation* (CUP 2002).

2 Panel members were from Anglican, Lutheran, Methodist, Reformed, Presbyterian, Baptist, Pentecostal, United, Roman and Eastern Catholic and the Eastern Orthodox churches. For the project and the *Statement*, see N Doe (ed), *Church Laws and Ecumenism: A New Path for Christian Unity* (Routledge 2021).

DOI: 10.4324/9780429264115-2

level, rather than internationally, though it may also belong to an international community within which it retains its autonomy.

The Roman Catholic Church (a global or 'universal' church in which 'subsists' the 'church universal') is 'established and ordered in this world as a society' which exists for 'the salvation of souls', 'to preach the Gospel to all people' and 'proclaim moral principles', to worship and administer the sacraments and to govern the faithful. An autonomous Anglican Church is a member of the worldwide Anglican Communion, each church in communion with the See of Canterbury, and asserts its place in the 'church universal'; it exists 'to minister the doctrine and sacraments and discipline of Christ', to respond to human needs and to establish 'the values of the Kingdom'. A Lutheran Church is a national or local association shaped by authoritative Reformation texts and its 'biblical foundations'; as 'part of the whole Church of Christ', its objects include to 'declare the teachings of the prophets and apostles and seek to confess in our time the faith' and to engage in 'worship and Christian service'; and it may also belong to the Lutheran World Federation. Similarly, a Methodist Church defines itself by its place in the church universal and World Methodist Council. Likewise, a Reformed, Presbyterian and Congregational church (which may belong to the World Communion of Reformed Churches) asserts: its place in the church universal, its Reformation doctrinal inheritance, its autonomy and its purposes, for example preaching the Gospel, worshipping and offering pastoral care. And within the Baptist World Alliance, Baptist Unions, Conventions and churches have the same outlook.[3]

The profound similarities between these juridical understandings of the nature and objects of each church are summed up in the *Statement of Principles of Christian Law*. A church as an institution may define itself by its autonomy, polity and objects. A church is a community which may be international, national, regional or local. It has a distinct body of persons associated with it. It is autonomous in its system of governance and it has among its objects the mission of Christ: proclaiming the Gospel, administering rites and serving wider society.[4]

The Sources, Forms, Effects and Purposes of Regulation

The Latin Church and the Protestant churches studied here share much in terms of the sources, forms, effects and purposes of their laws. For the Roman Catholic Church, 'the highest norm of human life is the divine law

3 These quotations are from *Codex Iuris Canonici* (CIC) (Code of Canon Law 1983 (of the Latin Church)), Bks. II–IV; *The Principles of Canon Law Common to the Churches of the Anglican Communion* (2022) (hereafter PCLCCAC); Evangelical Lutheran Church in America (ELCA), *Constitution and Foundational Texts*; Methodist Church in Great Britain (MCGB), *Constitutional Practice and Discipline*; Presbyterian Church of Wales (PCW), *Handbook of Rules*; and Baptist Union of Great Britain (BUGB), *Constitution*.

4 *Statement of Principles of Christian Law* (2016) (hereafter SPCL), I.1.

itself—eternal, objective and universal' and ascertained by the teaching of the church; and its Code of Canon Law (1983) often presents canons as derived from divine law. The Code is 'universal law' and binds all the faithful and 'particular laws', for example those of an Episcopal Conference bind locally. For Catholics, canon law 'facilitates . . . an orderly development in the life of both the ecclesial society and of the individual persons who belong to it'; indeed, canon law itself teaches that the 'salvation of souls [is] the supreme law'.[5]

Among Protestant traditions, Anglicans recognise that church 'Law should reflect the revealed will of God'; and their laws—'constitutions' and 'canons'—present Scripture as the ultimate standard and rule in matters of faith. Similarly, Lutherans recognise 'the Holy Scriptures . . . as the only infallible source and norm for all matters of faith, doctrine and life'; and they have 'church laws', 'constitutions', 'bylaws', doctrinal texts, 'ecclesiastical practices and customs' and 'guidance'. Methodists recognise 'God's Law'; see Holy Scripture as the record of divine revelation; and have 'Law' in a 'Constitution', 'Book of Discipline' or 'Manual of Law'.[6] And for Reformed and Presbyterian churches, 'the Word of God' is the supreme 'rule of faith and life', and their juridical instruments include 'law', a 'code', a 'book of church order' or a 'book of order' with 'legislation', a constitution, and normative doctrinal or confessional texts. Churches may also have a model constitution for a local church and regulate with soft law.[7]

In turn, Baptists recognise that Christ is 'the sole and absolute authority in all matters pertaining to faith and practice', and 'each Church has liberty, under the guidance of the Holy Spirit, to interpret and administer His Laws'; moreover, their norms recognise the authority of Holy Scripture as a revelation of God, and that the Holy Bible is part of 'the constitutions and laws' of a Convention or is 'the rule of church law'. A national Baptist Union or Convention normally has a 'constitution', with 'laws', and, sometimes, bylaws, as well as normative doctrinal standards (e.g. a Confession of Faith), guidelines,

5 CIC: cc. 1, 11–12, 19, 24, 207–223, 331, 1249, 1752. *Sacrae disciplinae leges* (1983), the Apostolic Constitution by which the Code was promulgated.

6 PCLCCAC; Lutheran Church of Australia (LCA), *Constitution*; Lutheran Church—Missouri Synod (LCMS), *Constitution* and *Bylaws*; Evangelical Lutheran Church of Southern Africa (ELCSA), *Guidelines*; Lutheran Church in Great Britain (LCGB), *Constitution* and *Rules and Regulations*; North American Lutheran Church (NALC), *Standards for Pastoral Ministry*; Free Methodist Church of North America (FMCNA), *Book of Discipline*; MCGB, *Constitutional Practice and Discipline*; Methodist Church in Ireland (MCI), *Constitution*; United Methodist Church in Northern Europe and Eurasia (UMCNEAE), *Book of Discipline*; Methodist Church of New Zealand, *Laws and Regulations*.

7 Presbyterian Church in Ireland (PCI), *Code*; Presbyterian Church of Aotearoa New Zealand (PACNZ), *Book of Order*; Presbyterian Church in America (PCA), *Book of Church Order*; JL Weatherhead (ed), *The Constitution and Laws of the Church of Scotland* (Board of Practice and Procedure 1997, hereafter CLCS); *Manual of Practice and Procedure in the United Free Church of Scotland*; *The Book of Church Order of the Reformed Church in America*; United Reformed Church, Great Britain (URC), *Model Constitution for Local Churches*.

policies, and codes. Within a Union or Convention, a regional association of local Baptist churches may have a constitution, and a local church has a constitution, trust instrument, members' 'covenant' and doctrinal texts.[8]

Protestants also provide for compliance with their laws. For example, within Presbyterianism: 'All members of congregations and any other person affected by any provision in the Book of Order must comply with the Book of Order'; Methodists require adherence to their 'laws and usages', Articles of Religion and 'guidelines'; and Baptists, 'strict adherence' to their 'rules'.[9]

As to the purposes of church law, Lutheran laws 'provide necessary organizational principles, structures, and policies for good order', which 'guide, direct, and assist [the church] in mission and ministry'. One Methodist Book of Discipline 'reflects our understanding of the Church and articulates [its] mission to make disciples of Jesus Christ for the transformation of the world'; it 'defines what is expected of [the] laity and clergy as they seek to be effective witnesses in the world as part of the whole body of Christ'; and it sets out the 'theological grounding of the [church] in biblical faith'. Rules of the Presbyterian Church of Wales seek 'to safeguard the unity of the Church, and to secure uniformity in the procedures of its courts'. Likewise, in the Baptist Union of Great Britain, a local Baptist church constitution seeks to 'govern', 'regulate' and 'enable' church life; and, for example, that of Riverside Baptist Church (Baltimore) is designed 'for the purpose of preserving and making secure the principles of our faith' so that 'this body be governed in an orderly manner'; 'for . . . preserving the liberties inherent in each individual member of the church'; and, for the presenting of 'this body to other bodies of the same faith'.[10]

The principles of Christian law reflect these approaches. First, laws are found in a variety of sources, including codes of canon law, charters and statutes, constitutions and bylaws, and books of church order. Customs may have juridical force to the extent permitted by church law. Ecclesiastical quasi-legislation (or soft law), such as guidelines and codes of practice, is designed to complement the formal laws of churches and consists of rules that may be prescriptive in form and also generate an expectation of compliance; and 'Church laws should conform to the law of God, as revealed in Holy Scripture and by the Holy Spirit'. Second, with respect to law as 'servant', church law exists to serve a

8 Baptist Union of Great Britain (BUGB), *Constitution*; Bethel Baptist Church (Choctaw, USA), *Constitution*; National Baptist Convention—USA (NBC-USA), *Constitution*; American Baptist Churches in the USA (ABC-USA), *Bylaws*; Canadian National Baptist Convention (CNBC), *Constitution*; Riverside Baptist Church (Baltimore, USA), *Constitution and Bylaws*; Jamaica Baptist Union (JBU), *Constitution*; Baptist Union of Southern Africa (BUSA), *Model Constitution for Local Churches*; BUGB, *Model Trusts*.

9 PCANZ, *Book of Order*; MCNZ, *Laws and Regulations*; UMCNEAE, *Book of Discipline*; JBU, *Constitution*.

10 Evangelical Lutheran Church in Canada (ELCIC), *Constitution*; UMCNEAE, *Book of Discipline*; PCW, *Handbook of Rules*; BUGB, *Model Trusts*; Riverside Baptist Church (Baltimore), *Constitution*.

church in its mission and in its witness to the salvific work of Christ; laws contribute to constituting the institutional organisation of a church and facilitate and order its activities; theology may shape law and law may realise theological propositions in norms of conduct and behaviour; and church laws should conform to the law of God, as revealed in Holy Scripture and by the Holy Spirit. Third, as to scope, structure and effect, the laws of churches deal principally with ministry, government, doctrine, worship, rites, admonition and discipline, and property; consist of various juridical formulae (e.g. precepts, prohibitions and permissions); may be cast as rules, rights and duties, functions and powers; and may be binding or exhortatory. Moreover, all members of a church are subject to its laws, to the extent that the law provides. Later laws may abrogate earlier laws. Laws should be prospective (not retrospective unless this is clearly provided for in them), as well as clear, stable and coherent. Also, a church may have a mechanism for the enforcement of its law.[11]

The Faithful

Catholics and Protestants have much in common legally with regard to the faithful. Roman Catholic canon law is particularly well-developed. First, Christ's faithful (*christifideles*) are 'incorporated into the Church of Christ through baptism'. The faithful constitute the 'people of God' and each 'participates in their own way in the priestly, prophetic and kingly office of Christ'; moreover, each is called according to his/her own condition 'to exercise the mission which God entrusted to the Church to fulfil in the world'. However, by 'divine institution, among Christ's faithful there are in the Church sacred ministers, who are in law also called clerics; the others . . . lay people'. Further, by virtue of baptism all Christ's faithful (lay and ordained) enjoy in the church 'a genuine equality of dignity and action' to contribute 'each according to his or her own condition and office, to the building up of the Body of Christ'.[12] A baptised non-Catholic may be 'received into' the Catholic Church on accepting full communion. Also, after lapse of a suitable period, 'persons who have manifested a willingness to embrace the faith in Christ are to be admitted to the catechumenate in liturgical ceremonies'; and '[t]hrough instruction and an apprenticeship in the Christian life catechumens are suitably to be initiated into the mystery of salvation and introduced to the life of faith, liturgy, charity of the people of God and the apostolate'; neophytes are instructed in the gospel and baptism.[13]

Second, whilst 'member' is not generally used, baptised persons 'are in full communion with the catholic Church here on earth who are joined with Christ in his visible body, through the bonds of profession of faith, the sacraments

11 SPCL (2016) I.2–4.

12 CIC: cc. 204, 207, 208; see also CCC, pars. 871–73.

13 CIC: cc. 11, 788: and their names are registered; c. 789: neophytes are instructed in the faith.

and ecclesiastical governance'.[14] At the local level, a parish is a 'community of Christ's faithful established within a particular church'. The parish priest must record in the register of baptism the names of baptised persons, the date and place of their birth, and the date and place of the baptism; there are also confirmation registers.[15]

Third, Roman Catholic canon law distinguishes the duties and rights of all the faithful, lay and ordained, as well as those specifically applicable to the laity. When incorporated by baptism into the Church of Christ, each of the faithful has 'such duties and rights which, in accordance with each one's status, are proper to Christians, in so far as they are in ecclesiastical communion and unless a lawfully issued sanction intervenes'.[16] The duties of all the faithful include: to preserve communion with the church, to lead a holy life, to show Christian obedience to what sacred pastors (who represent Christ) declare as teachers of the faith and rulers of the church, to provide for the needs of the church and to promote social justice; their rights include: to make known their needs and wishes to the pastors, to be assisted by their pastors, to worship God, to establish and direct associations (for e.g. charitable purposes), to have access to a Christian education and to vindicate and defend their own rights.[17] The laity have specific obligations and rights: to strive so that the divine message may be known throughout the world, to permeate the temporal order with the spirit of the gospel, to build up the people of God through marriage and the family and to acquire knowledge of and proclaim Christian teaching; they are also capable of admission to prescribed ecclesiastical offices.[18] These duties and rights derive from the fundamental dignity of the individual as a human person and as such are inalienable and inviolable.[19] Moreover, '[i]n exercising their rights, [the] faithful, both individually and in association, must take account of the common good of the church, as well as the rights of others and their own duties to others': the appropriate ecclesiastical authority is entitled 'to regulate, in view of the common good, the exercise of rights which are proper to Christ's faithful'.[20] All the faithful are subject to church

14 CIC: c. 205.

15 CIC: cc. 515, 877; see also c. 895: those baptised persons who have been confirmed are to be recorded in the confirmation register of the diocesan curia or when prescribed by the Bishops' Conference or the diocesan bishop in the register to be kept in the parish archive.

16 CIC: c. 96; a person has duties and rights: as well as the laity (cc. 224–231), there are those attaching to e.g. clergy (cc. 273–289), religious (cc. 662–672), married couples and parents (cc. 1135–1136).

17 CIC: cc. 208–223: 'obligations and rights of all the faithful'; sometimes, a duty and a right coincide: e.g. c. 211: 'All the Christian faithful have the obligation (*officium*) and the right (*ius*) to strive so that the divine message of salvation may . . . reach all people of all times and all places'.

18 CIC: cc. 224–231: the 'obligations and rights of the lay members of Christ's faithful'.

19 CIC: c. 208.

20 CIC: c. 223. The exercise of conscience is important here: CCC, pars. 1776–1802.

discipline—and provision is made for apostasy and 'the total repudiation of the Christian faith' as well as for excommunication.[21]

Similar rules are found in the laws of Protestants. For Anglicans: 'the *laos* is the whole people of God, but for the purposes of law, a lay person is a person who is not in holy orders'.[22] Unlike Catholics, Anglicans use the concept of church 'member'. Whilst a church 'should serve all who seek its ministry, membership in a church' may be based on any or all of: baptism; baptism and confirmation; baptism, confirmation and communicant status; or regular attendance at public worship. In turn, there are various classes of member: a communicant is a person who has received Holy Communion at such frequency and on such occasions as may be set by law; and a communicant in good standing is a communicant who for a prescribed period has been faithful in worship and has supported the work and mission of the church. Names may be entered on a parish roll or other membership register, subject to conditions prescribed by law, enabling eligibility for selection to participate in governance and other functions and offices; but names may be removed from the roll only in accordance with the law, justice and equity. Membership implicitly involves profession of the faith; acceptance of doctrine, government, law and discipline; and enjoyment of fundamental and other rights and duties of the faithful.[23]

Echoing the Lutheran norm that the 'people of God' embrace 'the priesthood of all believers', the Methodist Church in Ireland provides that 'every member of the Church is equal in spiritual privilege, has the same access to God through Christ, and is charged with the duty of establishing His Kingdom upon earth'—'this spiritual equality . . . has led to the recognition of laypersons as being of an equal status with ministers in all the Courts of the Church'. A local Baptist church may present the congregation as a manifestation of the Body of Christ, with 'members' and 'ministers' or else 'members' and 'ordained ministers'.[24] As to formal church membership, Lutheran norms are typical: a voting member is a baptised person aged 18 or over who has publicly confessed the faith after instruction in church teaching and is received into congregation membership by its council. Reformed, Presbyterian, and Baptist churches have similar conditions for admission to the church fellowship, and these normally include a mature profession of the faith and acceptance of church doctrine and discipline; for instance, the United Reformed Church admits persons if assured of 'the sincerity of their intention' and

21 CIC: c. 11: canon law binds those baptised or received into the church who enjoy the sufficient use of reason and have completed 7 years of age; for discipline, see cc. 1311, 1321–1323, 1341; c. 751: apostasy.

22 PCLCCAC, Principle 25.1.

23 PCLCCAC: Principle 27.

24 LCA, *The Ministry of the People of God, Commission on Theology and Inter-Church Relations* and *Constitution*; MCI, *Constitution*; BUGB, *Baptists in Local Ecumenical Partnerships*.

'adequate preparation', and on 'public profession of the faith and commitment to the Church'.[25]

With regard to discipleship, in Anglicanism, all the faithful, lay and ordained are responsible for church life and witness, and should regularly attend public worship, especially at Holy Communion; practise daily devotion, private prayer, Bible reading and self-discipline; bring the teaching and example of Christ into everyday life; uphold Christian values; be of personal service to church and community; and assist the church financially. Two types of right are envisioned: inherent rights and acquired rights:

> all persons, equal in dignity before God, have inherent rights and duties inseparable from their dignity as human beings created in the image and likeness of God and called to salvation through Jesus Christ; however, baptism is the foundation of Christian rights and duties, and a church should respect both sets of rights and duties.

Also, all the faithful enjoy such rights to government, ministry, teaching, worship, sacraments, rites and property as may flow from their human dignity, baptism, the duties of others 'and the law of that church'; indeed, there is to be no unlawful denial of equal rights, status or access to the life, membership, government, ministry, worship, rites and property of a church on grounds of race, colour, ethnic, tribal or national origin, marital status, sex, sexual orientation, disability or age.[26] All the faithful, as appropriate to their state, participate in teaching, governing and sanctifying; lay persons exercise authority in church in governance according to law, and are subject to discipline to the extent and in the manner set by law.[27]

Moving along the Protestant spectrum, Lutherans must, typically: 'make regular use of the means of grace, both Word and Sacraments'; 'live a Christian life in accordance with the Word of God'; 'support the work of the congregation'; 'lead godly lives'; 'proclaim the Gospel and renounce the evil one'; present their children for baptism; and if qualified they may participate in the governance of the church. Reformed, Presbyterian and Baptist churches are similar; members have 'rights' or 'privileges' and 'responsibilities' or 'obligations' to: attend meetings, provide help to each other, respect their ministers, receive baptism for their children, participate in Holy Communion, stand for election to church assemblies, engage in worship, study Scripture, proclaim the Gospel, lead a life consistent with the faith and accept discipline.[28]

25 LCGB, *Rules and Regulations*; URC, *Manual*; PCW, *Handbook of Rules*; Riverside Baptist Church (Baltimore, USA), *Bylaws*.

26 PCLCCAC: Principle 26.

27 PCLCCAC: Principle 25.1.

28 PCLCCAC; ELCA, *Model Constitution for Congregations*; MCI, *Regulations, Discipline and Government*; URC, *Manual*; PCW, *Handbook*; PCANZ, *Book of Order*; Central Baptist Church (Pretoria), *Constitution*.

Protestant laws also deal with the termination of membership. The Methodist Church in Ireland is typical: as well as termination on their death or resignation,

> a member, who in the judgment of the Church Council, has persistently failed to fulfil the Obligations of Membership, despite being reminded of these obligations, shall be regarded as having withdrawn from membership of the church and their name shall be removed from the Membership Register.[29]

All of these laws of Catholics and Protestants generate common principles of Christian law. In Christianity, 'Baptism constitutes the incorporation of a person into the Church of Christ'.[30] Some historic churches expressly use in their legal instruments the category church 'member', others do not. Yet, each church has an identifiable group of the faithful associated with it. The Christian faithful constitute the people of God. All the faithful should be equal in dignity. Baptism generates duties and rights for the faithful. The faithful includes lay and ordained people.[31] As to 'church membership' and other forms of belonging, a church is made up of those incorporated into it in accordance with its proper laws and customs. However, a church should serve, in appropriate ways, all who seek its ministry regardless of membership. Membership in a church, for the purposes of participation in its government, may be based on any of all of: baptism, baptism and confirmation or other mature demonstration of faith, and such other conditions as may be prescribed by law. The names of persons belonging to a church may be entered on one or more rolls or other registers of membership subject to such conditions as may be prescribed by law. Names may be removed from these in accordance with the law.[32] Whilst, theologically, the life of the faithful is governed by grace and the Holy Spirit, a church should generally set out the basic rights and duties of all its members. The laity should promote the mission of the church, and bear witness to the Christian faith through their lives in the world. A lay person should engage in the collective ecclesial life, in proclaiming the Word of God, participating in worship, and receiving the sacraments. Lay persons should maintain such Christian standards in their private lives as are prescribed by law, and are encouraged to practise daily devotion, private prayer, Bible reading and self-discipline, bringing the teaching and example of Christ into everyday life, upholding Christian values, and being of service to both the church and the wider community, and may exercise public ministry when allowed by law.[33]

29 MCI, *Regulations, Discipline and Government.*
30 SPCL (2016) VII.1.3.
31 SPCL (2016) II.1.1–4.
32 SPCL (2016) II.2.1–4.
33 SPCL (2016) II.3–4: see Chapter 3 in this volume.

Ordained Ministry

Historically, the effect of ordination in terms of the status, character and sacerdotal authority of ministers, and their hierarchical ranking as priests, bishops and the like, were the focus of much disagreement at and beyond the Reformation—and disagreements about the recognition of ordinations as between the separate churches continue to challenge ecumenism.[34] However, Catholics and Protestants both have laws on ordination and the functions of ordained ministers.

For the Roman Catholic Church ordination is a sacrament:

> By divine institution some among Christ's faithful are, through the sacrament of order, marked with an indelible character and are thus constituted sacred ministers; thereby they are consecrated and deputed so that, each according to his own grade, they fulfil, in the person of Christ the Head, the offices of teaching, sanctifying and ruling, and so they nourish the people of God;

the orders are the episcopate, the priesthood and the diaconate.[35] The Church has the duty and right to train persons for sacred ministries and the whole Christian community must foster vocations. Only men are ordained; a candidate must complete the required probation, possess the requisite qualities and be free of any irregularity or impediment—there is no right to ordination. The minimum interval between diaconate and priesthood is six months, and the right to determine the suitability for ordination rests with the bishop. Baptism and confirmation are required, as are sound faith, the right intention, requisite knowledge, a good reputation, moral probity, proven virtue and the physical and psychological qualities appropriate to the order received. The age for ordination is 25 for the priesthood and 23 for the diaconate. Marriage is an impediment to ordination, but there are exceptions. A deacon must make a profession of faith and take the oath of fidelity to the Pontiff. Ordinarily, ordination is celebrated during Mass. The minister is a consecrated bishop. Orders are conferred by the laying-on of hands and the prayer of consecration which the liturgical books prescribe for each grade; it is wrong to compel a man to receive orders.[36]

Turning to Protestantism, like Anglicans, Lutheran and Methodist ordained ministers engage in 'holy ministry', 'the gift of Christ to the church'—'the church does not create the office of the public ministry, but it does call and ordain persons into that office' who are 'qualified by personal qualities, gifts and training'. Moreover, in the laws operative in the Reformed tradition, ordained

34 See N Doe, *Christian Law* (CUP 2013) Ch. 3.

35 CIC: cc. 1008–1009; c. 207: clerics; c. 266: by admission to the diaconate, a person becomes a cleric.

36 CIC: cc. 1008–1054.

ministers, elders and deacons 'represent Christ'; and for Presbyterians, typically, Christ, 'for the edification of the visible Church . . . has appointed officers not only to preach the Gospel and administer the Sacraments, but also to exercise discipline for the preservation both of truth and duty'. Some Baptists practise 'ordination', whilst others do not.[37]

With regard to ordination, for Anglicans, no person is to be ordained a priest or deacon unless 'called, tried, examined and admitted according to the rite of ordination' effected through the imposition of hands by a bishop; orders are indelible. In Lutheranism, typically, '[b]y the rite of ordination the church sets a person apart' for ministry. In Presbyterianism, candidates must have an 'unimpeachable character', 'a deep experience of the truth of the Gospel', a vocation, 'the calling of God by the Spirit, through the inward testimony of a good conscience, the manifest approbation of God's people, and the concurring judgment of a lawful court of the Church'; a minister at ordination 'is set apart'. Churches also have norms on the appointment or election of ordained ministers to various ministry posts, tenure and termination of ministry.[38]

These shared legal norms are summed up in the principles of Christian law. The Catholic and Protestant churches designate persons for ministry in a special rite, for most called ordination. Ordained ministry is divine in origin and persons are set apart for it. A church may distinguish between different types of ordained ministers. Candidates for ordination must be called by God and by the church to ordained ministry. Vocation to and suitability for ordination are tested by the church through a process of selection, examination and training by competent authority. Persons are generally admitted to ordained ministry through ordination, which is administered by competent authority by means of the laying-on of hands and invocation of the Holy Spirit.[39]

Next, the functions of ordained ministers. Roman Catholic canon law provides a set of duties and rights applicable to all clerics, as well as specific functions applicable to parish clergy. First, since they all work to build up the body of Christ, clerics are united 'in the bond of brotherhood and prayer' and must 'seek to cooperate with one another', promote the mission of the laity, and show reverence and obedience to the Supreme Pontiff and their own Ordinary.[40] All clerics must seek holiness in their lives; fulfil their pastoral ministry; nourish their own spiritual life with Scripture, Eucharist, prayer and spiritual retreats; observe 'perfect and perpetual continence' and celibacy; refrain from associations

37 PCLCCAC; LCA, *The Ministry of the People and Public Ministry*; MCI, *Constitution*; RCA, *Book of Church Order*; PCA, *Book of Church Order*; Bethel Baptist Church (Choctaw), *Constitution*: ordained ministers; Riverside Baptist Church (Baltimore): *Bylaws*: pastors.

38 PCLCCAC; ELCA, *Constitution*; PCW, *Handbook of Rules*; PCA, *Book of Church Order*. For ministerial posts, see Doe (n 34) 86–93.

39 SPCL (2016) III.1.

40 CIC: cc. 273, 275; c. 274: only clerics exercise governance; c. 384: the bishop is to care for priests, defend their rights, ensure that they fulfil their duties and have an adequate means of livelihood.

inconsistent with the clerical state; hold church doctrine; reside in their diocese unless permitted otherwise by the Ordinary; wear suitable ecclesiastical dress; and do their utmost to foster peace based on justice—they are forbidden everything 'unbecoming to their state' (e.g. to assume public office involving the exercise of civil power, and practise commerce or trade except with lawful permission).[41] Secondly, deacons are the ordinary ministers of baptism, have various roles at the Eucharist, may celebrate marriages if delegated and may act as minister of the Word.[42] Thirdly, at parish level, the 'care of souls' (*cura animarum*) is reserved to priests, the co-operators of the bishops; the functions of a parish priest include administration of baptism, assistance at marriages, conducting funerals, celebrating the Eucharist on Sundays and holydays, instructing and prudently correcting the faithful, preaching and visiting the faithful entrusted to his care.[43] The parish priest acts on behalf of the parish, must ensure that parish goods are administered in accordance with law, and must reside in the parochial house (or elsewhere if the bishop permits).[44] As well as parish clergy, within the diocese, the bishop appoints a vicar general, episcopal vicars, and vicars forane to help govern the diocese and to oversee its clergy.[45]

There are many parallels between these Catholic norms and those of Protestants. For example, Anglican clergy teach, administer the sacraments and provide pastoral care, but 'must not engage in any secular employment or other occupation outside their ministry' without permission of the bishop. In Lutheranism, typically, 'Leaders in this church should demonstrate that they are servants by their words, life-style, and manner of leadership', recognising 'their accountability to the Triune God, to the whole Church, to each other, and the [church] . . . in which they serve'. Within Presbyterianism, as typified in the Presbyterian Church of Wales, a minister at ordination undertakes to lead the church in 'preaching the Word, the administering of the Sacraments, the pastoral care of members and their instruction in the Christian faith'.[46]

In turn, these norms may be reconciled in the form of principles of Christian law, among the historic churches, that ordained ministers must be duly authorised by their church in order to exercise ministry. Ministers are to preach the Word of God, teach the faith, administer the sacraments and provide pastoral care. They should fashion their ministries after the example of

41 CIC: c. 276: holiness, etc.; c. 277: continence and celibacy; c. 278: the right of association; c. 279: studies; c. 280: common life; c. 281: remuneration; c. 282: a simple way of life; c. 283: residence; c. 284: dress; c. 285: conduct inconsistent with their state; c. 286: commerce; c. 287: justice.

42 See e.g. CIC: c. 757: ministry of the Word; c. 288: permanent deacons.

43 CIC: cc. 149–150: cures; c. 757: co-operators; c. 527: possession; cc. 528–530: rights and duties.

44 CIC: c. 532: temporal goods; c. 533: residence; c. 535: registers; cc. 540–552: cases of absence.

45 CIC: cc. 475–481: a vicar general helps to govern the diocese; an episcopal vicar assists in a specific area or activity; cc. 553–555: a vicar forane oversees clergy, visits parishes and oversees property in a district.

46 PCLCCAC; ELCA, *Constitution*; MCI, *Constitution*; PCW, *Handbook of Rules*.

Christ and must lead their private lives in a way that befits their sacred calling. They may engage in such other occupations, including offices held beyond the local church, as they are not forbidden by church law or competent authority. Further, ministers are accountable for the exercise of their ministry to the competent church authority in the manner prescribed by law.[47]

There is also the matter of oversight. In the Roman Catholic Church, oversight vests in the bishop: 'By divine institution, bishops succeed the apostles through the Holy Spirit who is given to them. They are constituted pastors in the church, to be teachers of doctrine, priests of sacred worship, and the ministers of governance' (if in communion with the Pope and the other bishops). Bishops entrusted with a diocese are 'diocesan bishops'.[48] Appointed by the Pope,[49] the diocesan bishop has all ordinary, proper, and immediate power required for his office, legislative, executive and judicial, and oversees discipline; must protect and explain doctrine, preach frequently and oversee the ministry of Word and catechesis; and must set a personal example of holiness, promote that of the faithful, celebrate mass regularly, ordain clergy, reside in the diocese, and conduct a visitation every five years and report on this to the Pope.[50]

Anglicanism is similar: oversight by bishops is fundamental. A diocesan bishop is chief pastor, minister and teacher of the diocese, and a governor and guardian of discipline. For example, the bishop must foster the spiritual welfare and unity of the diocese, minister the Word and Sacraments, ensure the worthiness of public worship, preside at the Eucharist, administer ordination and confirmation, and uphold church doctrine; the bishop is also president of the diocesan assembly and resides in the diocese.[51] By way of contrast, the Methodist Church in Great Britain employs the concept of 'superintendence' for the oversight of a district (which consists of circuits of local churches). Each district has a chair who presides over the district synod which is responsible for 'the observance within the District of Methodist order and discipline'. It is also 'the duty of the Chair to exercise oversight of the character and fidelity of the ministers' and to make an annual visitation of the circuit churches. In Presbyterianism, the regional Presbytery exercises oversight, and similar functions are performed by the presidents in the United Reformed Church as well as by the presidents of regional Baptist associations.[52]

47 SPCL (2016) III.3.

48 CIC: cc. 375, 376.

49 CIC: c. 377: every three years, the Conference draws up a list of potential candidates.

50 CIC: cc. 273, 375, 380, 381–399: the bishop visits the Pope in the year of the report; cc. 401–402: the diocese is vacated when the bishop dies, resigns or is transferred/deprived; he may resign with papal consent, and at 75 should do so, or if cannot fulfil his office due to ill health or other reason.

51 PCLCCAC: Principles 15.10, 35, 36, 37.

52 MCGB, *Constitutional Practice and Discipline*; CSCL; PCW, *Handbook of Rules*; URC, *Manual*; NH Maring and WS Hudson, *A Baptist Manual of Polity and Practice* (Judson Press 1963) 233.

Provision may also be made for ministry at a global level, but this depends on the tradition. In the Roman Catholic Church, of course, the Pontiff exercises a teaching, sanctifying and governing authority over the faithful worldwide.[53] However, in Anglicanism, the Archbishop of Canterbury has no general jurisdiction exercisable over the autonomous churches of the worldwide Anglican Communion, but has a 'primacy of honour' as a 'focus of unity', but may exercise a limited metropolitical jurisdiction if this is assigned by the laws of a church.[54] Similarly, the president of the Lutheran World Federation, the president of the World Communion of Reformed Churches, and the president of the Baptist World Alliance each exercise a general oversight over these global bodies but exercise no coercive jurisdiction.[55]

And so, it is possible to sum up these various norms as principles of Christin law. Ministry is subject to oversight as an essential of ecclesial order. Oversight is exercised by such authority as is designated by law. A church may have a system of international oversight or leadership. A minister has such international functions of oversight or leadership as are permitted by the law. International church offices include those of pope, patriarch, primate, president, moderator or general secretary. They are appointed or elected to office by competent authority. A church may assign to an office of oversight a coercive jurisdiction or a moral authority.[56]

Church Governance: Legislative, Administrative and Judicial Bodies

There are significant differences between Catholics and Protestants as to church governance. In the Roman Catholic Church, with the Pontiff, the College of Bishops exercises power over the universal church, and its decrees, if confirmed by the Pope, are to be observed by all the faithful; administration is conducted by the Roman Curia.[57] Whilst there are also provinces, the national Episcopal Conference, 'the assembly of the Bishops of a country or of a certain territory', must draw up its own statutes (to be reviewed by the Apostolic See) which must deal with, *inter alia*, its plenary meetings, a permanent committee of bishops, a general secretary and other offices and commissions; each Conference must elect a president who presides over its plenary meetings and permanent committee. Plenary meetings are to be held at least once each year. The Episcopal Conference may issue decrees only in cases where the universal law so prescribes or by special mandate of the Holy See, on its own initiative or at the request of the Conference; a proposed conference decree must

53 CIC: c. 331: the Pontiff has 'supreme, full, immediate and universal ordinary power'.

54 PCLCCAC: Principle 11.4. See, for more detail, ch. 4.

55 LWF, *Constitution*, Arts. VII–VIII; WCRC, *Constitution*, Arts. XI–XII; BWA, *Constitution*, Art. VI.

56 SPCL (2016) III.4.

57 CIC: cc. 336–348, 360–361 and 754.

receive two-thirds of the votes at a plenary meeting; and '[t]hese decrees do not oblige until they have been reviewed by the Apostolic See and lawfully promulgated'; the competence of a diocesan bishop is also protected.[58] In turn, at the local level, there are for example parish councils and various committees alongside the priest.

With respect to Protestants, in Congregational and Baptist polity, authority resides primarily in the local church and ascends (for limited purposes of common action) to regional, national and international bodies—such as a Baptist Association (regional), a Baptist Union or Convention (national) and the Baptist World Alliance: but these cannot usurp the autonomy of the local church. In Anglicanism, Lutheranism, Methodism and Presbyterianism, authority is located in an institution at the national level (e.g. an Anglican or Lutheran General Synod, a Methodist Conference and a Presbyterian General Assembly, all composed of both lay and ordained persons); authority then descends to regional bodies (e.g. Anglican or Lutheran Diocesan Synods or Presbyterian Presbyteries) and local institutions (such as a Parish Council or Kirk Session)—in turn a limited authority ascends to international bodies but these have no general legislative power over member churches—this applies, for example, across the Anglican Communion, Lutheran World Federation and World Communion of Reformed Churches.[59]

At the local level, each church unit has its own governing body. For instance, a Methodist Circuit Meeting, composed of the circuit superintendent, ministers and elected representatives for each local church, is 'the principal meeting responsible for the affairs of a Circuit'; it exercises 'spiritual leadership and administrative efficiency' and oversees the 'pastoral, teaching and evangelistic work' of the churches in the Circuit each one of which has a Church Council, which is 'the principal meeting responsible for the affairs of a Local Church' with 'authority and oversight over' it. Presbyterians, too, have similar local bodies—(Kirk) Sessions and Congregational Meetings; and local Baptist churches have meetings and other assemblies.[60]

At national or regional levels, institutions may exercise control over the local church, but each local church enjoys such autonomy as is prescribed by the general law of the church. For example, in Lutheranism, 'The power of the Church shall be exercised through the General Synod', 'the highest constitutional authority of the Church', and each district synod exercises 'general supervision over . . . the congregations'; but a congregation has 'authority in all matters that are not assigned by the constitution and bylaws of [the church] to synods'. Likewise, a national Methodist Conference is responsible

58 CIC: cc. 435–455: Conference decides the manner of promulgation and the time decrees come into force.

59 See Doe (n 34) Ch. 4.

60 MCGB, *Constitutional Practice and Discipline*; ELCIC, *Constitution*; LCA, *Constitution*; BUSA, *Model Trust*; Central Baptist Church (Pretoria), *Constitution*.

for 'the management and discipline' of the church; and the District Synod is a link between Conference, circuits and local churches. Much the same applies in Presbyterianism; typically, a (national) General Assembly may 'enact, alter or abrogate a law of the Church', and a regional Presbytery is 'responsible for corporate oversight of the congregations and causes assigned to it by the General Assembly'—it 'superintends' the 'spiritual and temporal affairs of its congregations'. A Baptist national Union has more limited power—its Assembly may amend the Union constitution, and its policies and those of a regional association assembly may be adopted by the autonomous local churches.[61]

As the Catholic Church has its own system of tribunals, which are ordered hierarchically, so Protestant churches also have judicial institutions (usually styled courts or tribunals) for the resolution of ecclesial conflict and the enforcement of church discipline. With regard to the nature, purpose and scope of discipline, the Methodist Church in Ireland is typical:

> Discipline in the Church is an exercise of that spiritual authority which the Lord Jesus has appointed in His Church. The ends contemplated by discipline are the maintenance of the purity of the Church, the spiritual benefit of the members and the honour of our Lord;

moreover,

> All members and ministers of the Church are subject to its government and discipline, and are under the jurisdiction and care of the appropriate Courts of the Church in all matters of Doctrine, Worship, Discipline, and Order in accordance with the Rules and Regulations from time to time made by the [central and national] Conference.

Protestant laws make detailed provision for informal dispute resolution, due process, appeals, offences and sanctions.[62]

The commonalities which exist between these laws of Catholics and Protestants enable the articulation of several principles of Christian law. Christ is the ultimate head of the Church universal in all its manifestations. A system of government in a church reflects its conception of divine law. A church should have institutions to legislate, administer and adjudicate for its own governance. An ecclesial institution that has such power, authority or jurisdiction assigned to it by law must comply with the law, and may be subject to such substantive and procedural limitations as may be prescribed by law. Ecclesial institutions may be organised at international, national, regional and/or local

61 LCA, *Constitution*; ELCA, *Constitution*; MCGB, *Constitutional Practice and Discipline*; PCI, *Code*; BUGB, *Constitution*; ABCUSA, *Constitution*, XIII: regional association.

62 MCI, *Constitution* and *Regulations*. See also SPCL (2016) V.1–5.

levels.[63] Whilst an ecclesial tradition may have an international organisation in the form of a church, communion, federation or other global association, with a structure as may be constituted by or assigned to it under its doctrine and law, a tradition may have a national organisation. A church organised at the national level may have such institutional structure as is prescribed by the laws applicable to it. The functions of a national ecclesial entity, and its conference, synod, council or other central assembly, may include the authority to legislate, administer and adjudicate on matters within its competence.[64]

Doctrine and Worship

For the Roman Catholic Church, the teaching function (*magisterium*) belongs to the ordained ministers: supreme teaching authority vests in the Pontiff and the College of Bishops who may declare infallible doctrine, by which faith or morals on a matter of truth is solemnly defined, and proclaim truth, as contained in the written Word of God or in tradition and which exists in the deposit of faith entrusted to the church and proposed as divinely revealed.[65] Alternatively, the Pontiff or the College of Bishops may proclaim doctrine on faith or morals non-definitively, as might the bishops, both individually or collectively, in matters of faith.[66] The proclamation of the Word of God is a fundamental action of the church and a divine imperative for all the faithful.[67] Moreover, preaching is of 'great importance' and a homily must set out 'those things which it is necessary to believe and to practise for the glory of God and the salvation of all'.[68]

In Catholic canon law, worship is 'the first act of the virtue of religion', with adoration, prayer and the participation of the faithful.[69] Liturgy is 'an action of the church',[70] and its purpose is to enable the sanctification of the faithful through worship: the whole church, clergy and laity, shares in the exercise of the office of sanctifying, and liturgical actions are not private actions but corporate celebrations of the church with the presence and active participation of the faithful; and the faithful have the right to worship God according to rites approved by the legitimate pastors of the church.[71] It is for the Apostolic See

63 SPCL (2016) IV.1: Church Governance.

64 SPCL (2016) IV.3: National Church Structures.

65 CIC: c. 749.1: Pontiff; c. 749.2: College of Bishops; 749.3: 'No doctrine is understood to be infallibly defined unless this is manifestly demonstrated'; c. 750: Word of God and tradition; c. 748: all are bound to seek the truth but none to embrace catholic faith against their conscience.

66 CIC: cc. 752, 753, 386; the Dicastery for the Doctrine of the Faith is also active in this field.

67 Matt. 28.18–20; CIC: cc. 747–748.

68 See, respectively: CIC: 757, 759, 760–772.

69 CCC, pars. 2096–2098; 1069: liturgy is a 'public work' in 'the name of/on behalf of the people'.

70 SC: 1; CCC, pars. 1076–1109.

71 CIC: cc. 834–837; e.g. prayers, see c. 839; c. 217: the right to worship.

to order the sacred liturgy of the universal church and 'publish the liturgical books'; the Conference of Bishops may prepare both translations and particular ritual texts adopted to local needs and to publish them with the prior review of the Holy See.[72] As to its administration, worship takes place when it is carried out in the name of the church by persons lawfully deputed and through acts approved by the authority of the church; and liturgy is conducted under the presidency of the ordained ministers.[73] The supervision of liturgy depends solely on the authority of the church: liturgical supervision resides in the Pontiff and, under the law, the diocesan bishop, who may issue liturgical norms.[74] The liturgical books approved by competent authority must be faithfully observed in the celebration of sacraments: no one on personal authority may add, remove or change anything in them.[75] However, as liturgical law exists to facilitate worship, it should be applied flexibly, with choices and options. The bishop must supervise liturgical discipline and may dispense with the requirements of universal and particular liturgical law in this regard.[76]

Protestant laws echo many of the fundamentals of Catholic canon law on doctrine and worship. By way of illustration, doctrinal instruments include Catechisms, Articles of Religion, Confessions of Faith and other statements of belief. In the Presbyterian Church in New Zealand:

> The Church itself has the right, in dependence on the promised guidance of the Holy Spirit, to formulate, interpret or modify its subordinate standards, always in agreement with its superior standard and the fundamental doctrines of the Reformed Faith contained in its subordinate standards.

Anglican sermons 'must endeavour with care and sincerity to expound the word of truth according to Holy Scripture, to the glory of God and to edification of the people'. For Lutherans, preaching the Word is 'a means of grace' and must conform to the Confession of Faith. For Methodists, 'the main doctrines of the Christian faith should be more plainly and systematically set forth in public preaching, so that the Methodist people may be established in the faith'. Moreover, prescribed members who violate doctrine may be disciplined.[77]

72 CIC: c. 826: local ordinary; c. 838.2: Apostolic See; 838.3: Conference of Bishops; c. 455.2.
73 CIC: c. 834.2; LG 11.
74 CIC: c. 838; SC 22.
75 CIC: c. 846.
76 CIC: cc. 87–88: dispensation (see also c. 392.2); c. 89: ministerial compliance.
77 For doctrinal texts, see e.g. LCGB, *Rules and Regulations*, 'Statement of Faith'; PCI, *Code*: the Westminster Confession of Faith and Larger and Shorter Catechisms. For doctrinal change and preaching, PCANZ, *Book of Order*; PCLCCAC; LCA, *Bylaws*; ELCA, *Constitution*; MCGB, *Constitutional Practice and Discipline*; see also URC, *Manual*; Riverside Baptist Church (Baltimore), *Constitution*.

Protestant churches also have elaborate norms on worship and its public administration. For example, for the Presbyterian Church of Wales: 'Our purpose is to worship God and spread the Gospel'; the 'means of grace in a worshipping community are the reading of the Scriptures, prayer, the singing of hymns, the preaching and hearing of the Word and the administration and receiving of the sacraments'; their regular use is 'a duty to God and a necessity of the Christian life'. In the Methodist Church of Great Britain, service books are approved by Conference, and in the Church of Scotland: 'There is no prescribed liturgy . . . and ministers enjoy considerable freedom in matters of worship'; rather, the principles of worship are in accordance with the Directory for the Public Worship of God 1645 as that 'has been or may hereafter be modified by Acts of the General Assembly or by consuetude'. The General Assembly, therefore, may commend forms of service and has a modern Directory of Worship.[78]

From an ecumenical perspective, all these legal approaches of Catholics and Protestants come together in the form of common principles of Christian law. According to the statement of these principles, the worship of God is a fundamental duty of the church. It enables an intimate encounter between a church corporately and the faithful individually with the presence of God. Each church and those bodies within it competent to do so may develop liturgical texts or other forms of service for public worship provided these are consistent with the Word of God and church doctrine. The use of a form of service must be authorised. Forms of service may be found in a book of rites or liturgy, a book of common prayer, a directory of worship or other instrument, and these may include rubrics or other directions to facilitate worship.[79] A church must provide for public worship. Ordained ministers are particularly responsible for its conduct in accordance with forms of service. Regular attendance at worship, particularly on the Lord's Day, is an expectation on the faithful. The administration of worship in the local church is subject to supervision by those authorities designated by law to provide this.[80]

The fields of the rights of passage (baptism, confirmation, Holy Communion, marriage and funerals), ecumenical relations (including mutual recognition of the rites of passage), property (including places of worship), finances (including budgets, accounts, audit and church members' duties to contribute financially) and church-state relations also yield juridical unity as between the respective legal systems of the Catholic Church and the Protestant Churches.[81]

78 PCW: *Handbook of Rules*; MCGB, *Constitutional Practice and Discipline*; CLCS, 28–30.
79 SPCL (2016) VI.4: The Nature and Forms of Worship.
80 SPCL (2016) VI.5: The Administration of Public Worship.
81 Doe (n 34) Chs. 8 and 9; SPCL (2016) VIII and IX.

Conclusion

When compared, there are profound similarities between the basic elements of the laws and other regulatory instruments of the Roman Catholic Church and Protestant churches across the ecclesiastical traditions studied here. These similarities exist in relation to the nature and objects of the church; the sources, forms, effects and purposes of church laws; the faithful; ordained ministers; church governance; and doctrine and worship. There are many other areas of church life where a comparative account of Catholic and Protestant laws would yield further commonality. Moreover, these similarities have enabled both Catholics and Protestants to contribute imaginatively to the work of the ecumenical panel which issued its *Statement of Principles of Christian Law* in 2016. These principles reflect in large measure the laws of the Latin Church and the Protestant churches as they exist across the traditions in a multiplicity of legal instruments—from constitutions through to books of church order. There are, however, differences between the principles of Christian law and the laws of Catholic and Protestant churches in many fields—and further work needs to be done on how to reconcile these legal differences as a matter of interpretation, ecclesial practice and ecumenical endeavour. Whilst one legacy of the Reformation may indeed be institutional ecclesial separation, the concept of juridical ecumenism is a rich resource in identifying what Catholics and Protestants share today.

Bibliography

Baptist Union of Great Britain (BUGB 2020) *Constitution*

Codex Iuris Canonici (CIC) (Code of Canon Law 1983 (of the Latin Church) Bks. II-IV

Doe N, *Christian Law* (CUP 2015)

Doe N (ed), *Church Laws and Ecumenism: A New Path for Christian Unity* (Routledge 2021)

Maring NH and Hudson WS, *A Baptist Manual of Polity and Practice* (Judson Press 1963)

Methodist Church in Great Britain (MCGB 2023), *Constitutional Practice and Discipline*

Presbyterian Church of Wales (PCW 2022), *Handbook of Rules*

The Principles of Canon Law Common to the Churches of the Anglican Communion (2022) Evangelical Lutheran Church in America (ELCA 2022), *Constitution and Foundational Texts*

Witte J, Jr., *Law and Protestantism; The Legal Teachings of the Lutheran Reformation* (CUP 2002)

2 How the English and Scots Reformations Shaped Ecclesiastical and Secular Law in Great Britain

Frank Cranmer

Introduction: The English and Scots Reformations[1]

Like the other national Reformations, the English Reformation was not an event but a *process*—and a long drawn-out one at that. Unlike the Continental or Scottish Reformations, however, it was not predominantly about theology but largely about power politics or, if you like, sovereignty. English churchmen were by no means unaware of the theological ferments in Continental Europe—a group of Cambridge divines[2] was meeting regularly to discuss the theology of Luther and his associates in the White Horse Tavern, dubbed 'Little Germany'—and perhaps their awareness of those developments did make it easier to contemplate breaking with Rome. But when the English Church finally broke away during the reign of Henry VIII, though it was partly in the context of those wider theological movements for reform, it was principally because of the King's exasperation at the Pope's refusal to annul his marriage to Catherine of Aragon, which, claimed Henry, was invalid because she had previously been the wife of Henry's elder brother, Arthur.

The Act of Supremacy 1534 declared that Henry was to 'be taken, accepted, and reputed the only supreme head in earth of the Church of England, called *Anglicana Ecclesia*'. But that was a *political* statement, not a theological one; and the Statute of Six Articles 1539 declared that:

1 This chapter is a revised and expanded version of an article first published in *Law & Justice* in 2017. It has its origins in a paper presented at the *Kirchenrechtslehrertagung* in Halle in May 2017, to which I was kindly invited by Professor Dr Hans Michael Heinig. The initial paper was vastly improved by Professor Norman Doe's comments on my initial draft, by discussions at the Halle conference and by John Duddington's helpful comments, both as editor of *Law & Justice* and of this volume, but any remaining infelicities are mine. Websites were last accessed on 19 April 2023.

2 Which may—or may not—have included Thomas Cranmer. Diarmaid MacCulloch is sceptical about Cranmer's alleged participation: see D MacCulloch, *Thomas Cranmer: A Life* (Yale UP 1996) 25.

DOI: 10.4324/9780429264115-3

1. after the words of consecration [at Holy Communion], 'the natural body and blood of Our Saviour Jesu Christ' 'is present really, under the form of bread and wine';
2. 'communion in both kinds is not necessary *ad salutem*';
3. priests may not marry, 'by the law of God';
4. vows of chastity or widowhood made to God ought to be observed;
5. 'private masses be continued and admitted in this the King's English Church and Congregation'; and
6. auricular confession is 'expedient and necessary to be retained and continued'.

There was nothing in that to which a devout Roman Catholic could take exception—apart, of course, from the reference to 'the King's English Church'. Nor did Henry intend the Reformation to be any great new theological departure: he regarded himself as a Catholic and remained so all his life, albeit a Catholic no longer in communion with the Bishop of Rome, and his Prayer Book of 1549, which was largely based on the Sarum Rite, might be loosely described as 'reimagined Catholic'.

In short, the Henrician Reformation was not primarily about theology but about *governance*. The theological reformation came with Henry's death in 1547 and the accession of Edward VI, who came to the throne aged 9 and died aged 15. It was during the reign of Edward that the Church began to be influenced first by Lutheran ideas and then by Calvinism. One result was a shift in theological emphasis away from the reformed Catholicism of the *Prayer Book* of 1549 to the much more overtly Calvinist tone of the *Prayer Book* of 1552.

Then came the interlude from 1553 to 1558, when the Roman Catholic Mary I restored papal authority over the Church. But when Mary's sister, Elizabeth I, succeeded her, she consciously chose a theological compromise to accommodate so far as possible both those who had never wanted to break with Rome in the first place and those who had wanted a full-blown Reformed Church on Calvinist principles, for example by seeking to finesse the doctrine of the Real Presence with Zwinglian memorialism.[3] Perhaps the argument for continuity was most neatly summed up by Richard Hooker:

> [I]f against those things which have been received with great reason, or against that which the ancient practice of the Church hath continued

3 The words of administration in the 1549 *Book of Common Prayer* were 'The body of our Lord Jesus Christ which was given for thee, preserve thy body and soul unto everlasting life. The blood of our Lord Jesus Christ which was shed for thee, preserve thy body and soul unto everlasting life'. In the 1552 version that became: 'Take and eat this, in remembrance that Christ died for thee, and feed on him in thy heart by faith with thanksgiving. Drink this in remembrance that Christ's blood was shed for thee and be thankful'.

In an Elizabethan compromise, the 1559 version combined the two:

> The body of our Lord Jesus Christ, which was given for thee, preserve thy body and soul into everlasting life: and take and eat this in remembrance that Christ died for thee, and feed on him in thine heart by faith, with thanksgiving. The blood of our Lord Jesus Christ,

> time out of mind . . . the Church did give every man licence to follow what himself imagineth that God's Spirit doth reveal unto him, or what he supposeth that God is likely to have revealed to some special person whose virtues deserve to be highly esteemed, what other effect could hereupon ensue, but the utter confusion of his Church, under pretence of being taught, led and guided by his spirit: the gifts and graces whereof do so naturally all tend unto common peace.[4]

By the end of the English Reformation, when Charles II commissioned the 1662 *Book of Common Prayer*, the Church of England could perhaps be described as an ecclesiastical hybrid, with an ordered, fairly Catholic liturgy alongside some rather Calvinist statements of doctrine—and, in the process, Martin Luther seems largely to have been forgotten. And it is perhaps at that point that one can reasonably begin to talk about 'Anglicanism'.

Scotland was an entirely different proposition. There, a full-blown Reformed Church on Calvinist principles was *precisely* what the reformers intended, and the Scots Reformation proceeded on very different lines from that in England. It is generally held to have begun with the passing of the Confession of Faith Ratification Act 1560—under which the Scots Parliament approved the terms of the *Scots Confession*—and the Papal Jurisdiction Act 1560, under which it was 'statute and ordanit that the bischope of Rome haif na Jurisdictioun nor autoritie within this realme in tymes cuming'.

As in England, the power of the reformers ebbed and flowed. Under the so-called Black Acts of 1584, presbyteries were abolished—though they were reinstated in 1592—and King James VI assumed the power to appoint bishops. Charles I continued his father's attempt to impose episcopacy on Scotland, together with the 1637 *Book of Common Prayer*—the 'Wee Bookie'. When the two Parliaments came together during the English Civil War to oppose him, the Scots Covenanters promised their aid on condition that the episcopal system of church government would be abandoned once and for all. Under the terms of the Solemn League and Covenant,[5] the two parties met as the Westminster Assembly and formulated the *Westminster Confession of Faith*, and though it was never formally adopted in England it is still the principal subordinate standard of faith of the Church of Scotland[6] and of the other denominations in the Reformed tradition.

---

which was shed for thee, preserve thy body and soul into everlasting life: and drink this in remembrance that Christ's blood was shed for thee, and be thankful.

4 Richard Hooker, *Of the Laws of Ecclesiastical Polity*, Bk I.5.3, 1 (Cambridge Texts in the History of Political Thought 2008). The first four books were published in 1594.

5 Its full title was 'A SOLEMN League and Covenant, for Reformation, and Defense of Religion, The Honour and Happineſſe of the KING, And the Peace & Safety of the three Kingdoms of England, Scotland, and Ireland'.

6 Art. II of the Articles Declaratory of the Constitution of the Church of Scotland annexed to the Church of Scotland Act 1921 describes it as 'the sum and substance of the Faith of the Reformed Church'.

Church Law and the English Reformation: The Stubbs-Maitland Controversy

So: to the law. The first question is, 'What was the position of Roman canon law before the Reformation?' And this is where we encounter the nineteenth-century Stubbs-Maitland controversy.

William Stubbs[7] was an eminent constitutional historian whose *Constitutional History of England* was once a standard work. He believed that 'the canon law of Rome, though always regarded as of great authority in England, was not held to be binding on the courts'[8] and his *Historical Appendix* to the Report of the Royal Commission on Ecclesiastical Courts in 1883 gives three sources of law for the English church courts up to the time of the Reformation:

- the canon law of Rome contained in the six books of the *Corpus Iuris Canonici*;
- 'the civil law of Rome which from the reign of Stephen [*i.e. the mid-twelfth century*] onwards, was refused any recognition except as a scientific authority in England';[9] and
- 'the provincial law of the Church of England contained in the constitutions of the archbishops from Langton downwards and the canons passed in the legatine councils'.[10]

Crucially, Stubbs went on to suggest that the canon law of Rome was authoritative only if it had been ratified in national or provincial church councils, and that English church courts applied the native law even if in conflict with formal papal law.

Frederic William Maitland,[11] an equally eminent legal historian—and an agnostic—disagreed completely:

> In all probability, large portions (to say the least) of the 'canon law of Rome' were regarded by the courts Christian in this country as absolutely binding statute law. . . . Each of them was a statute book deriving its force from the Pope who published it, and who, being Pope, was

7 William Stubbs (1825–1901), Bishop of Oxford and sometime Regius Professor of Modem History at Oxford.

8 Royal Commission on Ecclesiastical Courts, *Report of the Commissioners Appointed to Inquire into the Constitution and Working of the Ecclesiastical Courts* (Eyre & Spottiswood 1883) xviii.

9 CH Donahue Jr, 'Roman Canon Law in the Medieval English Church: *Stubbs vs. Maitland* re-examined after 75 Years in the Light of Some Records from the Church Courts' (1973–74) 72 Michigan Law Revue 647, 648.

10 Ibid.

11 Frederic William Maitland (1850–1906), Downing Professor of the Laws of England at Cambridge.

> competent to ordain binding statutes for the Catholic Church and every part thereof.[12]

Maitland adduced three principal bodies of evidence to support his view: first, Lyndwood's *Provinciale*, compiled in about 1432; second, the system by which the Pope delegated authority to hear cases brought before him to judges in the area in which the case originated and gave instructions as to the law that would apply;[13] and, third, the various mediaeval English controversies between the Crown and the Pope in which the Church asserted the primacy of Roman canon law against English law and custom—the most famous of which led to the martyrdom of Thomas à Becket.[14] As Richard Helmholtz sums it up in *Roman Canon Law in Reformation England*, Maitland appeared to suggest that Stubbs and his supporters were seeking to demonstrate that 'the Church of England was Protestant before the Reformation and Catholic after it'.[15]

In volume I of *The Oxford History of the Laws of England*, Helmholz takes a balanced view of the controversy but comes down on the side of Maitland:

> [N]o one accepts the thesis of English independence from papal jurisdiction, the thesis attributed to Bishop Stubbs, at least in its extreme form. Maitland's side itself, however, . . . underestimated the role of custom in the law of the church and he treated the *Corpus iuris canonici* anachronistically. He treated it as if it had been a modern code. But he was right to stress that the mediaeval church was a subordinate part of a larger entity, the Catholic Church. It owed obedience and allegiance to the apostolic see.[16]

He goes on to point out that English synodical legislation was meant to *implement and augment* the general law of the Church: fundamental legislative change 'would come as the result of papal or conciliar initiative'.[17] But he also suggests that it is not a simple yes/no choice:

> [I]f put to choose between Maitland and Stubbs, we would certainly be right to follow Maitland. However . . . the choice need not be made, at

12 FW Maitland, 'Canon Law in England: I. William Lyndwood' (1896) 11 English Historical Review 446, 447–48.

13 FW Maitland, 'Canon Law in England: III. William of Drogheda and the Universal Ordinary' (1897) 12 English Historical Review 625, 632–33.

14 In passing it should be noted that the Archbishops' Commission on Canon Law in 1947 preferred Maitland's view: see Church of England, *The Canon Law of the Church of England: Being the Report of the Archbishops' Commission on Canon Law, Together with Proposals for a Revised Body of Canons* (SPCK 1947).

15 RH Helmholz, *Roman Canon Law in Reformation England* (CUP 1990) 4.

16 RH Helmholz, *Oxford History of the Laws of England: The Canon Law and Ecclesiastical Jurisdiction from 597 to the 1640s* (OUP 2004) 161–62.

17 Ibid 162.

> least in the stark form the original controversy took. In the years since Maitland wrote, a great deal has been discovered about the kinds of litigation actually heard in the mediaeval ecclesiastical courts. . . . Moreover, it is also possible to take a slightly longer look at the nature of Roman canon law than Maitland was able to manage. He himself claimed only a 'toe in the water' sort of familiarity with its traditions. A study of both of these puts the matters at issue between Stubbs and Maitland into a different light.[18]

The reason for that situation seems to be twofold. First, the Western Church was vast and communications were slow: if Rome disapproved of the way some obscure bishop in a distant part of the Church was enforcing canon law, the Papal Curia could not simply fire off a rude e-mail to the miscreant—always assuming that it knew what said miscreant had been doing. Secondly, there was no simple hierarchy of courts or precedent. Says Helmholz:

> the *ius commune* did not operate like modern legal systems in putting its hierarchy of sources into effect. The existence of appellate courts did not guarantee that local practices and customs would be 'corrected' by the process of appeal.[19]

In short, he suggests that Maitland was wrong in supposing that diocesan courts fell into line with the rulings of superior courts:

> That is not how things worked. The mediaeval canon law admitted, or at least tolerated, disparity between formal rule and local customary practice that was hard to grasp in the heyday of Austinian jurisprudence. Indeed, it is hard to grasp today.[20]

And in Chapter 3 of the present volume, Helmholz reminds us that the medieval and early modern canonists 'looked to custom, to local legislation, and to jurisprudential norms for substantial guidance in administering the law' as well as to canon law proper.[21]

So if we assume some degree of synthesis between the Stubbs view and the Maitland view of the independence of the English church courts at the Reformation, what happened?

18 Helmholz (n 15) 5.
19 Helmholz (n 16) 164.
20 Helmholz (n 15) 11–12.
21 See ch. 3, RH Helmholz, 'The Reformation and Legal Change: The Persistence of Medieval Canon Law' 64–65.

The English Church Courts at the Reformation and Its Impact on Domestic Canon Law

To the question 'How did the Reformation shape Anglican Church law?', I would suggest that the short answer is 'Not nearly as much as one might imagine'—or, at least, not immediately.

Western canon law had an enormous cultural influence on medieval Europe. Chapter 5 of Harold Berman's *Law and Revolution: The Formation of the Western Legal Tradition* is headed 'Canon Law: The First Modern Western Legal System'[22]—and that is not an unreasonable claim. There was a common system of church courts exercising a common jurisdiction. So, says Helmholz, by the middle of the fifteenth century in England, 'the courts of the Church exercised jurisdiction over broad though not unlimited areas of English life'[23]—and they went on doing so after 1534 . The other point that must be remembered is that the Church's courts—the 'courts Christian'—were functioning as proper courts in the modern understanding of that term, with books of canons and precedents, reports of rulings and the kind of apparatus that modern lawyers take for granted, and they were doing so at a time when the secular courts in England were still very primitive.

As Toby Milsom points out, the ecclesiastical courts were the earliest in England that looked anything like modern courts of law:

> Documents survive from actual litigation very nearly as old as the earliest rolls of the King's courts; and what we see is a single judge trying to find out what had happened by considering and comparing the evidence of witnesses, and applying to the facts so found rules of law which could be looked up in books.[24]

Moreover, the King's courts were extremely unsophisticated in comparison, even though there was an overlap of personnel:

> it was not just that the two kinds of process were going on in the same society and ordering the affairs of the same litigants. They were conducted by the same people. Until the process of centralisation [*of the royal courts of common law*] was complete at the end of the thirteenth century, the royal justices who brought it about were largely clerics with knowledge and often experience of the canon law.[25]

22 HJ Berman, *Law and Revolution: The Formation of the Western Legal Tradition* (Harvard UP 1983).

23 Helmholz (n 15) 2–3.

24 SFC Milsom, *Historical Foundations of the Common Law* (2nd edn, Butterworths 1969) 25.

25 Ibid.

And given that overlap of personnel, Milsom regards the disjunction between their methods as 'one of the odder contradictions of intellectual history'.[26]

Perhaps the difference between the two can be illustrated like this. Henry of Bracton wrote the first systematic study of English common law, *De Legibus et Consuetudinibus Angliae*, primarily before about 1235 and he did so from scratch. 'Though in almost all lands use is made of the *leges* and the *jus scriptum*', wrote Bracton, 'England alone uses unwritten law and custom'[27]—and the first 'modern' English law reports were not published until 1571 . In Spain, at almost the same time as Bracton, Raymond of Penyafort was composing the *Decretals of Gregory IX*—but what *he* was doing was rationalising previous collections of decretals. Bracton (with his associates) was writing on a blank sheet of vellum: Raymond of Penyafort was systematising existing material, as had Gratian before him. All that was not lightly to be discarded at the English Reformation—nor was it. So, apart from the change from papal to royal supremacy, the nuts and bolts of Church law continued much as before.

The Position in Scotland

In Scotland, the institutional changes were much more radical than in England—from an Episcopal form of government to a Presbyterian one—but, nevertheless, some of the mediaeval canon law persisted even if only in an attenuated form. The binding authority of canon law ended with the Reformation but, says William Gordon,

> where Canon law was already accepted as part of Scots law it continued to be applied in courts dealing with matters, such as status, which had been regulated by Canon law before the Reformation, in so far as Canon law did not conflict with Reformed doctrine. Canon law could also be referred to on questions not already settled but technically it was now only of persuasive authority.[28]

26 Ibid.

27 '*Cum autem fere in omnibus regionibus utatur legibus et iure scripto, sola Anglia usa est in suis finibus iure non scripto et consuetudine*': Henry of Bracton, *De Legibus et Consuetudinibus Angliae* (translated in GE Woodbine and SE Thorne, *Bracton on the Laws and Customs of England* (Belknap Press of Harvard University 1968–77)). In a comment on my initial draft, Norman Doe observed that Bracton relied greatly on the Italian jurist Azo. Further, Harvard Law School's *Bracton Online* suggests that 'it now seems that the bulk of the work was written in the 1220s and 1230s by persons other than Bracton himself': <>https://amesfoundation.law.harvard.edu/Bracton/> para 2.

28 W Gordon, 'Roman Law in Scotland' in R Evans-Jones (ed), *The Civil Law Tradition in Scotland* (Stair Society, supplementary series vol 2 1995): reprint at *Roman Law Resources* <>http://iuscivile.com/legacy/reprints/gordon-1.pdf> 14.

So, for example, it was simply a given that in Presbyterian Scotland women could not be ordained either as ministers of Word and Sacrament or as elders, because that had been the customary law of the Church since long before the Reformation.[29] The first Presbyterian denomination to ordain a woman as a minister was the United Free Church (Continuing), formed by the minority of the Free Church who did not rejoin the Church of Scotland in 1929.[30] Its first General Assembly passed a Deliverance that 'any member of the Church in full communion shall be eligible to hold any office within the Church' and, as a result, Elizabeth Brown Barr was ordained in 1935 as the first female Presbyterian minister in Scotland.[31] And when, in the 1960s, the General Assembly of the Church of Scotland changed its view on the ordination of women, it passed two Acts[32] to set aside what had been the customary canon law from before the Reformation.

Gradual Change

Obviously, there were changes over time. In England, issues of doctrine and worship came under the control of Parliament,[33] and the various Acts of Uniformity—1549, 1552, 1559 and 1662—established the various iterations of the *Book of Common Prayer* as the only legal form of worship.[34] Clerical celibacy was soon abolished—though not, it would appear, without some misgivings.[35] But the changes were gradual: the *ius commune*—the customary canon law of the undivided Church in the West—continued in force *as custom* unless expressly repealed by statute or implicitly repealed by custom to the contrary, and continued to be pleaded in the church courts. So the conclusion, *obiter*, of Tindal LCJ in *Millis*[36] that 'The canon law of Europe does not, and never did,

29 Though it might also say something about the position of women generally in the Christian Churches.

30 It dropped '(Continuing)' from its title in 1934.

31 She was moderator of the UFC General Assembly in 1960 and died in 1995. See Eun Soo Choi, 'The Religious Dimension of the Women's Suffrage Movement: The Role of the Scottish Presbyterian Churches, 1867–1918' (PhD thesis, Glasgow University 1996) 271 <>http://theses.gla.ac.uk/3943/>.

32 Act XXVIII, 1966 anent Admission of Women to the Eldership; Act XXV, 1968 anent Admission of Women to the Ministry.

33 In Scotland, they came under control of the General Assembly.

34 The Act of Uniformity 1662 was largely repealed by the Worship and Doctrine Measure 1974 but, even now, s 10 (about qualification for admission to a benefice) and s 15 (about the bishop's licence to preach) remain in force.

35 Queen Elizabeth I clearly had little enthusiasm for married clergy and is reported to have thanked the wife of Archbishop Parker after a feast at Lambeth Palace like this: 'Madam I *will* not call you—mistress I *may* not call you—but whatever you be, I thank you!' One of the many versions of this story is retailed in L Baldwin Smith, *The Elizabethan World* (Houghton Mifflin 1967) 73.

36 *R v Millis* (1844) 10 Clark and Finnelly 534; 8 ER 844 (HL).

as a body of laws, form part of the law of England'[37] looks, with hindsight, like something of an oversimplification.[38]

The detailed provisions of modern Anglican and Scots ecclesiastical law often bear little resemblance to the detailed provisions of Roman Catholic canon law, whether modern or mediaeval. That is hardly surprising: it is almost five centuries since the two Reformations, the ecclesiologies of the three Churches are not the same and their styles of lawmaking are very different. The supreme legislator for the Roman Catholic Church is the Pope.[39] Laws for the Church of England, on the other hand, are normally made nowadays by General Synod—which, crucially, includes lay members[40] as well as bishops and clergy,[41] and its courts are part of the general system of courts and operate a similar system of precedent. The Church of Scotland is governed primarily by the Articles Declaratory annexed to the Church of Scotland Act 1921 and the Acts and Regulations made by its General Assembly. But the basic concept of an ordered and orderly Church with a formal structure, properly understood lines of authority ***and rules*** remains common to all three. Whatever else the Reformations did in England and Scotland, they certainly did not produce an ecclesiological or legal free-for-all.

After the English Reformation

As noted earlier, the intention of Henry VIII, initially at least, was that the Church should be no longer subject to papal authority but not that it should undergo any major change in doctrine, and he appears to have taken a similarly

37 8 ER 898.

38 However, as to the substantive issue before the Court—whether a marriage entered into before a Presbyterian minister in Ireland 'was sufficiently a marriage to support an indictment against A for bigamy' (8 ER 845) after he had concluded a second marriage in England while his first wife was still living—see R Probert, '*R v Millis* Reconsidered: Binding Contracts and Bigamous Marriages' (2008) 28(3) Legal Studies 337–55. She concludes that the outcome was in fact correct, even though the reasoning of all but one of the judges was flawed.

39 Who is 'the head of the College of Bishops, the Vicar of Christ, and the Pastor of the universal Church here on earth. Consequently, by virtue of his office, he has supreme, full, immediate, and universal ordinary power in the Church, [*qui ideo vi muneris sui suprema, plena, immediate et universali in Ecclesia gaudet ordinaria potestate*] and he can always freely exercise this power': Canon 331.

40 Whereas, in the Roman Catholic Church, 'Those who are in sacred orders are, in accordance with the provisions of law, capable of the power of governance [*potestas regiminis*], which in fact belongs to the Church by divine institution': Canon 129 §1.

41 Hooker (n 4) Bk VIII: 'till it be proved that some special law of *Christ* has for ever annexed to the Clergy alone the power to make Ecclesiastical laws, we are to hold it a thing most consonant with equity and reason that no *Ecclesiastical* law be made in a *Christian Commonwealth* without consent as well of the laity as of Clergy but least of all without consent of the highest power'—by which he meant the Sovereign. It should also be noted that *in principle* the Canons do not bind the laity in general—see *Middleton v Crofts* (1736) 26 ER 788 (KB)—but lay officers such as churchwardens and readers are bound *in those capacities*.

conservative view of canon law. By ending appeals to Rome in matters of marriage and annulment, the Submission of the Clergy and Restraint of Appeals Acts 1533 made it possible for Henry to have his marriage to Catherine of Aragon annulled; however, that did not mean a total rejection of Western canon law. Under the Act, the 'divers constitutions, ordinances and canons' of the Church were to be submitted to the King, together with a commission to be appointed by him of 'two-and-thirty persons of the King's subjects'—16 from Parliament and 16 to be 'of the clergy of this realm'—and

> such of the said constitutions and canons as shall be thought and determined by the said two-and-thirty persons, or the more part of them, worthy to be abrogated and annulled, shall be abolished and made of no value accordingly; and such other of the same constitutions and canons as by the said two-and-thirty or the more part of them, shall be approved to stand with the laws of God and consonant to the laws of this realm, shall stand in their full strength and power, the King's most Royal assent first had and obtained to the same.[42]

Subject to the provisor in section 3 of the Act that 'no canons, constitutions or ordinance shall be made or put in execution . . . contrariant or repugnant to the King's prerogative royal, or the customs, laws or statutes of this realm', section 7 declared that

> such canons, constitutions, ordinances and synodals provincial being already made, which be not contrariant or repugnant to the laws, statutes and customs of this realm, nor to the damage or hurt of the King's prerogative royal, shall more still be used and executed as they were afore the making of this Act, till such time as they be viewed, searched or otherwise ordered and determined by the said two-and-thirty persons, or the more part of them, according to the tenor, form and effect of this present Act.

The report of the commission appointed under the Act was shelved;[43] however, section 3 remains in force—which is why section 1(3) of the Marriage (Same Sex Couples) Act 2013 declares that

> No Canon of the Church of England is contrary to section 3 of the Submission of the Clergy Act 1533 (which provides that no Canons shall be contrary to the Royal Prerogative or the customs, laws or statutes of this realm) by virtue of its making provision about marriage being the union of one man with one woman.

42 25 Henry VIII c 19 s 1.

43 N Cox, 'The Influence of the Common Law on the Decline of the Ecclesiastical Courts of the Church of England' (2001–2002) 3(1) Rutgers Journal of Law and Religion.

Commentators on English ecclesiastical law after the Reformation reckoned that Roman papal law continued to be operative in England after the Reformation *because it was accepted by the Crown and the local Church*; indeed, Helmholz suggests that ecclesiastical jurisdiction underwent rather *fewer* alterations during the Henrician Reformation than during the reigns of Elizabeth I and James I. Though virtually every statute enacted during their reigns that enlarged the scope of the common law jurisdiction contained a 'savings clause' for spiritual jurisdiction, over the longer term they tended to shrink the jurisdiction of the ecclesiastical tribunals.[44] What happened, he suggests, is that 'The common law courts took over substantial parts—though not all—of existing canon law in implementing the new statutes'.[45]

So John Godolphin, for example, writing in 1678, was able to claim that the pre-Reformation Roman canon law still continued to operate in England,

> not as to the observance of the Laws of any Foreign Prince, Potentate, or Prelate; but as to the accustomed and ancient Laws of this Realm, originally established as Laws of the same by the said sufferance, consent, and custome, and not otherwise . . . [*and could therefore be*] Dispenced with, abrogated, amplified or diminished by the King and his Parliament, or by such persons as the King and Parliament should authorize.[46]

Further:

> But as to those Canons which have been received, accepted, and used in any Christian Realm or Commonwealth, . . . those which have been embraced, allowed, and used in England, are made by such allowance and usage, part of the Ecclesiastical Laws of England; By which the interpretation, dispensation, or execution of these Canons . . . doth appertain sole to the King of England, and his Magistrates within his Dominions, and he and his Magistrates have the sole Jurisdiction in such cases, and the Bishop of Rome hath nothing to do in the interpretation, dispensation, or execution of those Laws in England, although they were first devised in the Court of Rome.[47]

What he was saying, in effect, was that the pre-Reformation canon law continued in force unless consciously revoked. And, as suggested, Elizabeth

44 Helmholz (n 15) 53.

45 Ibid 54.

46 J Godolphin, *Repertorium Canonicum, or, An Abridgment of the Ecclesiastical Laws of This Realm, Consistent with the Temporal Wherein the Most Material Points Relating to Such Persons and Things, as Come Within the Cognizance Thereof, Are Succinctly Treated* (Christopher Wilkinson 1678) 108.

47 Ibid 131.

I preferred consensus and compromise to confrontation, at least in ecclesiastical matters.

For the Church of England, possibly the most significant events in the seventeenth century were the restoration of Charles II after the English Civil War, the publication of the 1662 *Book of Common Prayer* and the accompanying Act of Uniformity 1662 : 'An Act for the Uniformity of Public Prayers and Administration of Sacraments, and other Rites and Ceremonies, and for establishing the Form of making, ordaining and consecrating Bishops, Priests and Deacons in the Church of England'. The Act provided that any minister who refused to conform to the new prayer book by St Bartholomew's Day (24 August) 1662 should be ejected from the Church: some 900 clergy refused to conform and were obliged to leave their parishes.[48]

I would suggest that it was the Act of Uniformity that finally settled the seat of authority for the Church of England for the next 250 years: henceforward, authority over the Church would be exercised unequivocally in the Crown in Parliament. The Provincial Convocations of Canterbury and York met in 1664 but then lapsed. Attempts to revive them in 1700 caused considerable disquiet to the authorities: they were prorogued in 1717, met once, formally, in 1741, and were not summoned again until 1854 (Canterbury) and 1861 (York). The Church did not start developing its own legislative institutions until 1855, when each Convocation established a House of Laymen to confer with it, elected by the diocesan conferences. A Representative Church Council was established in 1904, consisting of the two Convocations sitting together with the two Houses of Laymen—but it was still advisory.

It was not until the passing of the Church of England Assembly (Powers) Act 1919 that the Church was given a measure of control over its own law. The act provided for a National Assembly of three Houses—Bishops, Clergy and Laity—which would submit draft Measures through its Legislative Committee to an Ecclesiastical Committee of both Houses of Parliament, which would in turn report on their 'expediency'. The Synodical Government Measure 1969 extended those powers and conferred on General Synod the power to make canons—which, though not subject to parliamentary approval, are still subject to Royal Assent. Moreover, final *legislative* authority remains with Parliament, because no Measure of Synod can be presented for Royal Assent without an affirmative resolution of each House.[49]

48 See e.g. A Hunt, 'The Day the Shepherds Were Scattered' (*Church Times*, 21 September 2012).

49 During discussion at the *Kirchenrechtslehrertagung*, someone asked me what would happen nowadays if Parliament rejected a Measure. I cited the example of the Prayer Book Measure in 1927/28 and was asked whether a rejection would now engage Article 9 ECHR and whether Strasbourg might rule against the UK. On balance, I think not: the issue would certainly pass the test of cogency, but it could be argued that the mechanism for acceptance or rejection was both prescribed by law and necessary in a democratic society. There is also the issue of the prior exhaustion of domestic remedies: probably the only body with standing to seek judicial

So How Did Church Law Shape Secular Law?

Because the church courts had both a civil and a quasi-criminal jurisdiction, the canon law had a considerable influence on the development of secular law in both jurisdictions.[50]

Marriage

At the Reformation, though England renounced the doctrine that marriage was a sacrament, it still retained the idea that it was of divine institution, and reference continued to be made to customary canon law. Helmholz cites a Jacobean case on the validity of marriages of girls under the age of puberty in which one of the lawyers cited both the Lutheran Melchior Kling's *Tractatus de causis matrimonialibus*, first published in 1553 and in the preface to which he stated that he had based his text on the canon law,[51] and *Disputationes de sancto matrimonii sacramento* by the Jesuit Tomás Sánchez, published in 1602/03.[52]

Perhaps more surprisingly, England also adopted the principle laid down by Council of Trent's *Tametsi* decree of 1563, *De sacramento matrimonii*, that marriage was to be solemnised in church—even though Elizabeth I had by then succeeded Mary.[53] Moreover, matrimonial causes were ecclesiastical matters until the Matrimonial Causes Act 1857 moved them from the jurisdiction of the ecclesiastical courts to the civil courts.

However, because it had been promulgated three years after the Papal Jurisdiction Act 1560, *Tametsi* passed Scotland by. The classic principle of Scots law was the pre-Tridentine canonical principle that marriage is constituted by an interchange of mutual consent.[54] Traditionally, neither notice nor formality nor any kind of record was required to validate a marriage—and in the last quarter of the seventeenth century, Viscount Stair still felt able to cite the *ius commune* in support of that position:

> though the commixtion of bodies seem necessary for the constitution of Affinity arising from Marriage; yet the opinion of the Canon Law is

review would be the Archbishops' Council—and I cannot imagine it attempting to overturn a decision of Parliament to reject a draft Measure.

50 For a more general discussion of the influence of the *ius commune* on the development of the common law, see SL Bray, 'The Influence of the Catholic Intellectual Tradition on the Common Law' in R Domingo, GS Hauk and TP Jackson (eds), *Faith in Law, Law in Faith* (Brill 2024) <>https://papers.ssrn.com/sol3/papers.cfm?abstract_id=4439728>.

51 '*Sum autem in hoc scripto Ius Canonicum secutus*': see S Lettmaier, 'Marriage Law and the Reformation' (2017) 35(2) Law and History Review 461–510, 482.

52 Helmholz (n 15) 191.

53 The effect of the decree Tametsi is also considered by RH Helmholz in Chapter 3 at 62–63.

54 And, as MacCulloch points out, 'Christians (particularly when making categorical statements about Christian marriage) forget that there was no such thing as a church wedding in the first millennium of church history': D MacCulloch, 'One Enormous Room' (2013) 35(9) London Review of Books, 9 May.

> true, *consensus, non coitus, facit Matrimonium*; but this consent must specially relate to that Conjunction of Bodies, as being then in the consenters' capacity, otherwise it is void; . . . and the common essentials of consent, must also here be observed, so that, who cannot consent, cannot Marry.[55]

Religious marriage was very common in Scotland and was regulated by the Church. However, there was no statutory provision for non-religious civil marriage: one either got married in church or, instead, contracted one of the various forms of 'irregular marriage' under the common law. So irregular marriage 'with cohabitation by habit and repute' persisted as a valid legal form in Scotland until its abolition by the Family Law (Scotland) Act 2006, and, even then, its abolition did not affect the validity of subsisting irregular marriages. In short, post-Reformation Scotland held to the pre-Tridentine canonical view of marriage.[56] Until the jurisdiction was transferred to the Court of Session by s.1 Court of Session Act 1830, matrimonial causes were heard by the Commissary Courts as a remnant of the old ecclesiastical jurisdiction, and the principles of the canon law continued to be applied in their proceedings.[57] Matrimonial causes are still referred to in Scotland as 'consistorial jurisdiction'.

Perhaps surprisingly, the issue of the validity of marriage by mutual consent came before the Family Court in England and Wales as recently as 2018, in a case involving an application for a parental order under section 54 of the Human Fertilisation and Embryology Act 2008. The Act requires that the applicants 'must be . . . husband and wife'; in *X*,[58] however, though the applicants were married, one of them was gay—as the other had always known—and their relationship and marriage had been platonic. Sir James Munby P ruled at [7] that for the purposes of section 54(2)(a) of the Act they were nevertheless husband and wife: 'The fact that [*their marriage*] is platonic and without a sexual component is, as a matter of long-established law, neither here nor there and in truth no concern of the judges or of the

55 James Dalrymple, *Viscount of Stair, Institutions of the Law of Scotland* Bk I.6.26 (2nd edn, Edinburgh UP 1693).

56 For a detailed discussion of the background, see E Gordon, 'Irregular Marriage: Myth and Reality' (2013) 47(2) Journal of Social History 507–25. David Sellar argued that, historically, marriage with cohabitation by habit and repute derived from the canon law, in which it had been merely evidence of the parties' exchange of consent, and was not, therefore, an independent form of constituting marriage: 'Marriage by Cohabitation with Habit and Repute: Review and Requiem?' in DL Carey Miller and DW Meyers (eds), *Comparative and Historical Essays in Scots Law: A Tribute to Professor Sir Thomas Smith QC* (Butterworths 1992) 117–36.

57 DM Walker, 'Equity in Scots Law' (PhD thesis, Edinburgh University 1952) 477 <>https://era.ed.ac.uk/handle/1842/27594>.

58 *X (A Child: foreign surrogacy)* [2018] EWFC 15.

State'. Furthermore, at [8] he cited the traditional position at canon law in support of his conclusion:

> A sexual relationship is not necessary for there to be a valid marriage. The law was stated very clearly, if in Latin (for the use of which I apologise), by Sir James Wilde in *A v B* (1868) LR 1 P&D 559, 562: 'The truth is, *consensus non concubitus facit matrimonium*'. The law has always recognised that a couple may take each other as wife and husband *tanquam soror vel tanquam frater* (as sister and brother), as our ancestors would have put it, applying the canonists' maxim.

And even after the transfer of jurisdiction to the secular courts there were hangovers: Javier Martinez-Torrón attributes the persistence of the 'spousal exception' to rape—that a husband could not, in law, be held to have raped his wife—to its origins in Western canon law.[59] The fact of being married to the victim remained a defence to a rape charge until it was abolished by a judicial decision of the House of Lords in 1992.[60]

Probate, Succession and Intestacy

Jurisdiction over wills and testaments remained in the hands of the ecclesiastical courts in England and Wales until abolished by the Court of Probate Act 1857. As R.H. Helmholz notes elsewhere in this volume, 'by long established English custom, jurisdiction inheritance of personal property fell to the courts of the Church', where the combination of custom, synodal decrees and the *ius commune* 'remained relevant after the Reformation'.[61]

The Law of the Sea and Admiralty Jurisdiction

The jurisdiction of the Court of Admiralty over shipping and mercantile cases meant that its cases were often of international nature, which in turn meant that Admiralty law and procedure had a very strong element of Roman civil law. In the fifteenth and sixteenth centuries, the Court of Admiralty gradually acquired jurisdiction over many commercial areas properly belonging to the common-law courts—and to members of Doctors' Commons, as explained below.

Equity

In 1218, Pope Honorius III wrote to his legate in the conquered territories of the Byzantine Empire that the canon law had to be followed without

59 J Martinez-Torrón, *Anglo-American Law and Canon Law: Canonical Roots of the Common Law Tradition* (Duncker & Humblot GmbH 1998) 107.

60 *R v R* [1992] 1 AC 599, *per* Lord Keith of Kinkel 616.

61 See ch. 3 at 60.

exception in sacramental matters such as marriage law; however, in all cases without written rules of law the legate should act according to *aequitas 'in humaniorem partem'*—in response to human needs. The application of *aequitas* proved to be a major influence on English common law; and canon law contributed to its development—though, admittedly, not so much as other ideas like 'reason' and 'conscience'.[62]

In England, equitable principles evolved though the operation in the sixteenth century of the 'prerogative' courts (the Court of Chancery, the Court of Star Chamber and the Court of Requests) under which the King accepted petitions and authorised the Chancellor to make binding decisions in his name. The Chancellor could not restore land, but he could punish a party severely for not restoring it himself. The Chancellor, it should be remembered, was originally someone learned in canon law—and it was through the Chancellor's jurisdiction that the morality or otherwise of using one's neighbour's property crept back into the English law of property and tort. Later, the Court of Chancery evolved into the Court of Equity: 'modern' equitable principles developed in the sixteenth century and the larger moral idea of 'equity' became reduced to the 'rules/maxims of equity' in the eighteenth century.[63]

A good example of the rationale behind the evolution of equity was given by Lord Ellesmere in 1618—more than 80 years after the Henrician Act of Supremacy:

> Men's actions are so diverse and infinite that it is impossible to make any general law which may actually meet with every act and not fail. . . . The office of the Chancellor is to correct men's consciences for frauds, breach of trust, wrongs, and oppression of nature . . . and soften and nullify the . . . law.[64]

62 See, for more detailed discussion on equity, Ch. 10 of this volume:' Equity and Conscience'. It should be noted that the concept of 'equity of the statute' was much narrower: it was not about justice or fairness but about construction and application. Rather, it connoted the principle underlying a statute, its *ratio*, which justified a slight analogical extension outside its express terms. The core idea was that of similarity: '*equipollens lex est*, for similar cases are adjudged by the equity of the statute': see D Ibbetson, 'A House Built on Sand: Equity in Early Modern English Law' in E Koops and WJ Zwalve (eds), *Law & Equity: Approaches in Roman Law and Common Law* (Martinus Nijhoff 2014) 57, quoting from *Yearbook* T 7 Hen IV *f.*16 pl 6 (1406).

63 A Scott, *The Evolution of Resource Property Rights* (OUP 2008) 32. The last episcopal Chancellor was John Williams, Bishop of Lincoln and later Archbishop of York: he was Lord Keeper of the Great Seal (in effect, Lord Chancellor) from 1621 to 1625—almost a hundred years after the Reformation. It should also be remembered that the first common lawyer to be appointed Chancellor was Thomas More in 1529: prior to that date, most Chancellors had been clergy and, frequently, bishops. For a discussion of the canonical roots of equity, see J Martínez-Torrón, 'Comments on the Influence of Canon Law on the Common Law Legal Tradition' (1989) 20(1) Revue générale de droit 5–30 <>www.erudit.org/en/journals/rgd/1989-v20-n1-rgd04474/1058354ar/>.

64 *The Earl of Oxford's Case* (1618) *White & Tudor's Leading Cases* (Ch).

The development of equity led to special remedies such as injunction and specific performance—but those remedies operated under 'principles of equity' which echoed the canonist's or moral theologian's approach: for example, 'equity will not suffer a wrong to be without a remedy', 'he who seeks equity must do equity', 'he who comes to equity must do so with clean hands'.

As to Scotland, David Walker suggests that 'The adoption of civil law principles either direct from the *Corpus Juris* or through the influence of the canon law was considerable, and in either form these principles brought the elements of equity with them'.[65] While it was difficult to estimate the precise contribution of canon law to equity, because Scotland derived her Roman law more from the seventeenth century Dutch civilians who had repudiated much of the mediaeval canon law in favour of Justinian's *Institutes*, 'early judges were often canonists and cognisant of the conceptions of good faith and conscience, though these elements have not played an outstanding part in Scottish equity'[66] and '[t]he adoption of civil law principles either direct from the *Corpus Juris* or through the influence of the canon law was considerable, and in either form these principles brought the elements of equity with them'.[67] He also suggests that 'It seems at least possible that the interdict as we know it is derived from the canon law'.[68]

Contract/Obligations

There are conflicting views as to whether the doctrine of consideration in the English law of contract—that, unless it is made under seal, a contract cannot exist unless each party promises to give or do something for the other—is a development from mediaeval canon law. Willard Barbour[69] and Sir William Holdsworth[70] were both proponents of that theory; Sir John Baker is inclined to reject it.[71] My suspicion is that Baker's is the better view. If consideration *were* in fact a development from mediaeval canon law, one might reasonably expect that Scots law would have developed a similar doctrine—but it did not.

Though David Sellar suggests that, even after the Scottish Reformation, 'the canon law continued to be regarded as an important source of law, save inasmuch as it conflicted with the Reformation settlement' and that both

65 Walker (n 57) 219.
66 Ibid 679.
67 Ibid 219.
68 Ibid 310.
69 See WT Barbour, *The History of Contract in Early English Equity* (Clarendon Press 1914), especially 160–68.
70 WS Holdsworth, 'The Early History of Equity' (1915) 13 Michigan LR 301.
71 JH Baker, 'Origins of the "Doctrine" of Consideration' in *On the Laws and Customs of England: Essays in Honor of Samuel E Thome* (U of North Carolina P 1981) 351ff.

Craig[72] and Stair[73] were 'quite explicit about this',[74] the doctrine of consideration remains totally alien to the Scots law of obligations and under certain circumstances a unilateral promise can be binding—a principle reiterated by Lord President Hamilton as recently as 2007, relying on the exposition in Stair's *Institutions*.[75]

Doctors' Commons

Doctors' Commons was established at an uncertain date in the fifteenth or sixteenth century and incorporated in 1768. Its members practised in the ecclesiastical and admiralty courts and they were trained in Roman rather than common law. Like the mainstream legal profession, it was split between 'advocates' who pleaded causes and 'proctors' who were analogous to common law solicitors, and although its origin was in ecclesiastical law, it was concerned very largely with secular disputes.[76]

Doctors' Commons lost much of its *raison d'être* in the mid-1850s, when common lawyers were given the right to practise in areas which before had been the exclusive domain of the civilians. Under the reforms, the Court of Probate Act 1857 abolished the jurisdiction of the ecclesiastical courts over wills and succession, the Matrimonial Causes Act 1857 created a new divorce court in which barristers could appear, and the High Court of Admiralty Act 1859 liberalised rights of audience in the Admiralty Court.

There was a motion to dissolve Doctors' Commons in 1858 and its last meeting took place in 1865.[77] But it remains an interesting example of the

72 Sir Thomas Craig, *Ius Feudale*, I, 3.24. Craig (c1538–1608) wrote *Ius Feudale* (in Latin) on the Scots law of property in 1603 but it was not published until 1655: see JW Cairns, 'The *Breve Testatum* and Craig's *Ius Feudale*' (1988) 56(3) Tijdschrift voor Rechtsgeschiedenis 311–32.

73 *Stair* Bk I, 1.14.

74 WDH Sellar, 'Promise' in K Reid and R Zimmermann (eds), *A History of Private Law in Scotland, vol 2: Obligations* (OUP 2000) 263.

75 *Ilona and Ors v Vaughan* [2007] CSIH 3 at [15]:

> It is undoubted that the law of Scotland will recognise as obligatory a promise duly made. Delivery to or acceptance by the promisee is not necessary to the constitution of a promise (Stair—*Institutions of the Law of Scotland* Bk I.10.4), though, in my view, the presence or absence of communication to ther other party may be an adminicle of evidence in the question whether the statement amounts to a promise in law. Stair (op. cit.) I.10.2 distinguishes three acts of the will, namely, 'desire, resolution and engagement'. Only the third is obligatory. Having dealt with desire, Stair continues: 'Neither is resolution (which is a determinate purpose to do that which is desired) efficacious, because whatever is resolved or purposed, may be without fault altered, unless by accident the matter be necessary, or that the resolution be holden forth to assure others'. Neither of the two exceptions mentioned applies here.

76 Of 1,065 reported cases in the nineteenth century, only 124 concerned ecclesiastical matters: P Winckworth, *A Verification of the Faculty Jurisdiction* (SPCK 1953) 29.

77 The charter was never surrendered: Doctors' Commons came to an end with the death of its last Fellow, Dr TH Tristram, in 1912. For a short history, see P Barber, 'The Fall and Rise of Doctors' Commons?' (1996) 4(18) Ecclesiastical Law Journal 462–69.

continuing influence of civil and canon law on at least part of the secular legal system of England until long after the Reformation.

Conclusion

So how *did* the Reformation shape English and Scots church law? Perhaps unsurprisingly, there is no simple answer to that question. At the English Reformation, the *ius commune* persisted, with a transfer of supremacy from the Pope to the Crown. It was only after the death of Henry VIII that the two systems began gradually to diverge in their details. But the overall idea of canon or ecclesiastical law as a separate, if subordinate, system of law persisted, and ecclesiastical law as a distinct discipline still continues as a specialist area of legal practice. Equally, however, if canon law was shaped by the Reformation and by the gradual encroachment of secular law, that influence was by no means in one direction.

Canon law concepts continued to influence the common law in both jurisdictions. As we have seen, they influenced the secular law in England through the doctrine of equity and through the continuation of ecclesiastical jurisdiction over matters that are now dealt with by the secular courts.

As to Scotland, they seem to have had an important role in reminding the secular legal profession of the civilian roots of Scots law, and William Gordon goes so far as to assert that the civilian elements of Scots law *generally* are derived as much from the canonists as from the *Institutes* of Gaius and Justinian:

> [I]t is safe to say that in so far as Scotland has a share in the civilian tradition it has acquired that share essentially from later influence, initially through Canon law and then directly through contact with the Roman law taught in the universities.[78]

Like Sellar, though writing much earlier, Walker clearly regarded the pre-Reformation canon law as an important influence on Scots law, suggesting that it was 'impossible that ideas from the Roman and canon law should not have penetrated the law of Scotland'.[79] He offers as an example Lord President Normand's opinion in *F v F*[80]—an interim proceeding in an action by a husband for declarator of nullity on ground of his impotence—to the effect that 'the canon law, while not of binding authority affords a guide and will receive due weight in our law if it appears to be *secundum aequum et bonum*'.[81]

78 W Gordon (n 28) 4.
79 Walker (n 57) 99.
80 1945 SC at 208, [1945] ScotCS CSIH 1. The judgement is available at <>www.bailii.org/scot/cases/ScotCS/1945/1945_SC_202.html>.
81 Walker (n 57) 99. In his concurring opinion, Lord Moncrieff quotes Canons 1068 and 1971 of the *Codex Iuris Canonici 1917* and concludes that 'the title of the pursuer is thus . . .

Writing earlier still, Lord President Cooper concluded that the 'immense debt which Scots Law owes to Canon Law and Practice has never been sufficiently acknowledged'.[82] And as Helmholz observes in the present volume, 'Gero Dolezalek, John Cairns and Alan Wijffels . . . have demonstrated beyond doubt that the medieval canonical authorities continued to be cited and applied in courts north of the Tweed'.[83]

Inevitably, hard evidence for the influence of pre-Reformation canon law on secular law is scant, particularly in relation to Scotland—but such evidence as is available suggests that, so far as Western canon law was concerned, the broader legal effects of the English and Scots Reformations were by no means a clean break with what had gone before.

Bibliography

Baker JH, 'Origins of the "Doctrine" of Consideration' in *On the Laws and Customs of England: Essays in Honor of Samuel E Thome* (U of North Carolina P 1981)

Baldwin Smith L, *The Elizabethan World* (Houghton Mifflin 1967)

Barber P, 'The Fall and Rise of Doctors' Commons?' (1996) Ecclesiastical Law Journal 4(18) 462–69

Barbour WT, *The History of Contract in Early English Equity* (Clarendon Press 1914)

Berman HJ, *Law and Revolution: The Formation of the Western Legal Tradition* (Harvard UP 1983)

Bray SL, 'The Influence of the Catholic Intellectual Tradition on the Common Law' in R Domingo, GS Hauk and TP Jackson (eds), *Faith in Law, Law in Faith* (Brill 2024)

Cairns JW, 'The *Breve Testatum* and Craig's *Ius Feudale*' (1988) 56(3) Tijdschrift voor Rechtsgeschiedenis 311–32

Church of England, *The Canon Law of the Church of England: Being the Report of the Archbishops' Commission on Canon Law, Together with Proposals for a Revised Body of Canons* (SPCK 1947)

Cooper of Culross Lord, *Select Scottish Cases of the Thirteenth Century* (William Hodge & Co 1944)

Cox N, 'The Influence of the Common Law on the Decline of the Ecclesiastical Courts of the Church of England' (2001–2002) 3(1) Rutgers Journal of Law and Religion

Donahue CH Jr, 'Roman Canon Law in the Medieval English Church: *Stubbs vs. Maitland* re-Examined after 75 years in the Light of Some Records from the Church Courts' (1973–74) 72 Michigan Law Review 647

Eun Soo Choi, 'The Religious Dimension of the Women's Suffrage Movement: The Role of the Scottish Presbyterian Churches, 1867–1918' (PhD thesis, Glasgow University 1996) 271 <http://theses.gla.ac.uk/3943/>

Godolphin J, *Repertorium Canonicum, or, An Abridgment of the Ecclesiastical Laws of This Realm, Consistent with the Temporal Wherein the Most Material Points Relating*

supported by authority in Scotland, in England and even *Urbe et Orbi* [*sic*]; and, if only as so supported, ought to be sustained'.

82 Lord Cooper of Culross, *Select Scottish Cases of the Thirteenth Century* (William Hodge & Co 1944) xxii, quoted in S Thomson, 'Mixed Jurisdiction and the Scottish Legal Tradition: Reconsidering the Concept of Mixture' (2014) 7(1) Journal of Civil Law Studies 65.

83 See Ch. 3 at 59.

to Such Persons and Things, As Come Within the Cognizance Thereof, Are Succinctly Treated (Christopher Wilkinson 1678)
Gordon E, 'Irregular Marriage: Myth and Reality' (2013) 47(2) Journal of Social History 507–25
Gordon W, 'Roman Law in Scotland' in R Evans-Jones (ed), *The Civil Law Tradition in Scotland*, Supplementary Series (Stair Society 1995) vol 2
Helmholz RH *Roman Canon Law in Reformation England* (CUP 1990)
Helmholz RH, *Oxford History of the Laws of England: The Canon Law and Ecclesiastical Jurisdiction from 597 to the 1640s* (OUP 2004)
Henry of Bracton, *De Legibus et Consuetudinibus Angliae* (translated in GE Woodbine and SE Thorne, *Bracton on the Laws and Customs of England* (Belknap Press of Harvard University 1968–77)
Holdsworth WS, 'The Early History of Equity' (1915) 13 Michigan LR 301
Hunt A, 'The Day the Shepherds Were Scattered' (*Church Times*, 21 September 2012)
Ibbetson D, 'A House Built on Sand: Equity in Early Modern English Law' in E Koops, WJE Koops and WJ Zwalve (eds), *Law & Equity: Approaches in Roman Law and Common Law* (Martinus Nijhoff 2014) 57
MacCulloch D, *Thomas Cranmer: A Life* (Yale UP 1996)
MacCulloch D, 'One Enormous Room' (2013) 35(9) *London Review of Books*, 9 May
Maitland FW, 'Canon Law in England: I. William Lyndwood' (1896) 11 English Historical Review 446
Maitland FW, 'Canon Law in England: III. William of Drogheda and the Universal Ordinary' (1897) 12 English Historical Review 625
Martínez-Torrón T, 'Comments on the Influence of Canon Law on the Common Law Legal Tradition' (1989) 20(1) *Revue générale de droit* 5–30 <www.erudit.org/en/journals/rgd/1989-v20-n1-rgd04474/1058354ar/>
Martinez-Torrón J, *Anglo-American law and Canon Law: Canonical Roots of the Common Law Tradition* (Duncker & Humblot GmbH 1998)
Milsom SFC, *Historical Foundations of the Common Law* (2nd edn, Butterworths 1969)
Probert R, '*R v Millis* Reconsidered: Binding Contracts and Bigamous Marriages' (2008) 28(3) Legal Studies 337–55
Royal Commission on Ecclesiastical Courts, *Report of the Commissioners Appointed to Inquire into the Constitution and Working of the Ecclesiastical Courts* (Eyre & Spottiswood 1883)
Scott A, *The Evolution of Resource Property Rights* (OUP 2008)
Sellar D, 'Marriage by Cohabitation with Habit and Repute: Review and Requiem?' in DL Carey Miller and DW Meyers (eds), *Comparative and Historical Essays in Scots Law: A Tribute to Professor Sir Thomas Smith QC* (Butterworths 1992)
Sellar WDH, 'Promise' in K Reid and R Zimmermann (eds), *A History of Private Law in Scotland, vol 2: Obligations* (OUP 2000) 263
Stair—*Institutions of the Law of Scotland* Bk I.10.4 (2nd edn, Edinburgh 1693)
Thomson S, 'Mixed Jurisdiction and the Scottish Legal Tradition: Reconsidering the Concept of Mixture' (2014) 7 *Journal of Civil Law Studies* 51
Walker DM, 'Equity in Scots Law' (PhD thesis, Edinburgh University 1952) 477 <https://era.ed.ac.uk/handle/1842/27594>
Winckworth P, *A Verification of the Faculty Jurisdiction* (SPCK 1953)

3 The Reformation and Legal Change

The Persistence of Medieval Canon Law

R.H. Helmholz

Introduction

The Reformation was a dramatic event in European history—a sharp break from the religion established during the Middle Ages. In what would become the Protestant lands of Europe, the reformers threw off what they regarded as the illegitimate yoke of the papacy, abolished the Mass as if it were an idolatrous ceremony, sent monks and nuns packing, restored the Bible to a central place in the Christian life, and ended the requirement of clerical celibacy that the reformers of earlier centuries had fought so valiantly to establish. Strong stuff—apparent whether one regards what happened as a lamentable descent into heresy or a praiseworthy overthrow of superstition. The 'Wars of Religion' that pitted Catholic against Protestant princes appear the almost inevitable outcome of the latter's determination to rid their lands of the vestiges of the religion they had inherited from the later Middle Ages.

This chapter takes up one aspect of this story, a limited one. It assesses the extent of change in the use and enforcement of the classical law of the medieval church, the law contained in the *Corpus iuris canonici*, during the post-Reformation period. It recognises the existence of reforms during those years, no less in the Council of Trent's decrees than in the enactments adopted in Protestant lands. However, its focus is a more limited one. Its aspiration is to deal both with the canon law's place in the professional lives of the jurists whose careers were influenced by it and also with its impact on the ordinary men and women whose lives were affected by it. The chapter reaches a different conclusion about the extent of change than do most commonly received historical narratives on the subject. It is what emerges from looking to what happened in legal practice rather than to the hostile recrimination that marked the contests between Catholics and Protestants. Its coverage is thus concentrated upon the law as it was applied in the courts of European lands.

There is a particular reason for taking this approach. A great deal of systematic study of the judicial records of European lands has taken place during the past 50 years. It has opened a new window on this subject, one that had previously been closed to earlier historians. Most of them regarded individual cases simply as examples of what was found in the formal law and of

DOI: 10.4324/9780429264115-4

little importance on that account.[1] There was little reason for their study That has changed. More of today's historians link the study of theory and practice together, allowing us to see what happened 'on the ground' in this aspect of Reformation history, including developments within Catholic lands.[2] When coupled with an examination of the contemporary treatise literature, the scholarship that has emerged from this source provides a different and useful vantage point from which to assess the situation. It has produced some surprising results—particularly surprising because they do not match the dramatic changes in theology and religious practice that occurred.

The chapter's purpose is neither to challenge the recognition of the Reformation's historical effects nor to promote the ecumenical movement by minimising the differences between the doctrines espoused by Catholics and Protestants.[3] It is rather to sum up what recent research has revealed about the history of the medieval canon law as it was put to use during the post-Reformation era. These years confronted Protestant jurists with the need to deal with an inherited legal regime. They also witnessed the emergence of new problems in Catholic lands, calling for responses. Of course, what happened in Germany was not identical to what happened in Scotland. Nor was what happened in Italy identical to what happened in Spain. The subject calls for taking notice of events in both lands, and it invites an assessment of the differences among them. However, there were also widely shared assumptions and common reactions to the problems of life that had long been regulated by the canon law. Very few of the problems disappeared. Not all of them were upset by religious differences. Some were. Some were not. The chapter attempts to describe them both.

The Law's Foundations

The leaders of Protestant reform shared one relevant characteristic with contemporary Catholic jurists. They were not antinomians. They may have repeated the German maxim '*Juristen—böse Christen*',[4] but they did not use

1 JH Baker, *The Law's Two Bodies* (OUP 2011) 4–9. An example of the traditional conclusions about this subject in England is W Holdsworth, 'The Ecclesiastical Courts and their Jurisdiction' in *Select Essays in Anglo-American Legal History* (Boston 1908) II, 254–311, at 267: '[T]he great work of Henry's reign was to effect an entire change in the relations between church and state . . . the law of the church ceased to be the canon law of Rome'.

2 See e.g. the description of research in C Donati, 'Curie, tribunali, cancellerie episcopali in Italia durante i secoli dell'età moderna: percorsi di ricerca' in Cecilia Nubola and Angelo Tuchini (eds), *Fonti ecclesiastiche per la storia sociale e religiosa d'Europa: XV–XVIII secolo* (Il Mulino – Bologna 1999) , 213–29; C Donahue Jr., *Why the History of Canon Law Is Not Written*, Selden Society Lecture for 1984 (Stair Society 1986).

3 On this possibility, see the cautious approach of R Ombres, 'Ecclesiology, Ecumenism and Canon Law' in N Doe, M Hill and R Ombres (eds), *Essays in Honour of Bishop Eric Kemp* (University of Wales Press 1998) 36–47.

4 C Kenny, 'Bonus Jurista Malus Christa' (1903) 19 Law Quarterly Review 326–34.

that maxim as permission to cast off traditional sources of jurisprudence. On the contrary, they believed that law was a normal and a necessary part of Christian life, one built upon acceptance of the law of nature and the moral force of the positive law based upon it.[5] True, Luther himself may have cast the Gregorian Decretals into a fire, but he did not mean thereby to license a general freedom from law itself.[6] Attempts to ignore duties of earthly obedience to the law in response to the passages found in the Gospels earned only his indignation. And among the greatest of exponents of the legitimate place of natural law in human law there were many Protestant writers—Philip Melanchthon (1497–1560), Johann Oldendorp (1486–1567), Hugo Grotius (1583–1625) and Samuel Pufendorf (1632–1694), for example. If the law of nature has today been displaced in many Protestant circles by an emphasis on divine love as revealed in Scripture, as some think today, this has been a recent development rather than a consequence of the Protestant Reformation itself.

The early history of natural law in the Reformed tradition is not greatly different on this score. John Calvin was a lawyer by training, and he held to the then traditional view that 'the law of God which we call the moral law is nothing else than a testimony of natural law'.[7] In itself, natural law was not regarded as sufficient to lead men to God or to define the obligations of a Christian, but as one modern commentator put it, Calvin approached the question of natural law's rightful place in the world 'in a manner reminiscent of Aquinas'.[8] The Bible itself was said to embody the existing connection between the Christian religion and the premises of the law of nature. As with the Ten Commandments, natural law added divine endorsement to recognised sources of authority.

English contributions to the history of natural law thought may have been less foundational, but the adoption of Reformation principles spelled no retreat from its widespread acceptance. Richard Hooker (1553–1600) and Richard Cumberland (1631–1718) were the most prominent examples among the clerical elite who were authors and proponents of the relevance of natural law—the first the author of *The Lawes of Ecclesiastical Politie* (1593–1597), the second the author of *De Legibus Naturae Disquisitio Philosophica* (1672).

5 A Raunio, 'Natural Law in the Lutheran Tradition' in Norman Doe (ed), *Christianity and Natural Law: An Introduction* (CUP 2017) 77–97.

6 See e.g. M Heckel, *Martin Luthers Reformation und das Recht* (Tübingen 2016) 9–10; Kenneth Pennington, 'Protestant Ecclesiastical Law and the Ius Commune' (2015) 26 Rivista internazionale di Diritto Comune 9–35.

7 J Calvin, 'Institutes of the Christian Religion' in JT McNeill (ed), *The Library of Christian Classics*, vol XX (The Westminster Press 1960) 4.20.16.

8 See M van Huffel, 'Natural Law in the Reformed Tradition' in Norman Doe (ed), *Christianity and Natural Law: An Introduction* (CUP 2017) 125; see also D Van Drunen, *Natural Law and the Two Kingdoms: A Study in the Development of Reformed Social Thought* (Eerdmans 2010); J Witte, Jr., 'The Law Written on the Heart: Natural Law and Equity in Early Lutheran Thought' in Wim Decock et al. (eds), *Law and Religion: The Legal Teachings of the Protestant and Catholic Reformations* (Vandenhoeck & Ruprecht 2014) 174–85.

More than that, however, the evidence of natural law's acceptance among both English common lawyers as well as civilians is sufficient to show that the Reformation marked no real change to this subject's relevance in the courts of both the common and ecclesiastical laws on the other side of the English Channel.[9]

For assessing Catholic Europe's jurisprudence after the Reformation there is little need to demonstrate the continuity of the natural law tradition. It flourished then and it remains relevant to this day. Natural law has continued to occupy a place of influence within Catholic thought. Indeed its promotion has become something of a specialty among some conservative Catholic academics. The liveliest (and most famous) historical example from the early modern period was the debate centred in the Spanish School of Salamanca over the rights of the native peoples of South America. It encouraged, even depended upon, thought about natural law—an easy connection since the native peoples provided a 'test case' for the relevance of law for those in the discovered world who lived in something like a state of nature.

Of course, there have been developments in Catholic thought since then—the concentration on the writing on this subject by St Thomas Aquinas found in the work of modern Catholic writers on natural law is a change from the habits of the sixteenth century. His *Summa theologica* was rarely cited by Catholic (or Protestant) writers on law during those years.[10] Whatever that particular change signifies, it does not demonstrate any basic change in approach to legal questions among Catholic lawyers and theologians. Natural law was a constant. However much the two sides of the religious divide differed in 1600, law's philosophical foundation was not one of the things that kept them apart.

Secular Challenges

A second and quite different development had an impact on the law of churches on both sides of the Protestant-Catholic divide. Its character was expressed years ago by a famous French scholar. He described what happened at the close of the Middle Ages as a growth of an 'esprit laïque'.[11] Not caused by the Reformation and not without precedent in earlier centuries—this spirit took a more aggressive and decisive turn during the fifteenth century, and its effects grew during the Reformation. They took place in both Protestant and Catholic lands. In some places it broke what had been a virtual clerical

9 A fuller development of this subject is found in my article 'Natural Law and Human Rights in English Law: From Bracton to Blackstone' (2005) 3 Ave Maria Law Review 1–22.

10 For more evidence on this point, see my *Natural Law in Court* (Harvard University Press 2013) 5–7. For further discussion of natural law see chapters 6 and 7.

11 G de Lagarde, *La naissance de l'esprit laïque au déclin du Moyen Age*, 5 vols. (Paris-Louvain 1956–1970). English evidence on this subject is also found in E Kemp, *Counsel and Consent* (SPCK 1961) 145–61.

monopoly on the legal profession,[12] and in most it decisively curtailed the substantive scope of ecclesiastical jurisdiction. Virtually everywhere, even in territories that remained aggressively Catholic, the courts of the Church lost what had been a virtual monopoly over large parts of their medieval jurisdiction.[13] So one finds, for example, in early modern Venice the canonical rule that clerics accused of crimes were to be tried by their bishop, but we also find a series of exceptions in which secular courts exercised customary jurisdiction. Treason, assassination, murder, violent or great crimes all came within that expansive class.[14] It was very like the English experience of limiting the clergiable offenses in which clerics could claim benefit of clergy,[15] and it was also one part of a movement that led to a papal interdict being laid on the Venetian Republic.

The mediaeval church had never claimed jurisdiction over purely secular matters, but it did claim the right to define where the line should be drawn between the two. On this ground, French ecclesiastical courts therefore claimed the right to excommunicate debtors who had refused to pay their creditors, founding this right on the fact that it was a sin to violate a solemn promise.[16] The medieval consistory courts in England exercised a similar jurisdiction over sworn promises. It was widely used to secure the payment of ordinary debts.[17] Whether this assertion actually made sense to contemporaries is an open question. Contemporary canon lawyers defended it,[18] and it supplied weaknesses in the remedies available in the temporal courts. However, by the sixteenth century in both lands what amounted in practice to the process of debt collection had come to look more like an abuse.[19] The 'esprit laïque' stood against it. The result restricted the reach of the church's domain, and the church's jurisdiction over sworn promises to pay debts withered in consequence.

Something like this change of attitude towards debt collection had wider consequences in both Catholic and Protestant lands. Direct enforcement of statutes enacted in parliaments or other representative assemblies was one example of the drive to take greater control of the jurisdiction exercised by

12 H Thieme, 'Le rôle des *Doctores Legum* dans la société allemande du XVI siècle' in *Individu et Société a la Renaissance* (Presses Universitaires de Bruxelles 1967) 159–70.

13 G Dolezalek, 'Litigation at the Rota Romana, Particularly around 1700' in Alain Wijffels (ed), *Case Law in the Making, vol. 1: Essays* (Duncker & Humblot 1997) 339–73, at 342.

14 See Petrus de Zambonis (fl. 1600), *Isagoge in practicam criminalem ad leges Venetas accommodate* (1614) cap. 14.

15 JS Stephen, *History of the Criminal Law of England* (1883, repr. n.d.) I, 463–68.

16 Tyler Lange, *Excommunication for Debt in Late Medieval France: The Business of Salvation* (CUP 2016).

17 RH Helmholz, 'Assumpsit and Fidei Laesio' (1976) 91 Law Quarterly Review 406–32.

18 See W Lyndwood (ca. 1375–1446), *Provinciale seu Consitutiones Angliae* (OUP 1676) 315, s.v. perjurio.

19 P Cavill, 'Perjury in Early Tudor England' in R McKitterick, C Methuen and A Spicer (eds), *The Church and the Law* (Cambridge University Press 2020) 182–209; and see generally for France Jean Gaudemet, *Les Sources du droit canonique, VIII–XX siècle* (Routledge 1993) 190–91.

the courts of the Church.[20] English ecclesiastical lawyers learned to cope with the statutes enacted in Parliament, and that legislation entered into corners of practice in the ecclesiastical courts that had been left alone in the Middle Ages. Another example was the creation of new courts that acted as 'rivals' to the older ecclesiastical institutions. In Spain, for example, many of the offenses against morality once dealt with in ecclesiastical courts came to be dealt with in temporal courts as well.[21] A similar result was reached in parts of Italy.[22] In England, examples are the crimes of perjury and sodomy. The first became a secular crime in 1562–1563, the second in 1533.[23] During the Middle Ages, they had been prosecuted as ecclesiastical offenses.

In turn, this change of mind led to a greater use of mandates from kings and princes issued to the courts of the Church to prevent them from dealing with matters regarded as outside the scope of their jurisdiction. In England it led equally to an expansion in the scope of the jurisdiction exercised by the Court of Chancery and also to the creation of branches of the Court of High Commission. As royal courts, they drew litigation away from the ecclesiastical courts. In the courts of the Low Countries, something like the same process occurred. New statutes expanded the scope of the jurisdiction of temporal courts, which assumed jurisdiction over marriage and the family, charitable and testamentary bequests, and offences against morality.[24] In France, it led to the so-called Appel comme d'abus, which permitted the invalidation of acts of ecclesiastical judges that contravened royal interests or commands.[25]

Did this shared development serve as a force for European unity? Was it at least a source of empathy to be shared by ecclesiastical officials and ordinary lawyers in different European lands? Apparently not. The Catholic tribunals refused to treat the decisions of the ecclesiastical tribunals in Protestant lands as *res judicata*, even between the litigants themselves, much to the annoyance of Protestant judges and lawyers. But this is a different question. It was one expression of the antipathy the adherents of these branches of Christianity had for each other, not a declaration of unity or mutual respect. For the sake of completeness, therefore, this shared experience requires recognition nonetheless, primarily because it tells us something relevant to the evolution of the canon law as it was put into practice. Across most of Europe, the

20 For English evidence, see R Palmer, *Selling the Church: The English Parish in Law, Commerce and Religion 1350–1550* (The University of North Carolina Press 2002) 23–29.

21 R Barahuna, *Sex Crimes, Honour, and the Law in Early Modern Spain: Vizcaya, 1528–1725* (University of Toronto Press 2003) 97–100.

22 See e.g. D Lombardi, 'Marriage in Italy' in Silvana Seidel Menchi (ed), *Marriage in Europe 1400–1800* (University of Toronto Press 2016) 105–11.

23 5 Eliz. I, c. 9; 25 Hen. VIII, c. 6.

24 J Witte, Jr, 'The Plight of Canon Law in the Early Dutch Republic' in RH Helmholz (ed), *Canon Law in Protestant Lands* (Duncker and Humblot 1992) 134–64, at 157.

25 The process is expertly described in A Lefebvre-Teillard, *Les officialités à la veille du Concile de Trente* (1973) 130–43.

sphere of jurisdictional authority the courts of the Church had once enjoyed was being challenged from without. Secular courts began to offer alternatives and also purposefully to constrict the jurisdictional reach of the courts of the Church. The results that followed from an awakened 'esprit laïque' were similar, although they took somewhat different forms in different European lands.

European Legal Education

If the familiar adage 'Taught Law Is Tough Law' comes anywhere close to an accurate tribute to the results of a legal education,[26] the training of lawyers and judges in both Catholic and Protestant lands would have been a force for similarities between them. Reluctant similarity perhaps, but one that would have marked their attitudes towards what amounted to a proper legal education and also one of the sources of ideas they would have carried into their careers. It was a text-based kind of education. Law lecturers in Europe's universities began with and focused their attention on legal texts in their lectures. In teaching the civil law, they first read and then they explained the laws found in the *Corpus iuris civilis.* Not necessarily all of them, but to the exclusion of an exploration of decided court cases and questions of desirable policies that is bread and butter in today's law school. After the initial reading, lecturers followed with further textual references, and also with the parallels and distinctions found elsewhere in the *Corpus.* They did not start either with a law's social consequences or with descriptions of what their students could expect in practice.[27] The identical approach would have been taken in lectures for those students who went on to study canon law, except that the principal texts would have come from the Digest's canonical counterpart, the *Corpus iuris canonici.* In both cases, lecturers normally went slowly. Their object was to make clear the import of each legal text, comparing it with other texts and resolving apparent contradictions.

A quite remarkable phenomenon in the study of legal education is how slowly this system changed over the centuries. Legal humanism made very few inroads on this method of instruction, although it did widen the approaches many jurists and teachers took to the texts.[28] Of course, it was inevitable that the Reformation should have had a dramatic effect on the instruction offered in Protestant theological faculties. However, its impact on the subjects of instruction within the law faculties was much less.[29] A revealing result

26 See R Leflar, 'Taught Law Is Tough Law' (1982) 8 Wayne Law Review 465–80; FW Maitland, 'English Law and the Renaissance' in H. Cam (ed), *Selected Historical Essays of F.W. Maitland* (CUP 1957) 142.

27 Peter Stein, 'Roman Law' in *Cambridge History of Medieval Political Thought, c. 350–c. 1450* (CUP 1988) 37–47.

28 Mario Ascheri, *The Laws of Late Medieval Italy (1000–1500)* (Brill 2013) 353.

29 The evidence is presented and surveyed in H Coing, 'Die juristische Fakultät und ihr Lehrprogramm' in Helmut Coing (ed), *Handbuch der Quellen und Literatur der neueren europäischen*

was that the presence of 'foreign students' in law at universities outside their own countries was a common feature of the age, one not rivalled until the twenty-first century. For these students, it would have been no hindrance to returning to their native lands to begin their careers, since instruction in the authorities of the canon and civil laws would not have differed greatly from one land to another.[30] It proved to be of particular importance in Scandinavian lands, where the introduction of direct influence of the Roman and canon laws depended on the results of these scholarly migrations.[31]

No one should suppose that this continuity in method means that no lecturer in law made an irrelevant comment or expressed an opinion of his own. Only someone who has never met a member of a university law faculty could believe that. Nor should the disputations and informal study that accompanied the formal lectures be ignored.[32] The assertion made here is only that the lecturers of the time focused their attention on the meaning of individual texts and upon their relation to other texts. They rarely dealt with descriptions of practice in the courts or with the economic and social consequences of the laws. Any look at the *glossa ordinaria* that accompanied the texts of the Roman and canon laws will illustrate this feature of legal education in earlier centuries.

Education of English lawyers appears to have been an exception to this pattern of concentration upon the texts of the learned laws in medieval and early modern times. The education of most English lawyers took place in the Inns of Chancery and the Inns of Court in London, not in Cambridge or Oxford. Instruction and training there did not follow the normal Continental pattern of reliance on texts from the Roman and canon laws. This difference, however, is more apparent than real in the context of this investigation. The London Inns were for lawyers destined to practice in the royal courts. Education of English civilians, the lawyers who served as judges and advocates in the courts of the Church and other courts outside the common law's sphere, took place in the universities. Their education followed the European pattern.

When King Henry VIII's ministers shut the door on the canon law faculties at the English universities, the closure did not in itself eliminate references to the texts of the canon law. They found a place in lectures on the civil law.

Privatrechtsgeschichte, Zweiter Band: Neure Zeit (1500–1800) (C.H. Beck 1977) 3–102; for its continuity see also his 'L'insegnamento del diritto nell'Europa dell'Ancien Regime' (1970) 82 Studi Senesi 179–93.

30 See the text and references collected in G Dolezalek, 'French Legal Literature quoted by Scottish Lawyers 1550–1650' in *Mélanges en l'honneur d'Anne Lefebvre-Teillard* (PANTHEON ASSAS 2009) 375–91, at 381, nn. 20–24.

31 M Korpiola, 'On the Reception of the Jus Commune and Foreign law in Sweden, ca. 1550–1615' <www.cliothemis.com/Clio@Themis 2>.

32 E.g. Isidoro Soffietti, 'L'enseignement du droit à l'université de Verceil au Moyen Âge' (2021) 99 Revue historique de droit français et étranger 171–79.

Canon law was kept 'in commendam' with the study of Roman law,[33] and (to take a single example), when a late-seventeenth-century English lecturer in one of the English civil law faculties began what we would call his 'course description', he took careful note, saying that it would include references to both Roman and canon laws.[34] Even some English common lawyers of the period found it necessary, or at least useful, to do the same.[35] And in this inclusion, England was not alone among Protestant lands.[36] The overlap between the subjects treated in both laws was a regular feature of most of the Continental lectures on law.[37] It would have left many subjects quite incomplete had lecturers taken the closure of a canon law faculty to require them to ignore the canonical texts relevant to the subjects found in the Digest or Institutes.[38] One has only to consider subjects like the law on usury or on the powers of public officers to appreciate the utility of including texts found in the canon law.[39] Without it, the instruction offered would have been incomplete at best.

The Strength of the *ius commune*

Understanding the persistence of the canon law in post-Reformation Europe also requires some familiarity with the character of the European *ius commune*. It stood behind the lectures just discussed. This term itself is commonly used to describe the amalgam of Roman and canon laws that was fashioned by European jurists after the recovery of the texts of the Digest and the growth of

33 Thomas Fuller (1608–61), *History of the University of Cambridge* (1840), 167; William Fulbecke (1560–1603), *Parallele or conference of the civil law, the canon law, and the common law of this realme of England* (1618). Note also the famous dictum of Petrus Rebuffus (1487–1557), a Continental commentator: '[I]us canonicum et civile sunt adeo connexa, ut unum sine altero vix intelligi possit'. See 'Tractatus nominationum' in *Tractatus universi iuris* (1584), tit. 15.2.

34 British Library, London, MS. Harl. 6049 'On the Study of Law'. See also I Baumgärtner, 'Was muss ein Legist vom Kirchenrecht wissen? Roffredus Beneventanus und seine Libelli de iure canonico' in Peter Linehan (ed), *Proceedings of the Seventh International Congress of Medieval Canon Law* (S. Congregatio de Seminariis et Studiorum Universitatibus 1988) 223–45.

35 D Seipp, 'The Reception of Canon Law and Civil Law in the Common Law Courts before 1600' (1993) 13 Oxford Journal of Legal Studies 388–420.

36 See e.g. R Feenstra, 'Canon Law at Dutch Universities from 1575 to 1811' in RH Helmholz (ed), *Canon Law in Protestant Lands* (Duncker and Humblot 1992) 123–34.

37 See L Prosdocimi, 'Il diritto canonico di fronte al diritto secolare' in *La Formazione storica del diritto moderno in Europa* (OLSCHKI 1978) 431–46; H Liermann, 'Das kanonischen Recht als Gegenstand des gelehrten Unterrichts an den protestantischen Universitäten in den ersten Jahrhunderten nach der Reformation' (1955) 3 Studia Gratiana 541–66.

38 The academic literature is described in LJ Korporowicz, 'Was the Roman Catholic Canon Law Studied in Eighteenth-Century England?' (2018) 108 Studia Prawno-Ekonomiczne 83–102.

39 See T Rester, 'Roman Canon Law in Protestant Reformed Theologians as Both Touchstone and Foil' in *Law and Religion the Legal Teachings of the Protestant and Catholic Reformations* (Vandenhoek & Ruprecht 2014) 174–85; M Schmoeckel, 'Das kanonische Zinsverbot unde die Konfessionalisierung' in *Law and Religion The Legal Teachings of the Protestant and Catholic Reformations* (Vandenhoek & Ruprecht 2014) 186–212.

university study. It came to be the common inheritance of European lawyers,[40] one they had learned at university, although as they would have learned even then that it was subject to variation by local customary law or other statutory enactment, what was called the *ius proprium* of individual parts of all European lands.

The canon law part of medieval *ius commune* was never a Code in the modern sense. It was not meant to be. It did not displace existing laws or attempt to state the entire law of any region, as a Code seeks to do. It was rather an accepted reference point for lawyers and judges, one used regularly in dealing with legal questions of all sorts. So, for instance, if a question arose about whether one party had *dominium* over land, it was to the character of that concept found in the law of the Romans that would be used in answering the question. Canonists also used it to describe the ordinary law of the church rather than a particular law built upon a privilege or local custom, recognising also that in many circumstances the canon law itself had made use of the Roman laws. An old maxim—*ecclesia vivit iure Romano*—expressed the historical dependence and the continuing influence of this commonly accepted principle. In England, the same term in substance as *ius commune* was used to describe the general English law, as contrasted with special laws built upon either the royal prerogative or local custom.[41] It did not, however, prevent English ecclesiastical lawyers from making use of resources of the Roman and canon laws.

Why does this matter for understanding the persistence of canon law in the lands of Europe that accepted the Protestant forms of Christianity? It matters because the lawyers of these lands were accustomed to the European *ius commune*. It was the formal source of law they understood. It did not seem sensible to take a divergent path unless they were required to do so. Sometimes they were, but not always. For instance, under the common law of the church, the rector of a parish church was responsible for its maintenance and repair. By English custom inherited from the Middle Ages, however, the rector's responsibility was limited to responsibility for repair of the chancel. The parishioners themselves were required to maintain the nave. So when a question arose that was not clearly covered by this exception—say the need for repair of an outbuilding or the maintenance of the churchyard—it was to the church's law that English civilians looked for the answer. Rectors bore the responsibility, not the parishioners. Special customs were valid under their law, but they were not to be extended by implication—a lawyerly conclusion founded upon acceptance

40 The basic guide is M Bellomo, *The Common Legal Past of Europe 1000–1800*, Lydia Cochrane, trans. (1995); also insightful is J Gaudemet, 'Les transferts de droit' (1976) 27 L'année sociologique 29–59.

41 F Pollock and FW Maitland, *History of English Law before the Time of Edward* (2d edn, CUP 1898, reprinted 1968) I, 176–78.

and use of the *ius commune*, one they had first come into contact within the university lectures they had attended.

The *Corpus iuris canonici*

The largest part of the medieval church's law was contained in two large volumes, the first being Gratian's *Decretum*, the second being the so-called Decretals. Both contained many statements of legal rules. Both were arranged by subject matter. Using them does require some getting used to. The first of the two was a compilation of existing authorities—decrees of councils, passages from the Bible, writings of Church fathers, papal decrees and even civil law—brought together by a shadowy figure named Gratian—under the formal title *Concordia canonum discordantium*.[42] The title promised a concordance of existing and discordant canons, and that is what its compiler sought to supply. So, for instance, where some ancient texts required that the choice of bishops be made by the clergy and people of a diocese (*per clerum et populum*), whereas others reserved the same right to clerical electors alone, Gratian harmonised them by stating that the role of the people did exist, but that it was limited to 'acclaiming' the clergy's choice. This distinction brought the ancient canons into an understanding in line with evolving clerical attitudes against the active participation of the laity in the governance of the church.

The principal use made of the Gratian's *Decretum* in the Middle Ages was as a school book. Students were taken step by step through its contents. This requires a brief mention for two reasons. First, it brought students into immediate contact with some of the basic principles that underlay the medieval canon law—the great importance of *salus animarum* in shaping its enforcement or the independence of the clerical order, for instance. Second, it accustomed students to methods of textual interpretation that they would need in practice when, as often happened, they were required to confront and interpret existing laws. This chapter is about lawyers, whether Catholic or Protestant, and what they learned as preparation for their careers. The two shared in the approach to laws and statutes they would both have heard and experienced first in working through Gratian's *Decretum*.

It was, however, the latter of the two books, the Decretals, in which most of the rules that governed practice in the diocesan courts were stated, and it has been on its contents that modern church historians have focused the greater part of their attention. Most though not all of its contents were edited versions of answers to legal questions that had been appealed or otherwise submitted to the judgement of the supreme pontiff in Rome. It was divided into five books—the first dealt with the constitution and organisation of the

42 His identity and process of the formulation of the *Decretum* have long been matters of uncertainty; for the most recent understanding, see A Winroth, *The Making of Gratian's Decretum* (CUP 2000).

church, the second with procedural rules, the third with the rights and duties of the clergy, the fourth with marriage and divorce and the fifth with the penal law of the church. The same pattern was followed in the later additions to this corpus: the *Liber sextus* (1298), the *Clementines* (1317) and the *Extravagantes* (1325–1327).

For the purposes of this chapter's subject, there is no need to enter into a detailed analysis of the process by which either of these two volumes was compiled. Historical treatments of the formation of the medieval canon law are accessible, and they supply serviceable entry points for understanding the process by which the classical canon law came into being during the twelfth and thirteenth centuries.[43] All of them stress its lasting importance in European legal history, taking note both that these collections influenced litigation of all sorts and also retained their pre-eminent status for centuries. In fact, they were not fully displaced as statements of the basic law of the Catholic Church until the twentieth century.[44] There is one point about them, however, that is of particular relevance for this chapter. It is to emphasise how much of the medieval church's law modern historians have connected directly with the papacy. The great English historian, F.W. Maitland, described the Decretals as 'a statute book deriving its force from the pope who published it'.[45] Looking at most of the historical literature of Maitland's era and beyond suggests that its purpose must have been to establish and describe the legislative power of the papacy. It thus appears to follow that rejection of papal authority in Protestant lands would require rejection of texts that proceeded from papal authority.

That conclusion follows as a matter of logic, but looking at the actual contents of the Gregorian Decretals calls for hesitation in accepting it as a fair characterisation of the church's law. No title in its many pages was devoted to expanding or even defining the extent of papal authority. It did contain a title devoted to 'the office of archdeacons' and many others like it, but there was no title devoted to 'the office of the Roman pontiff'. Virtually all of what is found in the Decretals is actually private and procedural law. Its obvious intent was to establish working rules for the governance of the Church. True enough, individual decretals do define what their recipients are to do in response to directions emanating from the papal court. No real doubt exists that these decretals were assumed to rest upon legitimate authority of the papacy, but to see their purpose as the establishment of papal power is a stretch—something rarely to

43 See e.g. J Brundage, *Medieval Canon Law* (Routledge 1995); Harold J Berman, *Law and Revolution: The Formation of the Western Legal Tradition* (Harvard University Press 1983) 199–254; *History of Medieval Canon Law in the Classical Period, 1140–1234*, W Hartmann and K Pennington (eds) (Catholic University of America Press 2008).

44 It was, however, subject to the review of a special commission appointed to recover accurate texts of the church's law in line with legal humanist's principles, the *correctors Romani*, in the 1580s. See M Sommar, *The Correctores Romani: Gratian's Decretum and the Counter-Reformation Humanists* (Lit Verlag 2009).

45 FW Maitland, *Canon Law in the Church of England* (CUP 1898) 3.

be found in the contents of the decretals themselves. True, there were exceptions to this generalisation, texts defining papal power. This is undisputed, but there were not many of them, and it is a mistake to treat them as stating the dominant purpose of the compilations.[46]

Does this matter in the context of the question raised in this chapter? Yes, it does. In an age before law was routinely regarded as the command of a sovereign, one in which long established custom and the dictates of reason were treated as separate and legitimate sources of law, lawyers and commentators were freer than we are to take the individual laws found in the *Corpus iuris canonici*, assessing them for the intrinsic worth of their contents rather than for the authority of their author. We have largely lost this habit of mind today. The assumptions of legal positivism have become second nature to us. But when we factor in the limited range of choice lawyers of the sixteenth century had in finding statements of rules of private law and procedure, coupled with the possibility of the amendment or rejection of specific decretals which contradicted biblical or other Protestant authorities, the widespread use of the decretal texts by Protestant lawyers looks less strange than it does at first sight.[47]

An historical parallel is useful here. Consider the widespread acceptance of the rules of the English common law in the newly independent United States of America. This usage extended even to the acceptance and use of statutes enacted by the English King and Parliament, the very authorities whose yoke American lawyers had just cast aside. American lawyers proclaimed the establishment of a 'novus ordo saeculorum', but they made use of the laws from the old. They looked past the questions of legislative power to the substance of the existing English laws. So, as it turned out, did Protestant lawyers active in early modern Europe.

Continental and Scottish Examples

Demonstration of continuity in the application of the medieval canon law as is was found stated in the Gregorian Decretals is a subject best understood by a look at specific subjects, while also recognising the existence of a literature of criticism of the canon law that did come into being.[48] The most compre-

46 E.g. Extrav. Comm. 1.8.1, the famous *Unam sanctam* decree of Pope Boniface VIII, from 1302; it is found in translation in B Tierney, *The Crisis of Church & State 1050–1300* (University of Toronto Press 1964) 188–89.

47 A Watson, *Sources of Law, Legal Change, and Ambiguity* (University of Pennsylvania Press 1984) 51–75; this subject is also explored from a theological perspective in Anthony Milton, *Catholic and Reformed* (CUP 1995) 322–73.

48 See M Schmoeckel, 'Der Einfluss der Reformation auf die Kanonistik: Kontroversen um die Rechtsquellenlehre und das gemeine Recht' in Peter Erdö and Sz. Anzelm Szuromi (eds), *Proceedings of the Thirteenth International Congress of Medieval Canon Law* (Citta del Vaticano 2010) 707–30.

hensive collection of Continental examples of the former is found in a famous treatise of the eighteenth century, one that dealt specifically with Protestant laws that were in force in German lands. Its author, Justus Henning Böhmer (1674–1715), traced many of the similarities and also some of the differences between what was found in the *Corpus iuris canonici* and the church order then current. For instance, in his Second book, he discussed the place of the *litis contestatio* in litigation.[49] This was (roughly speaking) the civilian counterpart of the English common law's joinder of issue. It was an established part of the Church's procedural law, and Böhmer's style of presenting this subject appears today to have been a typical scholastic effort of the time. The work is full of references to the works of other jurists, both Protestant and Catholic. It contains little of interest to today's historians of religion. Nothing really. For purposes of this chapter, however, it does matter. It surely did in assessing the character of legal education and judicial practice characteristic of its time. The jurist's discussion of these subjects was taken from the definitions found in the Gregorian Decretals. Many of them also harkened back to the Roman law, as did the canon law on the subject itself. The point remains—what he wrote on the subject made frequent and unapologetic use of the *Corpus iuris canonici* and the commentators on it. Its texts were the principal (though not the sole) sources of Böhmer's understanding of his subject.[50]

Böhmer was far from unique in the attention he paid to the law of the medieval church. He was the most prolific of Protestant writers on its use in the courts of Protestant lands, but he was joined in his approach by many other contemporary jurists.[51] Not every writer, it appears, followed his lead, but the larger number of them did. When Matthias Berlich (1586–1638), a Saxon Protestant compiler of *Decisiones*, commented on a question involving the questions that could lawfully be put to witnesses, it was to the one of the Gregorian Decretals that he referred.[52] When a question of the legitimate power of a Protestant church assembly came up in Germany, the same source, taken together with a canon from Gratian's *Decretum*, provided the commonly

49 *Ius Ecclesiasticum Protestantium, usum modernum iuris caonici iuxta seriem Decretalium* (Halle 1714), Lib. II, tit. 5, cc. 1–17. For an introduction to the jurist's life and work, see U Wolter, 'Die Fortgeltung des kanonischen Rechts und die Haltung der protestantischen Juristen zum kanonischen Recht in Deutschland bis in die Mitte des 18. Jahrhunderts' in RH Helmholz (ed), *Canon Law in Protestant Lands* (Duncker u. Humblot 1992) 13–47, at 42–46.

50 See M Germann 'Das kanonische Recht in der protestantischen Kirchenrechtslehre an der Universität Halle zu Beginn des 18. Jahrhunders' in *Law and Religion the Legal Teachings of the Protestant and Catholic Reformations* (Vandenhoek & Ruprecht 2014) 63–90.

51 See the list in M Lipenus, *Bibliotheca realis iuridica* (1752, repr. 1970) I, 171–74, and also Wilhelm Maurer, 'Reste des Kanonischen Rechtes in Frühprotestantismus' (1965) 51 ZRG, Kan. Abt 190–253.

52 *Decisiones aureae: Casus admodum pulchros, controversos et utiles continentes usu practico et quotidiana experientia observatae et conscriptae* (1635), Dec. XVI, n. 1, the author's reference is to X 2.20.37 and earlier canonistic comment on it.

accepted answer.[53] The duties and powers of the clergy to lead ordinary men and women to right behaviour and ultimately personal salvation, were important matters to Protestants as well as Catholic thinkers. They were stated by the texts found in Gratian's *Decretum*, and most of what was found in them was accepted and endorsed by German Protestant lawyers.[54]

The continuing utility of the canonical legal texts is also particularly well illustrated in post-Reformation Scottish legal practice. The patient and admirable work of Gero Dolezalek, John Cairns and Alan Wijffels has enlarged that field by their thorough examination of Scottish court records, thereby opening a new window on characteristics of Scottish legal practice. They have demonstrated beyond doubt that the medieval canonical authorities continued to be cited and applied in courts north of the Tweed.[55] As Lord Bankton (1685–1760) would later comment about the procedural steps required to approve the alienation of lands held by the Kirk, 'We followed the canon law for the most part'.[56] He cited a text from the *Extravagantes* as evidence of the connection.[57] He did not mean to suggest that no change had occurred in the laws of Scotland. Papal consent to alienation of ecclesiastical property, a requirement of the medieval canon law in some circumstances, was obviously inconsistent with Protestant principles. As Bankton thought, the consent of the Scottish king was rightly substituted for it. It was equally obvious to him, however, that the justifications available to permit alienation of church lands which would otherwise have been prohibited act remained largely the same. They were found in the medieval canon law. Here Lord Bankton was following a thread commonly found in the work of Protestant jurists. It happened elsewhere. The reformers who compiled the 1571 Swedish Ordinance concluded that some of the matters it included belonged properly to the secular

53 E.g. *Larva Legis Aquiliae: A Legal Treatise by Christian Thomasius* § li (1655–1728), M Jewett, ed. (Hart 2000) 37 (dealing with the origins of a change in German law, attributing it to the canon law). See also Anneliese-Sprengler Ruppenthal, 'Das kanonische Recht im Kirchenordnungen des 16. Jahrhunderts' in RH Helmholz (ed), *Canon Law in Protestant Lands* (Duncker u. Humblot 1992) 57–58.

54 The foundational article demonstrating the extent of continuity was J Heckel, 'Das Decretum Gratiani und das deutsche evangelische Kirchenrechts' (1955) 3 Studia Gratiana 485–537. See also Pennington (n 6).

55 See A Murray and G Dolezalek, 'Legal Argumentation and Citation of *jus commune* sources in Pleadings in the Court of Session, 1549/1550' in AM Godfrey (ed), *Miscellany Eight* (Stair Society 67, 2020) 113–230; JW Cairns, '*Ius civile* in Scotland, ca. 1600' (2004) 2 Roman Legal Traditions 136–70. See also A Wijffels, *Qui millies allegatur: Les allégations du droit savant dans les dossiers du Grand Conseil de Malines (causes septentrionales, ca. 1460–1580)* (Brill Archive 1985).

56 *Institute of the Laws of Scotland in Civil Rights* II § 5 (Stair Society 42, 1994) 42. See also DM Walker, *A Legal History of Scotland, vol III: The Sixteenth Century* (Edinburgh UP 1995) 826–29: DB Smith, 'Canon Law' in *The Sources and Literature of Scots Law* (Stair Society 1, 1936) 183–92, at 188, 191–92; and T Green, 'The Sources of Early Scots Consistorial Law' in M Godfrey (ed), *Law and Authority in British Legal History* (CUP 2016) 120–39, at 127.

57 Extrav. Comm. 3.4.1.

side of life. However, their modern student concluded about many of them that that 'having been so long under ecclesiastical jurisdiction, they could remain there'.[58]

English Examples

When one enters England (with which most my own research concerns), the same pattern of reliance on the medieval canon law emerges. Indeed the parallel was closer. The diocesan structure, led by bishops and including most of the medieval rules, was retained in England. For this reason, the canons in the Decretals which defined the duties and powers of diocesan officers remained relevant. There was no reasonable alternative way to determine, for instance, what part archdeacons were to play in routine ecclesiastical administration than to look at the title *De officio archidiaconi* (X 1.23.1–10). The provisions in it could have been rejected, of course, but why should they have been? There was nothing inherently 'popish' about them. Lawyers have always been reluctant to start from scratch unless they had to.

One example of continuity is furnished by the law of last wills and testaments. It demonstrates the continuing influence of the Church's law on English practice. Although succession to most forms of real property was controlled by the common law, by long-established English custom, jurisdiction over inheritance of personal property fell to the courts of the Church. There the law was administered by a combination of custom, synodal decrees and the provisions found within the *ius commune*.[59] They remained relevant after the Reformation. When Henry Swinburne (1560–1623), the English civil lawyer whose treatise became the standard authority for this subject, came to discuss the rules limiting the testamentary capacity of 'manifest usurers' it was to the pages of the Decretals that he turned.[60] He did also take note of an Elizabethan statute on the subject.[61] It limited the reach of the canonical prohibition by defining illegal usury to taking in excess of 10 percent of the principal sum. Like other enactments of the English parliament, it controlled the effective reach of the laws found in the *Corpus iuris canonici* when a conflict existed. This particular statute specifically affirmed part of the canon law's condemnation of usury, but it also restrained its reach.

A second example, one which also demonstrates the continued relevance of the *Corpus iuris canonici* to English lawyers, comes from the law of tithes. Roughly speaking the tithe was a payment of a tenth of one's income to the

58 M Korpiola, *Between Betrothal and Bedding: Marriage Formation in Sweden 1200–1600* (Brill 2009) 272.

59 B Ferme, *Canon Law in Medieval England: A Study of William Lyndwood's Provinciale with Particular Reference to Testamentary Law* (1996); JM Torrón, *Anglo-American Law and Canon Law* (Duncker & Humblot 1998) 111–23.

60 *Briefe Treatise of Testaments and Last Wills* (1590) Pt. II, § 16. The text came from Sext 5.5.2.

61 13 Eliz. c. 8, § 4 (1577).

clergy serving every person's parish church. It was a complicated subject as well as a widely disputed obligation,[62] and it occupied a long chapter of the Gregorian Decretals (X 3.30.1–35). Its religious legitimacy was buttressed by several biblical references to its existence among the ancient Hebrews (e.g. Lev. 27:30–32). In various forms it remained a pan-European tax. In England the right to receive the basic tithe payments passed into the hands of many laymen as well as those of parochial clergy after the Dissolution of the Monasteries during the reign of Henry VIII. Concurrent jurisdiction over litigation brought to recover tithes also passed into the hands of courts of the common law, as was also true across the Channel in France. The relevant point for the subject of this chapter, however, is that the substantive law on the subject remained largely the same. When John Ayliffe, an English civilian and writer on the law of the English church in the eighteenth century, came to a description of the tithe obligation, the largest number of his references was to the relevant title of the Gregorian Decretals or to treatises based upon them.[63] This was not nostalgia on his part. Nor was he an historian. He was a lawyer. He did also cite cases dealt with in the royal courts, recognising the loss of the church's jurisdictional monopoly over the subject. But that was all. The basic law on the subject of tithes—its divisions, its coverage and its exceptions—was found in the Decretals. If a question arose about what to do with tithes that had become due but had not been collected during the lifetime of one incumbent, for example, it was in the canon law that the answer was found.[64]

A third English example, an important and lasting one in the professional lives of English civilians, comes from the church's procedural law. A fair part of what appeared in the Decretals came initially from Roman law sources. Incorporated and adapted in the texts of the canon law, they provided the basic guidelines to procedure in the consistory courts. Some of what was found there did become irrelevant in post-Reformation England, such as the rule that no appeal lay from a papal decision (X 2.28.56), but the greater part simply stated the rules that governed procedural practice, such as the one which prohibited more than two appeals from the same sentence (X 2.28.65). The laws regulating the use of oaths in court practice provide a similar example. They were in frequent usage. The usage and treatment found in contemporary English treatises on ecclesiastical court procedure, including the law of proof, contained abundant citation to canonical and civilian texts. Like Richard Cosin's *Apologie* for the English church's jurisdictional laws, they provide a clear example of the survival of the mediaeval church's laws into the sixteenth

62 See e.g. JAF Thompson, 'Tithe Disputes in Later Medieval London' (1963) 78 English Historical Review 1–17.

63 *Parergon juris canonici Anglicani* (1726), tit. 'Of Tithes, and the several Kinds of them, etc.' See also W Easterby, *History of the Law of Tithes in England* (1888) 47–61.

64 See e.g. the response of Dr. Thomas Eden, *Three Civilian Notebooks, 1580–1640*, RH Helmholz, ed. (Selden Society 127, 2010) 53.

century and beyond.[65] This seems to have been a choice. More fundamental reform had been proposed, and it produced the *Reformatio legum ecclesiasticarum*, a replacement for the *Corpus iuris canonici*.[66] Initially formulated under Henry VIII, it never became law. It has thus remained a 'might have been', interesting to modern historians but of no immediate use to the English civilians for whom it had been meant.[67]

Acceptance of Reforms

Continuation of the canon law's usage in European courts, as described earlier, was not regarded as inconsistent with the acceptance of specific legal reforms. In fact, reforms were adopted in both Protestant and Catholic lands. Continued usage of the *ius commune* in European courts, as described earlier, was not then regarded as inconsistent with reform any more than statutory amendments in modern practice often leave existing laws intact. This compatibility is shown most vividly in events within the Catholic church. The Council of Trent was convoked in part to debate and to enact needed reforms in the church's laws. It did so in a series of decrees listed under the title '*Canones super reformatione*'. Many of them struck at abuses in existing standards of conduct, such as the requirement of clerical residence in one's church or diocese. Abuses of that requirement had worked their way into practice over the years.[68] In these cases the Council's reform decrees simply required clear statement, renewed attention and stricter methods of enforcement. Reining in the asserted scope of privileges and establishing a more effective means of restriction is another example.[69] Others required changes in the rules for existing institutions, as in the law of expectant provisions to ecclesiastical office and benefices.[70] They had led to abusive uses and the Council's enactment declared they were not to be granted to anyone in the future 'even to cardinals of the holy Roman church'.[71]

Most dramatic (and consequential) among these decrees was Trent's decree *Tametsi*. The medieval canon law, found in the first title of the Fourth Book of the Decretals, held that the exchange of words of present consent between

65 See his *Apologie for Sundrie Proceedings by Jurisdiction Ecclesiastical* (1593); see also H Conset (fl. seventeenth century), *Practice of the Spiritual or Ecclesiastical Courts* (1685), Pt. III, c. 4 § 3.

66 Its full text appears in *Tudor Church Reform: The Henrician Canons of 1535 and the Reformatio Legum Ecclesiasticarum*, G Bray (ed) (Church of England Record Society 8, 2000) 150–737.

67 G Bray, 'The Strange Afterlife of the *Reformatio Legum Ecclesiasticarum*' in *English Canon Law, Essays in Honour of Bishop Eric Kemp* (University of Wales Press 1998) 36–47.

68 H Jedin, *A History of the Council of Trent*, Ernest Graf (trans) (Thomas Nelson and Sons Ltd. 1961) II, 317–69.

69 See N Tanner (ed), *Decrees of the Ecumenical Councils* (Sheed & Ward 1990) II, * 765.

70 Ibid * 770.

71 Ibid * 772.

a man and a woman constituted a valid marriage; this without the consent of their family, without calling of the banns, and without other ecclesiastical intervention. It was binding even where the man and woman had gone their separate ways, without having consummated the union or even lived together. This result was followed even in cases in which they had married someone else in a fully public union, one blessed by the church. *Tametsi* overturned that regime. It declared the presence of the parish priest necessary for a man and women to enter a valid and enforceable union.[72] At least when seen in historical perspective, this was a wise step. It can even be defended as a legitimate outgrowth of the Christian view of marriage.[73] However, for the subject of this chapter, the result is that it was in the courts of the Church of England, not in those in lands that remained loyal to the papacy, that the medieval canon law on this particular subject retained a large share of immediate relevance.[74] The consistory courts retained their medieval jurisdiction over this subject, and they made use of this part of the medieval canon law. The *Treatise of Spousals* written by Henry Swinburne (1560–1623) contains the evidence,[75] as do many contemporary court records. In Scotland, the old law on the subject lasted even longer than it did south of the border.[76]

Conclusion

It would be a mistake to read this essay as a depiction of the medieval canon law triumphant after the Reformation even in Protestant lands. Reforms in the law occurred in both Protestant and Catholic lands. In Protestant lands, severance of traditional ties with the Roman pontiffs also mattered in practice as it surely did in theory. Parts of the canon law became irrelevant, and in some of them still in use, their juridical status became controversial. In a pamphlet published during the reign of James I, for instance, an English controversialist asserted that 'the Papall and foreign canon law is already taken away and ought not to be used in England'.[77] That result appears to be what he thought had happened. It is assuredly what he desired. Recognition of the failure of

72 Ibid * 755.

73 P Aimoné, 'Le mariage dans le Compendium d'un canoniste praticien du 12e siècle' (2016) 66 Revue de droit canonique 89–113, at 113; see also J O'Malley, *Trent: What Happened at the Council* (Belknap Press 2013) 223–35.

74 This is apparent in the seventeenth-century case recorded in a manuscript now in Canterbury Cathedral Library, MS. Z.3.27, citing X 4.1.23. See my 'The English Ecclesiastical Courts: Appendix' in Alain Wijffels (ed), *Case Law in the Making*, vol 2 (Duncker & Humblot 1997) 98–99.

75 *A Treatise of Spousals or Matrimonial Contracts* (1686).

76 D Sellar, 'Marriage by Cohabitation with Habit and Repute: Review and Requiem?' in DL Carey Miller and DW Meyers (eds), *Comparative and Historical Essays in Scots Law: A Tribute to Professor Sir Thomas Smith QC* (Edinburgh UP 1962) 117–36. See also Chapter 2. pp. 36–38.

77 W Stoughton, *An Assertion for True and Christian Church-Politie* (1604) 39. Similar is E Hall, 'Certen Considerations Why the Spirituell Jurisdiction Wold Be Abrogatt and Repelled or at

that desire turns out to be required by the evidence of the law that was being put to use by Protestant lawyers in England, and the same conclusion applies in varying measures to what occurred in Continental Europe. It is, of course, a plausible reading of the evidence to conclude that the canon law survived the Reformation because these Protestant lawyers had little else to fall back on. Undoubtedly they did have a restricted choice, and they could even have regarded many parts of the canon law as among their own land's customary regime.

We cannot suppose, however, that this can be a complete explanation for the survival of so much of the canon law inherited from the Middle Ages. Encouragement in looking beyond this conclusion actually comes from by the very words used by F.W. Maitland on this subject, the same man who taught us to look at the papal law books. He remarked, 'We have all of us been nationalists of late. Cosmopolitanism can afford to await its turn'.[78] Perhaps that turn has come. The situation in Protestant lands was akin to what is now being called 'legal pluralism' or 'legal hybridity'.[79] These terms recognise the coexistence of multiple sources of law within a given community, treating it as a common feature of legal regimes.[80] Its students point to the common use in many lands of wider sources of law than the commands of the sovereign. Customary law, international law, religious law, trade union rules, mercantile practices and natural law all figure as legitimate sources of law.[81] That seems very like what Maitland meant by the term 'Cosmopolitanism' as applied to the history of European law.

The medieval canon law is itself now more often understood in this enlarged sense than it had when Maitland wrote. The medieval and early modern canonists themselves recognised more than papal commands as legitimate sources of law.[82] They looked to custom, to local legislation and to jurisprudential

---

the Leest Reformed' in M McGlynn (ed), *The Rights and Liberties of the English Church* (Selden Society 129, 2015) 159–66.

78 See Maitland (n 26) 138.

79 See A Giuliani, 'Jurisdictional Complexity in the Ecclesiastical State: A Discussion on the Diversity of Laws in Legal Education and Legal Practice' in P Donlan and D Heirbaut (eds), *The Laws' Many Bodies: Studies in Legal Hybridity and Jurisdictional Complexity, c 1600–1900* (Duncker and Humblot 2015) 35–56.

80 See W Twining, 'Legal Pluralism 101' in B Tamanaha, C Sage, and M Woolcock (eds), *Legal Pluralism and Development: Scholars and Practitioners in Dialogue* (CUP 2012) 112–28; B Tamanaha, *Legal Pluralism Explained. History, Theory, Consequences* (OUP 2021).

81 The medieval canon law is itself treated as an example of legal pluralism in some recent treatments; see e.g. C Rolker and A Thier, 'Introduction' in C Rolker (ed), *New Discourses in Medieval Canon Law Research* (Brill 2019) 2–3. As K. Pennington nicely stated it, in the world of the canonists, 'legal systems had very permeable borders'. See his 'Canonical Jurisprudence and other Legal systems in the Medieval and Early Modern Periods' in Jesús Miñambres (ed), *Nel centenario del Codex Iuris Canonici del 1917, Atti del XVI Congresso Internazionale della Consociatio Internationalis Studio Iuris Canonici Promovendo* (EDUSC 2019) 109–18.

82 See e.g. A Scappi (fl. 1575–85), *Tractatus Iuris non scripti, quod in utroque foro observatur* (1586).

norms for substantial guidance in administering the law. The parallel between the modern understanding of legal pluralism and this description of the medieval canon law is probably not exact, but it is close enough to show that functioning legal regimes which admit more than one source of law often do exist. In them, a variety of sources shape legal practice, sometimes without much concern for their origins. Such a situation appears to have characterised European legal systems after the Reformation. Protestant lawyers looked beyond the papal connection to the content of decretal laws. They looked to their substance and to their utility, fastening onto an encouraging dictum in Gratian's *Decretum*: 'Laws are set up when promulgated; they become firm when approved by their usage'.[83] Such a principle shaped the use made of texts found in the *Corpus iuris canonici* by both Catholic and Protestant jurists. The great modern historian of the medieval canon law, Stephan Kuttner, was right when he spoke of the canon law's 'universal scope that has always characterized the law of the Christian Commonwealth'.[84] On the evidence, this is a fair description of what an exploration of legal practice in post-Reformation Europe has taught us.

Bibliography

Anneliese-Sprengler Ruppenthal, 'Das kanonische Recht im Kirchenordnungen des 16. Jahrhunderts' in RH Helmholz (ed), *Canon Law in Protestant Lands* (Duncker u. Humblot 1992)

Ascheri, M, *The Laws of Late Medieval Italy (1000–1500)* (Brill 2013)

Ayliffe J, *Parergon juris canonici Anglicani* (1726)

Baker JH, *The Law's Two Bodies* (OUP 2011)

Barahuna R, *Sex Crimes, Honour, and the Law in Early Modern Spain: Vizcaya, 1528–1725* (University of Toronto Press 2003)

Baumgärtner I, 'Was muss ein Legist vom Kirchenrecht wissen? Roffredus Beneventanus und seine Libelli de iure canonico' in Peter Linehan (ed), *Proceedings of the Seventh International Congress of Medieval Canon Law* (S. Congregatio de Seminariis et Studiorum Universitatibus 1988) 223

Bellomo M, *The Common Legal Past of Europe 1000–1800*, Lydia Cochrane (trans) (1995)

Berman HJ, *Law and Revolution: The Formation of the Western Legal Tradition* (Harvard University Press 1983)

Bray G, 'The Strange Afterlife of the *Reformatio Legum Ecclesiasticarum*' in *English Canon Law, Essays in Honour of Bishop Eric Kemp* (University of Wales Press 1998)

Brundage J, *Medieval Canon Law* (Routledge 1995)

Cairns JW, '*Ius civile* in Scotland, ca. 1600' (2004) 2 Roman Legal Traditions 136

Calvin J, *Institutes of the Christian Religion*, JT McNeill (ed) (The Westminster Press 1960)

83 D.p. Dist. 4 c. 3: 'Leges instituntur cum promulgantur, firmantur cum moribus utentium approbantur'.

84 See Joseph Goering, 'Chronicle of the Congress' in *Proceedings of the Fifth International Congress of Medieval Canon Law* (Biblioteca Apostolica Vaticana 1980) xix.

Cavill P, 'Perjury in Early Tudor England' in R McKitterick, C Methuen and A Spicer (eds), *The Church and the Law* (CUP 2020) 182

Coing H, 'Die juristische Fakultät und ihr Lehrprogramm' in *Handbuch der Quellen und Literatur der neueren europäischen Privatrechtsgeschichte, Zweiter Band: Neure Zeit (1500–1800)* (1973)

Conset H, (fl. 17th century), *Practice of the Spiritual or Ecclesiastical Courts* (1685)

Coing H (ed), '(Munich 1977) 3–102; for its continuity see also his 'L'insegnamento del diritto nell'Europa dell'Ancien Regime' (1970) 82 Studi Senesi 179–93

Cosin R, *Apologie for Sundrie Proceedings by Jurisdiction Ecclesiastical* (1593)

de Lagarde G, *La naissance de l'esprit laïque au déclin du Moyen Age* (1956–1970) 5 vols

de Zambonis P, (fl. 1600) *Isagoge in practicam criminalem ad leges Venetas accommodate* (1614)

Decrees of the Ecumenical Councils, N Tanner ed. (1990)

Dolezalek G, 'French Legal Literature Quoted by Scottish Lawyers 1550–1650' in *Mélanges en l'honneur d'Anne Lefebvre-Teillard* (PANTHEON ASSAS 2009)

Dolezalek G, 'Litigation at the Rota Romana, Particularly around 1700' in Alain Wijffels (ed), *Case Law in the Making, vol 1: Essays* (Duncker & Humblot 1997)

Donahue C Jr., *Why the History of Canon Law is Not Written*, Selden Society Lecture for 1984 (Stair Society 1986)

Donati C, 'Curie, tribunali, cancellerie episcopali in Italia durante i secoli dell'età moderna: percorsi di ricerca' in Cecilia Nubola and Angelo Tuchini (eds), *Fonti ecclesiastiche per la storia sociale e religiosa d'Europa: XV–XVIII secolo* (Il Mulino- Bologna, 1999) 213–29

Easterby W, *History of the Law of Tithes in England* (1888)

Feenstra R, 'Canon Law at Dutch Universities from 1575 to 1811' in RH Helmholz (ed), *Canon Law in Protestant Lands* (Duncker and Humblot 1992) 123

Ferme B, *Canon Law in Medieval England: A Study of William Lyndwood's Provinciale with Particular Reference to Testamentary Law* (LAS 1996)

Fulbecke W, *(1560–1603), Parallele or Conference of the Civil Law, the Canon Law, and the Common Law of This Realme of England* (1618)

Fuller T, *(1608–61), History of the University of Cambridge* (1840) 167

Gaudemet G, *Les Sources du droit canonique, VIII–XX siècle* (Routledge 1993) 190

Gaudemet J, 'Les transferts de droit' (1976) 27 L'année sociologique 29–59

Giuliani A, 'Jurisdictional Complexity in the Ecclesiastical State: A Discussion on the Diversity of Laws in Legal Education and Legal Practice' in P Donlan and D Heirbaut (eds), *The Laws' Many Bodies: Studies in Legal Hybridity and Jurisdictional Complexity, c 1600–1900* (Duncker and Humblot 2015)

Goering J, Chronicle of the Congress, *Proceedings of the Fifth International Congress of Medieval Canon Law* (Biblioteca Apostolica Vaticana 1980)

Green T, 'The Sources of early Scots Consistorial Law' in M Godfrey (ed), *Law and Authority in British Legal History* (CUP 2016) 120

Hall E, 'Certen Considerations why the Spirituell Jurisdiction wold be abrogatt and Repelled or at the leest Reformed' in M McGlynn (ed) *The Rights and Liberties of the English Church* (Selden Society 129, 2015)

Heckel J, 'Das Decretum Gratiani und das deutsche evangelische Kirchenrechts' (1955) 3 Studia Gratiana

Heckel M, *Martin Luthers Reformation und das Recht* (2016) 9–10; Kenneth Pennington, 'Protestant Ecclesiastical Law and the Ius Commune' (2015) 26 *Rivista internazionale di Diritto Comune* 9

Helmholz, RH, 'Assumpsit and Fidei Laesio' (1976) 91 Law Quarterly Review 406–32

Helmholz RH, 'Natural Law and Human Rights in English Law: From Bracton to Blackstone' (2005) 3 Ave Maria Law Review 1

Helmholz RH (ed), *Three Civilian Notebooks, 1580–1640*, (Selden Society 127, 2010)

Helmholz RH, *Natural Law in Court* (Harvard University Press 2013)
History of Medieval Canon Law in the Classical Period, 1140–1234, W Hartmann and K. Pennington (eds) (Catholic University of America Press 2008)
Holdsworth W, 'The Ecclesiastical Courts and their Jurisdiction' in *Select Essays in Anglo-American Legal History* (Boston 1908) II
Jedin H, *A History of the Council of Trent*, Ernest Graf (trans) (Thomas Nelson and Sons Ltd. 1961)
Kemp E, *Counsel and Consent* (SPCK 1961) 145–61
Kenny C, 'Bonus Jurista Malus Christa' (1903) 19 *Law Quarterly Review* 326
Korpiola M, 'On the Reception of the Jus Commune and Foreign law in Sweden, ca. 1550–1615' <www.cliothemis.com/Clio@Themis 2>
Korpiola M, *Between Betrothal and Bedding: Marriage Formation in Sweden 1200–1600* (Brill 2009)
Korporowicz LJ, 'Was the Roman Catholic Canon Law Studied in Eighteenth-Century England?' (2018) 108 Studia Prawno-Ekonomiczne 83
Larva Legis Aquiliae: A legal treatise by Christian Thomasius § li (1655–1728), Zimmermann R, M Jewett (ed) (2000)
Lefebvre-Teillard A, *Les officialités à la veille du Concile de Trente* (1973) 130
Leflar R, 'Taught Law Is Tough Law' (1982) 8 Wayne Law Review 465
Liermann H, 'Das kanonischen Recht als Gegenstand des gelehrten Unterrichts an den protestantischen Universitäten in den ersten Jahrhunderten nach der Reformation' (1955) 3 Studia Gratiana 541–66
Lipenus, M, *Bibliotheca realis iuridica* (1752, repr. 1970)
Lombardi D, 'Marriage in Italy' in Silvana Seidel Menchi (ed), *Marriage in Europe 1400–1800* (University of Toronto Press 2016)
Lyndwood W, (ca. 1375–1446), *Provinciale seu Consitutiones Angliae* (OUP1676) 315
Maitland FW, 'English Law and the Renaissance' in *Selected Historical Essays of F. W. Maitland* (CUP 1957)
Maitland FW, 'English Law and the Renaissance' in H Cam (ed), *Selected Historical Essays of F.W. Maitland* (CUP 1957) 142
Maitland FW, *Canon Law in the Church of England* (CUP 1898)
Murray A and Dolezalek G, 'Legal Argumentation and Citation of *jus commune* sources in Pleadings in the Court of Session, 1549/1550' in AM Godfrey (ed), *Miscellany Eight* (Stair Society 67, 2020)
O'Malley J, *Trent: What Happened at the Council* (Belknap Press 2013)
Ombres R, 'Ecclesiology, Ecumenism and Canon Law' in N Doe, M Hill, and R Ombres (eds), *Essays in Honour of Bishop Eric Kemp* (University of Wales Press 1998) 36
Paimoné P, 'Le mariage dans le Compendium d'un canoniste praticien du 12e siècle', *Revue de droit canonique* 66 (2016) 89–113
Palmer R, *Selling the Church: The English Parish in Law, Commerce and Religion 1350–1550* (The University of North Carolina Press 2002) 23
Pennington K, 'Canonical Jurisprudence and other Legal systems in the Medieval and Early Modern Periods' in Jesús Miñambres (ed), *Nel centenario del Codex Iuris Canonici del 1917, Atti del XVI Congresso Internazionale della Consociatio Internationalis Studio Iuris Canonici Promovendo* (EDUSC 2019)
Pollock F and Maitland FW, *History of English Law before the Time of Edward 1st* (2d edn, CUP 1898, reprinted 1968)
Prosdocim L, 'Il diritto canonico di fronte al diritto secolare' in *La Formazione storica del diritto moderno in Europa* (OLSCHKI 1978) 431
Raunio A, 'Natural Law in the Lutheran Tradition' in Norman Doe (ed), *Christianity and Natural Law: An Introduction* (CUP 2017) 77
Rester, T, 'Roman Canon Law in Protestant Reformed Theologians as Both Touchstone and Foil' in Law and Religion (above note 000) 174–85

Rolker C and Their A, 'Introduction' in C Rolker (ed), *New Discourses in Medieval Canon Law Research* (Brill 2019)
Scappi A (fl. 1575–85), *Tractatus Iuris non scripti, quod in utroque foro observatur* (1586)
Schmoeckel M, 'Das kanonische Zinsverbot unde die Konfessionalisierung' in Law and Religion (above note 000) 186–212
Schmoeckel M, 'Der Einfluss der Reformation auf die Kanonistik: Kontroversen um die Rechtsquellenlehre und das gemeine Recht' in Peter Erdö and Sz.Anzelm Szuromi (eds), *Proceedings of the Thirteenth International Congress of Medieval Canon Law* (Citta del Vaticano 2010)
Seipp D, 'The Reception of Canon Law and Civil Law in the Common Law Courts before 1600' (1993) 13 Oxford Journal of Legal Studies 388
Sellar D, 'Marriage by Cohabitation with Habit and Repute: Review and Requiem?' in DL Carey Miller and DW Meyers (eds), *Comparative and Historical Essays in Scots Law: A Tribute to Professor Sir Thomas Smith QC* (1962)
Smith DB, 'Canon Law' in *The Sources and Literature of Scots Law* (Stair Society 1, 1936)
Soffietti I, 'L'enseignement du droit à l'université de Verceil au Moyen Âge' (2021) 99 Revue historique de droit français et étranger 171
Sommar M, *The Correctores Romani: Gratian's Decretum and the Counter-Reformation Humanists* (Lit Verlag 2009)
Stein P, 'Roman Law' in *Cambridge History of Medieval Political Thought, c. 350–c. 1450* (CUP 1988) 37–47
Stephen S, *History of the Criminal Law of England* (1883, repr. n.d.) I, 463
Stoughton W, *An assertion for true and Christian Church-Politie* (1604) 39
Swinburne H, *Briefe Treatise of Testaments and Last Wills* (1590)
Tamanaha B, *Legal Pluralism Explained. History, Theory, Consequences* (OUP 2021)
Thieme H, 'Le rôle des *Doctores Legum* dans la société allemande du XVI siècle' in *Individu et Société a la Renaissance* (Presses Universitaires de Bruxelles 1967) 159–70
Thompson JAF, 'Tithe Disputes in Later Medieval London' (1963) 78 English Historical Review
Tierney B, *The Crisis of Church & State 1050–1300* (University of Toronto Press 1964)
Torrón JM, Anglo-*American Law and Canon Law* (Duncker & Humblot 1998)
Tudor Church Reform: The Henrician Canons of 1535 and the Reformatio Legum Ecclesiasticarum, G Bray (ed) (Church of England Record Society 8, 2000)
Twining W, 'Legal Pluralism 101' in B Tamanaha, C Sage and M Woolcock (eds), *Legal Pluralism and Development: Scholars and Practitioners in Dialogue* (CUP 2012) 112–28
Tyler Lange T, *Excommunication for Debt in late Medieval France: The Business of Salvation* (CUP 2016)
Van Drunen D, *Natural Law and the Two Kingdoms: A Study in the Development of Reformed Social Thought* (William B. Eerdmans 2010)
van Huffel M, 'Natural Law in the Reformed Tradition' in *Christianity and Natural Law* (above note 000) 125
Walker DM, *A Legal History of Scotland, vol III: The Sixteenth Century* (Edinburgh UP 1995)
Watson A, *Sources of Law, Legal Change, and Ambiguity* (University of Pennsylvania Press 1984)
Wijffels A, *Qui millies allegatur: Les allégations du droit savant dans les dossiers du Grand Conseil de Malines (causes septentrionales, ca. 1460–1580)* (Brill Archive 1985)
Winroth A, *The Making of Gratian's Decretum* (CUP 2000)
Witte J Jr, 'The Plight of Canon Law in the Early Dutch Republic' in RH Helmholz (ed), *Canon Law in Protestant Lands* (Duncker and Humblot 1992) 134

Witte, J Jr., 'The Law Written on the Heart: Natural Law and Equity in Early Lutheran Thought' in Wim Decock et al (eds), *Law and Religion: The Legal Teachings of the Protestant and Catholic Reformations* (Vandenhoeck & Ruprecht 2014) 174

Wolter U, 'Die Fortgeltung des kanonischen Rechts und die Haltung der protestantischen Juristen zum kanonischen Recht in Deutschland bis in die Mitte des 18. Jahrhunderts' in RH Helmholz (ed), *Canon Law in Protestant Lands* (Duncker u. Humblot 1992)

Zimmermann R, *Larva Legis Aquiliae A legal treatise by Christian Thomasius* § li (1655–1728), M. Jewett ed. (Oxford and Portland, Or 2000)

Part Two

Catholic and Protestant Approaches to Law in the Life of the Church

The focus remains on law in the life of the visible Church but for now turns inwards, in contrast to succeeding chapters where the focus is more on the effect of the Reformation on Church principles and Church law and its interaction with civil society. So, in Chapter 4, Richard Deadman gives a detailed description of how legislative authority operates in the Anglican Communion and concludes by noting that the absence of an overarching Anglican law, whilst still formally a principle of Anglican polity, has proved problematic in recent decades. In Chapter 5, Luke Beckett OSB, in his chapter on Roman Catholic canon law emphasises that the codification of the Church's law in 1917 brought with it important advantages of legal clarity and ease of application but there is the need to distinguish between theology in canon law and the theology of canon law, and there is a discussion of the theory of Cardinal Ghirlanda as an important recent contribution to the theology of canon law. Then in Chapter 6, Paul Goodliff, from a Calvinist perspective, noting that early Baptists drew much of their theology from John Calvin, explains that this is reflected both in Calvin's doctrine of natural law and in the place of conscience within that. His chapter then examines both of these and notes the link between the thought of Aquinas and Calvin. The chapter ends by arguing that a fusing of Thomist and Calvinist theories of natural law and conscience 'may speak eloquently to the challenges faced by late modernity'.

DOI: 10.4324/9780429264115-5

4 Legislative Authority in the Anglican Communion

Richard Deadman

Introduction

Anglicanism emerged to serve a very particular political and cultural context. It was one in which the monarch had taken control of the Church in England and religious affiliation was a key element of loyalty to the state. In the intervening centuries, the relationship between church and state has changed considerably, in many ways pulling the rug from under the original rationale for the Church of England. The migration of the Church of England throughout the British Empire and the development of an Anglicanism, which was not rooted in English society or English law, has further prompted adaptations of the original 'model'. The following will consider briefly how Anglican Communion law has interwoven with the developments of self-understanding across the provinces of the communion.

The Thirty-nine Articles of Religion routinely appended to the Book of Common Prayer[1] furnished a standard of Faith for the reformed Church of England. They were adopted by various provinces established by Anglicanism as it spread throughout the world.[2] During the twentieth century the authority of these Articles waned,[3] but one provision has proved an enduring influence on Anglican Communion law.

Article XXXVII states that:

> THE King's Majesty hath the chief power in this Realm of *England*, and other his Dominions, unto whom the chief Government of all Estates of this Realm, whether they be Ecclesiastical or Civil, in all causes doth appertain, and is not, nor ought to be, subject to any foreign Jurisdiction.

1 The volume is still used by the Church of England—though now supplemented by other provisions.

2 See e.g. for New Zealand: Fundamental Provisions 1.

3 See N Doe and R Deadman, 'The Resolutions of the Lambeth Conference and the Laws of Anglican Churches' in P Avis and BM Guyer (eds), *The Lambeth Conference* (T&T Clark 2019) 290f.

DOI: 10.4324/9780429264115-6

The immediate impetus for this provision was to circumscribe Papal influence,[4] for which canon law was seen as a conspicuous conduit. Structurally, this influence was constrained by the Ecclesiastical Appeals Act 1532;[5] and, in terms of content, by the suppression of the study of canon law, which was heavily influenced by continental scholarship.[6] This assertion of national autonomy as opposed to a universal jurisdiction has proved a resilient feature of Anglican Communion law and polity.

Law in the Anglican Communion

The Role of the Lambeth Conference

In 1867, the views of Bishop Colenso of Natal had for a while been causing concern in various parts of the Anglican Church.[7] In response to an ongoing battle of jurisdictions, Archbishop Longley of Canterbury convened a meeting of the 'Indian and Colonial Episcopate . . . and the Home Bishops for brotherly counsel and conference'.[8] In proposing the meeting,[9] the Archbishop stated that, 'no declaration of Faith shall be made . . . I should refuse to convene any assembly which pretended to enact any canons of affected to make any decisions binding on the Church'.[10]

In fact, he would have had no authority to convene such a council, which would have required the consent of the Sovereign in Parliament. Furthermore, as the Primus of the Scottish Episcopal Church observed, not all of the bishops were subject to his jurisdiction.[11] We might also infer in hindsight from the Primus's words that this was the moment when the Anglican Communion began to emerge from the Church of England.

4 See later in Article XXXVII—'The Bishop of Rome hath no jurisdiction in this realm of England'.

5 24 Hen. 8. c. 12—this suppressed the right to appeal to Rome.

6 See RH Helmholz, *The Oxford History of the Laws of England*, vol 1 (OUP 2004) 243 though the process was slow: continental jurists were still being cited in ecclesiastical courts into the seventeenth century—247ff.

7 See WL Sachs, 'Sexuality and Anglicanism' in J Morris (ed), *The Oxford History of Anglicanism*, vol IV (OUP 2017) 99.

8 The Archbishop of Canterbury's Letter of invitation—22 ii 1867 in GR Evans and J Robert Wright (eds), *The Anglican Tradition, A Handbook of Sources* (SPCK 1988) 329f.

9 To the Lower House of the Convocation of Canterbury.

10 GR Evans and J Robert Wright (eds), *The Anglican Tradition, a Handbook of Sources* (SPCK 1988) 328.

11 The Scottish Primus at the Lambeth Conference of 1867 in the Historical Records of the Church of the Province of South Africa (pp84f) and reproduced in: Evans and Wright (n 10) 328.

Anglican Polity of Autonomous Provinces

This disavowal of a juridical[12] or legislative[13] role for the Lambeth Conference has perdured the decades and has crystallised in the almost legal doctrine of the autonomy of Anglican provinces.[14] Neither the Lambeth Conference nor any other Anglican institution has the competence formally to create law for the communion; and there is no pan-Anglican equivalent to the universal *Corpus Juris Canonici* of the Roman Catholic Church.

However, this does not leave the Lambeth Conference as a gathering without meaning or significance. From the outset it was intended '[t]hat the Resolutions adopted by such Conferences should be formally communicated to the Anglican Communion for their consideration, and for such action as may seem to them desirable'.[15]

This has been characterised as 'quasi-legislation'[16] or 'persuasive authority'[17] in that the resolutions should have moral authority throughout the communion and be incorporated into the law of the autonomous provinces. In this, there is something of the structure of councils of the early Church and the subsequent reception (or not) of their canons. The unity and character of the Anglican Communion is determined not so much by law as by the network of relationships between the various provinces—what are sometimes termed 'bonds of affection'.[18]

There was one power, however, which was inherent to the communion and that was to decide who was in and who was not. So, for example, why did the Church of South Africa qualify, but not the Church of England in South Africa?[19] These matters were more important, as churches which did not emerge from the Church of England[20] sought to join.

The Lambeth Conferences did give consideration as to what makes a Church Anglican;[21] doubtless, these resolutions influence the decisions that

12 LC 1878 rec 8 (a); see also LC 1930 res 51.

13 *The Principles of Canon Law Common to the Churches of the Anglican Communion*, Anglican Communion Legal Advisers Network (Anglican Communion Office 2008) (details of this document follow). Principle 11.2: 'the churches . . . are bound together, not juridically by a central legislative, executive or judicial authority, but by mutual loyalty sustained through the instruments of Anglican unity'; see also Canon A7 of the Church in Chile.

14 See e.g. LC 1930 res 48.

15 Res 3.

16 See N Doe, *Canon Law in the Anglican Communion* (Clarendon Press 1998) 347.

17 See L Leeder, *Ecclesiastical Law Handbook* (Sweet and Maxwell 1997) 424 para 12.6.

18 PCLCCAC, p97.

19 Known since 2013 as *The Reformed Evangelical Anglican Church of South Africa;* see: E Wild-Wood, 'Anglicanism in Sub-Saharan Africa c 1829–1910' in R Strong (ed), *The Oxford History of Anglicanism*, vol 3 (OUP 2017) 264.

20 See JS Pobee, 'Newer Dioceses of the Anglican Communion—Movement and Prospect' in S Sykes and J Booty (eds), *The Study of Anglicanism* (SPCK 1988) 393.

21 E.g. LC 1930 resn 48f.

are made to admit a province[22], but the choice is not made by the Conference, but another of the so-called *Instruments of Communion*[23]—the Archbishop of Canterbury.

Archbishop of Canterbury

For quite some time, the decision about whom to invite was a personal prerogative of the Archbishop as part of his presidential role.[24] It is quite a powerful means of maintaining a level of discipline (assuming that bishops wish to be invited) and its reach was apparent from the beginning: Dr Colenso (a significant subject of debate) was not invited to the inaugural conference.[25] In 1978, there was the beginning of a move to encourage the Archbishop to exercise his presidential functions in a more collegial way.[26]

In 2023, responding to the decision of the Church of England's General Synod to accord limited liturgical recognition of same-sex marriages,[27] GSFA[28] issued a release stating that their members no longer recognised the Archbishop of Canterbury as the head/leader of the Anglican Communion.[29] What is not clear is how they propose the gap should be filled—either with an 'anti-Pope' type figure or the election (for which there is no mechanism) of a person who would be acceptable to all sides in the debate.

Anglican Consultative Council

Another avenue of influence over membership is via the work of the Anglican Consultative Council (ACC). Unlike the other Instruments, the ACC is a constituted body, the constitution of which was approved by all the provinces at the time.[30] Meetings of the entire Council[31] are infrequent;[32] but there is a

22 'Province' in this sense is almost a tern of art, used to denote any of the assorted ecclesiastical polities, which comprise the Anglican Communion.
23 These are the institutions, around which the relationships of the Anglican Communion revolve; they comprise: Lambeth Conference, the Anglican Consultative Council, the Archbishop of Canterbury and the Primates' Meeting—see LC 1998 sII.2b.
24 LC 1968, res 65(a).
25 The Scottish Primus at the Lambeth Conference of 1867 in the Historical Records of the Church of the Province of South Africa (pp84f) and reproduced in: Evans and Robert Wright (n 10) 329.
26 Resn 13f; restated ten years later, LC 1988 Res 18.2(a).
27 www.churchofengland.org/media-and-news/press-releases/prayers-gods-blessing-same-sex-couples-take-step-forward-after-synod
28 Global South Fellowship of Anglican Churches—a grouping within the Anglican Communion.
29 www.churchtimes.co.uk/articles/2023/24-february/news/world/archbishop-of-canterbury-no-longer-our-leader-after-synod-vote-say-gfsa-primates
30 LC 1968 res 69.
31 Which comprises members from each of the provinces—LC 1968 res 69 Constitution Membership.
32 Once every two years—LC1968 res 69(7).

standing committee, which, so to speak, represents the perpetual functioning of the Anglican Communion between meetings.[33]

Like the Lambeth Conference, it has no formal legislative power, but the policies it produces,[34] as with the resolutions of the Conference, have a level of persuasive authority.[35] In terms of membership of the Anglican Communion, this is particularly apparent in the role of the ACC in advising new provinces as they devise their constitutions.[36]

The Anglican Communion

Persuasive authority, of course, relies on the willingness of people to be persuaded; if they refuse, the Anglican Communion has no means of coercion. For a time, the relational model of autonomous provinces worked quite well. However, as the years have passed, the weaknesses of this approach have become apparent.

In 1944, in the extreme situation of the war, the Bishop of Hong Kong decided that 'God's work would reap better results if [the deaconess Florence Li Tim-Oi] had the proper title [of priest]';[37] so he ordained her priest. The Lambeth Conference of 1948 condemned the ordination and refused to recognise Florence's priesthood.[38]

Thirty years later, several provinces had decided to admit women to the priesthood and did so. The ins and outs of all of this, though interesting, are not really the point here. Rather, we should focus on the failure of the Lambeth Conference to contain the momentum of the move towards ordaining women priests or, at least to lead the initiative rather than follow feebly in its wake.[39] The Lambeth Conference had failed to persuade, and the communion was heading towards disarray with the elegant phrase of 'impaired Communion'[40] describing the fact that some provinces of the communion did not recognise the Orders of other provinces. A protocol was produced to try and contain the fractured relationships;[41] but a communion wherein some provinces do not recognise the Orders of other provinces is approaching something of an oxymoron.

33 LC 1968 res 69(8).
34 LC 1968 res 69.
35 See Doe (n 16) 350.
36 Constitution s 5.3.
37 Quoted in the entry for Florence Li Tim-Oi in 'Lesser Feasts and Facts 2003' (2004 Church Publishing Incorporated).
38 Ress 113–16.
39 LC 1978 res 21.
40 LC 1988 Res 1 (4).
41 *The Lambeth Commission on Communion—the Windsor Report 2004* (Moorhouse 2004); LC 1988 res 1 (3).

However, worse was to come when the issue of homosexuality broke into the open. Whether there was a cumulative effect of multiplying crises or the question of homosexuality being, of itself, a profound issue, the Anglican Communion was thrown into turmoil. Some bishops were not present at the Conference of 2008 and no attempt was made to produce resolution.[42]

This followed the failure of some provinces to respect the resolutions of 1998 urging restraint in the matter of ordaining practising homosexuals.[43] In response, the *Anglican Covenant*[44] was proposed. This was a mechanism by which a coerced penalty could by imposed by a judicial process: it would have been, in other words, an introduction of hard law into the global level of the Anglican Communion. The problem for the proposal was that it would require all of the provinces to incorporate its provisions into their provincial law: some were willing, others were not, fearful of incipient papalism.[45]

It is, of course, only possible to speculate on why people voted against the proposals. It is likely that there was a realpolitik wariness of what might be imposed by the uncertain outcomes of synodical legislation. It is also possible that references to incipient papalism were not anti-Roman Catholic sentiments as such, but represented a residual attachment to the Reformation principle that churches should be governed nationally. Although in England this was motivated by Henry VIII's desire to divorce Queen Katharine and promoted the very questionable assertion that England was anciently an empire (and so higher than papal authority), it also drew on the Reformation ideas that the papal jurisdiction had no scriptural warrant and was contrary to the practice of the early Church.[46]

With this impasse, it might have seemed that the Covenant was a dead duck. However, events took a different course. In 2016, a communiqué[47] announced that The Episcopal Church (of the US—TEC) had been suspended from participation in the Instruments of Communion and representing the Anglican Communion on ecumenical bodies for a period of three years: this does not seem to have included excommunication of the Province. This sanction looks remarkably similar to what was proposed in the Anglican Covenant.[48]

In a way, this reflects an English common law process rather than a continental code-based approach. There is no stated law which TEC has breached. Instead, a law has been inferred from the context of norms and conventions on which the Anglican Communion rests.

42 See *Lambeth Indaba* (2008) s A3.

43 LC 1998 res 1: 10 (e).

44 For an account of the *Anglican Covenant* see N Doe, *The Anglican Covenant* (Canterbury Press 2008).

45 See e.g. S Noll, 'Sea-change in the Anglican Communion' (2013) <www.anglican.ink/article/sea-change-anglican-communion>.

46 See A Ross, *A Still More Excellent Way* (SCM 2020) 28ff.

47 www.anglicannews.org/features/2016/01/communique-from-the-primates-meeting-2016.aspx

48 s 4.2.

Primates' Meeting

In this instance, TEC acquiesced in the decision; but it is possible that we see here a first step in the creation of precedent, which in due course will become so persuasive as to be almost indistinguishable from hard law. This is an instance of an apparently administrative act taking on a quasi-judicial character and the role of the Primates' Meeting is interesting.

When Norman Doe published his book on Anglican Communion law in 1998, there was little to say about the Primates' Meeting.[49] In the same year, however, the Lambeth Conference stated that 'the exercise of . . . responsibilities by the Primates' Meeting should carry moral authority calling for ready acceptance throughout the Communion';[50] in other words the conference was delegating its moral authority to the Primates' Meeting. At the same conference, numerous resolutions specifically delegated decisions and actions to the Primates' Meeting.[51]

It is impossible to predict at this point the extent to which (if at all) the administrative acts of the Primates' Meeting will morph into some sort of law.[52] At present, it still seems that some degree of conscious acquiescence by the individual provinces would be necessary for such a development and one can only speculate as to whether that is a possibility. For the time being, the quasi legal doctrine of autonomous provinces endures. So, the question arises, where the provinces locate the authority to make law and to impose discipline.

Sources of Legislative and Judicial Authority

The Church of England

Paradoxically, given its place within the development of the Anglican Communion, the Church of England is something of an outlier when it comes to legislative authority. Owing to the Reformation settlement which established the Church in England in law,[53] it is not the Church structures themselves which are generally the source of legislative authority, but the UK Parliament. Although the European Convention on Human Rights[54] holds, in principle, to the separation of church and state, the European Court of Human Rights tolerates established churches within the *margin of appreciation*.[55]

49 Doe (n 16) 346.
50 Res III.6(c).
51 See Ross (n 46) Ch. 7.
52 See MD Chapman, 'The Dull Bits of History: Cautionary Tales for Anglicanism' in MD Chapman (ed), *The Anglican Communion Covenant* (Mowbray 2008) 81.
53 By a series of Acts of Parliament—see Evans and Wright (n 10) 130.
54 For details of how the ECHR impacts on the Church of England see: M Hill, *Ecclesiastical Law* (4th edn, OUP 2018) 12.
55 See R Ahdar and I Leigh, *Religious Freedom in the Liberal State* (OUP 2005) 137.

For centuries after the Reformation, most significant legislation relating to the Church of England was enacted by Parliament. By the beginning of the twentieth century, pressures were militating against the continuation of this arrangement. The Church of England was losing its religious pre-eminence and increasing numbers of parliamentarians, particularly in the House of Commons, were not Anglican. From within the ranks of practising Anglicans there was disquiet at the state interference in internal church matters.[56]

An initial consequence of this was the passing of the Enabling Act.[57] The act enabled the Church Assembly (later the General Synod)[58] to present legislation to Parliament by a prescribed procedure,[59] which could be accepted or rejected, but not amended.[60] These 'Measures' have the status of Acts of Parliament,[61] even to the point of being able to amend any other Act of Parliament.[62] The Act does not preclude Parliament legislating for the Church of England on its own initiative.[63] It is rare for Parliament to reject Measures, but not unknown.[64]

At the Reformation, the convocations'[65] function of making canons was not abrogated, but it was constrained by a number of limitations. Among these were the need for a royal licence[66] and a requirement that they were not 'repugnant or contrariant' to the laws and customs of the realm.[67]

Relationship Between State and Church Law

A concrete instance of this occurred in the nineteenth century when Parliament legislated for the remarriage of divorcees.[68] Clergy were permitted in conscience to refrain from conducting the weddings of divorcees (with a

56 P Butler, 'From the Early Eighteenth Century to the Present Day' in S Sykes and J Booty (eds), *The Study of Anglicanism* (SPCK 1988) 35.
57 Church of England Assembly (Powers) Act 1919 (9 & 10 Geo. 5 c. 76).
58 Synodical Government Measure 1969 (No. 2) s 2(2).
59 ss 2–4.
60 s 4.
61 Ibid.
62 s 3(6).
63 Some MPs suggested legislation on their own initiative after the initial failure of the General Synod to pass legislation for the consecration of women bishops—Hansard, HOC 22 xi 2012 cols 722f (David Tredinnick MP).
64 The Churchwardens Measure (2001) was sent back to the Synod for further consideration and amendment—see J Behrens, 'The Churchwardens Measure' (2001) 29(6) Ecclesiastical Law Journal.
65 There are two provinces in England—Canterbury and York.
66 Act for the Submission of the Clergy to the King's Majesty (1534; 25 HenVIII c19) s1.
67 s 3.
68 Divorce and Matrimonial Causes Act (1857) 1 Vict c 85.

spouse still living).[69] In 1937–1938 a further statute[70] liberalised the law further. The convocations met and called on the clergy not to conduct such weddings.[71] This was as far as they could go: the statute permitted clergy to conduct the weddings of divorcees and, therefore, the convocations could not forbid it or make it an ecclesiastical offence.

More than that, however, the Church of England was not permitted to act in any way which impugned the validity of these marriages contracted by divorced persons. This is inferred from a case involving not the marriage of divorced persons but of people who had married within previously prohibited degrees.[72] Under the relevant Act,[73] a priest had the right not to conduct the wedding, but also not to refuse Holy Communion to the couple. The effect is that, constitutionally speaking, marriage in a Church of England church and marriage in registry office were and are the same thing.

This fact has, more recently, thrown up another challenge when Parliament legislated for same-sex marriages.[74] To avoid a clash with religious organisations, an exemption to protect them from action under equality legislation was included.[75] Additional reference was made to the clergy of the Church of England;[76] and it was stated that Church of England canons were immune to challenge if they stated that marriage is contracted only between one man and one woman with a specific reference to the Submission of the Clergy Act.[77]

If the Submission of the Clergy Act constrained the convocations, in 1969[78] their prerogative to create canons was subsumed into the General Synod (see more on this later) and canons now clearly have the status of secondary legislation.[79]

In a similar vein, the ecclesiastical courts are courts of the realm: they are subject to supervision by the High Court;[80] and a bishop is required to consult with the Lord Chancellor before the appointment of a diocesan chancellor (judge).[81] Chancellors are required to have held high judicial office or be of equivalent standing in the temporal legal sphere.[82] A more recent consequence of the status of ecclesiastical courts is that the provisions of the Human

69 1 Vict c 85 s 63: at this stage, the minister was required to permit his church building to be used: this was later changed (Matrimonial Causes Act (1937) s 12).
70 The Matrimonial Causes Act (1937).
71 See N Doe, *The Legal Framework of the Church of England* (Clarendon Press 1996) 377.
72 *Bannister v Thompson* [1908] P 362.
73 Deceased Wife's Sister's Marriage Act (1907) s 1.
74 Marriage (Same Sex Couples) Act (2013).
75 ss 2, 4.
76 s 1(5) a.
77 s 1(3).
78 Synodical Government Measure 1969 s 1.
79 See Hill, M. Ecclesiastical Law (4th edn.) OUP 2018.
80 Ecclesiastical Jurisdiction Measure (1963) s 82(3) c.
81 Ecclesiastical Jurisdiction and Care of Churches Measure (2018) s 2(6) a.
82 Ecclesiastical Jurisdiction and Care of Churches Measure (2018) s 2(4).

Rights Act 1998 are directly applicable to their proceedings.[83] Furthermore, Measures and Canons, being state legislation, must be read and interpreted in conformity with the Act regardless of when they became law.[84]

Lawyers who appear before them are also drawn from the temporal sphere[85] proceedings inevitably largely reflect the practices in the temporal courts. This might have been envisaged when the study of canon law at the universities was abolished[86] in an attempt to clip continental influence[87] in the affairs of the realm.[88] However, the creation of the Ecclesiastical Law Society in 1987, together with the journal which it publishes,[89] and the establishment of an LLM at Cardiff Law School in 1991 have fostered a greater level of knowledge and expertise in the field.[90] Furthermore, Anglican canonists have been at the forefront of sustaining law-based discussions in the ecumenical[91] and interfaith[92] arena.

The Conflict Between Spiritual and Temporal

One of the slightly curious byways of establishment is that a few issues, which would usually be considered 'spiritual' (that is concerned with the workings of the Church), are justiciable in the temporal courts. Perhaps the most contentious of these[93] is patronage—the right to present a priest to an ecclesiastical living.[94] The reason for this is that patronage is considered a piece of property.[95] *Gorham v Bishop of Exeter*[96] concerned the presentation of a priest to

83 s 6(3) a—see M Hill, 'Judicial Review of Ecclesiastical Courts' in N Doe, M Hill and R Ombres (eds), *English Canon Law* (University of Wales Press 1998) 13.
84 s 3—see Hill (n 54) 12.
85 The ecclesiastical courts were opened to civilian lawyers in 1545—Ecclesiastical Jurisdiction Act (37 Henry VIII c 17). However, it was not until the demise of the Doctors Commons (which studied and practised Canon Law—see n 59) in 1857, the Court of Probate Act opened the ecclesiastical courts to common lawyers.
86 Hill (n 82) 04.
87 GR Elton, *The Tudor Constitution* (2nd edn, CUP 1992) 340 n22.
88 As it turned out, this process took rather longer than might have been imagined—see RH Helmholz, *Roman Canon Law in Reformation England* (CUP 1990) 152.
89 The Ecclesiastical Law Journal.
90 In 2024, the LLM ceased to be offered; and was replaced by a module within the Durham University MA in Theology: <lawandreligionuk.com/2024/06/04/a-new-chapter-in-the-acadmeic-study-of-canon-law-in-britain>.
91 See e.g. N Doe, *Church Laws and Ecumenism* (Routledge 2021).
92 See e.g. N Doe, *Comparative Religious Law: Judaism, Christianity, Islam* (CUP 2019).
93 See T Sutton, 'Advowsons and Private Patronage' (2019) 21 Ecclesiastical Law Journal 267.
94 Though, in fact, this is the end of a very long thread of dispute between the Church and temporal powers about such a right, which erupted periodically across Europe in what are sometimes termed, 'Investiture' crises. At this time, Church of England bishops were appointed by the Queen on the advice of the Prime Minister; as is still the case today, albeit with modified processes. Appointment of Bishops Act 1533 (25 Hen 8 c 20) s 3.
95 P Smith, 'The Advowson: the History and Development of a Most Peculiar Piece of Property' (2000) 5 Ecclesiastical Law Journal 320.
96 *Gorham v Bishop of Exeter* (1850) 15QB 52; Gorham v Bishop of Exeter (185) 5 Exch 630. For a detailed analysis of the judgement, see A Jordan, 'George Cornelius Gorham, Clerk v

a living and the eventual overturning of the bishop's refusal to institute him. High Church Anglicans considered this a notorious intervention by temporal powers in a spiritual matter. The events caused a furore in those high church circles: it was a principal factor in Cardinal Mannings's decision to secede to the Roman Catholic Church.[97] More recently, in a case[98] which the judge considered analogous to the precedents of advowson cases and in view of the status of Church of England canon law as secondary legislation,[99] the High Court issued an injunction against a proposed (and unlawful) Ordination in the Diocese of Newcastle.

In recent decades, there has been an exponential increase in the use of guidelines. These are often termed quasi-legislation.[100] Although its provenance is sometimes obscure and it does not undergo legislative scrutiny, like its temporal parallels, it is considered to have considerable force in terms of being binding on those to whom it refers.[101] This was reiterated in connexion with the duty to have due regard to such guidelines connected with children and vulnerable people by a formal legal opinion in 2020.[102] The opinion was circulated by e-mail to the clergy[103] shortly before the welter of guidelines addressing the Covid pandemic (when almost everyone was vulnerable) began to tumble out from the centre. These included the interdict announced by the Archbishops, which they had no formal legal power to impose.[104]

The Rest of the Anglican Communion

Apart from Wales, where the Anglican Church retains some vestiges of establishment,[105] the other provinces of the Anglican Communion are not established; though there are one or two relics of Colonial era establishment.[106] In their respective territories, therefore, they have the character of what are termed in English legal circles private associations; the state does not determine

---

Henry Phillpotts', Bishop of Exeter (1998) 5 Ecclesiastical Law Journal 104. The case involved the refusal of the bishop to institute Gorham to the living to which he had been presented by the patron on account of his theological views.

97 Butler (n 56) 362.

98 *Gill v Davies* QB div 19th December 1997: judgement printed in Hill (n 54) 2nd edn 707f.

99 At 709.

100 Hill (n 54) 15.

101 *R (on the application of Munjaz) v Mersey Care NHS Trust* [2006] 4 All ER 736 at 69 per Lord Hope.

102 NCI Legal Office, *Duty to 'Have Due Regard' to the House of Bishops Safeguarding Guidance* (NCI Legal Office, February 2020).

103 Including the author.

104 This was discussed by the Archbishop of Canterbury with Andrew Marr on the BBC, reported by: Thornton, E Church Times (15 iv 20); <www.churchtimes.co.uk/articles/2020/17-April/news/uk/we-have-give-guidance-not-instruction-says-welby-on-andrew-marr-show>.

105 The Welsh Church was largely disestablished by the Welsh Church Act 1914; but the state retains some authority over weddings (e.g. Marriage (Wales) Act 2010) and burial grounds (s 24).

106 See Ross (n 46) 179.

their canon law, nor enforce it, except insofar as it creates contractual relationships between members, which might be justiciable in the temporal courts.[107] In the United States, the religious character of the Episcopal Church gives it constitutionally based[108] broad exemptions from supervision by the courts;[109] whereas in South Africa there is a history of the temporal courts intervening in the decisions of church courts, where an injustice of one sort or another is thought to have been perpetrated.[110]

In theory, every province is free to formulate its law as it pleases. However, as a study in 2008 discovered, there is a considerable degree of commonality between the provinces. *The Principles of Canon Law Common to the Churches of the Anglican Communion* (*PCLCCAC*)[111] laid the laws side by side and pulled out common themes. As the preamble makes clear, these are principles, not common laws;[112] some of them are fairly broadly drawn[113] and some are not of universal applicability.

There are a number of factors which explain this similarity. First, of course, a number of the provinces emerged directly from the Church of England and some of them, at least, preserve this as a part of their identity.[114] In Central Africa, there remains an appeal to English bishops on matters of doctrine.[115] However, in the United States, most ecclesiastical law was abrogated after the Revolution and legal development there took a very different course.[116] Secondly, new provinces are guided in creating their constitutions and laws by the ACC (discussed earlier). Finally, a notion of Anglicanism is strengthened by participation in the Lambeth Conferences and other institutions of the Anglican Communion, as well as the programmes of links and exchanges, which characterise the communication between the provinces.

107 See e.g. IA Akinloye, 'Legal Issues Involving Succession Disputes among South African Churches: Some Issues' (2021) 23(2) Ecclesiastical Law Journal 160.
108 First Amendment—Freedom of expression and religion; which is commonly supposed (though not uncontroversially) to have erected a 'wall of separation' between Church and state (see *Reynolds v US* (1878)).
109 See C Evans and A Hood, 'Religious Autonomy and Labour Law: A Comparison of the Jurisprudence of the United States and the European Court of Human Rights' (2012) 1 Oxford Journal of Law and Religion 81.
110 RB Frank, 'Historical Milieu of Tribunals in South Africa: the Role of Church Tribunals' (2021) 23(1) Ecclesiastical Law Journal 75.
111 *The Principles of Canon Law Common to the Churches of the Anglican Communion*, Anglican Communion Legal Advisers Network (Anglican Communion Office 2008); a revised edition of the text was produced in 2022.
112 p15.
113 E.g. Principle 22(3) 'Lay participation in church government is subject to the conditions prescribed in the law of a church . . .'—these conditions vary between the churches.
114 Fundamental Provisions 1, 4.
115 Can 26.
116 C Podmore, 'The Tale of Two Churches, the Ecclesiologies of the Episcopal Church and the Church of England Compared' (2008) 10(1) Ecclesiastical Law Journal 38.

Laity

Theologically speaking, membership of the laity is secured by baptism. For some churches, this is sufficient to participate in the life of the Church.[117] Many provinces add confirmation to this requirement; and often regular (variously defined) reception of Holy Communion.[118] Many provinces specify the maintenance of membership rolls.[119]

In the Church of England and the Church in Wales, the situation is more complex as a result of the established or erstwhile established status. In both churches, residence in a parish (regardless of baptismal or other status) affords rights to marriage (other legal requirements being satisfied) and burial.[120] With regard to weddings in England, the situation was complicated further in 2008[121] when certain historic 'qualifying connexions' with a particular parish also created a right to marry in the church there on the same basis as if they were (still) resident in the parish. The continuing establishment of the Church of England has, without defining who is a member, created a range of rights and types of membership, which are not necessarily tied to baptism.[122] Similar issues have been identified in the disestablished Church in Ireland.[123] In all three countries, we see here a hangover from the time when almost everyone living within their territories was or was expected to be a member of the established Church.

One of the features which all of the provinces share (even the Church of England by authority delegated by Parliament) is that their legislative authority lies with synods of clergy and laity, developing the convocations of former times. It is the formal inclusion of the laity in the governance of the Church by right which was an important development in twentieth-century Anglicanism; and one which distinguishes it from other branches of the Church, which have a Catholic identity.

This synodical framework was consciously embraced by the communion during various Lambeth Conferences. In 1920, resolutions encouraged the development of synods as legislative authorities;[124] and PCLCCAC states that, '[r]epresentative government is fundamental to church polity, and in matters which touch all, all should have a voice'.[125]

117 E.g. TEC (USA) Canon I 17.1.
118 E.g. Tanzania Const. 1.2; see also PCLCCAC principle 27.2.
119 PCLCCAC principle 27.6.
120 Doe (n 16) 274.
121 Church of England Marriage Measure 2008.
122 See Hill (n 54) 49.
123 See P Colton, 'The Pursuit of a Canonical Definition of Membership in the Church of Ireland' (2008) 10 (1) Ecclesiastical Law Journal 3.
124 Ress 14, 43f.
125 Principle 18(1).

Exactly how that synodical framework is structured is a matter for the individual provinces.[126] Typically, there are houses of bishops, clergy and laity, though there are a few instances of bi-cameral synods[127] (bishops in one, other clergy and laity in the other).[128] In some provinces, legislation is the prerogative of the national synod alone;[129] in others, dioceses may legislate for their territory.[130] In Australia, the diocese is the basic unit of governance onto which a federal structure has been superimposed,[131] indeed, dioceses are so powerful vis-a-vis the central institutions, let alone the provinces, and, historically, have guarded their autonomy to such an extent that the situation has come to be termed 'Diocesanism'.[132]

Whilst, of course, the Reformation era requirement of a Royal Licence for meetings of the synods only remains in England,[133] there might be a remnant of it transferred to the synods themselves, since bishops do not have the power to legislate,[134] either individually for their own dioceses,[135] nor corporately for the province unless that power is accorded to them in specific circumstances.[136] Equally, bishops do not have the power to dispense from laws unless it is accorded to them by law in particular circumstances;[137] and bishops are subject to the law in exactly the same way as any other member of the Church.

At the same time, bishops are often accorded privileged positions in regard to some areas of legislation: for example, although they do not constitute a magisterium (see more on this later), in many jurisdictions, they are sometimes accorded a particular role in legislation connected with the definition of doctrine.[138] In some provinces, this principle has been somewhat qualified by the increasing resort to quasi-legislation.[139]

Judicial authority is derived from synodical legislation.[140] As in England, many provinces require their legal officers to be qualified and practising lawyers

126 LC 1920 Res 43f.
127 E.g. TEC Art I ss 1–4; Ireland Constitution Pt 1 s 2.
128 See Doe (n 16) 43.
129 PCLCCAC prin 19.
130 PCLCCAC prin. 20 (5).
131 B Kaye, 'From a Colonial Chaplaincy to Responsible Governance: The Anglican Church of Australia and its Ecclesiological Challenge' (2021) 23(1) Ecclesiastical Law Journal 43.
132 See Ross (n 46) 162.
133 Synodical Government Measure 1969 s 1(1).
134 Though in some dioceses bishops do have the right of veto over legislation proposed in their synods: PCLCCAC prin. 20(6)—though not all, see Podmore (n 113) 35; and a House of Bishops can block some legislation in the national synod—when the consent of the several houses is required rather than a simple majority of those voting.
135 PCLCCAC prin. 20(6).
136 PCLCCAC prin. 18(6).
137 PCLCCAC prin. 7(6).
138 E.g. Wales Const. II: 34–43; North India Const. I.III.
139 See Doe (n 16) 3.
140 PCLCCAC prin. 24.

in the secular realm;[141] and, unsurprisingly, the requirements of secular justice are incorporated into ecclesiastical laws.[142] It would seem that the abolition of the study of canon law under Henry VIII continues to influence the provinces in that there is no specifically ecclesiastical culture and technique to the administration of canon law; rather it reflects the law as practised in the territories in which it exists. This impression is reinforced by the fact that the Lambeth Conferences make no reference to the process of making laws.

Temporal Legislation

All provinces are subject to the generally applicable laws in which they are found unless those laws give them a specific exemption[143] or, as the in the case of the United States, there is a constitutional presumption of exemption (discussed earlier).

Whilst, of course, this can impact on many areas of Church life, there is a particular area of engagement. Churches do not usually legislate for all areas of their activity. Until very recently,[144] the Church of England did not directly[145] regulate monastic communities,[146] for example (possibly as a relic of the abolition of conventual life at the Reformation). Other provinces have regulated monastic life for quite some time,[147] as the Lambeth Conference of 1930 recommended.[148] However, there are many organisations, particularly of laity,[149] which are legally separate from the provinces. These various organisations are governed by their own constitutions, which they are free to craft as they please. They might include some references to the Church[150] and her laws, but this is not required.

141 See Doe (n 16) 174.
142 PCLCCAC, Prins. 7; 8; 15(12–14; 17).
143 E.g. in England: Equality Act 2010 Sch 9, pt 1 s 2.
144 In 2020 Canon D was amended to include Canon DA. Ostensibly, this is to provide a framework for officially recognising Church of England religious communities; but it includes a provision (s 3) for the House of Bishops to create fairly detailed regulation as a condition of recognition.
145 There may be indirect regulation if their communities include licensed clergy or others, who are covered by legislation or, for example, if their churches are consecrated, in which case they fall under faculty jurisdiction.
146 There are a couple of minor exceptions such as the allocation of seats to monastic communities in the General Synod—see e.g. Church Representation Rules 2020 rule 46 1(c).
147 E.g. The Episcopal Church: Canons and Constitutions Title III Canon 14 (2006).
148 Res 74.
149 The prime example being the Mothers' Union, a worldwide organisation founded in 1876 originally for married mothers; but over the years, membership has expanded—even, now, to including men.
150 E.g. The constitutions of Monastic houses and clerical societies often prescribe the appointment of a bishop as 'Visitor'. E.g. The Constitution of the English Province of the Community of the Mission Sisters of the Holy Name of Jesus s 6.

An extreme example of this is found in the United States, where older parish churches in some states are, in fact, private trusts[151] for historical reasons. Subsequent to their foundation, the synodical structures of the Episcopal Church were superimposed on the network of these independent trusts. This has led to property disputes, which were heard in the temporal courts.[152] These independent trusts are therefore generally supervised not by ecclesiastical bodies but by temporal institutions. These are often the courts of the territory in which a province is located; and there must be at least a possibility that a temporal context will render a different judgement than might have been handed down in the church courts.

The issue is all the more acute in places like England where many of these organisations register as charities to secure the tax exemptions which come with such a status. In 2006,[153] the UK Parliament replaced the structure of recognising charities, based largely on judicial precedent, with statutory provisions now in the Charities Act 2011.[154]

In this new statutory regime, the 'public benefit test' has come to the fore.[155] In the past, religious organisations were considered intrinsically beneficial so long as they disseminated religion in some way, but this is no longer the case.[156] Church organisations wishing to retain their charitable status are vulnerable to being pushed in particular directions to meet the criteria set by the Charity Commission; and this brings us to one of the keys issues: the impact of changing attitudes in the state.

Church and State 'Pulling Apart'

The Church of England

Along the winding road of establishment,[157] there developed a fusion of church and state as described by Richard Hooker[158] under which dispensation, it was for the Godly Magistrate[159] to make laws for the laity.[160] The Church of England was a national church which ministered to the nation shaped by the

151 Though this is not wholly unknown in England, where there are a number of 'Proprietary Chapels', which are owned and governed by their trustees. The history of Saint Ninian's, Whitby, demonstrates the independence that such establishments enjoy.
152 See Podmore (n 113).
153 Charities Act 2006; now incorporated into the Charities Act 2011.
154 See M Harding, 'Trusts for Religious Purposes and the Question of Public Benefit' (2008) 71 (2) MLR 159.
155 Charities Act 2011 pt 1, ch 1, s 4.
156 Harding (n 151) 175.
157 See J Rose, 'The Godly Magistrate' in A Milton (ed), *The Oxford History of Anglicanism*, vol 1 (OUP 2017) 103.
158 *Of the Laws of Ecclesiastical Polity* Bk VIII 1.2.
159 It was never certain whether this was the Monarch or Parliament.
160 Rose (n 154) 107.

Godly Magistrate.[161] In some senses, the Church of England is cast as much in the role of national chaplaincy as an independent institution pursuing its mission in the world. It was the view of the principal branches of the Reformation that the work of redeeming society must be pursued from within that society rather than as a separated institution of the virtuous calling to a sinful world.[162] However, of course, this was based on a polity in which the state shared the religious outlook of the Church to a great extent: '*cuius est regio, illius est religio*' was a popular mantra in Reformation era circles.[163] No real thought was given to what happened when the 'regio' had no 'religio'.

In England, as time has passed, the state has gradually withdrawn from its identity of Godly Magistrate, but the principle that ecclesiastical canons cannot legislate for the laity has endured. This was articulated in a judgement concerning the applicability (or otherwise) of the Canons of 1603[164] to laypeople who have contracted a clandestine marriage.[165] The judgement was subsequently acknowledged[166] by the Court of Arches.[167]

So, for example, the specification in canon law of marriage being contracted by a man and a woman is not a legally enforceable instruction to the laity about who may marry, but to the clergy about whose marriages they are permitted to solemnise. In the seventeenth century, this might have appeared something of a conceptual distinction (if it was recognised at all); but today there are categories of people, whose marriages the Church must (at least to all intents and purposes) acknowledge as valid and regular, whilst not being permitted to solemnise them. So, for example, if a man had contracted a same-sex marriage and then divorced to marry a woman, the Church of England would treat him as a divorced person in the procedures to be followed for the subsequent marriage. Furthermore, following the logic of *Bannister v Thompson*,[168] no disciplinary action can be taken in respect of people living in a same-sex marriage.

The Church may have teaching about human morals and ethics, but she cannot impose these on lay English subjects, who resort to her ministrations;[169] and the question then arises as to how the Church's law responds to these gaps. The response to the provisions for divorce is perhaps instructive. After decades of living with an increasing number of clergy conducting marriages

161 Ibid 106.
162 WL Sachs, 'Sexuality and Anglicanism' in J Morris (ed), *The Oxford History of Anglicanism*, vol 4 (OUP 2017) 96.
163 DL Dusenbury, *The Innocence of Pontius Pilate* (Hurst & Co 2021) 225.
164 A set of canons enacted without parliamentary authority.
165 *Middleton v Crofts* 1736 2Atk 650.
166 *Phillimore v Machon* (1876) 1 PD 481 per Lord Penzance.
167 The ecclesiastical Court of Appeal for the Province of Canterbury.
168 See n63.
169 Canon B16 does provide for excommunication in certain rather vaguely framed circumstances; but this would not include conduct explicitly legitimised by temporal legislation. In practice, excommunication is very rare in the Church of England.

discouraged by the resolutions of the Convocations, in 2002, the General Synod passed a set of principles to apply to the remarriage of divorcees.[170]

Still conscious of being the Church of the nation, similar pressures apply to the canon law when it conflicts with the prevailing attitudes in the land. So, in 2014 the Church enacted legislation to consecrate women bishops.[171] Proposals to permit the blessing of same-sex marriages have not succeeded thus far, though a compromise step—perhaps along the way—has been agreed.[172]

A particular problem can arise when the disciplines relate to the clergy. In 1990, provision was made to enable divorced persons to be ordained.[173] At present, the Church of England is struggling to provide a coherent legal response to those of her clergy who enter into same-sex marriages.[174]

At the same time, the Church of England does not simply glide along in the slip-stream of the state. Bryan Spinks has observed that, 'The ambiguity [of the Elizabethan Settlement] would be a Trojan horse in a Church that regarded itself as thoroughly Protestant'.[175] Whilst Spinks was writing from a liturgical perspective, his assessment is equally valid for the Elizabethan Settlement as a whole. During the nineteenth century, rumblings from inside the horse broke into the open through the influences of renewal movements, such as the Oxford Movement; as well as the state moving away from the church, elements in the church were pulling away from the inherited understanding of the Established Church.[176] In due course, the assumption of membership of the Church of England, manifested in the right to baptism,[177] marriage[178] and a funeral in the parish church[179] were mingled with 'Electoral Rolls'—quasi-membership lists.[180] The two approaches do not sit altogether comfortably together,[181] which might indicate the tension between a defined membership and being the Church of the nation.

Furthermore, the Church of England periodically clashes with the government over policy, notably in a ferocious criticism of economic policy;[182] and, in the wake of the Falklands conflict, the refusal of the then Archbishop of

170 *Marriage in Church after Divorce* GS 1449 (2002).
171 Bishops and Priests (Consecration and Ordination of Women) Measure 2014.
172 See n27.
173 Clergy (Ordination) Measure 1990.
174 See N Patterson, *Ecclesiastical Law, Clergy and Laity* (Routledge 2020) 141.
175 BD Spinks, *The Rise and Fall of the Incomparable Liturgy* (SPCK 2017) 27.
176 J Pereiro, 'The Oxford Movement and Anglo-Catholicism' in R Strong (ed), *The Oxford History of Anglicanism*, vol III (OUP 2017) 190.
177 Can B22 (4).
178 Hill (n 54) 143.
179 Cano B38 (2).
180 Church Representation Rules 1(1).
181 Hill (n 54) 49.
182 E.g. Archbishop of Canterbury's Commission on Urban Priority Areas: *Faith in the City: a call for action by Church and Nation* (London 1985).

Canterbury to countenance a triumphalist service of celebration:[183] something, which, in former generations, would have been considered a routine part of the Church of England's duties.

Other Provinces of the Anglican Communion

With the exception of the Church in Wales, the other provinces have had little experience of establishment and of being the church of the nation. Even in those provinces which emerged in the British Colonial expansion, whatever elements of establishment there might have initially been, were falling away by the middle of the nineteenth century.[184] Notions of being a national church in the sense that the Church of England claims or claimed to be are even more meaningless where a province's territory spans across different cultural contexts or even national boundaries.[185]

Nonetheless, provinces do tend to reflect in their laws the prevailing attitudes of the countries in which they are set.[186] Various Lambeth Conferences considered the accommodation that some provinces made with the practice of polygamy, which was prevalent in their territories;[187] whereas the most energetic proponents of solemnising same-sex marriages have come from those places where it is becoming the norm in the society around them.

TEC has included in its canons a prohibition of discrimination, which fully reflects issues of diversity current in the United States.[188] The Church in Nigeria followed a rather different course, removing from its canons references to the Archbishop of Canterbury in response to his comments on sexuality.[189] In a way, all of this could be understood as implementing the Lambeth resolution that autonomous provinces should 'promote within each of their territories a national expression of Christian faith, life and worship';[190] which, in turn, might be construed as an updated idea of being a 'national' church: a concept adopted as Anglicanism made a conscious attempt to move away from the colonial era.[191]

183 M Grimley, 'The State, Nationalism and Anglican Identities' in J Morris (ed), *The Oxford History of Anglicanism*, vol IV (OUP 2017) 134.

184 E.g. for Australia see B Kaye, 'From a Colonial Chaplaincy to Responsible Governance: The Anglican Church of Australia and Its Ecclesiological Challenge' (2021) 23(1) Ecclesiastical Law Journal 39.

185 W Adam, 'Communion and Jurisdiction' (2021) 24(2) Ecclesiastical Law Journal 206.

186 Other factors come into play, such as the theological perspectives of those whose missionary work established the Anglican presence in particular places.

187 LC 1888 resn 5; LC 1958 resn 120; LC 1968 resn 23; LC 1988 resn 26.

188 Can I.17.5.

189 See EF Kuehn, 'Instruments of Faith and Unity in Canon Law: The Church of Nigeria Constitutional Revision of 2005' (2008) 10(2) Ecclesiastical Law Journal 161.

190 LC 1930, Res. 48 and 49.

191 The concept of the 'National Church' is discussed in Ross (n 46) Ch. 4.

The Church in South India's law includes a canon which takes this a stage further, requiring members to,

> contribute to the total ministry of the Church . . . by responsible participation in secular organizations, legislative bodies . . . and in other areas of public life, [so that] the decisions which are made in these areas may be controlled by the mind of Christ and the structures of society transformed according to His will.[192]

The laws of other provinces provide for similar engagement with the society around them. In Venezuela, the Church must contribute to the 'moral and spiritual' welfare of society;[193] in the Philippines Anglicans should promote justice in the world.[194]

All the same, this is action, as it were, from outside the state establishment, even when it involves individuals becoming members of that establishment: their participation does not integrate their church into the machinery of state. There is, therefore, no temporal arm to handle the day-to-day discipline of the churches and they must look to their own internal resources. PCLCCAC infers that, 'The laity are subject to discipline to the extent and in the manner prescribed by law'.[195] Several provinces state that their canons are binding on the laity;[196] and likewise their judicial proceedings.[197]

However, in recent years, the power of the state to press Anglican churches to change their discipline has become apparent in the wake of the abuse scandals, which have beset in the Church across much of the world: as well as the willingness of some provinces at least to consider aligning their law with the national agenda.

In the UK, a government commissioned report[198] made extensive criticisms of the Church of England.[199] Many recommendations were made to address the issue;[200] and the guidance has been updated to reflect these conclusions.[201] The report refers to a misunderstanding on the part of many clergy of the force of these provisions in connexion with the requirement to have, 'Due

192 South India: Const. VI.2.
193 Const. II.
194 See e.g. Philippines: Const. Art. 1.1; Canons 1.2.2(d): amongst the functions of the Provincial Synod's Commission on Social Concerns is the 'study [of] the nature and root causes of poverty and underdevelopment in the country and review[ing] the participation of the Church in the development process'.
195 Principle 25.4.
196 E.g. Wales Const. 1.2; Australia Const. XII.70.
197 E.g. Scotland can 58; Burundi Const. art 5.
198 Independent Inquiry Child Sexual Abuse: *The Anglican Church* (October 2020).
199 s B6.2; the report also considered the Church in Wales.
200 s D1.
201 Details of guidance are provided on the Church of England Website.

regard',[202] which led to an e-mail being circulated to all the clergy on the subject (discussed earlier at p. 83). In response to a welter of terrible revelations, the Church of England has amended its law,[203] as well as introducing extensive guidelines and policies, which, as we have seen function as quasi-legislation.[204]

In Australia, there has been a similar process in response to the Royal Commission commissioned on the same subject.[205] Like its English parallel, it included all manner of recommendations, including a criticism of the 'diocesanism' (discussed earlier), which undermines the effectiveness of safeguarding measures; some parts of the Australian Anglican Church are making some progress towards redressing this situation, changing the balance of power between dioceses and the provinces.[206]

However, there is another issue raised by both inquiries, which reaches deeply into the spiritual dimension of ecclesiastical life: the Seal of the Confessional.[207] The roots of legislation on this matter lie, for Anglicans, in the Canons of 1603, which assert the centuries old Catholic prescription of the inviolability of the confessional.[208] At the same time, reports have suggested that perpetrators of abuse have disclosed their actions to confessors and the refusal or inability of those priests to report what they have heard enables the perpetrators to continue with their offences and even, perhaps, illegitimately to quieten their consciences.

Over some years, there had been a leisurely debate as to whether the seal would be respected by English courts, given that it is included in the Canons, which have the status of secondary legislation:[209] a question which has relevance in the unfolding of the abuse scandal. Now, in the wake of the inquiries, however, the law regarding the Seal is being reconsidered by the churches themselves; and whether it can be retained in connexion with disclosures of abuse. In Australia, the national canons have been amended to permit disclosure of abuse;[210] these canons will need to be adopted by the individual dioceses. The Church of England has not changed the law at present but has determined to improve training for clergy about the hearing of confessions.[211]

202 s D1 para 42.
203 The introduction of the canon concerning the recognition of religious communities was part of this programme, along with, *inter alia*, the Safeguarding (Code of Practice) Measure 2021.
204 E.g. House of Bishops, *Parish Safeguarding Handbook* (CHP 2018).
205 The final report was published in 2017, childabuseroyalcommission.gov.au/final-report.
206 Ross (n 46) 178ff.
207 ICCSA Final report sB.5.3.
208 Can 113.
209 See C Grout, 'The Seal of the Confessional and the Criminal Law of England and Wales' (2020) 22(2) Ecclesiastical Law Journal 138.
210 Can 10 (1992) amended by Can 16 (2017) and Can 17 (2017).
211 The Church of England, *Report of the Seal of the Confessional Working Party* (The Church of England, March 2018).

It is far from certain that this will be the last word on the subject;[212] and in 2023 a further commission was established to reconsider the question.[213]

Of course, it is impossible to gauge how much of the work that has been done results from the pressure of the inquiries. Both in Australia and England, the response to the scandal had begun long before the reports were produced—even on the issue of the Seal of the Confessional.[214] However, it is difficult to suppose that the pressure made no impact; and what is certain is that models from secular institutions were imported into the law of both churches.[215]

In England, there was a clearer instance of government pressure. Following the promulgation of an EU Directive[216] (when the UK was still a member of the EU), the DTI required the Church of England to revise the basis on which clergy hold their offices.[217] The result was *Ecclesiastical Offices (Terms of Service) Measure 2009*[218] and associated secondary legislation.

Conclusion: The Doctrinal Constraints on Anglican Law

The question arises, therefore, of what constraints being Anglican place on the law that is enacted; and the answer must lie in the doctrinal tenets of the Church. However, Anglicanism as an entity has neither a magisterium nor a confessional statement to define what that doctrine might be.[219] The canons of the Church of England hold that doctrine was to be inferred from the Thirty-nine Articles of Religion, the Book of Common Prayer (BCP) and the Ordinal.[220] However, the BCP does not form part of every Anglican province's

212 It was reported in the Church Times (30 May 2018) that the Diocese of Canterbury had issued guidelines, instructing priests to warn penitents: 'If you touch on any matter in your confession that raises a concern about the well-being or safeguarding of another person or yourself, I am duty bound to pass that information on to the relevant agencies, which means that I am unable to keep such information confidential'; though this seems to have been withdrawn.

213 www.churchofengland.org/media-and-news/press-releases/further-work-seal-confessional

214 An initial alteration of the canons was agreed in 2014; but that amendment was repealed in 2017 and replaced with another. See G Blake, 'The Confidentiality of Confessions in the Anglican Church of Australia' (2015) 17(1) Ecclesiastical Law Journal 46.

215 Such as the notion of 'Professional Standards'. See G Blake, 'Ministerial Duty and Professional Duty in the Anglican Church of Australia' (2010) 12(1) Ecclesiastical Law Journal 53; Church of England, *Guidelines for the Professional Conduct of the Clergy* (Church of England, Revised 2015).

216 EU Directive (2000/78/EC of 27 xi 2000).

217 Threatening to use the Employment Relations Act (1999) s 23 (4).

218 The Measure has been amended since 2009.

219 See Doe (n 16) 197.

220 Canon A5. Something similar pertains in the Australian canons—Canon 13(4).

heritage,[221] the Scottish Church set it aside in 1867;[222] TEC, likewise in 1979;[223] and the canons of Melanesia do not mention it at all. In 1974, the Church of England made provision for the creation of new liturgies without the need to resort to Parliament;[224] and the prominence of the BCP—the flagship of the English Reformation—in the past 50 years or so, has faded considerably (although it is enshrined in many Province's Laws),[225] more to a position of honour than influence,[226] revisions being driven not by doctrinal impulses but by ecumenism and academic investigation.[227]

The fate of the Thirty-nine Articles of Religion was similar. Again, early on the Lambeth Conference recognised that they would not be a feature of every province's doctrinal patrimony.[228] Today, very few provinces treat them as the 'Standard of Faith' they were once considered to be.[229] The Law of Melanesia would seem to capture the situation in most places, that

> The Church of Melanesia accepts:
> 1. the Thirty-Nine Articles of Religion as the historic statement of the Anglican position in faith and practice at the time of the Reformation, without thereby subscribing to every statement contained therein.[230]

The Irish Church is an outlier in this regard (reflecting perhaps, its particular affinity with the inheritance of the Reformation), requiring candidates for Ordination to 'be able to yield an account of such person's faith according to the Articles of Religion'.[231]

PCLCCAC, as well as reflecting the current status of the 'historic formularies', locates doctrinal authority in the Holy Scriptures, the Apostles' and Nicene Creeds and the 'undisputed' General Councils (typically the first four, in the rare cases[232] when they are identified).[233] These reflect to some

221 Doe states that the 'vast majority of Anglican Churches have received or adopted' the BCP; i.e. not all—Doe (n 16) 225.

222 Preamble s 8.4.

223 Title II, Canon 3.1.

224 Worship and Doctrine Measure (1974) s 1 (1).

225 E.g. Canada: Declaration of Principles 1 (Solemn Declaration); Southern Africa: Declaration of Fundamental Principles and Constitution Art X; Central Africa: Art 12; SE Asia Fundamental Declarations 1.

226 As early as 1897, the Lambeth Conference recognised that the BCP would inevitably be adapted as Anglican Churches embedded in their context—resn. 45f.

227 LC1958 resn 73, 74(c).

228 LC1888 res 19.

229 *Gorham v Bishop of Exeter* (1849) 2 Rob Ecc 1 at 55 per Sir Jenner Fust (Ct of Arches).

230 Standing Resolution 10. A similar sentiment is found in the Church of England Declaration of Assent, where a candidate is required to assent to the 'historic formularies' on insofar as they 'bear witness' to the Faith.

231 Const. IX 21 (3) (c).

232 Kenya (cited in Doe (n 16)) identifies them as the 'First four Councils'.

233 Princ 49 (1–3).

extent statements found in the Articles of Religion as sources of doctrine.[234] The emphasis is placed on the authority of Holy Scripture as befits churches descended from the influence of the Reformation. However, it is one thing to assert the authority of Holy Scripture, it is quite another to determine how its texts should be interpreted.[235] As the English Law puts it, 'The Church is called upon to proclaim afresh [the Faith] in each generation';[236] echoing a Lambeth Resolution of 1930.[237]

The law in a few provinces makes reference to the doctrinal authority of the Anglican Communion[238] or even the Church of England.[239] However, the preponderance of opinion is reflected in the sentiments of the Church in Kenya that she has the right, 'To draw up its own formularies of faith and to set forth in terms that it considers suitable to the present day and to the needs of the people of this Province, the Faith which this church holds'.[240]

In support of this process of proclaiming the Faith afresh, many provinces have established doctrinal commissions.[241] These do not make doctrinal law but reflect and advise. In every province the prerogative of defining doctrine rests with the highest legislative body;[242] and requires the consent of the House of Bishops.[243] There may also be particular procedures for the passing of doctrinal legislation.[244]

In some ways, this brings us back to the point where we started and tensions in the Anglican Communion. Over the past 50 years or so, provinces have headed off in different doctrinal directions. To a large extent, this reflects the impetus from conceiving of oneself as a national church reflecting the culture in which one is set. At the same time, another Reformation principle of fidelity to Holy Scripture makes these developments problematic for some provinces. The danger of this divergence was foreseen by the Lambeth Conference of 1930,[245] but subsequent conferences have proved unable to constrain the trend. In many provinces the problem is writ little in that the same debates raging in the Anglican Communion are also being fought out within

234 Arts VI and VIII (though this includes the *Quicunque Vult*); art XXI denies the authority of a General Council.

235 This has beset the churches of the Reformation from the outset; see, Rex, R: *The Making of Martin Luther* (Princeton University Press 2017) pp. 226f.

236 The Declaration of Assent—Canon C15.

237 Res 2.

238 E.g. West Indies Declaration of Fundamental Principles (e).

239 Central Africa Can 26.

240 Const. Art II (c).

241 See e.g. Australia General Synod Commissions Canons 1998–2007 part V; West Indies Can 33.1.A; England GS 1782; Scotland Can 52.23.

242 PCLCCAC Principle 50 (3).

243 PCLCCAC Principle 50 (5).

244 PCLCCAC Principle 50 (4).

245 Res 3.

provinces: though unlike the communion as a whole, individual provinces do have the legislative authority to impose their will.[246]

In a communion, in whose 'Mother Church' the study of canon law was once abolished, law has become an important factor in defining its identity in changing times and contexts. The absence of an overarching Anglican law, whilst still formally a principle of Anglican polity, has proved problematic in recent decades. Time will tell whether that principle can survive—though nobody should underestimate the challenge of creating a legal framework for the communion to which all provinces could assent.

Bibliography

Adam W, 'Communion and Jurisdiction' (2021) 24(2) Ecclesiastical Law Journal 206

Ahdar R and Leigh I, *Religious Freedom in the Liberal State* (OUP 2005)

Akinloye IA, 'Legal Issues Involving Succession Disputes among South African Churches: Some Issues' (2021) 23(2) Ecclesiastical Law Journal 2021 160

Behrens J, *The Churchwardens Measure* (2001) 29(6) Ecclesiastical Law Journal

Blake G, 'Ministerial Duty and Professional Duty in the Anglican Church of Australia' (2010) 12(1) Ecclesiastical Law Journal 53

Blake G, 'The Confidentiality of Confessions in the Anglican Church of Australia' (2015) 17(1) Ecclesiastical Law Journal 46

Butler P, 'From the Early Eighteenth Century to the Present Day' in S Sykes and J Booty (eds), *The Study of Anglicanism* (SPCK 1988)

Chapman MD, 'The Dull Bits of History: Cautionary Tales for Anglicanism' in MD Chapman (ed), *The Anglican Communion Covenant* (Mowbray 2008)

Church of England, *Guidelines for the Professional Conduct of the Clergy* (Church of England 2015)

Church of England, *Report of the Seal of the Confessional Working Party* (Church of England, March 2018)

Colton P, 'The Pursuit of a Canonical Definition of Membership in the Church of Ireland' (2008) 10 (1) Ecclesiastical Law Journal 3

Doe N, *Canon Law in the Anglican Communion* (Clarendon Press 1998)

Doe N, *The Anglican Covenant* (Canterbury Press 2008)

Doe N, *Comparative Religious Law: Judaism, Christianity, Islam* (CUP 2019)

Doe N and Deadman R, 'The Resolutions of the Lambeth Conference and the Laws of Anglican Churches' in P Avis and BM Guyer (eds), *The Lambeth Conference* (T&T Clark 2019)

Dusenbury DL, *The Innocence of Pontius Pilate* (Hurst & Co 2021)

Elton GR, *The Tudor Constitution* (2nd edn, CUP 1992)

Evans C and Hood A, 'Religious Autonomy and Labour Law: A Comparison of the Jurisprudence of the United States and the European Court of Human Rights' (2012) 1 OJLR 81

Evans GR and Robert Wright J (eds), *The Anglican Tradition, A Handbook of Sources* (SPCK 1988)

246 So, for example, in 1986 Canada withdrew its conscience clause concerning the Ordination of women (General Synod 14–16 vi 1986 Act 91) on the basis that future ordinands knew what the Church now taught: see W Hemmerick, 'The Ordination of Women—the Canadian Experience' (1992) 2 Ecclesiastical Law Journal 180.

Florence Li Tim-Oi in 'Lesser Feasts and Facts 2003' (2004 Church Publishing Incorporated)

Frank RB, 'Historical Milieu of Tribunals in South Africa: the Role of Church Tribunals' (2021) 23(1) Ecclesiastical Law Journal 75

Grimley M, *The State, Nationalism and Anglican Identities* in *The Oxford History of Anglicanism*, J. Morris (ed) (OUP 2017) vol IV

Grout C, 'The Seal of the Confessional and the Criminal Law of England and Wales' (2020) 22 (2) Ecclesiastical Law Journal 2020 138

Harding M, 'Trusts for Religious Purposes and the Question of Public Benefit' (2008) 71 (2) MLR 159

Helmholz RH, *Roman Canon Law in Reformation England* (CUP 1990)

Helmholz RH, *The Oxford History of the Laws of England* (OUP 2004) vol 1

Hemmerick W, 'The Ordination of Women—the Canadian Experience' (1992) 2 Ecclesiastical Law Journal 180

Hill M, *Ecclesiastical Law* (2nd edn, OUP 2001)

Hill M, 'Judicial Review of Ecclesiastical Courts' in N Doe, M Hill and R Ombres (eds), *English Canon Law* (U of Wales P 1998)

Hooker R, *Of the Laws of Ecclesiastical Polity* Bk VIII 1.2 (Note: one recent edition of this is published in Cambridge Texts in the History of Political Thought (2008) ed.)

House of Bishops, *Parish Safeguarding Handbook* (CHP 2018)

Kaye B, 'From a Colonial Chaplaincy to Responsible Governance: The Anglican Church of Australia and its Ecclesiological Challenge' (2021)23(1) Ecclesiastical Law Journal 2021 43

Kuehn EF, 'Instruments of Faith and Unity in Canon Law: The Church of Nigeria Constitutional Revision of 2005' (2008) 10(2) Ecclesiastical Law Journal 2008 161

Leeder L, *Ecclesiastical Law Handbook* (Sweet and Maxwell 1997)

Lesser Feasts and Facts 2003 (2004 Church Publishing Incorporated)

Marriage in Church after Divorce GS 1449 (2002)

Noll S, *Sea-change in the Anglican Communion* (2013) at www.anglican.ink/article/sea-change-anglican-communion

Patterson N, *Ecclesiastical Law, Clergy and Laity* (Routledge 2020)

Pereiro J, 'The Oxford Movement and Anglo-Catholicism' in R Strong (ed), *The Oxford History of Anglicanism* (OUP 2017) vol III

Pobee JS, 'Newer Dioceses of the Anglican Communion—Movement and Prospect' in S Sykes and J Booty (eds), *The Study of Anglicanism* (SPCK 1988)

Podmore, C, 'The Tale of Two Churches, the Ecclesiologies of the Episcopal Church and the Church of England compared' (2008) 10(1) Ecclesiastical Law Journal 38

Rex, R: *The Making of Martin Luther* (Princeton University Press 2017)

Rose J, 'The Godly Magistrate' in A Milton (ed), *The Oxford History of Anglicanism* (OUP 2017) vol 1

Ross A, *A Still More Excellent Way* (SCM 2020)

Sachs WL, 'Sexuality and Anglicanism' in J Morris (ed), *The Oxford History of Anglicanism* (OUP 2017) vol IV

Sachs WL, *Sexuality and Anglicanism the Oxford History of Anglicanism*, J Morris (ed) (OUP 2017) vol 4

Smith P, 'The Advowson: The History and Development of a Most Peculiar Piece of Property' (2000) 5 Ecclesiastical Law Journal 320

Spinks BD, *The Rise and Fall of the Incomparable Liturgy* (SPCK 2017)

Sutton T, 'Advowsons and Private Patronage' (2019) 21 Ecclesiastical Law Journal 267

The Principles of Canon Law Common to the Churches of the Anglican Communion, Anglican Communion Legal Advisers Network (Anglican Communion Office 2008)

Wild-Wood E, 'Anglicanism in Sub-Saharan Africa c 1829–1910' in R Strong (ed), *The Oxford History of Anglicanism* (OUP 2017) vol 3.

5 The Theology of Canon Law

A Catholic Perspective on the Fundamentals

Luke Beckett OSB

Introduction

The attempt to identify the fundamentals of the Catholic approach to canon law needs to start with a consideration of the theology of canon law, to root the whole legal order of the Church in a theological vision rather than one that is simply philosophical or anthropological. Unless this is done, it is not simply the case that some of the legal institutions specific to canon law will be difficult to understand, but (worse) that the whole project will seem to be in important ways contestable and perhaps even simply an attempt at the imposition of power. The codification of the Church's law in 1917 brought with it important advantages of legal clarity and ease of application. The accusation was subsequently made that this merely enabled a legalistic system of governance in the Church that displaced authority with mere power. While even in 1917 it was not true that all the Church's law was contained in the Code (and it remains true today that it is not) the Code was universal in its scope and was a powerful symbol of what one recent author has called legal modernity[1]—in a world in which law elsewhere, in the light of legal positivist theories, seemed to be more about power than anything else. Unless canon law can be shown to be something which necessarily brings about an indispensable aspect of the life of the Church, such an allegation would be hard to respond to. The question, therefore, has to be put as to whether there is anything theological about canon law. This is a question that may well resonate with Anglican audiences, for although there are important differences between the two systems[2] there are also many similarities; if canon law has a theological root, we should expect these to be merely the result of neither the hangover of pre-Reformation historical matter nor sociological pressures surrounding the need to organise a community, but rather of something intrinsic to the notion of ecclesial community.

1 Carlo Fantappiè, *Chiesa romana e modernità giuridica* (Giuffrè 2008).
2 It is unlikely that many will see the English Reformation as primarily about canon law, though the claims of Royal Supremacy can be read in this way.

DOI: 10.4324/9780429264115-7

The notion of the theology of canon law has only recently become a subject of considerable study in the Catholic Church. The single most important stimulus to this study in recent times seems at first sight to have been an unlikely one. In 2002 the Congregation for Catholic Education published the decree *Novo Codice* reforming the syllabus for the study of canon law in ecclesiastical universities.[3] This decree, among other changes, introduced as an obligatory subject into the course for the Licence in Canon Law[4] the new subject of the 'theology of canon law'. Suddenly a topic which had been the subject of occasional monographs and particular interest in some restricted canonical circles had to be taught in every faculty of canon law. Moreover, since the 2002 reforms extended the duration of the Licence in Canon Law from two years to three, there was plenty of time to fill. The challenge could not be ignored, and it was a large one. The approach to the teaching of canon law since the promulgation of the 1917 Code of Canon Law had been one closely focused on the text of the Code itself. The position of canon law in the Church seemed obvious, and beyond the need for justification. All that was required was the acquisition of a body of professional expertise. The suggestion that the theology of canon law was a necessary element of canonical study, backed up by the insistence of *Novo Codice* that students of canon law had a full and thorough theological formation[5] meant that theological reflection was now something required for all students (and therefore for all faculties) of canon law.[6] The basis for canon law was identified not simply as a theology which could be derived from within canon law itself but rather as theology in the widest sense of the term: the theology which is appropriated by an authentic theological formation such as is envisaged in *Optatam Totius*, the decree of the second Vatican Council on priestly formation.

This decree, when discussing the curriculum of priestly studies, made comments which go well beyond that particular sphere in their importance. It stated that

> theological subjects should be renewed through a more lively contact with the mystery of Christ and the history of salvation . . . [and] . . . the

3 By a decree *Novo Codice* dated 2 September 2002, in AAS 95 (2003) 281–85. There is a survey of this decree by B Esposito 'Il nuovo piano degli studi delle Facoltà di diritto canonico' in *Quaderni della Mendola* 12, 257–92.

4 The Licence is the essential qualification for working as a Canon Lawyer in the Catholic Church. By way of example, see canon 1420 §4.

5 The specific reforms proposed for both the first and second cycles of study underline this: see *Novo Codice* I, II and III.

6 It may not be too fanciful to imagine the effect on Law Faculties in England and Wales if the relevant government department and the relevant professional bodies were to require that the Philosophy of Law were to be a compulsory subject in every law degree in England and Wales. In the canonical context it is worth remembering that the philosophy of law had long been a required course.

> teaching of canon law and church history should take account of the mystery of the church as presented in the dogmatic constitution 'On the Church' of this holy council.[7]

There are a number of important points for canon law to be taken from this paragraph, including the importance of Holy Scripture and the church's magisterium as constant sources for teaching, which support the reference quoted here. Given that the presentation of the Church in *Lumen Gentium* is richly based in Scripture and tradition and offers a constant sense of the mystery of Christ being made present in the Church, no distinction should be seen between the first part of the passage quoted and the words specifically applied to canon law. These words go well beyond mere indications about syllabus content and offer a pathway towards the renewal of theological study more generally, and as a consequence of that to the renewal of the aspects of church life which are the object of those theological studies. There is clearly a sort of virtuous circle envisaged here, where the mystery of the Church illuminates the theological disciplines,[8] and those disciplines, because they are of their nature deeply ecclesial, further illuminate the mystery of the Church. The importance of the link with Church history cannot be more than touched on here, but the underlying reference to the work of the Spirit in the life of the Church is important to bear in mind.

Theology in Canon Law and Theology of Canon Law

A discussion of the theology of canon law needs to start with a distinction. We could speak of the theology in canon law, and the theology of canon law. The second of these is our primary object here, but the first is an important element in understanding it. The notion of theology in canon law is itself a relative novelty in modern canon law, at least at the explicit level: anyone who has seriously considered the canons of the former Code will see that a theological vision inspires them all. Those who were formulating the 1917 Code of Canon Law very consciously endeavoured to exclude all theological statements from the text of the Code, to produce a purely legal text. The most obvious evidence of this was the very structure of that Code, whose books were divided using the Roman law categories of Persons, Things and Actions, but the canons themselves were drafted so as to offer texts that made no apparent theological reference.

7 *Optatam Totius* 16. An accessible source of the documents of the Second Vatican Council is *Vatican Council II Constitutions, Decrees, Declarations* (Dominican Publications 1995) *Optatam Totius* is at 365. The dogmatic constitution 'On the Church' is better known as *Lumen Gentium* see 1 of *Vatican Council II Constitutions, Decrees, Declarations.*

8 *Optatam Totius* 16 begins 'Theological studies should be taught in the light of faith'.

The way in which the revision of the law that led to the 1983 Code decided not to follow such a path can be seen in many ways. A helpful way of entering into this is to take a specific example. The group that was entrusted with producing a new draft of the law on Religious Life decided, at its first meeting, to set out a series of principles which would guide their work. The first of these was that the new texts of the canons should have an explicitly theological content: even if this content were expressed in a way that was a brief synthesis; such a presentation would tend towards the elimination of the mentality that (it was feared) had become widely spread within the religious life which believed that this life could be fully lived out by formal fidelity to the rules of canon law, both universal and proper to the Religious Institute.[9] At the early stage of drafting the hope was to achieve this aim by offering an almost skeletal common law, and inviting each Institute to fill out the details with a proper law that was drafted in the light of their own charism. Although this latter aim was later viewed as perhaps too utopian, the desire to retain canons whose theological content was evident remained.

The next step in this analysis is to look at individual canons to see how they reflect this aim. My own work on canons 617 to 619 attempted to do this for these canons on the nature and role of the Superior in a Religious Institute, and to demonstrate how these canons reflected the developments in the theology of religious life concerning obedience that had been stated in the decree *Perfectae Caritatis* of the second Vatican Council.[10] The attempt to do this involved tracing the sources of the conciliar text in the renewal of religious life that was going on in the twentieth century, and seeing how that text was then translated into canonical form.[11] Here the text of the Code has its theological basis visible in the very words of the laws. This visibility is not always the case, but theology is always there. The words of the Council offer a resource for checking the adequacy of the Code—and sometimes the Code is judged to have failed. The most notorious example of this is the way in which the warm recommendation of Diocesan Pastoral Councils made at Vatican II is expressed with much greater tepidity in the Code.[12]

This way of looking at the theology in the 1983 Code does not simply operate at the level at which considers one or two canons individually. The recent reform of Book VI of the Code,[13] concerning the Church's penal law, can be examined as an implementation of the second Vatican Council. An example of this is a recent analysis of the duties laid on the bishop by this

9 *Communicationes* 18 (1986) 179.

10 Luke Beckett, *The Canonical Understanding of Spiritual Leadership in Religious Life: From the Compilation of the 1917 Code to the Coming into Force of the 1983 Code* (Rome 2011).

11 A similar project in the same area of canon law can be seen in Simone Pereira de Araujo, *Il consiglio dei Superiori nella storia e nella legislazione attuale* (Venice 2019).

12 Compare *Christus Dominus* 27 with Canon 511.

13 See the Apostolic Constitution *Pascite gregem Dei*, reforming Book VI of the Code of Canon Law (23 May 2021).

reform, which suggests that the conciliar understanding of the Church was not sufficiently mature by the time of the work of the revisers of the Code to offer an immediately applicable vision for penal law. Mosconi suggests that the work of the revisers reveals a hesitancy about the appropriateness of penal law in an ecclesial context (as well as a mentality which had not fully moved on from a *societatis perfecta* ecclesiology), which in turn led to an excessive preference for 'pastoral' rather than 'penal' remedies which were seen as better expressing the need to demonstrate Christian mercy. The influence of this view in the immediate post-conciliar period can be seen in the words of Ladislas Orsy:

> It would be immoral to ask an intelligent and free person to perform an act, even in obedience to a law, if he had not reached a personal judgment that the act was in pursuance of a true value and if he had not decided freely to do it.[14]

On this analysis there seems little point in a penal law, and the church seems to have little power to deal with abuses. By way of contrast, the move to a renewed vision of the Church and a rereading of the Council, seen clearly in words of Pope Benedict XVI,[15] led in its turn to the renewal of Book VI. The principles which guided the revision are rooted in a theological approach which is not a repudiation of Vatican II but an attempt to implement it better.[16] The Council was an attempt to renew the whole of Christian life to make the action of the Church a more truly pastoral: reflection on what is required to be genuinely pastoral generated both the perception that the text of 1983 needed to change and the direction in which that change needed to be made.

The Apostolic Constitution *Sacrae Disciplinae Leges*

This small-scale detail is important, as it leads into a consideration of one of the most important claims made about the 1983 Code of Canon Law. This is found in the Apostolic Constitution *Sacrae Disciplinae Leges*, by which Pope St John Paul II promulgated the new Code:

> Indeed, in a certain sense, this new Code could be understood as a great effort to translate this same doctrine, that is, the conciliar ecclesiology, into canonical language. If, however, it is impossible to translate perfectly into canonical language the conciliar image of the Church, nevertheless,

14 See Ladislas Orsy, *Theology and Canon Law* (Collegeville 1992) pages 42–42.

15 Benedict XVI, *Letter to the faithful in Ireland*, 19 March 2010, paragraph 4.

16 Marino Mosconi, 'L'avvio della procedura per l'applicazione della sanzione penale nella revisione del libro VI del CIC, tra opportunità e dovere per l'ordinario diocesano' (2022) 35 *Quaderni di Diritto Ecclesiale* 264–88, especially at pages 265–68.

> in this image there should always be found as far as possible its essential point of reference.

At this point the notion of the theology in canon law begins to lead us to the theology of canon law. *Sacrae Disciplinae Leges* itself offers an example which also helps to make this transition.

> Therefore the Code, not only because of its content but also because of its very origin, manifests the spirit of this Council, in the documents of which the Church, the universal 'sacrament of salvation', is presented as the People of God and its hierarchical constitution appears based on the College of Bishops united with its Head.

The organisation of the new Code (albeit not perfectly) is arranged around the concepts of *Lumen Gentium*, and its conceptual foundation is presented in the second book, which treats of the People of God first as individuals and then as organised into the hierarchical constitution of the Church. The importance of this insight is demonstrated by the way in which the 1990 Code of Canons of the Eastern Churches begins not with General Norms (as the 1983 Latin Code does) but with a treatment of the basic nature of Christ's faithful seen in a legal context, and then goes on to look at the structures of the Church, with the material covered in the 1983 book I on General Norms coming at the end of the 1990 Code. The reference to 'origin' in these words of *Sacrae Disciplinae Leges* is expanded by that document to suggest that the production of the new Code, with its wide involvement of bishops around the world, followed a methodology that was 'as far as possible collegial'. But it is the content of the Code which is the primary ground for this claim to manifest the spirit of the Council. As the Apostolic Constitution goes on to say:

> Among the elements which characterize the true and genuine image of the Church, we should emphasize especially the following: the doctrine in which the Church is presented as the People of God (cf. *Lumen Gentium*, no. 2), and authority as a service (cf. ibid., no. 3); the doctrine in which the Church is seen as a 'communion', and which, therefore, determines the relations which should exist between the particular Churches and the universal Church, and between collegiality and the primacy; the doctrine, moreover, according to which all the members of the People of God, in the way suited to each of them, participate in the threefold office of Christ: priestly, prophetic and kingly. With this teaching there is also linked that which concerns the duties and rights of the faithful, and particularly of the laity; and finally, the Church's commitment to ecumenism.

Here we see that the primary claims made about the theology which is to be found in the Code are about ecclesiology. With good reason we may agree with Robert Ombres that canon law is best seen as applied ecclesiology.[17] This insight invites us to further consideration: we may ask, what sort of tool is canon law for the application of ecclesiology? Is it a legal tool, which has no independent theological value of its own? Or is it a theological tool, which has its own theological nature? The first of these answers can be found in the literature, and today is perhaps most associated with the so-called Navarre school of canon law,[18] whose rigorous legal analysis of canon law has greatly helped to bring depth and precision to the understanding of canon law. But is this all?

The Contribution of St Thomas Aquinas

Can we, and should we, look for more? To answer this question, we need to step back to look at the roots of the Catholic approach to reflection on canon law, which lies in the work of St Thomas Aquinas on law generally.

To begin with, the position of St Thomas Aquinas is important not simply because of the clarity of his concept of law, but also because of the influence that his theology had in the Catholic Church in the early twentieth century. Since Pope Leo XIII's *Aeterni Patris*,[19] Thomist theology had enjoyed a privileged position in Catholic thought—and this was also reflected in theological education. Within that matrix, reflection on law had an additional reason for starting with St Thomas.

St Thomas offered a definition of law as 'an ordinance of reason for the common good made by the authority who has care of the community and promulgated'.[20] This justly famous definition has, however, to be seen in its context, and to understand how it offers a basis for the theology of canon law this is essential. Two points are important.

Firstly, the definition is the culmination of a process of reasoning, and one of the first steps in that process is vital. At the beginning of his discussion of law, St Thomas asks whether law is a product of reason, and starts his answer to that question with the statement 'law is a kind of direction or measure for human activity through which a person is led to do something or held back'.[21] This beginning point reminds us of two important points. The first is that the notion of reason implies an intellectual hinterland which could provide reasons. For St Thomas this is most obviously evident in the position of this question in the wider world of his *Summa Theologiae*: it comes roughly half

17 An argument put forth in several pieces: see R Ombres, 'Why Then the Law?' (1974) New Blackfriars 296–304; 'Canon Law and the Mystery of the Church' (1996/1997) The Irish Theological Quarterly 200–12; and 'Ecclesiology, Ecumenism and Canon Law' in N Doe, M Hill and R Ombres (eds), *English Canon Law* (Wales 1998) 48–59.

18 The founder of this approach, Prof. Pedro Lombardia, was a professor in the faculty of canon law in the University of Navarre.

19 Issued on 4 August 1879.

20 *Summa Theologiae* 1a2ae, 90, 4.

21 *Summa Theologiae* 1a2ae, 90, 1; the question is 'utrum lex sit aliquid rationis'.

way through the extended treatment of moral theology which comprises the second part of the *Summa*. Already from this it is evident that the reference to action in his preliminary statement about the nature of law is one that is oriented towards moral theology. This context informs the treatment of the power of human law: St Thomas first asks whether law should restrain all the vices, and then whether it should command all the acts of the virtues, and only then what the response should be to a bad law. His view is clearly that law

> does not forbid all the vices, from which upright men can keep away, but only those very grave ones which the average man can avoid, and chiefly those which do harm to others and have to be stopped if human society is to be maintained, such as murder and theft and so forth.[22]

Similarly,

> human law does not enjoin every act of virtue, but only those acts which serve the common good, either immediately, as when the social order is directly involved from the nature of things, or mediately, as when measures of good discipline are passed by the legislator to train citizens to maintain justice and peace in the community.[23]

His treatment of bad laws is contained in a response to the question as to whether laws bind in conscience—which begins by asserting that a just law does bind in conscience because it is derived from God's eternal law. Only once this has been said does he go on to ask how a law can be unjust and suggests that the basic reasons are when a law is not fair in human terms or is against God's rights. He is clear that the second case (his example is a law which promotes idolatry) can never be obeyed. The first case receives a more complex answer. He supposes as an example the case of a ruler who taxes his subjects 'for his own greed or vanity rather than for the common good'. Laws in this situation of unfairness, says St Thomas, do not bind 'unless perhaps to avoid scandal or riot'.[24]

In these words we begin to see St Thomas' approach to law taking a more definite shape, and being influenced by the second key point that underpins his arguments. His view rests on an implicit confidence that rulers will act to promote the common good: their authority has the backing of divine support (a conclusion he draws from *Romans* 13) to enable them to do this. While the common good is preserved to some degree by any ruler who preserves a

22 *Summa Theologiae* 1a2ae, 96, 2.
23 *Summa Theologiae* 1a2ae, 96, 3.
24 *Summa Theologiae* 1a2ae, 96, 4. See also the point made *ad tertium*: a law which inflicts an unjust grievance on subjects 'exceeds the power of command divinely granted, and in such cases a man is not obliged to obey, if without scandal or greater damage he can resist'.

minimum level of social peace, the confidence that St Thomas shows towards rulers (I will not essay to say whether this was justifiable in his own day) seems to be to say the least over-optimistic in the present. For St Thomas law is a necessary part of the moral universe, and this grounds his positive view even of the laws of secular rulers. His *Summa Theologiae*, it must be remembered, is a guide to theology which is strictly practical. The longest sections are all about moral theology, and that moral theology is ordered to action. Law is put on a footing which offers to both ruler and subject a vision for legislation and obedience to legislation—and also perspectives on what happens when those visions are lost. However, it seems a vision which is equally applicable to the law of a state and the law of the Church: we might justly say that his concept of law is univocal when applied to civil law and canon law. Perhaps this is unsurprising for his time: the recent rediscovery in the Latin West of the legal treasures of the Roman law (and especially of Justinian's *Digest*) was transforming legal science and techniques and issuing in an explosion of creative legislation in the Church under the guidance of great canon lawyer Popes. There was also great confidence in the idea of a partnership between church and state, so that both could co-operate in the pursuit of the common good. Moreover, the theology of the Church was still in a relatively undeveloped state with the great advances in this area made in the nineteenth and twentieth centuries still long in the future. Perhaps it is unsurprising then that St Thomas has little to say about the theology of canon law as something distinct. The whole medieval tradition left canon law vulnerable to the damaging Erastianism of the post-Reformation world, when rulers (whether formally Catholic or Protestant) claimed to legislate for the Church on the basis that they were the ones who had care of the community. In such a perspective, canon law could only be another branch of the essentially secular law of the early modern state, with nothing intrinsically special about it.

By the end of the nineteenth century, the door will be open to the critique of Rudolph Sohm, the German Protestant scholar who argued that since the Church was the realm of grace, law as such had no place in it, and that canon law was a fundamental error. Sohm's detailed historical presentation of his theory was attacked and essentially refuted by Adolf von Harnack and Pierre Batiffol, but the question he poses remains a source of uneasiness for the project of canon law and for the institutional church as a whole.[25] The foundations of the answer had already been laid in the decree *Dei Filius* of the first Vatican Council, but the ecclesiological developments that both led to and followed from that Council would be vital for providing a satisfactory answer. Only a fuller understanding of the Church could provide the context in which the erroneous interpretation of Sohm, with its vision of a church without law, could be corrected.

25 See e.g. P Erdo, *Teologia del Diritto Canonico* (Torino 1996) 54.

The Theory of Cardinal Ghirlanda

Cardinal Gianfranco Ghirlanda, the distinguished Jesuit canon lawyer who was for many years a professor at the Gregorian University in Rome, has set out a comprehensive theology of canon law. The examination of this theory will give a basis for understanding one of the most influential of modern strands in contemporary Catholic approaches to theology and canon law.[26]

Ghirlanda begins his study with an examination of the anthropological foundations of law: for him the notion of the human being as a person in relationships with other persons is fundamental. Each person is not merely the qualities which identify him or herself (that is, not merely the personal attributes, but also the values and the rights that make them up) but has also an openness to relationship which is realised in social relationships. Since the freedom which is a human quality can be exercised both in actions which express that relationship in positive and in negative terms, the nature of humanity requires an authority which can both prevent negative interactions and indicate the obligations which have to be fulfilled for the dignity of the other to be respected. Thus human sociability both creates relationships and brings with it the necessity for law—a necessity which is responded to in every human society by some kind of positive law. This dignity of the other person is as a consequence recognised and expressed in Ulpian's maxim that justice is the stable and permanent will to render to the other what is his right,[27] these words offer a pithy summary of the basis of justice both as the positive law which is expressed in every human society and the natural law which is the moral foundation of that positive law as well as the basis of the value of law's certainty. When all the positive laws of a given society are viewed together one can speak of an institution, or a legal system, which aims at the common good—a situation in which all can pursue what is the good of the group alongside their individual good, with this latter being secured by some notion of the human rights of each individual.

On the basis of this anthropological foundation, Ghirlanda goes on to indicate the importance of the philosophy of law, which he specially identifies with the question of the relationship between the moral order and the legal system. In this the role of the legislator is of supreme importance, having the task of rendering it possible for people to live together in the society governed by the legal system in question. While he acknowledges the importance of pluralism and the different opinions present in a society, this task cannot simply be some form of compromise to allow co-existence but must rest on the necessary foundation of the need to protect and foster the dignity of the person. Positive law rests on the objective foundations of the rights which this need generates: it cannot only be something technical but must carry within itself

26 The survey here draws on his *Il diritto nella Chiesa mistero della communion*, now in its (4th edn, Rome 2014).

27 Digest 1,1: constans et perpetua voluntas ius suum cuique tribuendi.

fundamental human values. While Ghirlanda is fully open to the way in which positive law needs to be an expression of the culture of the particular social group, the universality of human rights is more fundamental than culture, and having these rights at its heart enables the law of any human system to transcend its own cultural expressions with all their limitations. This points to the problem that positive law, regulating as it does the external actions of human beings, does not exhaust the full range of human possibility. The internal sphere necessarily eludes law's reach, expressing as it does the fundamental privacy of each human being and offering a space for a moral critique of the laws (and indeed the whole legal system) as they stand. Law offers both a means for promoting moral action in the realm of human relationships and a stimulus to its own improvement in the light of these more profound moral values.

This dialectic is where Ghirlanda places the first aspect of law as an historical phenomenon, always expressing the current state of human self-understanding in the moral and social sphere and at the same time being open to moral critique. He goes on to see in this the first opening to transcendence in the legal system, which necessarily invites a reflection on human experience which goes beyond the particular to look at the universal human nature which underpins the universality of law. This universality is the basis of the authority of law, which thus rests not simply on brute force but on the authority of the Creator who brought into being human nature with its moral conscience. Conscience is where the transcendent voice of the Creator is heard and made immanent through laws which reflect its demands. Having said this, Ghirlanda acknowledges that a merely phenomenological and philosophical account of law is inadequate in itself to explain the reality of law. He sees the need for a deeper inquiry into human nature, and an account of the link between divine justice and human justice, between divine law and human law.

Theological Anthropology

Ghirlanda's theological anthropology begins with the statement in Genesis that humanity is created in the image and likeness of God: this points out that the fundamental human relationship is with God. Relationships with all else in creation are secondary to this divine-human relationship, which constitutes the foundation of human dignity. Each human life is sacred, and the most basic and important law in any human society must be to respect this: indeed, without such respect human life together would soon reveal itself to be impossible. Life in the image and likeness of God is ordered towards communion with God and with other people. Although sin has made this a practical impossibility, the old and new Covenants reveal God's plan for the restoration of this communion. The Old Testament vision of justice becomes a way for humans to come to know the will of God, and this points forward to the justice of the new Covenant (which finds its perfection in the love of Christ) whereby a human can come into communion with God.

As he makes this link between charity and justice, Ghirlanda acknowledges that although the justice of the gospel does not deny the experience of human justice—rather, it completes it as it goes beyond it—this going beyond indicates to us that the relationship between these two expressions of justice is not univocal but analogical. This was the same view as that of St Thomas, despite some crude criticisms of the latter for holding to a position of univocality in this respect.

This leads into a brief consideration of the link between nature and grace—important because of challenges to the position of canon law in the Church arising from post-Reformation currents of thought with a less positive view of fallen nature. Ghirlanda affirms the Catholic position that man, although created in the image and likeness of God, with the accompanying potential for relationship firstly to God and then to other people, has fallen by sin. However, the effect of the fall is to damage but not destroy this image and likeness. The grace which God offers can arouse the response of faith and by this faith each person can have a relationship with God and a relationship with others that is illuminated by that relationship with God. These relationships can be described as relationships of communion—both in their inception and in their fullness in the kingdom of heaven. The grace God offers can also offer a path to the identification of a natural law, which is (as St Paul puts it in Romans) written in the human heart. Unaided human reason may be able to recognise this law, but grace is required to live it out. The attempt in history to cooperate with grace to recognise this eternal law results in positive law which states the natural law, as well as going beyond it. And although these statements may be partial and incomplete and reflect the historical context from which they come; they nonetheless offer us a path towards a law which perfectly reflects God's justice—even if that path will never arrive at its destination in this life.

Communion

So far Ghirlanda's theory does not seem to be radically different from that of St Thomas (even if its detailed presentation is much more obviously Biblically rooted) and seems to be open to the same problems. Can he offer an account of canon law which enables it to be recognised as an essential element of the Church, and not an obstruction to its charismatic essence? He starts to do this with an insight of Pope St Paul VI, who saw that the nature of canon law can only be defined adequately by deepening one's understanding of the mystery of the Church. For Ghirlanda the essential means to this is the vision of the Church as communion. This approach is already glanced at in *Sacrae Disciplinae Leges*, but Ghirlanda offers a development which takes the notion of communion as a path not simply to identifying the theology in canon law (as might seem to be the limit of the Apostolic Constitution) but to identifying the theology of canon law. Moreover, an approach rooted in communion also offers the possibility of a way in which to acknowledge the contingent reality of the form which canon law takes at any given historical moment, and to go beyond that to enter into the mystery of the Church in precisely such a way that the contingent historical reality of ecclesial existence at any given moment is what prevents the vision of the Church from being a merely unreal phantom. Thus the divine law, which is given both by nature and Revelation, expressing the will of the Church's divine founder, exists within the institutional Church of any given day, and that institutional Church (albeit in a fragmentary and imperfect manner) expresses that mystery, both revealing it and being given shape by it.

In this context one can do no more than recall the theology of communion found in the New Testament, but even a brief account must point out how communion has both a Christological and an ecclesiological aspect. St Paul offers a vision of how communion with the Father is mediated through communion with the Son, established through communion in his body and blood. On the basis of this communion the Spirit works to bring about spiritual communion among believers, which they express by adhering to that original teaching for which he uses the traditional term the Apostolic Tradition—and from this all Christian solidarity flows. This solidarity is rooted in adhesion to the doctrines handed down and to a way of life that is in accordance with the demands of the gospel: when these are present we can speak of a visible ecclesial communion: even though at that stage it is too early to identify the institutionalised form of that communion, we have here the matrix from which that will emerge. Indeed, the need the Church feels to remain in continuity with its foundations, and with the beliefs and practices handed down by its Founder, is the foundation for law in the Church, since it is law which operates to ensure that fidelity. However, since the Tradition (that is, what is being handed on) is most basically Christ himself and is handed on in the Spirit which animates the Church, this fidelity is not something essentially static. The active presence of the Spirit both prompts the confession of faith and guides action, and in doing so builds the Church as a communion of believers. Rooting himself in an analysis of New Testament texts, Ghirlanda proposes a definition of the Apostolic Tradition as the active handing on of a deposit which contains doctrinal teaching, norms of practical comportment and ministerial structures to which believers should orient themselves as authoritative.

This notion of the Apostolic Tradition develops through the patristic period as the Church lives the reality of the communion it embodies, and this lived experience comes to constitute a new development: the ecclesiastical tradition. This is not as fully normative as are Scripture and the Apostolic Tradition, but it is none the less important. In this context communion comes to express the bond of union between the bishop and his flock and between bishops themselves, which finds its visible expression in eucharistic communion. The practical expressions of the bond of communion in the early Church, the so-called letters of communion, consolidate this, and also express in practice its opposite, the rupture in relationship of excommunication. The complex history of these practices shows that from the earliest times communion has also been a legal as well as a sacramental institution—and that these two elements however theoretically separable cannot be separated in practice.

Communion in the Second Vatican Council and the Code

Much history has been passed over here, as is inevitable in a short sketch, but the direction of travel which was to lead to the renewal in ecclesiology of the second Vatican Council had been set. In its first section *Lumen Gentium* defines the Church as a sacrament—that is a sign and an instrument—of union with God and between human beings; as such the Church both signifies and brings about communion with God and others. Communion between the faithful is not simply the external structure of communion between the churches, but neither is it only a spiritual communion which has no concrete form whatsoever. Rather, the impulse of the Holy Spirit constitutes a spiritual communion which is both invisible and humanly structured. The Council, however, does not want to disappear into the purely abstract, into a vision of spiritual communion which has no contact with reality. Instead, that spiritual communion requires the legal forms of ecclesiastical communion and hierarchical communion to compose an organic reality whose fullness is found in full communion with the Catholic Church. Ghirlanda identifies five essential elements of the Church: baptism, the differentiation between the faithful within the Church by means of different hierarchical and charismatic gifts, the acceptance of the visible Church and its visible means—most notable among which are the proclamation of the gospel and the celebration of the eucharist, union with Christ in the Church through the bonds of the profession of faith, the sacraments and ecclesiastical government and the role of Pope and bishops in the Church. It is not merely the case that these visible structural elements are always present wherever there is communion, but more deeply that their presence is generated by the communion itself. He presses this analysis further to look at the manner in which the communion of the faithful which the Spirit constitutes similarly generates three levels of structural communion: the local (typically experienced as parish), the particular (that is, diocesan) and the universal. Each of these includes the elements he identifies as necessary, and the communion they express requires the institutional structure that gives shape not merely to their own inner being but also to the complementarity between them.

Ghirlanda looks at other ways of talking about the Church which are prominent in the work of the second Vatican Council. His consideration of the Church as Sacrament leads him particularly to the eighth chapter of *Lumen Gentium*, which points out an analogy of proportionality between the unity of the humanity and divinity in Christ and the way in which the Church has within itself elements both human and divine which are inseparably united. This is the basis of the way in which the Church can become a prolongation of the Incarnation at the service of the salvation of humanity in all ages. Similarly, viewing the Church as the Body of Christ also offers a way of talking about the Church as a visible reality accessible to experience which is not merely a human or this-worldly thing. The image of the body as animated by the soul suggests how the Church can be both humanly structured and also spiritually animated. In considering both these images, Ghirlanda's concern is to point out how a vision of the Church demands a human element which expresses itself in human ways, and to go on from there to argue that the divine element which lies within conditions the way in which that human element emerges.

The structure of the visible Church, a community which manifests communion, is as a consequence one which also shows forth the ultimate and most profound reality towards which the Church is on pilgrimage, the life of the Trinity. The double aspect of both communion and mission is rooted in the fact that the Church is a communion of equals, between whom a radical equality in dignity is the fruit of baptismal regeneration, and a community of difference in which there are different functions and conditions which serve the Church's mission. Acknowledging the hierarchical ordering of the Church as the most obvious expression of this difference, Ghirlanda argues that this valid element of the pre-conciliar ecclesiology of the public ecclesiastical law school is complemented and completed by the vision of the Council which points to the deeper dimension of communion. The hierarchy so importantly identified by that older school is necessary, for the Church cannot renounce being a legally perfect society (thus independent of any state) which needs a governmental principle within itself so that the laws it needs to emanate to be true to its inner identity are genuinely its own in every aspect.

This ability to identify both equality and difference in the Church is the basis of Ghirlanda's development of the relationship between charism and institution. He is clear that the analogy of *Lumen Gentium*[28] prevents us from conceding any opposition between these two, but rather calls for an understanding of the way in which they mutually imply each other. The gift of the Spirit to the Church for mission made to the individual believer is not merely a personal gift for the one who receives it but is instead something for the whole Church. In order that it can be so, it carries within it an immanent structure, since both duties and rights arise from the exercise of the charismatic gift. Once these begin to extend themselves in time and space away from the original recipient, then we see the charism becoming a canonical institution. This analysis is clearly seen in the way a religious institute develops from the initial

28 See *Lumen Gentium* 8:

> the society structured with hierarchical organs and the Mystical Body of Christ, are not to be considered as two realities, nor are the visible assembly and the spiritual community, nor the earthly Church and the Church enriched with heavenly things; rather they form one complex reality which coalesces from a divine and a human element. For this reason, by no weak analogy, it is compared to the mystery of the incarnate Word. As the assumed nature inseparably united to Him, serves the divine Word as a living organ of salvation, so, in a similar way, does the visible social structure of the Church serve the Spirit of Christ, who vivifies it, in the building up of the body.

charism of the founder to enable that same charismatic gift to be available to disciples and through them to the whole Church, even after the death of the founder.

The fundamental structure of the Church can be seen as a communion constituted by both charismatic and ministerial gifts. Both are gifts of the same Spirit which is why they can be united in communion even as they maintain their necessary plurality. At the same time they generate different duties and rights which go beyond the task of organising the life of the Church in a purely administrative manner. A briefly stated example must suffice: lay people profess the faith and live that out according to a lay charism which is to live in the world and engage in temporal affairs directing them according to God's will in such a way that by doing this they announce God's message of salvation. From this flows the institutional and canonical condition of the laity which has its own proper duties and rights (most fundamentally the duty and right to lead a holy life and preach the gospel)[29]—and within these specific and personal charisms can nest and flourish (such as might be exercised within the right of association).[30] Law within the Church has the function of being at the service of the visible unity which manifests communion and at the same time serving the various Spirit-given missions which build up the whole Body of Christ. Thus this law is of its nature something spiritual, not something opposed to the Church of *agape* or to the double nature of communion and mission which belongs to the Church. It is rooted in the charismatic and institutional nature of the sacramental Church, whose very nature requires and engenders the fundamental legal institutions of the Church. Ghirlanda does not hesitate to say that this entails that we are able to speak of these institutions as willed by Christ and produced by the action of the Spirit.

Law in the Mystery of the Church

Having seen the way in which the self-understanding of the Church generates legal duties and rights, one must go on to integrate this with the understanding of law that was seen to emerge from a philosophical and anthropological perspective in which law arises as a consequence of the social and relational nature of humanity. The relationships which arise are patterned by duties and rights which are a consequence of the very nature of humanity, and law is the means whereby these are structured. This fundamental legal pattern can be identified as the natural law (or the law of human rights);[31] in the Church, as in any other human society, these legal rights need to be recognised—even as they are acknowledged in the light of the fuller revelation given through Christ only to be partial. The essence of the law of the Church is conveyed

29 See canons 210 and 211.

30 See canon 215.

31 The notion that natural law and the law of human rights are coterminous is contested, but I sketch an account of how this might be understood later in this chapter.

by the charisms, sacraments and ministries given by Christ, which create (in various senses) rules of conduct. The Church offers positive legislation and creates a legal order to ensure that these duties and rights are observed and protected (as the state does, or should do, for natural human rights)—but the source of the rights is Revelation, and because of this law in the Church must be considered as theologically founded (not merely anthropologically or philosophically founded) and thus its study to be a sacred science. The bases of law in the church are thus theological anthropology (enabling it to treat of the problems of nature and grace), moral theology (especially the attempt to reconfigure the concept of justice in the light of the Beatitudes) and ecclesiology (which especially deals with the necessity and limits of positive Church law and its relationship to the divine law whether natural or revealed).

This difference enables us to approach the question of natural law and human rights in the Church. In as much as these belong to humans, they are a question for the Church and should be expressed in Church law. However, this is not to assume a total identity between the expressions of human rights in any given state and those found in the Church. The natural human rights found in the state arise from anthropological foundations, not from political ones. The human who is baptised carries into his new life in Christ these human rights which belong to him by virtue of his humanity, but this new perspective adds its own proper and original contribution which goes beyond the natural domain which is discoverable by anthropology. While the Church seeks to establish a legal order in which the communion between believers which is the most fundamental expression of its common good is secured, it does so knowing that this also requires that the full dignity of each as an individual is safeguarded. The need to integrate these two aspects is vital.

However, the dynamism imparted by grace can change the way this would operate, so that an individual may renounce his fundamental rights or be exonerated from performing his fundamental duties. An example would be that one might renounce the exercise of the right to life and be exonerated from the duty to protect one's own life, in order to offer one's own life for another.[32] There is a more complex way in which this operates. The right to liberty of conscience and religious freedom, another of the fundamental human rights, has an obvious relevance for the Church in as much as it establishes that a person cannot be prevented from fulfilling her duty to know and freely embrace faith in Christ in his Church. Once having entered into the Church, the person remains human but at the same time ascends to a higher level, that of grace, in which adhesion to faith in Christ becomes the highest value so that her free adherence of heart and mind to the saving faith of the Church becomes the true object of the natural right of freedom of conscience. Even here, though,

32 By the Motu Proprio *Maiorem hac dilectionem*, on the offer of life (11 July 2017) Pope Francis made such an action a ground for canonisation. Readers may wish to consider these thoughts on natural law and human rights in the light of the views expressed in Ch. 11 of this book.

the human right of conscience remains, so that if someone no longer wishes to preserve communion (or even wishes to embrace another religion) the Church may not compel that person to remain.

The rights and duties that are the common patrimony of all humanity are not the only ones that exist in the Church: baptism by which one is incorporated into Christ also incorporates the believer into the Church and therefore into its legal system with all its supernatural duties and rights. Most fundamentally, these are the duties (already noted) to live a holy life, to preach the gospel and to maintain the communion of the Church. However, there is an important conceptual difference between these duties and rights of the faithful and those that exist in the society of the state. In the latter the individual person is the foundation of society and precedes it, and the society has the most fundamental duty of recognising the dignity of the individual, by recognising and enabling the fulfilment of her duties and the exercise of her rights. In the Church things are different, because it is the grace of the Holy Spirit which brings human sociability to its greatest possible fulfilment (even at the human level) by leading the individual into the Church which is not a purely human product but the effect of the saving work of God. Legal incorporation into the Church is not simply something legal, but more deeply is something theological as it also involves being drawn into communion with God.[33] This drawing is done at baptism, which is an action of the Church before it is an action of the one being baptised, and it is the Church which, through baptism, confers the duties and rights that belong to the faithful. These duties and rights thus do not precede baptism (as civil rights and duties precede civil society) but are granted by God in that sacramental moment. However, the fact that the Church is also a human society which must exist to be at the service of its members as persons means that it has to provide means for these duties and rights to be fulfilled and exercised to bring the baptised to their natural and supernatural fulfilment. Here the image of the Church as sacrament helps us: the visible structures of its legal order become the means of invisible communion. But this legal order, which is genuinely legal, has as its aim the building of a communion of charity; law is not opposed to charity, which is the antinomy which is the basis of the challenge to canon law associated with Sohm, but rather charity requires law in order that rights can be effectively exercised.

Ghirlanda shows a constant concern to root this exercise in the context of what he identifies as the primary and most fundamental duty, that of maintaining communion with God and the Church, expressed in the profession of faith and the life of active charity: this is the priority, not the vindication of individual rights, which have to be ordered to this. This responds to the basic truth of Christian life, that what comes first is God's gratuitous gift of salvation. It follows from this that the exercise of rights by any individual believer has to take account of the common good of the whole Church—a common

33 Canonically, we may say that this is why canon 96 needs the completion provided by canon 204.

good which cannot simply be conceived of as the legally organised society of the Church but needs to reach beyond this to the level of the divine mystery of the Church which offers the grace by which all are called to be adopted as sons of God and share in the life of the Trinity. If the exercise of a right by one believer puts ecclesial communion in peril, then the more fundamental duty of charity requires the renunciation of that right, lest one injustice should be met with a still greater injustice—the breaking of communion. The Church is called to live as a communion of saints, in which the good of all becomes the good of each individual, and the good of each individual becomes the good of all.

Baptism is not the only source of duties and rights: the other sacraments and charisms given by the Spirit are also such sources. These are the basis of the fundamental structure of the Church and the institutions which form it, and like the sacraments and charisms they come from divine gift not human arrangement, and their purpose is the divine purpose of salvation, not any human purpose. Ghirlanda sees in this dogmatic foundation the basis of a divine law structure of the Church. He is clear that there is a delicate and not always easy task to undertake in distinguishing what in the Church belongs to this necessary basis and what is of positive ecclesial law which is intended to give it shape and form in any given human cultural context. The divine law, even if through history it comes to be known more clearly, is immutable, and the task of the canon lawyer is understanding the canonical order in such a theological way that this divine law can be seen and lived out. Canon law cannot simply be understood as the product of human wisdom and political compromise. Here we may refer back to the words of *Optatam Totius*,[34] which desired that both canon law and Church history should be studied in such a way as to attend to the work of the Spirit in the Church. In the project of assessing the necessarily historical aspect of canon law, such a perspective is essential.

Thus the nature of canon law can be seen as not simply positive laws created by Church leaders[35] but also as divine law, whether natural or revealed, and as a necessary aspect of the Church itself. Of the two elements the divine is the most important; because the Church is most fundamentally the Mystical Body of Christ, the sacrament of salvation and the communion created by the Holy Spirit, and the most important analogy for understanding it is the mystery of the Incarnate Word, not the state. Canon law derives its purpose from that of the Church of which it is part: the eternal salvation of all as individuals in communion with God and each other. Its common good is not simply external peace and good order in the human community but the internal reality of communion with God and neighbour. Each separate norm of canon law has to take account of this deeper reality of each human's relationship with God and

34 See *Optatam Totius*, 16.

35 Those responsible for the care of the community, in St Thomas' phrase.

her being called to salvation and renewed. Since, however, no human positive law in its abstract and general formulation can foresee and provide for every human situation (no matter how carefully it is framed nor how long it has been tested) it is not sufficient that these laws should regulate the external situation of the faithful, even if this is on the basis of a genuine distributive justice ascertained according to the highest human ideals. Canon law must always aim to reflect divine justice, animated by charity. To this end, when positive ecclesiastical laws are being applied, the situation of the individual with regard to her salvation must be considered, since without this the common good cannot be achieved.

From this need a number of legal institutions which are typical of canon law are derived. Above all among these is the notion of canonical equity,[36] which is derived from the Roman law notion of equity but finds both a deeper motivation and a new foundation in the context of the Church. When specific, concrete circumstances, which could not be foreseen, are present this provides a corrective where the application of the law would be excessively rigorous and would not lead to the supernatural good of the individual concerned. Canonical equity is thus an intrinsic quality of canon law and a rule for its application but goes beyond this to be an attitude of spirit which those in authority should foster in themselves. It recalls them to the divine justice which they should make present in any situation, rooted as that is in charity, and is the element of canon law which above all makes the essentially pastoral character of canon law shine through.

This basic attitude finds expression in a number of distinct legal institutions. The most obvious is the dispensation from merely ecclesiastical laws,[37] which should not be seen harming the notion of law, but as its necessary complement, because it makes active the fundamental principle that canon law aims at the spiritual good of the individual in the concrete situation in which she finds herself. To this one might add the notions of factors which excuse from or diminish responsibility[38] and the practices of *epikeia*, tolerance and dissimulation, and also the distinction between the internal and external forum. Through all these charity comes to play a role in the canonical system, and through that role in turn charity influences the whole way in which authority is exercised in the Church—whether at the level of the production of laws, or that of their interpretation or that of their application. Charity thus cannot be described as a something which is outside the legal world. Rather it is the foundation of the Church's legal order, being the visible expression of that divine justice which is the basis of justice in the Church. Since the commandments which relate to all human relationships can be summed up in the

36 The classic modern statement of this notion is found in an allocution of Pope St Paul VI to the Roman Rota, on 8 February 1973 (see *Acta Apostolica Sedis* 65 (1973) 98–102).

37 See canon 85ff.

38 Canons 1323 and 1324.

commandment to love one's neighbour as one's self, the Church's legal order as much as its moral vision is a way in which this is expressed. The charity which they express enables the Church's laws to be the external form of the bond of the Holy Spirit which unites the Church, in so far as it deals with the visible, social and legally disciplined ways in which that relationship is lived out under the authority of the Church's hierarchy.

Ghirlanda concludes by observing that positive ecclesiastical laws are at the service of the Word of God, the sacraments and divine worship, and the holiness of Christian life. As such these laws cannot be solely a product of human reason which aims at a common good which is conceived of in wholly external terms. Rather they must be a product of human reason illuminated by faith and shaped by that love which the Holy Spirit bestows and must be promulgated not by any merely human authority but by the Church itself to aim at the common good conceived of in all its fullness.

Conclusion

The precious contribution that Ghirlanda makes is to enable us to speak theologically about the necessary place of canon law in the Church, in such a way that canon law is seen not simply to be some regrettable concession to fallen humanity's weakness, nor even an instrumental means to hand on certain theological truths. It is, of course, both of these. But it is more. The very understanding of the Church itself, especially as communion, has within it a logic which requires and generates a legal system. It is the attempt to see how this operates, and how it more deeply reveals the nature of the Church itself, that is the theology of canon law—and also the true foundation of the Church's legal order.

Bibliography

Acta Apostolica Sedis 65 (1973) 98–102: allocution of Pope St Paul VI to the Roman Rota www.vatican.va › aas › AAS-65-1973-ocr

Apostolic Constitution *Pascite gregem Dei*, reforming Book VI of the Code of Canon Law (23 May 2021) <www.vatican.va/content/francesco/en/apost_constitutions/documents/papa-francesco_costituzione-ap_20210523_pascite-gregem-dei.html>

Aquinas T, *Summa Theologiae*. (Note: Of the countless editions of this, one recent publication is that by the Aquinas Institute (2023)—*ed.*)

Beckett L, *The Canonical Understanding of Spiritual Leadership in Religious Life: From the Compilation of the 1917 Code to the Coming into Force of the 1983 Code* (2011)

Erdo P, *del Diritto Canonico* (1996)

Esposito B, 'Il nuovo piano degli studi delle Facoltà di diritto canonico' 12 *Quaderni della Mendola* (2020) 257–92

Fantappiè C, *Chiesa romana e modernità giuridica* (Giuffrè, Milano 2008)

Ghirlanda, Cardinal, *Il diritto nella Chiesa mistero della communion* (4th edn, Gregorian University Press 2014)

Motu Proprio, *Maiorem hac dilectionem*, on the offer of life (11 July 2017) www.vatican.va/content/francesco/en/events/event.dir.html/content/vaticanevents/en/2017/7/11/maioremhacdilectionem-motuproprio.html

Ombres R, 'Why then the Law?' New Blackfriars (1974) 296–304

Ombres R, 'Canon Law and the Mystery of the Church' (1996/1997) The Irish Theological Quarterly 200–12
Ombres R, 'Ecclesiology, Ecumenism and Canon Law' in N Doe, M Hill and R Ombres (eds), *English Canon Law* (University of Wales Press 1998)
Orsy L, *Theology and Canon Law* (Liturgical Press 1992)
Pereira de Araujo S, *Il consiglio dei Superiori nella storia e nella legislazione attuale* (Marcianum Press 2019)
Vatican Council II Constitutions, Decrees, Declarations (Dominican Publications 1995)

6 Conscience and Natural Law

A Calvinist Perspective

Paul Goodliff

Introduction

The genesis of this chapter lies in the work of the Christian Law Project and its development of a new form of ecumenical instrumentality called juridical ecumenism. Drawing together representatives of major Christian traditions from across Europe, all with an understanding of the legal aspects of those traditions (a number were canon lawyers), it produced a report that demonstrated that there is remarkable synergy between the legal codes, regulatory schemes and broad expectations of those traditions at the macro scale.[1] Flowing from that ecumenical work was an allied, if separate, project to deepen the understanding of the place of natural law in those traditions, resulting in the publication of a book in 2017, edited by Norman Doe, *Christianity and Natural Law*.[2] In that volume I wrote the chapter on Baptists and natural law,[3] arguing that much of the early Baptist polity was inherited from the Calvinist tradition. That issued an invitation to present that research at a symposium at Heythrop College, London, in 2019, and also an invitation to present the Calvinist theme of conscience in the present chapter. Also in that 2017 volume was a chapter by Mary Anne Plaatjies van Huffel, 'Natural Law in the Reformed Tradition',[4] to which I am indebted.

In this chapter, therefore, I want to present the understanding of conscience as a central theme of John Calvin's doctrine of natural law, aware that this is similar to the ways in which early Baptists understood it. This is particularly important among the various Reformation traditions, such as Lutheranism

1 This issued in a *Statement of Principles of Christian Law*, agreed by the panel in Rome 2016, and published as an appendix in Norman Doe (ed), *Church Laws and Ecumenism. A New Path for Christian Ecumenism* (Routledge 2021) 270–86; and originally in N Doe and M Hill, 'Principles of Christian Law' (2017) 19(2) Ecclesiastical Law Journal 138–55.

2 N Doe (ed), *Christianity and Natural Law. An Introduction* (CUP 2017).

3 PW Goodliff, 'Natural Law in the Baptist Tradition' in N Doe (ed), *Christianity and Natural Law. An Introduction* (CUP 2017) 140–61.

4 Plaatjies van Huffel and Mary Anne, 'Natural Law in the Reformed Tradition' in N Doe (ed), *Christianity and Natural Law. An Introduction* (CUP 2017) 121–40.

DOI: 10.4324/9780429264115-8

and Zwingli's more radical polities, as Jean Calvin was not only a major theological reformer, but began his professional life as a lawyer at the University of Orleans in 1528–1529. The classic exposition of Calvin's theological thinking is found in his *Institutio Christianae religionis* of 1559[5] (hereafter, *'The Institutes' or 'Institutes'* in citation), which had its first version issued in 1536, and which was substantially revised in 1539, by which time Calvin was in Geneva and starting his life's work of reforming that city. The final Latin version of 1559 was almost 80 percent longer than its predecessor, and it is this version which today is regarded as the definitive '*Institutes*'. While it might be viewed as a form of Reformed scholastic dogmatics in the tradition of the Late Medieval scholasticism, epitomised by Thomas Aquinas' *Summa Theologicae*, it is rather a *summa pietatis*, a work of gratitude, love and obedience, rooted in the conviction that the sense of deity is indelibly imprinted on the soul and mind, and that speculation about God's existence is available to all, even if

> men are so damaged by the heritage of sin entailed by Adam's fall that they miss this testimony of creation to the Creator, and grope blindfold in this bright theatre of the universe with only erroneous and unworthy notions of the God who made it.[6]

However, this was written not as an end in itself but rather as a work in support of Calvin's much larger project, the commentaries on Scripture. It is no surprise, then, that Calvin's understanding of natural law[7] is deeply shaped by the New Testament, and Romans 2:1–16 in particular.

In my earlier discussion of Calvin's understanding of natural law, I argued that,

> To develop a natural law theory, it is necessary to demonstrate that: (1) it is possible to establish a set of empirical generalisations about human nature that is constant, both spatially (cross-culturally) and temporally (historically); (2) it is possible to move from a set of generalisations about how people do act to a set of prescriptions regarding how they ought to act; (3) the Christian must also be able to show in what sense human nature, although corrupted by sin, is still a reliable guide independent of Christian obligation; and (4) relate his generalisations about natural moral obligation to Christian belief and obligation. Calvin attempted to do just this.[8]

5 J Calvin, 'Institutes of the Christian Religion' in JT McNeill (ed) and Ford Lewis Battles (trans), *The Library of Christian Classics*, vol XX (The Westminster Press 1960).

6 JT McNeil, 'Introduction' to *The Institutes, op. cit.*, liii.

7 *in lege naturali*, which Calvin sometimes describes as *lex illa interior*, inward law, as in *Institutes* 2.7.1.

8 Goodliff (n 3) 145.

Thus, as we first give an exposition of Calvin's theory of natural law, we do so in order to attempt to answer the following questions: does the origin of positive laws lie in some aspect of human reason derived from an evolving social contract, or has it an origin external to the human sphere and rooted in the divine revelation of its Creator? If the latter, then what access has human reason to such a set of laws, and is that access universal, or restricted to a certain religious or theological elite? If it is universal, or in other words, 'general', by what mechanism of the human psyche are those universal or natural laws apprehended, and under what conditions, if any, are they rendered more or less opaque, or indeed, perhaps, invisible—or, to raise the question in other ways, is it possible to live as a human completely unaware of a set of universal and natural laws, rooted in the will of the Creator, and otherwise apprehended by reason?

In summary, we will see that for Calvin, and many of the traditions that flowed from him (for Calvinism is by no means an uncontested tradition), our knowledge of the ethical and moral values of conduct that become expressed as positive laws are part of the creaturely characteristics of being human and have their origin in the divine will and revelation. Amongst those who followed this without adopting a thoroughgoing Reformed polity were Baptists, on the one hand, and the Anglican divine Richard Hooker,[9] on the other. They are not some merely human programme ensuring the maximum safety and well-being of human life, or its most peaceable manner of existence, evolved over millennia of experience and evolution, and therefore open to further adaptation as the processes of evolution continue. It is, rather, fixed for all time, in all places and in all contexts as an expression of the divine will that human life should flourish. So, Calvin would most likely reject any notion that there are a set of 'human rights' that are derived from an agreed set of human values that are cut loose from revelation, or a set of laws derived from 'modern liberal autonomy'.[10] The knowledge of that will, of that natural law, is available to every human society, and is somehow 'hard-wired' into the soul, so that even those who lack any special revelation of God through Israel and Jesus Christ, can apprehend it sufficiently to live accordingly. I say 'sufficiently', because Calvin also balances the universality of apprehension with the universality of that sinful breach in the relationship with God which Scripture and theology sometimes refers to as 'the fall'. It is not necessary to subscribe to some literal and historical event whereby an original man, Adam, took matters into his own hands,[11] despite Calvin in some ways having done so, to affirm the universal sinfulness of humanity (even if the Biblical record ascribes the origins of that sinful character to such an event). Thus, while natural law is universally

9 Richard Hooker, *On the Laws of Ecclesiastical Polity* (1593–97).

10 Cf. Jacqueline A Laing, 'Law, Liberalism and the Common Good' in JA Laing and R Wilcox (ed), *The Natural Law Reader* (Wiley Blackwell 2014) 379–91.

11 Genesis 3:1–7.

grasped and implanted in every human soul, it is also universally, more or less, rendered opaque through sin. Thus, by dint of keeping this natural law to the best of one's ability alone, access to eternal life is always unavailable, and therefore salvation through faith in the redeeming work of Christ always remains the only means by which a person might be saved from the consequences of an imperfect keeping of the law, which is death. The mechanism in the human psyche that is attuned to this natural law is conscience, and so as well as exploring Calvin's doctrine of natural law, we shall also sketch the ways in which Calvin understood the conscience, the means by which the laws of God are apprehended and the signal of their transgression.

Calvin's Doctrine of Natural Law

The Augustinian Teaching on Natural Law

Calvin, in his discussion of the Ten Commandments in *The Institutes*, writes:

> Now that inward law, which we have above described as written, even engraved upon the hearts of all, in a sense asserts the very same things that are to be learned from the two Tables. For our conscience does not allow us to sleep a perpetual insensible sleep without an inner witness and monitor of what we owe God, without holding before us the difference between good and evil and thus accusing us when we fail in our duty. But man is so shrouded in the darkness of errors that he hardly begins to grasp through this natural law what worship is acceptable to God.[12]

Here, his understanding of *in lege naturali*, natural law, is associated with conscience, and follows Augustine and Aquinas.[13] Augustine in his Commentary on the Sermon on the Mount writes,

> For who but God has written the law of nature in the hearts of men?—that law concerning which the apostle says: 'For when the Gentiles, which have not the law, do by nature the things contained in the law. . .'. And therefore, as in the case of every rational soul, which thinks and reasons, even though blinded by passion, we attribute whatever in its reasoning is true, not to itself but to the very light of truth by which, however faintly, it is according to its capacity illuminated, so as to perceive some measure of truth by its reasoning.[14]

12 Calvin (n 5) 2.7.1., 367–68.

13 Thomas Aquinas, *Summa theologiae*, I.II, questions xci. 1–3; xciv; c. 1–5: here, the principles of the Decalogue are identified with those of natural reason.

14 St Augustine, *De Serm. Dom. in Mont.*, 2.9.32 (*Commentary on the Sermon on the Mount*) cited in Jacqueline A Laing and Russell Wilcox (eds), *The Natural Law Reader* (Wiley-Blackwell

Augustine looks to St Paul's Epistle to the Romans for the assertion that 'every rational soul' has access to that light, and Calvin in *The Institutes* similarly quotes Romans 2.14–15 as evidence that 'There is nothing more common than for a man to be sufficiently instructed in a right standard of conduct by natural law (of which the apostle is here speaking)'.[15] Calvin puts severe limitations upon the efficacy of natural law in providing a clear picture of the will of God, and ascribes to the Ten Commandments 'a clearer witness of what was too obscure in the natural law'. Nonetheless, there is a natural law written upon the conscience and derived from the created nature of humanity that is independent of specifically Judeo-Christian revelation.[16]

Natural Law in the Teaching of Aquinas

Thus, through the ubiquity of this Catholic understanding at the time of Calvin's education, it was also adopted by Calvin. Aquinas argues at length in *Summa Theologiae*, I.II. that humans, as creatures made in the image of God, have genuine moral agency (the individual has free will and power over their actions.) Ethics is, therefore, a question of responding positively to the will of God and imitating him. This is enabled by reason, 'a law is nothing other than a certain dictate of practical reason',[17] and that reason is orientated to the divine wisdom, the eternal law of God. He writes, 'that law is something pertaining to reason'.[18]

Specifically, Aquinas ties natural law to both reason and the common good. Helen Costigane writes, of Aquinas' understanding,

> if a law has no rational basis, then it cannot bind and so is not truly a law. Additionally, a law must be for the sake of the common good and as such binds only because it is directed to this end. Next, if the purpose of the law is the good of the community, then it must be promulgated either by the whole community or by someone whose role is to act for the good of that community.[19]

2014) 94. Also in *Commentary on the Sermon on the Mount*, trans. William Findlay, from Philip Schaff (ed), *Nicene and Post-Nicene Fathers*, First Series, vol 6 (Christian Publishing Co. 1888).

15 *Institutes*, 2.2.22, Calvin, McNeill (n 15) 281.

16 Cf. *Institutes*, 3.19.15, where Calvin argues for the natural law outworked in the temporal jurisdiction, the political kingdom.

17 Aquinas, *Summa Theologiae*, I.II.91.1C.

18 Aquinas, *Summa Theologiae*, I.II.90.1C.

19 H Costigane, 'Natural Law in the Roman Catholic Tradition' in N Doe (ed), *Christianity and Natural Law. An Introduction* (CUP 2017) 17–35. 19.

Aquinas then suggest that there are 'four kinds of law—eternal, divine, natural and human positive'.[20] The eternal law is the divine wisdom that governs the whole universe, and which is revealed in 'divine law', that is the 'Old Law' of the Old Testament Decalogue, and the 'New Law' revealed in Christ and the gospel. This brings us to natural law, the rational human's participation in the eternal law, revealed in the divine law found in Scripture. Being rational creatures, humans understand the good, as revealed in God's law, and through the exercise of free will, orientate their actions towards that end, unless they are in sinful rebellion towards their Creator. It is possible, even without any special grace offered through baptism, for humans to grasp what is good, and avoid what is evil. Such orientation inherent in natural law moves from general principles to 'more particular determinations of certain matters. These particular determinations, devised by human reason, are called human laws'.[21]

Natural law for Aquinas is rooted in natural instincts for survival and procreation, and rational tendencies such as the knowledge of good and existence in society. 'These natural tendencies incline a human being towards his natural good and therefore form the foundation for the natural law. These precepts are universal and naturally knowable by all human beings'. It is a capacity for moral discernment, as Jean Porter argues,

> natural law . . . is intrinsic to the character of the human soul as made in the image of God, and therefore it cannot altogether be obliterated; and it is expressed or developed through moral precepts which are confirmed as well as being completed and transcended through the operation of grace. Even though the natural law understood in its primary sense does not consist of specific moral rules, it does find immediate expression in the fundamental precepts of the Golden Rule or the two great commandments of love of God and neighbour; these in turn yield the more specific norms of the Decalogue, which can be further specified as warranted by the circumstances of human life.[22]

Porter continues by noting that there is room for considerable 'legitimate variation and sinful distortion at the level of particular norms'.[23] Furthermore, there is always room for the exercise of prudential judgement, and the understanding of natural law is always, for Aquinas, accompanied by what is now termed 'virtue ethics', the capacity to do what is right originating in a habituated orientation of life towards the good, and not always directly related to the adherence to some positive law or moral precept.

20 Ibid.

21 Aquinas, *Summa Theologiae*, I.II. 91.3C.

22 Jean Porter, *Nature as Reason: A Thomistic Theory of the Natural Law* (Eerdmans 2005) 14. Cited in Costigane (n 19) 20–21.

23 Ibid.

We have paid some attention to Aquinas because his framework is the one inherited by Calvin, albeit with revisions, and to his articulation of natural law we now turn.

Calvin's Teaching on Natural Law

As with Augustine, Calvin places his doctrine of natural law within a Scriptural framework, specifically, Romans 1:19–20, and so some attention to the exegesis of this section of Paul's argument about the universality of God's judgement against human sinfulness is warranted.[24] First, it should be noted that this portrayal of universal accessibility of knowledge about God has parallels in the Jewish apocryphal book Wisdom of Solomon, written by a Hellenistic Jewish author between 50 BC and 10 AD, thus a generation or so before Paul writes Romans in the winter of 56–57 AD.[25] Widely read by Jews and Jewish Christians of Paul's day, the resemblance to the whole argument of Romans 1 is striking, even if direct quotation is absent. God has revealed through creation some of the basic elements of his existence, leaving all people without excuse for ignoring him. Calvin in his commentary upon this verse says that this knowledge is 'that God exists and is powerful, that he is humanity's creator and that therefore all people are to glorify God'.[26] This is clear to all because God has made it plain to them (ὁ θεὸς γὰρ αὐτοῖς ἐφανέρωσεν) and so what can be known about God ('his eternal power and divine nature', ἥ ἀΐδιος αὐτοῦ δύναμις καὶ θειότης) is evident from what he has made (τοῖς ποιήμασιν νοούμενα καθορᾶται). Paul, in drawing upon Greek philosophical thought about the ability of human reason in every culture, both Jewish and Gentile, to work back from what is present in creation to the first unmoved mover, is not following Jewish thought at this point, which, rather, emphasises that while there is implanted in creation 'a revelation that calls on all of God's creation, both personal and non-personal, to respond to God, the creator, appropriately',[27] this knowledge was unavailable to Gentiles (so Wisdom of Solomon 13:1). Thus, rather than this awareness of God being primarily a product of human reasoning, it is a response to revelation that is woven through the fabric of creation, and it is to this that all people can, and should, respond, in whatever time, place or circumstance. Paul is revising his Jewish inherited understanding by reference to Greek thought.

24 We should note here that the purpose of this section is contentious, with a minority position advocated by Douglas Campbell, arguing that this section is a cameo of the teaching in Rome that Paul is contradicting, rather than advocating. cf. Douglas A Campbell, *The Deliverance of God. An Apocalyptic Re-reading of Justification in Paul* (Eerdmans 2009) 542–50.

25 R Jewett, *Romans, Hermeneia* (Fortress Press 2007) 21.

26 John Calvin, 'Romans' in THL Parker (trans. and ed.), *John Calvin's New Testament Commentaries* (SCM 1971) 8.30–31.

27 RN Longenecker, *The New International Greek New Testament Commentary. The Epistle to the Romans* (Eerdmans 2016) 209.

However, it is a considerable step to move from the awareness of the existence and power of a creator to the assertion that there is an innate knowledge of his moral laws established in every human mind. Yet, that is the move which Calvin makes in response to Paul. The step he makes is to establish the trajectory of such basic knowledge through the absence of its proper consequences, as Barrett says,

> As God's creature, man [humanity] was bound to render glory and thanksgiving to his Creator; this means not merely to acknowledge his existence, and to employ the words and rites of religion, but to recognise his lordship and live in grateful obedience—in fact (in the Pauline sense) to believe, to have faith. This, men [people] failed to do; instead they rebelled against God, and their fault lay not in their lack of knowledge but in their rebellion.[28]

The lack of the first responses of praise and thanks leads to the darkening of the heart and mind (ἐσκοτίσθη ἡ ἀσύνετος αὐτῶν καρδία, 1:21) and by which the clear knowledge of God's law becomes opaque. Calvin understands that there are vestiges of the natural law in every human mind, but it has been corrupted and rendered obscure. 'God's self-revelation is partial and elusive. Whether this revelation occurs subjectively within each person's conscience or publicly within each cultural group is impossible to determine from the phrase ἐν αὐτοῖς'.[29]

> In contrast to most forms of natural theology in which qualified humans have access to divine knowledge, Paul relies upon the classic biblical doctrine of divine self-disclosure to explain the truth that humans attempt to suppress. . . . With rhetorical finesse, Paul fuses the biblical doctrine of revelation and creation with the Graeco-Roman doctrine of divinity visible in the natural world.[30]

Calvin takes the Thomist understanding of the awareness of God's divine wisdom and law in every soul and subjects it to a more thoroughgoing Pauline insight into the *limits* of that awareness. The relative optimism with which Aquinas attests to the presence of natural law in every human soul is turned to the relative pessimism of Calvin's articulation of the same phenomenon, with a

28 K Barrett, *A Commentary on the Epistle to the Romans. BNTC* (Black 1957 2nd ed. 1991) 36.
29 R Jewett, *Romans, Hermeneia* (Fortress Press 2007) 153.
30 Ibid 154.

deeper awareness of the 'darkness' of the human mind and the opacity of that law as a result of sin. He says,

> Now when you hear of a universal judgment discriminating between good and evil, do not consider it to be sound and whole in every respect. . . . The light of nature is extinguished before he even enters upon this abyss. While the philosophers label the immoderate incitements of the mind as 'vices', they have reference to those which are outward and manifest by grosser signs. They take no account of the evil desires that gently tickle the mind.[31]

Some Dutch Reformed commentators upon Calvin refuse to admit the existence of natural law in Calvin, but Paul Helm has demonstrated that, while Calvin accepted and worked with Aquinas' concept of natural law, for him, 'our *epistemic access* to this moral order is more prone to negligence and error than in the tradition he inherited'.[32]

In their sinful state humans are unable to fully know the natural law of God and possess only a relic of this. However, despite sin, there are certain vestiges, 'crumbs of righteousness' remaining to direct human action towards the good, enabling people to distinguish that good from its opposite. In other words, humanity continues to possess—minimally, to be sure—some conscious awareness of the demands of natural law, which for Calvin might be summarised as the law of love. As David Little observes:

> These crumbs or vestiges make up Calvin's explicit doctrine of natural law. Despite all the corruption, God has left His law implanted in man's nature for two reasons: to prod man in the direction of his true end, and, second, to convict and condemn him because he must be prodded and is not voluntarily disposed to act in accord with love of God and man.[33]

Calvin also accepts a qualified place for human reason. In matters of heavenly understanding, reason is 'utterly blind and stupid' (*Institutes*, 2.2.19), but in matters earthly or political, natural reason would appear to stand partly on its own. Men naturally affirm the duties of humankind, which were put into the second table of the Decalogue.

31 *Institutes*, 2.2.24.

32 Andrew JB Cameron, 'How "Ethics" Works: An Engagement with John Calvin' in Mark D Thompson (ed), *Engaging with Calvin* (Apollos 2009) 242, citing P Helm, *John Calvin's Ideas* (OUP 2004) 346–88.

33 D Little, 'Calvin and the Prospects for a Christian Theory of Natural Law' in GH Outka and P Ramsey (eds), *Norm and Context in Christian Ethics* (SCM Press 1968) 186.

In other words, Calvin has a theory of natural law, but he is not interested in developing a self-contained, independent doctrine. He has

> a derivative theory of natural law, one that has always to be seen in a more inclusive theological and moral design. The theory starts from the notion of love (or mutuality, co-operation, benevolence) as the central ethical principle embodied in revelation, and then works back to make room for those generalisations of human nature considered the conditions or prerequisites for making the realization of love possible.[34]

The roots of this adoption of natural law within a Judeo-Christian revelatory framework is an early move in Christian history. David Little demonstrates how primitive Christians understood Christ as completing the way the world was meant to be.[35] The coming kingdom represented a decisive break with the old, and a fulfilment of that for which the whole creation has been longing, and that it would be realised within the generations following Jesus. However, after the waning of eschatological fervour, the church readily embraced the Stoic doctrine of natural law to help cope with the complications of the everyday world. As Little puts it:

> If any contemporary 'rehabilitation' of Christian natural law theory is to be accomplished, it is safe to say that the way Calvin tried to solve some of the abiding problems demands careful attention.[36]

Calvin begins with the theological assumption that all things are ordered according to a divine design. Second, right human action is not fully possible without acknowledging from the heart the divine author of the design. What Calvin calls the 'moral law' or 'true and eternal rule of righteousness, prescribed for men of all nations and all times', is simply that God be worshipped by us all and we love one another.[37] Moreover, all legal and moral regulations derive from and point toward the 'perpetual rule of love', which is the same as God's eternal law:[38]

> For God's will is so much the highest rule of righteousness that whatever he wills, by the fact that he wills it, must be considered righteous. . . . But the will of God is not only free of all fault, but is the highest rule of perfection, and even the law of all laws.[39]

34 Ibid.
35 Little (n 33) 175–97.
36 Ibid 177.
37 *Institutes*, 4.20.15.
38 *Institutes*, 2.8.11.
39 *Institutes*, 2.8.13; cf. 1.17.1.

The second table of the Decalogue is 'engraved upon the hearts of all men'.[40] He says that the prohibitions of the Law recommend certain positive obligations, and that these derive from the perpetual rule of love.[41]

On the sixth commandment, 'You shall not kill', Calvin says: 'The purpose of the commandment is: the Lord has bound mankind together by a certain unity; hence each man ought to concern himself with the safety of all',[42] that is, the obligation is not simply to resist murder, but to go out of our way to enhance the physical and spiritual well-being of our neighbour. On the eighth commandment, the aim is benevolence and cooperation.[43] Neighbour 'includes even the most remote person. It includes the whole human race'.[44] Calvin takes strong exception to the Scholastic position on counsels of perfection which limited the more radical precepts of Christian love to monks.

Andrew Cameron summarises Calvin's approach to natural law by reference to the tradition which Calvin inherited:

> Aquinas had already described how divinely ordered moral reality is experienced by humanity as a 'natural law', which is graciously 'republished' for humanity by God in the Bible. Calvin was sufficiently persuaded by this approach to deploy it in broad outline. 'Moral law' expresses 'natural law'; ceremonial law was a specific instance of the moral law to order worship of God; and civil law was a specific instance of the moral law to order human desires and human society. It follows that the specific instances (the ceremonial law and civil law) are no longer directly relevant to Christians (although there remains much to be learnt in them about Christ and about equity). But those in Christ are regaining access to moral order, so moral law remains relevant to them.[45]

For Calvin, as for other reformers, the natural law, or universal moral law, has two purposes: to act as that mirror which convicts everyone of sin, thus driving us to repentance and faith (following Paul's arguments in Romans 7), and, second, to act as a restraint against evil in society, and enable communities to live in relative harmony:

> at least by fear of punishment to restrain certain men who are untouched by any care for what is just and right unless compelled by hearing the dire threats in the law . . . the law is like a halter to check the raging and otherwise limitlessly ranging lusts of the flesh.[46]

40 *Institutes*, 2.8.1.
41 *Institutes*, 2.8.9.
42 *Institutes*, 2.8.39.
43 *Institutes*, 2.8.46.
44 *Institutes*, 2.8.55; cf. 4.12.7.
45 Cameron (n 32) 230–53, at 248.
46 *Institutes*, 2.7.10.

But to these two Calvin adds a third: the law is 'the best instrument' for believers to 'learn more thoroughly each day the nature of the Lord's will'.[47] Biblical moral law is an expression of natural law, and thus aids us in self-denial and acts as an antidote to self-love. Far from being a threat to our conscience, within the context of participation in Christ, the law functions as the gentle act of the heavenly Father to rehabilitate our understanding of reality, or the provocations of an athletic coach to stimulate our running of the race of faith.

The psychological and spiritual mechanism by which the demands and transgressions of the natural law are perceived is the conscience, and to this aspect of Calvin's theological anthropology we now turn.

The Role of Conscience

The first aspect to note is that Calvin's understanding of conscience is framed by the central theological motif of his theology, that the Christian life is one of participation in union with Christ. This is very different to the notion in modernity that we might seek to emulate the life and morals of an attractive and heroic figure, and by our own efforts live accordingly. That figure might be an advocate for human rights, or gender justice, or political freedoms, and the modern individual seeks to share in those ideals and live accordingly. Participation in Christ is not some attempt to follow Christ's example, however heroic that might seem. Calvin certainly sees Jesus Christ as a 'man who acts in love, whose emotions are well ordered, who is moderate in adversity, who perseveres and who "has been set before us as an example, whose pattern we ought to express in our life" [*Institutes* 3.2.3]'.[48] But we seek to imitate him only in the context of our union with him.

> When Calvin speaks of our conformity to the pattern of Jesus Christ, it is usually in the context of union between the Head and members of the body. It is within the relationship of union with Christ that we are exhorted to imitate Christ as our example. The conformity to Christ at which we are to aim is not a mere 'conformity of example',[49] Christ being viewed 'at a distance'[50] from us and we painfully seeking by ourselves and in our own strength to shape our lives after his pattern. It is a conformity that is to be sought within a close union with Him who is the pattern, and that can result only from such a union. . . . It is because Christ lives and is powerful within us that we become conformed to His

47 *Institutes* 2.7.12.

48 Cameron (n 32) 236.

49 Calvin, *Commentary on Romans* 6:5, *Insitio non exempli tantum conformitatem designat, sed arcanam coniunctionem* (grafting, by example, not only designates conformity, but a mysterious union).

50 *Institutes*, 3.1.3.

> image. He is for us not only the example of righteousness but the cause of righteousness.[51]

Calvin's understanding of participation in union with Christ is hard for Modern Western people to accept, as it contrasts what such individuals know and accept as reality (and which is almost exclusively their frame of reference) with the reality we have in Christ, hidden from sensory perception.

> Yet more: we experience such participation in him that, although we are still foolish in ourselves, he is our wisdom before God; while we are sinners, he is our righteousness; while we are unclean, he is our purity; . . . while we still bear about with us the body of death, he is yet our life.[52]

We need to see the work of the conscience within this most intimate of relationships, whereby Christ shares his life with us,[53] and is made effectual whereby 'the Holy Spirit is the bond by which Christ effectually unites us to himself'.[54] This participation brings us into contact with the proper order of the universe, which is both a description of the relationships between the Persons of the Godhead (infinite love), and the manner in which all other persons and things participate properly in that moral order. This participation, enabled by the Spirit (note, not by our own moral ability, which Calvin deems ineffective), avoids three cul-de-sacs: an overemphasis upon (but not abolition of) the imitation of Christ as a moral exemplar; a legalism that places an over-reliance upon rules (so, we operate by regulatory guidance, rather than by the leading of the Spirit); and a lawlessness, or moral carelessness, that places confidence merely in the forgiveness of God in a forensic justification (and which the Apostle Paul challenges in Romans 6:1–15). Freedom from legal obligation to God does not free us from relational obligation, for who could possibly sin all the more if the one offended is wonderfully close:

> (We do not . . . contemplate him outside ourselves from afar in order that his righteousness might be imputed to us but because we put on Christ and are engrafted into his body—in short, because he deigns to make us one with him. For this reason we glory that we have fellowship of righteousness with him.)[55]

The second thing to note is that the dimension of the person that gains epistemic access to the moral law, the conscience, is not by any means an

51 RS Wallace, *Calvin's Doctrine of the Christian Life* (Oliver and Boyd 1959) 47.
52 *Institutes*, 3.15.5.
53 Calvin, *Sermon on Ephesians* 5:28–30, cited in Cameron (n 32).
54 *Institutes*, 3.1.1.
55 *Institutes*, 3.11.10.

infallible guide to natural law. Calvin advocates a daily examination of life in order to confess sin and receive absolution, and by such daily examination in the presence of God, who sees all things, we come to deeper self-knowledge of our guilt.

> in this matter of self-examination we have no natural ability nor willingness to come to true self-knowledge. . . . We cannot trust our own conscience in this matter, for even the saints are so entangled in the snares of Satan that they are unconscious even of their grosser sins, quite apart from the hundred lesser sins of ignorance and inadventure [Calvin, Commentary on Psalm 19:12]. Left to our conscience alone we are full of guile and we cover over our nakedness with leaves [Commentary on Psalm 32:2].[56]

Self-examination in the light of the Word of God—the articulation in Scripture of the natural law—trains the conscience and fits it the better for the task of an internal moral compass. It cannot be purified apart from the Word of God, which alone teaches us the true use of the benefits of this life.

Calvin first ascribes to the conscience a sign of the immortal spirit within a human life, 'Surely the conscience, which, discerning between good and evil, responds to God's judgement, is an undoubted sign of the immortal spirit'.[57] It is a feature universally present in humanity, and quoting Romans 2:14–15, Calvin says,

> If the Gentiles by nature have law righteousness engraved upon their mind, we cannot say they are utterly blind as to the conduct of life. There is nothing more common than for a man to be sufficiently instructed in a right standard of conduct by natural law (of which the apostle is here speaking).[58]

So, for the unbeliever,

> conscience stands in place of law; this is sufficient reason for their just condemnation. The purpose of natural law, therefore, is to render man inexcusable. This would not be a bad definition: natural law is that apprehension of the conscience which distinguishes sufficiently between just

56 Wallace (n 51) 226. Calvin writes, '*Quisquis ergo se non examinat coram Deo quin potius Dei iudicium fugitans, vel se abdit in tenebras, vel foliis obtegit: secum dolose agit, et cum ipso Deo*'. 'Whosoever, therefore, does not examine himself before God, but rather shuns the judgment of God, or hides himself in darkness, or covers himself with leaves: he acts deceitfully with himself, and with God himself'.

57 *Institutes*, 1.15.2.

58 *Institutes* 2.2.22.

> and unjust, and which deprives men of the excuse of ignorance, while it proves them guilty by their own testimony.[59]

The degree to which the role of the 'fear of God' for the 'elect and believers' in enabling them not to provoke the wrath of God against them by committing the same offenses, is a balance between the restraint of presumption, 'which sometimes creeps upon the saints from the vestiges of the flesh', and to be so overwhelming so as to 'dishearten the conscience with fear that it cannot rest with full assurance of God's mercy'.[60] Here is one danger of excessive use of the conscience—to be so acutely aware of the sinfulness of the person as to rob them of assurance of faith (a so-called scrupulous conscience)—while the other extreme is a conscience unlettered by the Word of God and reliant upon that more obscure origin in the natural law.[61] While the existence of the conscience for Calvin is an aspect of our unregenerate humanity, its development is only possible through the right 'fear of God' that drives us to the Word of God to educate and refine it.

Calvin contrasts this 'good conscience' with those that 'have no repose'[62] because they are over-scrupulous with things that are 'indifferent' (ἀδιάφοροι). There was considerable discussion among Calvin's contemporaries about things that were 'indifferent'. So, Melanchthon said 'For love's sake we do not refuse to observe adiaphora with others'.[63] Calvin says,

> regarding outward things that are of themselves 'indifferent', we are not bound before God by any religious obligation preventing us from sometimes using them and other times not using them, indifferently. And the knowledge of this freedom is very necessary for us, for if it is lacking, our conscience will have no repose and there will be no end to superstitions. Today we seem to many to be unreasonable because we stir up discussions over the unrestricted eating of meat, the use of holidays and of vestments, and such things, which seem to them vain frivolities. But these things are more important than is commonly believed. For when consciences once ensnare themselves, they enter a long and inextricable maze, not easy to get out of. . . . To sum up, he will come to the point of considering it wrong to step upon a straw across his path, as the saying goes.[64]

59 Ibid.

60 *Institutes* 3.2.22.

61 cf. *Institutes* 3.3.15, 'For he who is touched by a lively feeling of dissatisfaction with self . . . may not afterward fall away from the governance of the Holy Spirit, nor be lulled into a sense of security'.

62 *Institutes,* 3.19.7.

63 Melanchthon, *Apology of the Augsburg Confession* XV.52.

64 *Institutes* 3.19.7.

Calvin here describes the conscience entrapped in debates about the propriety of things that are not encompassed by the natural law. A compulsive and progressively severe austerity was also widely admonished against in early monastic counsels. This amounts to the conscience set adrift from both the relationship with Christ, and so reduced to a monitor of rules, and set loose from the engraved demands of natural law upon the soul. The liberty of conscience that Calvin advocates does not amount, however, to a violation of conscience. 'To violate conscience even in an apparently insignificant matter is to destroy our faith, for so closely is faith bound up with conscience that Calvin can say that faith is of itself goodness of conscience'.[65] For the Christian, conscience should be brought into bondage to nothing other than the Word of God, maintaining an integrity of heart before God that is 'a good conscience'. However, Calvin maintains the dangers of scrupulosity when it comes to matters that are 'indifferent' (such as vestments or the prohibition on eating meat at certain times and seasons). Calvin writes frequently in his sermons about these matters of indifference, and

> the danger of falling into such extreme scrupulosity over trivial matters was a real and common one in Calvin's time, partly owing to the attitude of mind encouraged by the teaching and customs of the Roman Church. Calvin reminds his hearers that a man can be brought into such bondage of conscience, not only by other men, but also by following his own uncontrolled imagination and imposing on himself moral burdens that have no relation to the Word of God, and by bringing to the interpretation of Scripture an attitude that is slavishly literal and legalistic.[66]

The outcome might be either an extreme state of bondage to scruples that leads to despair, or the throwing off of all restraints and plunging into a licence to which there are no bounds.

Implications for Western Culture and Ethics

We saw that there are three things which Calvin seeks to avoid by placing the apprehension of natural law and the exercise of conscience within the context of an intimate relationship of union with Christ enabled by the indwelling of the Holy Spirit and a regular practice of daily examen: a piety that seeks simply to emulate Jesus, an over-reliance upon an ever-more complex and comprehensive set of regulations to enable moral discernment (legalism) and

65 Wallace (n 51) 308, citing Calvin Commentary on Phil 1:23, *O bona conscientia, quantum polles ac valles! Bonae autem conscientiae fundamentum est fides: imo ipsa est conscientiae bonitas.* 'Oh good conscience, how powerful and strong you are! But faith is the foundation of a good conscience; yea, it is the goodness of conscience'.

66 Ibid 310.

an antinomian lawlessness that casts off all restraint. It is precisely these three excesses which, it could be argued, characterise the moral framework within which modernity (modern liberal and Late-Capitalist) societies operate. Calvin's notion of the place of conscience as the tool by which the requirements of natural law are enacted has some significance for a Christian apologetic in the face of such excesses.

First, a kind of religious piety that seeks to emulate, if not Jesus of Nazareth, at least some heroic figure of note, is resisted by Calvin. It might be true that for the secular individual, the person of Jesus is most interesting as a moral teacher, cut loose from any theological or metaphysical notion of his divinity or the salvific purpose of his life, but the ability to emulate that life and follow his teaching soon fails at the hurdles of radical self-sacrifice or the ability to love one's enemies without the grace of God. (Twitter storms about slight infringements of a perceived just cause are but one example of the way in which modern people can tend to 'take no prisoners' when it comes to debate.) A moral exercise based simply upon hero worship is doomed to fail, either because of the inability of the worshipper to live up to the perceived ideas or the subsequent demonstration of the very human and imperfect character of the heroic figure themselves. Idols tend to have feet of clay, be they Mahatma Gandhi or Martin Luther King Jr.

The second excess Calvin seeks to avoid is a legalistic approach to morality, whereby the goal of eradicating evil behaviour is attempted by regulation and associated sanctions for infringement. A technocratic society within late modernity is so imbued with this manner of regulating itself that it is hard to see how inadequate this is. It makes all sorts of assumptions about human existence that Calvin would be swift to contradict, and an approach that seeks to regulate away human failure, rather than attempt a programme of godly transformation that seeks to form virtuous individuals, will always be one step behind the next form of wickedness, scam or criminality (the example of fraud in financial institutions or through the internet is but one, and the regulatory and technocratic attempts to eradicate child abuse, another). Positive laws that punish wickedness are by no means resisted by Calvin, and the expression of those will be various and subject to human reason and political will, but they are not the sole means to the godly society that Calvin attempts to build in Geneva. The replacement of deontology, with its focus upon acts (which may or may not be deemed illicit), with virtue ethics as the substantive framework is in this regard to be welcomed.

Finally, Calvin sees that the exercise of conscience outside of a relationship with God leads some to a bifurcation between an excess of scruples and a radical deficit in propriety—the exaltation of minor matters (which Calvin would describe as 'indifferent' in the sense that Scripture does not attempt to arbitrate upon their goodness) to the status of totemic signs of the overall moral character of a person, or the loss of all restraint in other matters. Both can exist within the same person. The former might be seen in the kind of outrage that some experience when, for instance, others challenge their assertion that biological sex is not immutable, but utterly fluid (an aspect of the culture wars in 2020–2022, at least), while seemingly indifferent to other ills that the writers of Scripture denounce with some clarity. The latter could be illustrated by the almost universal weakening of the ethics of sexual restraint in a liberal society that views sexual activity as a form of entertainment governed by personal choice, rather than an activity regulated by covenant (either by its avoidance by the unmarried—the sins of fornication or adultery—or, in Catholic ethics, its detachment from procreation). An unrestrained pursuit of economic growth, and its concomitant damage to the environment, or the liberal economic structures that increasingly seem to benefit the rich at the expense of the poor in an increasingly unequal world might be a second illustration of the way in which conscience untutored by Scripture quickly avoids those uncomfortable challenges that arise from natural law.

Calvin's is but one approach to a legal system based upon natural law, with predecessors in the ancient Stoics, the New Testament and Aquinas, and more recent approaches by, for instance, John Finnis,[67] Germaine Grisez[68] and Jean Porter,[69] but his positioning of it within a Christological context, and its outworking in conscience and Christian discipleship and associated disciplines of regular self-examination, provides a thoroughly theological outworking that continues to have serious application within today's cultures. As St Paul fused Greek philosophy and Jewish revelation in his explication of natural law, so a fusing of Thomist and Calvinist theories of natural law and conscience may speak eloquently to the challenges faced by late modernity.

Bibliography

Aquinas T, *Summa Theologiae* (Note: Of the countless editions of this one recent publication is that by the Aquinas Institute (2023)—*ed.*)

Barrett KA, *Commentary on the Epistle to the Romans. BNTC* (Black 1957 2nd edn 1991)

Calvin J, 'Institutes of the Christian Religion' in JT McNeill (ed) and Ford Lewis Battles (trans), *The Library of Christian Classics* (The Westminster Press 1960) vol XX

Calvin J, 'Romans' in THL Parker (trans. and ed), *John Calvin's New Testament Commentaries* (SCM 1971)

Cameron AJB, 'How 'Ethics' Works: An Engagement with John Calvin' in MD Thompson (ed), *Engaging with Calvin* (Apollos 2009)

Campbell DA, *The Deliverance of God. An Apocalyptic Re-reading of Justification in Paul* (Eerdmans 2009)

67 J Finnis, *Natural Law and Natural Rights* (2nd edn, OUP 2011).

68 G Grisez, 'The First Principle of Practical Reason: A Commentary on the *Summa theologiae*, 1-2, Question 94, Article 4' (1965) 10 *Natural Law Forum* 168–201.

69 J Porter, *Natural Law and Divine Love: Reclaiming the Tradition for Christian Ethics* (Eerdmans 1999).

Commentary on the Sermon on the Mount, trans. William Findlay, from Philip Schaff (ed), *Nicene and Post-Nicene Fathers*, First Series (Christian Publishing Co. 1888) vol 6
Costigane H, 'Natural Law in the Roman Catholic Tradition' in N Doe (ed), *Christianity and Natural Law. An Introduction* (CUP 2017) 17–35
Doe N (ed), *Christianity and Natural Law. An Introduction* (CUP 2017)
Doe N and Hill M, 'Principles of Christian Law' (2017) 19(2) Ecclesiastical Law Journal 138–55
Finnis J, *Natural Law and Natural Rights* (2nd edn, OUP 2011)
Goodliff PW, 'Natural Law in the Baptist Tradition' in N Doe (ed), *Christianity and Natural Law. An Introduction* (CUP 2017) 140–61
Grisez G, 'The First Principle of Practical Reason: A Commentary on the *Summa theologiae*, 1–2, Question 94, Article 4' (1965) 10 Natural Law Forum 168–201
Helm P, *John Calvin's Ideas* (OUP 2004)
Hooker R, On *the Laws of Ecclesiastical Polity* (1593–7). (Note one recent edition of this is published in Cambridge Texts in the History of Political Thought (2008)—*ed.*)
Jewett R, *Romans, Hermeneia* (Fortress Press 2007)
Laing JA, 'Law, Liberalism and the Common Good' in JA Laing and R Wilcox (eds), *The Natural Law Reader* (Wiley Blackwell 2014) 379–91
Little D, 'Calvin and the Prospects for a Christian Theory of Natural Law' in GH Outka and P Ramsey (ed), *Norm and Context in Christian Ethics* (SCM Press 1968)
Longenecker R, *The New International Greek New Testament Commentary. The Epistle to the Romans* (Eerdmans 2016)
Melanchthon, *Apology of the Augsburg Confession* XV.52
Plaatjies van Huffel MA, 'Natural Law in the Reformed Tradition' in N Doe (ed), *Christianity and Natural Law. An Introduction* (CUP 2017) 121–40
Porter J, *Natural Law and Divine Love: Reclaiming the Tradition for Christian Ethics* (Eerdmans 1999)
Porter J, *Nature as Reason: A Thomistic Theory of the Natural Law* (Eerdmans 2005)
Statement of Principles of Christian Law, agreed by the panel in Rome 2016, and published as an appendix in Norman Doe (ed), *Church Laws and Ecumenism. A New Path for Christian Ecumenism* (Routledge 2021)
Wallace RS, *Calvin's Doctrine of the Christian Life* (Oliver and Boyd 1959)

Part Three

Catholic and Protestant Approaches to Church, State and State Law

These two chapters focus first on the extent to which the Reformation and its legacy affected both the relationship between natural law, seen as a Christian concept, and human law and, then, in Chapter 8, on approaches to church-state relations from Roman Catholic, Anglican, Lutheran and Calvinist perspectives. This chapter, starting from the period of the Reformation, then moves to the period of the Enlightenment through to the modern era.

There are strong links in this part with other chapters in this book where Chapter 7, for instance, follows the exploration of Calvinist thought on natural law in Chapter 6. Moreover, given that the Anglican Church is the established Church in England, readers may wish to read the exploration of church-state relations in Chapter 8 in conjunction with Chapter 2, which considered the impact of the Reformation on Anglican Church law, and then the place of law in the Anglican communion today, dealt with in Chapter 4.

DOI: 10.4324/9780429264115-9

7 Natural Law and Human Law

The Reformation Legacy—an Ecumenical Approach

Stephen Coleman and Norman Doe

Natural Law in the Work of Christian Theologians

In Christianity, natural law discourse has to do with, fundamentally, the existence of God-given universal principles which God 'revealed' to humankind at creation. This original revelation shapes practically what it is to be a human being and the social character of human nature and life. The 'original' revelation is distinct from the 'special' revelation of God in Christ which concerns our relationship with God, the perfection of natural law and, ultimately, our salvation. Natural law is a form of divine law. Through it God implanted in the minds or hearts of every person the capacity to know right and wrong and so discern these universal principles. In turn, these principles are normative: they provide moral standards, or ethical constraints on human conduct, and determine what acts are right and wrong in our relations with others. These standards are applicable to all humans. They are discoverable through the use of reason, and the exercise of conscience, and should be used as a criterion to assess the legitimacy of action. Needless to say, there are many views about the content of natural law.

The germ of natural law in Christian thought is commonly traced to Paul's Letter to the Romans: 'When Gentiles who have not the law do by nature what the law requires, they are a law to themselves, even though they do not have the law. They show that what the law requires is written in their hearts' (Romans 2.14–15).[1] Among the early Fathers of the Church, Origen of Alexandria (185–254) saw natural law not only as the physical law governing the cosmos but also as a body of ethical norms binding humans and centred on the 'Golden Rule'—do to others as you would have them do to you (Luke 6.31); however, while all humans have the capacity to obey natural law, we need Christ the redeemer whose teaching on morals goes beyond natural law so as to share in God's righteousness.[2] For Augustine (354–430) too there is a

1 See e.g. *The Threads of Natural Law: Unravelling a Philosophical Tradition* FJ Contreras (ed) (Springer 2013).

2 BL Dunkle, 'A Development of Origen's View of the Natural Law' *Pro Ecclesia* 13 (2004) 337–51.

DOI: 10.4324/9780429264115-10

'law which is called supreme reason, which must always be obeyed, by which the evil deserve an unhappy life and the good a blessed life'; this is the eternal law: 'the divine reason or will of God which commands that the natural order be preserved and forbids that is be disturbed'. But unless humans are united to the salvation won by Christ with the grace of the Holy Spirit, they cannot sufficiently obey natural law.[3]

In the Middle Ages, Aquinas proposes (along Aristotelian lines) that humans are rational creatures; by using reason we may discover the specific ends towards which we naturally tend (e.g. to live, reproduce, have an ordered society and worship God), and the general end for which God created us, that is, salvation in eternal communion with God. It is also possible for us to determine the means required to achieve these ends. God's plan for humans, implanted in us by His act of creation, is natural law—a participation in the eternal law of God—and from natural law may be induced moral duties and rights.[4] Aquinas also proposed (echoing Augustine) that a human law violating natural law is no law at all, but, rather, a corruption.

The Reformation did not end the medieval appeal of natural law. For Calvin: 'It is a fact that the law of God which we call the moral law is nothing else than a testimony of natural law and of that conscience which God has engraved upon the minds of men'; as a result: 'the entire scheme of this equity of which we are now speaking has been prescribed in it. Hence, this equity alone must be the goal and rule and limit of all [positive] laws'.[5] In a similar vein, for Luther, the commandment of love, the Golden Rule and the Decalogue are expressions of natural law insofar as they *both* concern the inner orientation of a person and external action; but for Melanchthon, natural law consists of precepts, resembling the Ten Commandments, which demand *only* external action, not an inner disposition of love. In turn, later Lutherans echo these two approaches; for instance, Leibniz follows Luther and combines natural with the idea of divine love, whereas Pufendorf echoes Melanchthon.[6]

The nineteenth century, though, saw a more sceptical approach among Protestants which generally rejected the competence of fallen human reason to engage in natural theology. For instance, Karl Barth (1886–1968) writes:

> What is pleasing to God comes into being when all human righteousness is gone, irretrievably gone, when men are uncertain and lost, and when they have abandoned all ethical and religious illusions, and when they have renounced every hope in this world and in this heaven;

3 See generally M Levering, 'Natural Law and Christianity' in AM Emon, M Levering and D Novak (eds), *Natural Law: A Jewish, Christian and Islamic Trialogue* (OUP 2014) Chapter 2.
4 See generally J Finnis, *Natural Law and Natural Rights* (Clarendon Press 1980).
5 *Institutes*, 4.20.16. See also here Ch.6 where Calvinist thought on natural law is fully dealt with.
6 A Raunio, 'Divine and Natural Law in Luther and Melanchthon' in V Mäkinen (ed), *The Lutheran Reformation and the Law* (Brill 2006) 21–61.

indeed, when gentiles 'show that what the law requires is written on their hearts' (Romans 2.15), they show precisely that they no longer cling to any human resources, including 'natural law'.[7]

Increasingly, those unsympathetic to natural law thinking argued, for example, that (1) natural law theory is flawed because it moves from observable facts to moral principles; it attempts to base ethics (ought) on a non-moral account of what human beings are like (is)—what humans are like does not tell us what they ought to be like morally; (2) the picture of human nature is likely to be as controversial as the moral conclusions at which it arrives—that picture is itself the product of a moral outlook rather than an independently established basis by which a moral outlook can be supported; (3) that human reason alone (and fallen human reason at that) has the capacity to understand God's will for us, undermines the need for God's grace, and so devalues the revelation in Christ—if humans can know what is good in God's eyes, this unacceptably exalts human reason; and (4) natural law theory plays down or denies specifically Christian ethics—whereas Christianity actually requires a radically new set of imperatives instituted by the ministry of Christ.[8]

By way of contrast, today many Catholic,[9] Lutheran,[10] Reformed[11] and other scholars[12] use the idea that God imprints on all a capacity to discern through our natural inclination and human reason the ordering which God has given us—whether the discoverability of universal principles is affected by sin,[13] or not.[14] The Anglican theologian Nigel Biggar is a good example. To 'affirm natural law' means that there is a form of flourishing given in and with the nature of human beings; reflection on human nature can achieve an

7 K Barth, *The Epistle of Paul to the Romans* (OUP 1933) 68.

8 GJ Hughes, 'Natural Law' in JF Childress and J Macquarrie (eds), *A New Dictionary of Christian Ethics* (SCM Press 1986) 412–14; Stanley Hauerwas, *The Peaceable Kingdom: A Primer in Christian Ethics* (U of Notre Dame P 1983); Paul Ramsey, *Basic Christian Ethics* (Westminster-John Knox Press 1993) 84–85.

9 G Grisez, 'The First Principles of Practical Reason: A Commentary on the *Summa Theologiae,* 1-2, Question 94, Article 2' (1965) 10 *Natural Law Forum* 168–201; Javier Hervada, *Critical Introduction to Natural Law*, M. Emmons (trans) (Wilson and Lafleur 2006).

10 CE Braaten, 'A Lutheran Affirmation of the Natural Law' in RC Baker and RC Ehkle (eds), *Natural Law: A Lutheran Reappraisal* (Concordia Publishing House 2011) 3–16.

11 See e.g. D VanDrunen, *Natural Law and the Two Kingdoms: A Study in the Development of Reformed Social Thought* (Eerdmans 2010) 95, and his *A Biblical Case for Natural Law* (Acton Institute 2006), and Stephen J Grabill, *Rediscovering the Natural Law in Reformed Theological Ethic* (Eerdmans 2006).

12 J Daryl Charles, *Retrieving the Natural Law: A Return to Moral First Things* (William B. Eerdmans 2008); Jean Porter, *Natural Law and Divine Law: Reclaiming the Tradition for Christian Ethics* (Eerdmans 1999) Chapter 3.

13 R Hittinger, *The First Grace: Rediscovering the Natural Law in a Post-Christian World* (ISI Books 2003) 3–37, 63–91 and 93–112.

14 J Porter, 'Does the Natural Law provide a Universally Binding Morality?' in LS Cunningham (ed), *Intractable Disputes about Natural Law: Alistair MacIntyre and Critics* (UP of Notre Dame 2009) 53–95.

understanding of that flourishing and its basic goods; reflection on our experience enables a grasp of dispositions and actions that respect and promote those goods in our relations with others; all humans are, despite their sinfulness, *somewhat* capable of an accurate grasp of basic goods and their practical requirements. However:

> None of this . . . makes the Christian theological salvation narrative ethically irrelevant. It does not say that sinful humans have the motivation to do sufficiently what they know to be right, apart from penitence, faith, gratitude, and hope that the story of God's salvific initiative inspires,

nor 'that they have the power, unaided by biblical tradition, to know completely what is good, what is virtuous, or what is right'.[15]

Matthew Levering reflects these ideas and argues that the principles of natural law are capable of specific articulation and should function as the basis for any just legal system. First, natural law does not negate the need for the grace of the Holy Spirit and the work of Christ. Knowing its precepts does not mean that we will observe them, or if we do observe them that this reflects our interior disposition. As human sinfulness obscures natural law and makes it impossible to know its precepts adequately and observe them rightly, so we need to be transformed by the grace of the Holy Spirit and the work of Christ to be reconciled to God. Second, when humans follow their conscience and strive to act justly to God and neighbour, they may be moved by grace that unites them to the salvation won by Christ, even without knowing God explicitly. Third, like all humans, Christians possess natural law and are required to follow its precepts. Indeed, imitating Christ would not be possible, if Christians lacked natural law; and 'Part of the task of Christian [approaches to] natural law . . . is to remind Christians of what Christians should be doing, rather than solely to call upon others to value the dignity of all human persons'. Fourth, natural law doctrine helps to affirm God's universal providence and desire to save all humans, affirms the worth of each, shows that there are certain things that no human may do to other humans and upholds the value of free choice. Fifth, natural law is our participation in God's eternal law, and it is constituted and promulgated by the Creator God, who imprints it on our hearts. It requires recognition of a divine lawgiver. Sixth, human positive law is properly grounded in natural law. Law is not a solely cultural constraint, according to which some actions are right or wrong depending on time/place. Some actions are simply wrong because they violate God's law, which we know however imperfectly by natural law. Finally, human sinfulness obscures but does not eliminate our ability to discover the precepts of natural law, though humans may not be able to agree on its content. However, over the course of

15 N Biggar, *Behaving in Public: How to Do Christian Ethics* (Eerdmans 2011) 41–42.

history, and for all sorts of reasons, different individuals and societies will see the precepts of natural law more or less clearly.[16]

Natural Law and the Official Teaching of Churches

Natural law thinking is not the preserve of theologians. The official teaching of churches also deploys natural law. For instance, the American Methodist Church's conference declared in 1780: 'Slavery is contrary to the laws of God, man and nature, and hurtful to society; [and] contrary to the dictates of conscience'; and this is echoed by Wesley himself: 'Can law, human law, change the nature of things? . . . Notwithstanding ten thousand human laws, right is right and wrong is wrong still'.[17] Likewise, the Roman Catholic Church's International Theological Commission in 2009 proposed that 'natural law is the basis of collaboration among all persons of good will, whatever their religious convictions'. Indeed, there are 'convergences' in the great religious traditions that 'bear witness to a largely common moral patrimony that forms the basis of all dialogue on moral questions'. So it is possible to speak of discovering common moral values, beginning with their insertion into a network of human relationships from birth, which allow individuals to become aware of themselves, of others and of the context in which they live. In turn, natural law is the foundation of a universal ethic and yardstick against which to measure the political order, discoverable from observing and reflecting on a common human nature; inscribed on the human heart; dynamic rather than static; and, instead of being a list of definitive immutable precepts, 'a spring of inspiration always flowing forth for the search for an objective foundation for a universal ethic'.[18]

Natural law has also entered ecumenical dialogue between Christians as in the case, for example, of the Anglican and Roman Catholic International Commission. First, there is the idea of 'natural morality': 'Reflection on experience of what makes human beings, singly and together, truly human gives rise to a natural morality, sometimes interpreted in terms of natural justice or natural law, to which a general appeal for guidance can be made'. In Jesus Christ 'this natural morality is not denied' but 'renewed, transfigured and perfected, since Christ is the true and perfect image of God'.[19] Second, the Commission notes how Roman Catholic moral teaching emphasises 'the absoluteness of some

16 M Levering, 'Natural Law and Christianity' in AM Emon, M Levering and D Novak (eds), *Natural Law: A Jewish, Christian and Islamic Trialogue* (OUP 2014) Ch. 2.

17 J Harrod, 'Natural Law in the Methodist Tradition' in N. Doe (ed), *Christianity and Natural Law* (CUP 2017) Ch. 6.

18 *In Search of a Universal Ethic: A New Look at Natural Law* (2009) pars. 9, 11, 38, 113: see H Costigane, 'Natural Law in the Roman Catholic Tradition' in N Doe (ed), *Christianity and Natural Law* (CUP 2017) Ch. 2.

19 The Second Anglican-Roman Catholic International Commission (ARCIC II) report *Life in Christ: Morals, Communion and the Church* (1994) par. 9: see L Koffeman, 'Natural Law

demands of the moral law and the existence of certain prohibitions to which there are no exceptions'. By way of contrast Anglicans, 'while acknowledging the same ultimate values, are not persuaded that the laws as we apprehend them are necessarily absolute'—for instance,

> it might be right to incorporate contextual and pastoral considerations in the formulation of a moral law, on the grounds that fundamental moral values are better served if the law sometimes takes into account certain contingencies of nature and history and certain disorders of the human condition.

As a result, Anglicans 'do not make the clear-cut distinction, which Roman Catholics make, between canon law, with its incorporation of contingent and prudential considerations, and the moral law, which in its principles is absolute and universal'.[20] It is to church laws that we now turn.

Natural Law and the Regulatory Instruments of Churches

This section explores the extent to which natural law thinking appears in the modern juridical texts of churches—that is, in the form of concepts of divine law, the revealed law of God, as well as moral ideas rooted in ethical standards perhaps conceivable as universal in scope. However, it does so in the context of their dominant, largely positivist view of church law.

On the one hand, therefore, this juridical positivism (with its focus on the positive law of churches) is expressed in a variety of legal principles in which, at best, there is an implicit moral content. First, the ecclesial traditions studied here have a system of church law, order or polity—and these are understood as a bodies of rules without any obvious and explicit connection to morals. As we saw in Chapter 1, the Roman Catholic Church has its 'Code of Canon Law' (1983), which is a juridical text (albeit with theological foundations) issued by the supreme legislator of that Church, the Pontiff; Anglican churches have a 'constitution' and 'canons'; Methodist churches have 'Methodist Law' in a variety of sources; Reformed and Presbyterian churches have 'laws' or a 'book of church order'; and a Baptist Union or Convention has 'laws' or 'bylaws'; and a local church, a constitution or 'covenant'. These are, as their titles indicate, systems of law not morals. Second, compliance with church law: obedience. The Presbyterian Church in New Zealand is typical: 'All members of congregations . . . must comply with the Book of Order'; and Baptist norms require 'strict adherence' to the 'rules and regulations'. Nevertheless, church laws may enable the relaxation of rules by various devices, such as that

---

in the Ecumenical Movement' in N Doe (ed), *Christianity and Natural Law* (CUP 2017) Ch. 9.

20 Ibid § 52.

of dispensation in the Roman Catholic canon law: 'the relaxation of a merely ecclesiastical law in a particular case'. Third, matters are regulated by law, not morals; for example in the Methodist Church of Ireland:

> All members . . . are subject to its government and discipline and are under the jurisdiction and care of the appropriate Courts of the Church in all matters of Doctrine, Worship, Discipline, and Order in accordance with the Rules and Regulations . . . made by the Conference.[21]

In all of these examples, there is no explicit connection of church laws to morality—church laws are simply bodies of positive rules created by authorities within those churches which possess legislative competence. Natural law thinking may at best be implicit in the examples offered: for example—it is morally right for a church to have a system of law, order or polity to enable that church to fulfil its mission and ministry as witness to Christ; it is morally right for church members to comply with the law which they or their representatives have made (as an expression of applied ecclesiology); and it is morally right for decisions to be made in a church in accordance with the rules it has created on a matter of ecclesial life.

On the other hand, there is evidence that the legal texts of churches also, at the same time, deploy explicitly concepts associated with natural law thinking. First, they use the idea of 'the law of God'. For instance, under the Roman Catholic canon law, a custom is void if it is contrary to divine law; in the Lutheran Church Missouri Synod: 'no resolution of the Synod imposing anything upon the individual congregation is of binding force if it is not in accordance with the Word of God'; according to the book of order of the Presbyterian Church of America: 'the Word of God' is the supreme 'rule of faith and life'; and for Baptists the Bible is part of 'the constitutions and laws' of a Convention, or 'the rule of church law'.[22]

Second, the regulatory instruments of some churches provide that the law of the state applies to the church provided it is just: for example, the Roman Catholic canon law states that civil law applies to the church unless contrary to divine law; and the Catechism of the Church (a teaching document) states: 'unjust laws . . . would not be binding in conscience'; the polity of the Methodist Church in New Zealand requires ministers to declare that 'While respecting the law, I will act to change unjust laws'; and in the Baptist Union New Zealand, ministers must 'obey the laws of [the] government unless they require disobedience to the law of God'.[23]

Third, the juridical instruments of churches also enable and regulate the pursuit of philanthropic activities in wider society; they oblige or exhort care

21 See N Doe, *Christian Law: Contemporary Principles* (CUP 2013) 19–29.
22 Ibid 33–36.
23 Ibid Ch. 10.

for others on the part of the faithful individually and/or collectively. In doing so, these juridical instruments very commonly deploy large moral ideas of 'justice' reminiscent of natural law thinking generally.

For example, in the Roman Catholic Church, under canon law all the faithful must promote social justice and help the poor and they may establish associations for charitable purposes;[24] and each parish priest is 'to help the sick and especially the dying in great charity' and he is 'to endeavour to ensure that the faithful are concerned for the community of the parish', and 'to foster works which promote the spirit of the gospel, including its relevance to social justice'.[25] In Anglicanism the objects of a church may include the duty to contribute to the 'moral and spiritual' welfare of society;[26] to promote justice in the world;[27] 'to transform unjust structures of society, caring for God's creation, and establishing the values of the Kingdom';[28] and to engage in 'educational, medical, social, agricultural and other service'.[29]

Similar ideas appear in the legal instruments of the Protestant churches. One object of the Evangelical Lutheran Church in America is 'to meet human needs, caring for the sick and the aged, advocating dignity and justice for all people, working for peace and reconciliation among the nations, and standing with the poor and powerless and committing itself to their needs'.[30] Moreover, the church 'shall seek to meet human needs through encouragement of its people to individual and corporate action, and through establishing, developing, recognizing, and supporting institutions and agencies that minister to people in their spiritual and temporal needs'. It must also 'establish affiliations and alliances within this church and within society and carry out a comprehensive social ministry witness'.[31] As such, its central organisation must respond to 'human need, caring for the sick and suffering, working for justice and peace, and providing guidance to members on social matters',[32] and its Church Council 'shall have responsibility for the corporate social responsibility of this church'.[33]

24 Code of Canon Law 1983, *Codex Iuris Canonici* (CIC), c. 215: the faithful; c. 222.2: social justice.
25 CIC, cc. 528–529.
26 Anglican Church in Venezuela: Constitution, II.
27 See e.g. Episcopal Church in the Philippines: Constitution, 1.1; Canons 1.2.2(d): one of the functions of the Provincial Synod's Commission on Social Concerns is 'to study the nature and root causes of poverty and underdevelopment in the country and review the participation of the Church in the development process'.
28 Anglican Church in Aotearoa, New Zealand and Polynesia: Constitution, Preamble.
29 United Church of North India: Constitution, II.I.II; see also Anglican Church of Chile: Statutes, 2.
30 ELCA: Constitution, 4.02.
31 ELCA: Constitution, 8.33.
32 ELCA: Constitution, 11.20–21.
33 ELCA: Constitution, 14.21.10–16.

It is a principle of Methodist social responsibility that the church has a duty 'to apply the Christian vision of righteousness to social, economic and political issues'; as such, a local church council is to 'give attention to local and larger community ministries of compassion, justice and advocacy' including 'religion and race, and the status and role of women'; moreover, the faithful individually should engage in 'healing the sick, feeding the hungry, caring for the stranger, freeing the oppressed, being and becoming a compassionate caring presence, and working to develop social structures that are consistent with the gospel'.[34]

Similarly, in Presbyterianism, a national General Assembly may take action for 'the well-being of the community';[35] the regional Presbytery must provide for pastoral care 'within the wider community';[36] the local Kirk Session must seek to further Christian witness and service in the local community and raise funds for prescribed 'philanthropic objects';[37] ministers must visit the sick and provide leadership in the humanitarian activity of the local church;[38] and members must themselves witness to society.[39] And the North American Baptist Conference: 'Christians, individually and collectively . . . [must] promote truth, justice and peace', and 'aid the needy and preserve the dignity of all races and conditions'.[40]

Conclusion

In Christianity, one legacy of the Reformation is the persistence of natural law thinking. Natural law has a wide variety of meanings, but it is generally seen as the law implanted in nature by God which rational creatures can discern through the use of natural reason; it is thus contrasted with the revealed law, though aspects of divine law may also be precepts of natural law. At its core is the Golden Rule, which applies to all human relations regardless of religion. However, there are differences of opinion about the content of natural law beyond broad agreement that good is to be done and evil avoided; this

34 United Methodist Church in Northern Europe and Eurasia (UMCNEAE): Book of Discipline (BOD), pars. 101, 122 and 252.

35 Presbyterian Church in Ireland (PCI): Code: Book of the Constitution and Government (Code), VII.II.104; Presbyterian Church of Wales (PCW): Handbook of Order and Rules (HOR), 3.4.2: social issues; Presbyterian Church in America (PCA): Book of Church Order (BCO): General Assembly is 'to recommend measures for the promotion of charity . . . through all the churches under its care'.

36 Presbyterian Church of Aotearoa New Zealand (PCANZ): Book of Order, 8.4(4).

37 PCI: Code, II.II.35 and 38; PCA: BCO, 4.4: the local church must make offerings 'for the relief of the poor'.

38 PCI: Code, IV.73: Presbytery must ensure that visits to the sick are carried out; PCW: HOR, 4.2: humanitarian activity in 'the local community, nation and world'; PCA: BCO, 8.4: pastors; 9.2: deacons.

39 PCW: HOR, 2.2: members must 'give freely of their service to society'.

40 North America Baptist Conference (NABC): Statement of Beliefs, 8: this cites e.g. Matt. 5.13–16, Hebrews 13.5, Luke 9.23 and Titus 2.12.

suggests that natural law underwrites morality as such, rather than any particular moral code. Nevertheless, Christians across the traditions in the regulatory instruments of their various churches oblige or exhort the engagement of the faithful in pastoral care for the other. On the one hand, the dominant approach of Christians to church law (or other systems of church order or polity) is positivist—one which focuses on church laws as systems of rules which on the face of the legal text have no explicit link to morality, or universal principles of right and wrong. Laws are rules and they must be complied with, though they exist to enable and regulate the mission of the church in its witness to Christ. On the other hand, the regulatory instruments of churches today also link law to large moral ideas, which itself may be understood as a form of natural law thinking. They provide that the law of God is the supreme rule of faith and life; the civil law applies to the church only in so far as it is not inconsistent with divine law, and that the faithful may disobey unjust civil law; and the church should engage in charitable work on the basis that this is required by justice (to meet the needs, for example of the poor and needy).

All the echoes, so to speak, of natural law thinking, which have survived the golden age as it were of natural law in the early and medieval church, are summed up in elements of the Statement of Principles of Christian Law (issued by the Ecumenical Christian Law Panel in 2016)—these too, it is suggested, are expressions of natural law; for instance: 'Church law and church order exist to serve a church in its mission and in its witness to the salvific work of Christ'; 'Church laws should conform to the law of God, as revealed in Holy Scripture and by the Holy Spirit'; 'A law may be relaxed, by competent ecclesial authority, by means of dispensation, economy or other form of equity'; 'The right to exercise discipline [is based on] divine and spiritual authority'; 'Christians must be judged in the church according to law applied with equity, and disciplinary procedures must secure fair, impartial and due process'; and 'Sanctions should be lawful and just'.[41] In all this, it is clear that the Reformation has left a challenging legacy in the subsequent development and deployment of natural law thinking.

Bibliography

Barth K, *The Epistle of Paul to the Romans* (OUP 1933)
Biggar N, *Behaving in Public: How to Do Christian Ethics* (William B. Eerdmans 2011)
Braaten CE, 'A Lutheran Affirmation of the Natural Law' in RC Baker and RC Ehkle (eds), *Natural Law: A Lutheran Reappraisal* (Concordia Publishing House 2011)
Church Laws and Ecumenism, N Doe (ed) (Routledge 2021)
Costigane H, 'Natural Law in the Roman Catholic Tradition' in N Doe (ed), *Christianity and Natural Law* (CUP 2017) Chapter 2
Daryl Charles J, *Retrieving the Natural Law: A Return to Moral First Things* (William B. Eerdmans 2008)

41 See *Church Laws and Ecumenism*, N Doe (ed) (Routledge 2021) Appendix II, 270–86.

Doe N, *Christian Law: Contemporary Principles* (CUP 2013)
Dunkle BL, 'A Development of Origen's View of the Natural Law' (2004) 13 Pro Ecclesia
Finnis J, *Natural Law and Natural Rights* (Clarendon Press 1980)
Grabill SJ, *Rediscovering the Natural Law in Reformed Theological Ethic* (William B. Eerdmans 2006)
Grisez G, 'The First Principles of Practical Reason: A Commentary on the *Summa Theologiae*, 1–2, Question 94, Article 2' (1965) 10 Natural Law Forum
Harrod J, 'Natural Law in the Methodist Tradition' in N Doe (ed), *Christianity and Natural Law* (CUJP 2017) Ch. 6
Hervada J, *Critical Introduction to Natural Law*, M. Emmons (trans) (Wilson and Lafleur 2006)
Hittinger R, *The First Grace: Rediscovering the Natural Law in a Post-Christian World* (ISI Books 2003)
Hughes GJ, 'Natural Law' in JF Childress and J Macquarrie (eds), *A New Dictionary of Christian Ethics* (SCM Press 1986)
In Search of a Universal Ethic: A New Look at Natural Law (2009) pars. 9, 11, 38, 113 <www.vatican.va/roman_curia/congregations/cfaith/cti_documents/rc_con_cfaith_doc_20090520_legge-naturale_en.html>
Koffeman L, 'Natural Law in the Ecumenical Movement' in N Doe (ed), *Christianity and Natural Law* (CUP 2017)
Levering, M, 'Natural Law and Christianity' in AM Emon, M Levering and D Novak (eds), *Natural Law: A Jewish, Christian and Islamic Trialogue* (OUP 2014) Ch. 2
Porter J, 'Does the Natural Law Provide a Universally Binding Morality?' in LS Cunningham (ed), *Intractable Disputes about Natural Law: Alistair MacIntyre and Critics* (UP of Notre Dame 2009)
Porter J, *Natural Law and Divine Law: Reclaiming the Tradition for Christian Ethics* (William B. Eerdmans 1999) Ch. 3
Ramsey P, *Basic Christian Ethics* (Westminster-John Knox Press 1993)
Raunio A, 'Divine and Natural Law in Luther and Melanchthon' in V Mäkinen (ed), *The Lutheran Reformation and the Law* (Brill 2006)
Stanley Hauerwas H, *The Peaceable Kingdom: A Primer in Christian Ethics* (U of Note Dame P 1983)
The Threads of Natural Law: Unravelling a Philosophical Tradition, FJ Contreras (ed) (Springer 2013)
VanDrunen D, *A Biblical Case for Natural Law* (Acton Institute 2006)
VanDrunen D, *Natural Law and the Two Kingdoms: A Study in the Development of Reformed Social Thought* (William B. Eerdmans 2010)

8 Catholic and Protestant Approaches to Church-State Relations

Helen Costigane

Introduction

The period of the Reformation was a pivotal moment of change and development in the government, beliefs and practices of the Christian Church. Therefore, this discussion in terms of Catholic and Protestant approaches to church-state relations will take that as a starting point, follow through to the period of the Enlightenment, and then to the modern era beginning in 1850. In looking at the often-vexed question of these relations, four perspectives will be considered—the Roman Catholic, Anglican, Calvinist and Lutheran. Though the Roman Catholic perspective is global, others such as the Church of England will be more localised. While it is acknowledged that Anglicanism too has a global perspective, the situation of the Church in England is a good example of the operation of a 'state' church. From a Calvinist perspective, we will consider the Church of Scotland which, too, has a unique relationship with the state. Finally, the Lutheran Church began in a specific geographical place, so we will consider that but also refer to other countries where Lutheranism is predominant. What will emerge is that, despite best efforts, there has often been an intertwining of the secular and ecclesiastical in internal Church matters such as the appointment of bishops or in terms of spiritual or doctrinal matters, the right of the Church to hold property independently of the control of the state, or where the Church has intervened to protect its interests.

The Roman Catholic Church

Reformation

The issue of ensuring the independence of the Roman Catholic Church from various states has been an ongoing issue for centuries before the Reformation. That secular states had an interest in the Catholic Church was not least due to the fact that by the end of the ninth century, the Church's property had grown to ownership or administration of nearly 30 percent of all revenued land in Europe. The Church's rich endowment provided hospitals, orphanages and social services for the medieval community. Its assets made possible

DOI: 10.4324/9780429264115-11

the magnificent cathedrals and churches of Europe, as well as the universities and institutes of education at all levels. The separation of church and state, and maintaining the independence of the episcopate from secular rulers was addressed at the Second Council of Nicaea in 787, and again at the Fourth Council of Constantinople (869–870) which condemned the election of bishops carried out through 'the power and intrigues of civil authorities'.[1] Further, bishops were forbidden to alienate ecclesiastical property,[2] and any attempt by a 'secular person' to wrest such control was considered to be sacrilegious.[3] Subsequent Councils addressed similar themes. Alongside this was the considerable autonomy and power of the Church, exercised by popes and bishops. Pope Gregory VII (1073–1085) elevated the Pope to the rank of the supreme and unchallenged leader of the universal Church. Bishops and kings alike were submitted to his authority, and the worldly power of the pope reached its zenith in the twelfth and thirteenth centuries.[4]

It is against this backdrop that we can view the Protestant Reformation movements which fractured the unity of the Church and resulted in a remodeling of relationship between church and state. It might be argued that Reformation movements crystallised trends that had long been in evidence, such as the conflict between secular rulers and papal authority, and what was perceived as spiritual corruption within the Catholic Church. The Council of Trent (1545–1563) succeeded in enacting a series of decrees on the internal reform of the Church in addition to major doctrinal clarifications—this despite significant political obstacles and two long interruptions. Careful consideration was given to questions relating to Church life and discipline, including the Church's use of temporal goods. Clear responsibilities were assigned to bishops and parish priests, and the Council outlawed simony, the possession of multiple benefices and absenteeism. Though the Council did not enact any new legislation regarding church property, it declared that it was renewing and restating all the ordinances of former sacred canons and general councils which sought to protect the Church's immunity.[5] The most flagrant violations of this immunity had already been committed by Henry VIII (1509–1547), when in 1534 he published the Act whereby he established himself to be the supreme head of the Church of England.[6] That the Council directly admonished secular princes of their duties towards the Catholic Church might be interpreted as a response to this.[7]

1 N Tanner, *Decrees of the Ecumenical Councils*, 2 vols. (Sheed & Ward 1990). Canon 12, (Tanner, 175).
2 Canon 15 (Tanner, 177).
3 Canon 18 (Tanner, 180).
4 See Gregory VII's 'Dictatus Papae' 1090 <https://sourcebooks.fordham.edu/source/g7-dictpap.asp> accessed 10 February 2022.
5 Cf Session 25 (Tanner, 728, 784, 788–794).
6 Act of Supremacy, 1534.
7 Council of Trent, session 25, chapter 24 (Tanner, 795).

The Enlightenment

The belief that the Catholic Church had no right to acquire property unless the state gave its permission was a logical deduction from the tenets of Gallicanism and Febronianism. The legal basis for this teaching was the concept that the Church received its juridical personality from the civil law of the land. As the teaching spread and its effects became apparent, it was met by the insistent teaching of the ecclesiastical authorities that the Catholic Church by its very nature was a perfect society and thus possessed a legitimate and natural right to property. The term 'Gallicanism' was used to designate a certain group of religious opinions peculiar to the church in France and its theological schools. The quarrel between Louis XIV and Pope Innocent XI, where the king sought to extend his powers over the church's temporal goods, led to the king making a show of force by requiring the French clergy to reaffirm his powers in the so-called Gallican Articles of 1682. This 'Declaration of the Clergy of France' declared that the pope had spiritual power only, and not temporal or civil power. Secondly, papal primacy within the Church was limited in that although the pope had the main role in questions of faith, his decrees lacked infallible authority in themselves; it was the bishops who, by giving their consent, gave his decrees that authority.

In 1763, Johann Nikolaus von Hontheim, Auxiliary Bishop of Trier, wrote a work under the pseudonym Justinus Febronius. Based on Gallican principles, it advanced to a radicalism far outstripping traditional Gallicanism. According to Febronius, and denying the monarchical constitution of the Church, the power of the keys was entrusted by Christ to the whole body of the Church, which was exercised through the bishops. The pope comes first among these, but he is subordinate to the Church as a whole. Schatz tells us that 'Febronianism' was translated into ecclesio-political reality at the Congress of Ems in 1786, which was the last great uprising of German prince-bishops of Rome.[8] The Congress protested against Roman centralism and demanded a return to the situation that existed before Pseudo-Isidore. This was the conventional name for the unknown Carolingian-era author (or authors) behind an extensive corpus of influential forgeries. Though not the main objective, these 'false decretals' expanded the legal jurisdiction of the Bishop of Rome, and the Congress demanded a return to the situation where the Pope was the principal overseer and primate of the whole Church, but that his power and privileges did not undermine the jurisdiction of bishops.

Febronius believed that the final court of appeal was the ecumenical council to which the pope was subordinate. The delegates to the congress demanded more authority for the bishops, the removal or restriction of nuncios and the restoration of the rights of metropolitans as they existed in the ancient Church. However, while it was foreseen that all this would be accomplished with the assistance of the emperor, the reality was that the Holy Roman Empire was

8 K. Schatz, Papal Primacy: From its Origins to the Present, Collegeville, Minn., (Liturgical Press) 1996 at 141

dying and Joseph II of Austria was more concerned with his own territorial problems, and the fragile unified front of the archbishops collapsed.

Joseph II (1741–1790), the son of Maria Theresa of Austria, was the father of 'Josephinism', a desire for an episcopal and territorial church. Its beginnings can be traced to thirteenth-century Austria but was fostered in the eighteenth century by the spread of Febronian ideas. The basic ideas were that the state was supreme over the Church, any canonical legislation conflicting with the interests of the state is opposed to natural law, and the actions of the Church are undertaken with the consent and sanction of the state. The fundamental underlying idea was that the state was the administrator of the Church's temporal property. Joseph enacted laws merging the funds of all churches, religious houses and endowments within his territories. All ecclesiastical property was to be held as part of a new fund which would be applied for the various requirements of public worship. The state took over the training of clergy and the regulation of worship, with the foundation of 12 theological seminaries (many of which were badly managed).

The loss of the papal states, recounted by Pius IX in *Respicientes* (1870), in which he notes that the papal states were 'stolen from Us',[9] restricted the Church's temporal and civil power; and what remained related to the realm of the spiritual and moral. Much of the papal encyclicals from this time report the persecution of the Church in different countries, either outright persecution in terms of expulsion or suppression, or in terms of laws enacted which restricted rights and freedoms. In 1863, Pius notes the way in which the government of New Grenada 'impedes, disturbs, and tears asunder the Catholic Church',[10] through a number of measures including confiscating and selling ecclesiastical property, and enacting laws and decrees attacking the right of the Church to acquire and possess property. Pius later denounced happenings in Switzerland, Austria and Germany where seminaries were dissolved, Catholic schools being taken away from the care of the Church, and where laws were enacted intending to subjugate the Church to civil authorities.[11] Leo XIII wrote about the threat to Catholic schools in Manitoba, Canada,[12] addressed what he saw was a conspiracy against Christianity in France, in terms of the separation of church and state,[13] deplored laws enacted in Hungary which restricted the Church's capacity to act,[14] together with the war which he saw being waged generally against the authority of the Church.[15] Leo, recounting the loss of the papal states and addressing some of the issues in Italy, suggested that 'the Catholic

9 *Respicientes*, 1870, paragraph 11. The text of this and other encyclicals can be found on the Vatican website (www.vatican.va) and/or at Papal Encyclicals Online (https://papalencyclicals.net).

10 *Incredibili*, 1863, paragraph 1.

11 See *Etsi Multa* (1873), *Vix Dum a Nobis* (1874), *Quod Numquam* (1875).

12 *Affari Vos* (1897).

13 *Au Milieu Des Sollicitudes* (1892).

14 *Constanti Hungarorum* (1893).

15 *Diuturnum* (1881).

Church in Italy was gradually robbed of her elements of life and action as well as of her native secular influences in public and social life'.[16]

Modern Era

Pius X spoke of the situation in France where there had been the separation of church and state which he denounced as 'a thesis absolutely false, a most pernicious error'.[17] Among the documents dealing with resultant problems are *Gravissimo Officii Munere* (1906) in which he mentions laws injurious to the Catholic Church there, and also *Une Fois Encore* (1907), where he states that the property of the Church 'has been wrested from her'.[18] Portugal too was guilty of an 'incredible series of excesses and crimes . . . enacted . . . for the oppression of the Church'.[19] Tensions between the church and the state of Germany are recorded in Pius XII's *Mit Brennender Sorge* (1937), which noted with unease the rise of Hitler and political and social developments which might have a negative impact on the Church and society in general. The lack of improvement of the conditions for Catholics in China (and the expulsion of the Apostolic Nuncio) was discussed in by Pius XII in *Ad Sinarum Gentem* (1954), and the aftermath of the Second World War in Europe, with the establishment of the Communist bloc in Central and Eastern Europe, led to much discussion on the persecuted churches in Hungary, Poland and Czechoslovakia (to name but some), where schools were closed, clergy were imprisoned (sometimes tortured) and Catholic publications silenced.[20]

In the face of such tensions and difficulties, the Church wanted to protect herself and her mission in different countries. During the Second Vatican Council, Pope Paul VI had expressed a wish that the role and functions of papal legates be more clearly defined. His *motu proprio, Sollicitudo omnium Ecclesiarum*, issued on 24 June 1969, dealt precisely with such issues. Paul notes the contribution made by papal legates living in different countries which allowed for a greater knowledge of their needs and aspirations, and how legates might enable both church and state to work together for the good of humanity. These legates represent 'in a stable manner the person of the Roman Pontiff . . . in the States and the public authorities to whom they are sent'.[21] Further, 'those also represent the Apostolic See who are appointed to pontifical Missions as Delegates or Observers at international Councils or at Conferences and Meetings'.[22] The papal legate acts as an envoy to a state to promote the relationship between the Apostolic See and the state, and the

16 *Spesse Volta* (1898), paragraph 4.
17 *Vehementer Nos* (1906), paragraph 3.
18 *Une Fois Encore* (1907), paragraph 11.
19 *Iamdudum* (1911), paragraph 1.
20 See, for example, Pius XII's *Meminisse Iuvat* (1958).
21 1983 Code of Canon Law, canon 363.
22 Canon 363 §2.

common good, and may be involved in discussions on education, health, the temporal goods of the church and confiscated property.[23] Secondly, the legate deals with questions between the church and state, particularly where a concordat exists. Such questions might focus on the establishment of religious schools, access to places of worship and the teaching of religion. In so doing, he will seek the opinion of the bishops of that ecclesiastical jurisdiction, as the latter have the right to be involved in the affairs of their own country.[24]

So, as we can see, there has been much conflict in terms of church-state relations over many centuries. The Church has faced many challenges in terms of its autonomy in both spiritual and temporal matters. No less is the case today when national laws may challenge its doctrinal stance, examples of this being the content of religious education in Catholic schools in England; the dilemma faced by Catholic adoption agencies over the issue of legislation allowing adoption by homosexual couples; recent calls by sexual abuse inquiries (and in some cases proposed legislation) in Australia, Ireland and England to require priests to break the seal of the confessional in some circumstances; and Church control over charitable structures which may challenge doctrinal orthodoxy.[25] Nevertheless, the Code of Canon Law makes it possible for collaboration (even harmony) between civil law and canon law unless the former is contrary to divine law.[26]

The Anglican Church and State Relations

Reformation

At its inception the Anglican Church had the closest of relationships with the state in the person of the King. Henry VIII's break with Rome, removed the church in England from papal jurisdiction and effectively nationalised it. His Act of Supremacy 1534 made it clear that the monarch was now 'the only supreme head in earth of the Church of England, called *Anglicana Ecclesia*'. In terms of law, the Submission of the Clergy Act 1533, provided for the existing canon law to remain in force so far as it was not 'contrary or repugnant to the laws, statutes and customs of this realm'.[27] This preserved the church

23 Canon 365. One example of this in recent history is the restitution of church property in countries that formed the Eastern Communist bloc, such as the Baltic States (Lithuania, Latvia and Estonia), Poland, Bulgaria, Hungary and what was at the time Czechoslovakia.

24 Canon 287 §2.

25 See H Costigane, 'Catholic Education in England—What Is to Be Taught?' (2009) 163 Law & Justice, 103–9; 'Catholic Adoption Agencies and "Gay Adopters"' (2008) 161 Law and Justice, 98–110; 'A Protected Rite? Defending the Seal of Confession from Legal Challenge' (2013) 209(4) America 15; R Meakin, 'What Are the Implications of Being a Church-Controlled Charity in the Church of England and the Roman Catholic Church?' (2016) 176 Law & Justice 18–38.

26 Canon 22.

27 Act of Supremacy 1534 (as discussed earlier); Submission of the Clergy Act 1533.

courts, the episcopal system and rules applying to the holding of property connected with ecclesiastical offices. This closest of relationships between church and state is manifested in further legislation which set out matters of doctrine. The Statute of the Six Articles (1539), approved by Convocation and enacted in Parliament, arose from Henry's personal conservatism. These upheld the doctrine of transubstantiation, the practice of auricular confession, the discipline of priestly celibacy and the continuation of private masses, and which he was prepared to enforce under heavy penalties, including death by burning for heresy and the forfeiture of property.[28]

The six-year reign of Edward VI saw a swing towards Protestantism, then back towards Catholicism when Mary I assumed the throne in 1553, though her time as Queen was short, lasting only five years. During her reign she had no success in her attempt to restore annates to the papacy and return church property. Though she gave back the monastic lands that she herself held, she could not persuade the members of Parliament to do the same. Williamson observes that: 'here the will of Parliament was so obviously to the contrary'.[29] She gave several manors back to the Archbishop of York and restored the colleges of clergy at Manchester and Southwell, and granted lands to the Bishop of Chester, but other attempts to re-endow the church were thwarted. Haigh reports that she met parliamentary resistance to revive the See of Durham, which had been dismembered, restored six religious houses from crown resources, but the cost of the war against France from 1557 halted the process. As Haigh notes: 'Mary had done what she could afford, but her conscience over Church property was shared by few of her subjects'.[30]

The reign of Elizabeth I (1558–1603) demonstrated again the close relationship between church and state. Less than a year after Elizabeth's accession to the throne, the first Elizabethan Parliament passed the Act of Uniformity, which effectively prohibited Catholic worship.[31] One form of Protestant worship was prescribed for the entire realm, ending 30 years of vacillation between Catholic and Protestant forms of worship under Henry VIII, Edward VI, and

28 The text of the Six Articles can be found on <http://anglicanhistory.org/reformation/henry/sixarticles.html> accessed 12 February 2022.

29 JA Williamson, *The Tudor Age* (D. McKay 1961) 225.

30 C Haigh, *English Reformations: Religion, Politics, and Society under the Tudors* (Clarendon Press 1993) 226.

31 Act of Uniformity, 1559. The goal of this legislation was

> to drive Catholicism out of England by cutting off access to Catholic clergy, holy sites, sacraments and symbols. . . .The law also banned the further ordination of any Catholic priests, a measure aimed at gradually depriving lay communities of Catholic priests and sacraments. Over time this is just what happened in many areas. The government hoped that its efforts to wipe out any vestiges of the Roman Church's presence in England would also end the practice of Catholic recusancy—the refusal of Catholics to attend Protestant religious services—and eventually result in a unified and unchallenged Protestant Church of England.

See L McClain, *Lest We Be Damned: Practical Innovation and Lived Experience Among Catholics in Protestant England 1559–1642* (Routledge 2004) 19.

Mary Tudor. Elizabeth insisted that all subjects adhere to her new 1559 prayer book, attend services on Sundays and holy days and participate in Protestant communion three times a year. The effects of the changes in the organisation of worship meant that Catholic priests were removed from their offices, the physical sites of worship—churches and cathedrals—were transferred to the control of Protestant ministers, and many of the artefacts were confiscated or destroyed.[32] The response from Pope Pius V was a bull of excommunication, *Regnans in Excelsis*, in 1570, and there has been much debate as to how this affected the loyalty of Catholics to the crown, given that Elizabeth was labeled as a heretic and all her subjects were absolved from obeying her.[33] Parliament

32 McClain (n 30) 3.

33 Did this bull dispense Catholics from their obligation of loyalty to the sovereign? Opinion on this is divided. Reading paragraphs 3 to 5 of the Bull suggests that it did. It says:

> We, seeing impieties and crimes multiplied one upon another the persecution of the faithful and afflictions of religion daily growing more severe under the guidance and by the activity of the said Elizabeth -and recognizing that her mind is so fixed and set that she has not only despised the pious prayers and admonitions with which Catholic princes have tried to cure and convert her but has not even permitted the nuncios sent to her in this matter by this See to cross into England, are compelled by necessity to take up against her the weapons of justice, though we cannot forbear to regret that we should be forced to turn, upon one whose ancestors have so well deserved of the Christian community. Therefore, resting upon the authority of Him whose pleasure it was to place us (though unequal to such a burden) upon this supreme justice-seat, we do out of the fullness of our apostolic power declare the foresaid Elizabeth to be a heretic and favourer of heretics, and her adherents in the matters aforesaid to have incurred the sentence of excommunication and to be cut off from the unity of the body of Christ (3). And moreover (we declare) her to be deprived of her pretended title to the aforesaid crown and of all lordship, dignity and privilege whatsoever (4). And also (declare) the nobles, subjects and people of the said realm and all others who have in any way sworn oaths to her, to be forever absolved from such an oath and from any duty arising from lordship. fealty and obedience; and we do, by authority of these presents, so absolve them and so deprive the same Elizabeth of her pretended title to the crown and all other the above said matters. We charge and command all and singular the nobles, subjects, peoples and others afore said that they do not dare obey her orders, mandates and laws. Those who shall act to the contrary we include in the like sentence of excommunication (5).

However, Adrian Hastings writes: 'While there were among them a very few who would have welcomed a Spanish victory in the 1580s and a few more who were prepared to plot on their own internal dynastic revolution . . . there is no doubt of the deep loyalty of the English Catholic community as a whole to its Protestant rulers'. See A Hastings, *Church and State: The English Experience* (University of Exeter Press 1991) 35. This is supported by David Lunn who suggests that 'the tragedy was that the vast majority of them [Roman Catholics] bent over backwards to show their loyalty to the Queen, without seeming faithless to the pope, by not mixing themselves up in politics at all'. He also quotes the last words of Edmund Campion, Jesuit priest, before his execution: 'Elizabeth, your Queen, my Queen'. See D Lunn, *The Catholic Elizabethans* (Bath, Downside Abbey 1998) 58.

At the same time, it might be argued that by breaking the laws enforced individuals were de facto demonstrating disloyalty, in harbouring priests or helping them escape. For stories of such individuals, see R Connelly *Women of the Catholic Resistance in England 1540–1680* (Pentland Press 1997). However, there were protestations that all individuals wished to do was to practice their Catholic religion which, as Robert Southwell pointed out in his prison writings, had been

passed new penal laws in 1571, and it became treasonable to question the monarch's religion, challenge her right to the throne on religious grounds, bring or receive papal bulls, or reconcile anyone to the Catholic Church.

Enlightenment

From the sixteenth century onwards, much legislation concerning issues connected with the church were dealt with by Parliament in the same way as legislation on any other subject. Church-state relations therefore remained closely entwined. Apart from 11 years of the period known as the Protectorate when England was a republic (1653–1659), the House of Stuart ruled from 1603 until 1714. James I of England (and the VI of Scotland) was the son of the Catholic Queen of Scots, Mary (executed by order of Elizabeth in 1587 under suspicion of plotting against her). He was heavily influenced by Catholicism, as his wife, Anne of Denmark, was Catholic, and she had corresponded with Pope Clement VIII to support James's claim to the throne. James had also made informal overtures to Catholic powers such as Spain, Savoy, and Tuscany to gain support for his claim.[34] This, together with the view of some commentators that the Church of England he inherited in 1603 was in 'a state of uneasy equilibrium'[35] created hopes that he might restore Catholicism or relax the penalties against Catholic recusants. However, he quickly made it clear that he would not restore Catholicism as the state religion, though he did waive the steep financial penalties against Catholics who refused to attend Protestant services. The Gunpowder Plot of 5 November 1605 caused James to reimpose the Elizabethan fines and punishments, and added a few more and required all of his subjects to take an Oath of Allegiance.

His successor, Charles I, who reigned from 1625 to 1649 is noted for having been the only English king to have been executed and was subsequently

practiced openly in England for 1400 years prior to the establishment of the new religion. In appealing to the Queen to soften her measures against Catholic priests, he contended that they were only in England for religious purposes and not to plot against the government. Indeed he asserted Catholic loyalty, writing: 'It is a point of the Catholique faith . . . that subjects, bound in Conscience, under pains of forfeiting their right in Heaven, and incurring the guilt of eternal torments, do obey the just lawes of their Princes'. See P Strauss, *In Hope of Heaven: English Recusant Prison Writing of the Sixteenth Century* (Peter Lang 1995) 97. However, this does not quite accord with Marie Rowlands's view that, as the papal bull excommunicated Elizabeth, 'in medieval theory, an excommunicate monarch could not lawfully reign, and his subjects were to withdraw their allegiance'. While others believed that Catholics could not be loyal, Rowlands points out that the bull 'was never properly promulgated in England, and English Catholics protested their loyalty to the crown and ignored it'. M Rowlands, 'English Catholics in the Reign of Elizabeth' (2007) History Review 59.

34 See P Croft, 'The Gunpowder Plot: Pauline Croft Explains the Origins of Bonfire Night by Reconstructing Events 400 Years Ago' (2005) 52 History Review 9–13.

35 See GE Seel, *The Early Stuart Kings 1603–1642* (Routledge 2001) 18.

hailed as a martyr by the High-Church wing of the Anglican Church.[36] While Parliament alleged that he had committed treason, there is still much discussion on the reasons for his trial and execution. Commentators tend to discount any religious motivation, focusing more on Charles's insistence on the 'divine right of kings', his side-lining of Parliament[37] and his 'utter political stupidity'.[38] After the period of the Protectorate, Charles's son, Charles II, was restored to the throne in 1660, and he revived official Anglicanism, with Parliament passing a series of laws known as the Clarendon Code (1661–1665) and the Test Act (1673), which required holders of public office to take various oaths of loyalty and to receive the sacrament of the Church of England. As well as penalising Roman Catholics, these laws also affected Protestant nonconformists. In 1678 the Act was extended to require that all members of the Houses of Commons and Lords should make a declaration against transubstantiation, the invocation of saints and the sacrifice of the mass.

His successor, James II, was his brother, married to a Catholic princess, Mary of Modena. Although a Catholic himself, James's two daughters, Mary and Anne, had been raised as Protestants on the orders of Charles II. James's reign demonstrated a tolerance towards Catholics, and his *Declaration of Indulgence* of 4 April 1687 was seen as one sign that there might eventually be a Catholic restoration, further compounded by the birth of a male heir, James Francis Edward, in 1688. This raised fears that the next monarch would be Catholic, endangering the future of Protestantism in England. The anti-Catholic movement culminated in defeat of James during the Glorious Revolution of 1688 and the succession to the throne of William and Mary (James's older daughter). An Act of Toleration in 1689 relieved many Protestant nonconformists of many of their disabilities, though they remained excluded from public office. As for Catholics, they were now subjected to new laws limiting their property and means of education, and still excluded from political office and from universities. Mary died in 1694, and William ruled alone until 1702, when he was succeeded by his sister-in-law, Anne, the younger daughter of James II. Fearing that Anne would die without issue (as out of 16 pregnancies none of her children had survived to adulthood), and that the Catholic Stuart line of succession would be revived, Parliament passed the Act of Settlement in 1701 which excluded the Catholic branch of the house of Stuart from the throne. This settled the throne on the descendants of the Electress Sophia of Hanover. The guarantee of Protestant succession was further strengthened with the Treaty of Union of 1707 which united the kingdoms of England and

36 See E Wingfield-Stratford, *King Charles the Martyr* (Hollis & Carter 1950); A Lacey, *The Cult of King Charles the Martyr* (Boydell Press 2003).

37 After four disastrous parliaments, Charles ruled for 11 years before calling another, and only then out of absolute necessity. See LJ Sirico, 'The Trial of Charles I: A Sesquicentennial Reflection' (1999) 16(1) Constitutional Commentary 51.

38 See B Coward, 'Why Charles I was Executed in 1649' (1998) History Review 32.

Scotland. One article declared that: 'all Papists, and Persons marrying Papists, shall be excluded from, and for ever incapable to inherit, possess, or enjoy the imperial Crown of Great Britain, and the Dominions thereunto belonging, or any Part thereof'.[39] This legislation has only recently been repealed by the Succession to the Crown Act, 2013.

Modern Era

In more recent times, legislation was enacted giving powers to a new body, the National Assembly of the Church of England (known less formally as the Church Assembly) by the Church of England Assembly (Powers) Act of 1919. Behind this was the idea that, for greater efficiency, the national church needed, and was seeking from Parliament, more freedom to manage her internal affairs. These legislative powers are now exercised by the General Synod which became the Church Assembly's successor body through the Synodal Government Measure of 1969. A Measure passed by the Synod may relate to any matter concerning the Church of England and can be presented for the Royal Assent but only if both Houses of Parliament agree. While Parliament may reject a Measure (but very seldom does), it does not have any power to amend its text. The scope of the Church's autonomy was tested in 1992, when the General Synod voted to allow the ordination of women. Opponents of this legislation sought judicial review on the grounds that the 1919 Act did not allow the Synod to rule on the ordination of women. The High Court refused to restrict the plain language of the 1919 Act and ruled that the Church should have the right to debate matters such as women's ordination, make its own legislation, and place this before Parliament for acceptance or rejection.[40] This case confirmed the breadth of the legislative authority delegated to the Church by Parliament.

In terms of the ongoing relationship between the Church of England and the state, the latter still retains a say in the appointment of bishops, 26 bishops have seats in the House of Lords, and in the Commons, an MP is chosen by the party in government to speak officially on behalf of the Church of England. This Second Church Estates Commissioner ensures that the established Church is accountable to Parliament by answering questions from Members, and guiding church legislation through the House. Finally, the Speaker appoints a Church of England chaplain, whose duties include leading the Commons in prayer every day and offering pastoral and spiritual care for all who work in the Palace of Westminster. That the idea of being a 'National Church' has been affirmed by a report from the House of Bishops who note

39 See CA Whateley, *Bought and Sold for English Gold? Explaining the Union of 1707* (Tuckwell Press 2001) 101.

40 *R v Ecclesiastical Committee of the Houses of Parliament, ex parte the Church Society* [1993] EWHCJ 1028–4.

that, as the Church of England has a special place within the constitution, it continues to have a special contribution to make to the life of the nation.

The Church of Scotland (Calvinist)

Reformation

The Reformation in Scotland was a process rather than an event but took root in Scotland when the Scottish Parliament passed bills in its favour in 1560. The Confession of Faith Ratification Act of 1560 followed a new confession written by six leaders of the Protestant Reformation in Scotland, including John Knox. Knox's aim was to reform the church along the lines of Calvinist doctrine. Along with the *Book of Discipline* and the *Book of Common Order*, this Act is considered to be the foundational document for the church at this time. The Act became part of the Scottish constitution that envisaged an exclusively Protestant nation, while two further Acts effectively abolished the Mass and papal jurisdiction.[41] Though the issue of the episcopacy continued to provide trouble, supporters of the Presbyterian model (that is to say a Church made up of local communities who delegate representatives to regional and national bodies) outweighed their opponents and in 1592 a full Presbyterian system was adopted by the Scottish Church and Parliament, comprising an ascending series of courts made up of ministers and elders. However, while the Scottish reformed Church became a national Church, it remained separate from the state, as Knox aimed at preserving the spiritual influence of the Church.[42] Thus the monarch was not the head of the Church as was the case for the Church of England.

Enlightenment

Following the unification of the Scottish and English crowns under James VI and I in 1603, James aimed at establishing church uniformity north and south of the border on Episcopalian lines. Therefore, during his reign and that of his successors, the Scottish Church alternated between Presbyterianism and Episcopacy. Strong believers in the divine right to rule both church and state, the Stuart monarchs had to deal with the Covenanters who believed that Jesus Christ and God were at the head of the Church and not temporal rulers. Andrew Melville (1545–1622), who was the successor of John Knox, was an enthusiastic defender of the Presbyterian system. A former Moderator of the Church's General Assembly, he was unflinching in his opposition to

41 There were four acts in all in 1560: The Confession of Faith Ratification Act, The People Jurisdiction Act, The Abolition of Idolatry Act, and The Abolition of Mass Act.

42 The Confession of Faith makes it clear that Jesus Christ 'is the only head of the kirk [church]'. See Article 16, The Scots' Confession, ed. D Bratcher, 2018 <www.crivoice.org/creedscots.html> accessed 20 February 2022. See also Ch. 2 on Church law in Scotland.

the episcopal form of church governance, so much so that he acquired the name 'the Scourge of Bishops'. However, following Melville's imprisonment in 1606, the king imposed a return to episcopalism on Parliament in 1610.

The conflict worsened in the reign of his son Charles I (1625–1649), who wanted to set up the Church of Scotland on the same lines as the Anglican model in 1637 by introducing the *Book of Common Prayer*. Although this had been drawn up by three Scottish bishops, it closely resembled the English *Prayer Book*. When this new liturgy was first used in Edinburgh cathedral the congregation were furious and anger spread through most of the country. The National Covenant of 1638 rejected the attempt of King Charles I to force the Scottish Church to conform to English liturgical practice and Church governance, but also urged loyalty to the King at the same time. The Solemn League and Covenant (1643) was an Anglo-Scottish agreement whereby the Scots (believing it to be a guarantee of their religious freedom) agreed to support the English Parliamentarians (who saw it as a civil agreement) in their disputes with the Royalists. At the time, both countries aimed to work for a civil and religious union of England, Scotland and Ireland under a Presbyterian-parliamentary system. It was accepted by the Church of Scotland (17 August 1643) and by the English Parliament and the Westminster Assembly (25 September 1643). After Charles I surrendered in 1643, Oliver Cromwell gained control of England, but the covenant was not honoured by him and though Charles I ultimately accepted it, it was to no avail as he was executed in 1649. The future Charles II signed the covenants in 1650 and 1651 but failed to honour them after the Restoration in 1660, when the episcopal system was reintroduced in both Scotland and England. In 1688, the Catholic King James II was overthrown and replaced with his Protestant daughter, Mary, and son-in-law, William. In November 1690, the General Assembly met and rejected the episcopacy that had been forced on the Church by the Stuart kings. The Settlement of 1690 thus finally settled the reformed Scottish Church as Presbyterian. At the time of the union between England and Scotland considerable pains were taken to safeguard the position of the two established churches. Parliament passed the Protestant Religion and Presbyterian Church Act in 1707 which affirmed the Presbyterian nature of the Church as the only form of government within the Kingdom of Scotland.

Modern Era

After the Act of Union in 1707, the next major event relevant to the legal position of the church was its disruption in 1843. The basis of the dispute was the right of the state to intervene in church affairs to disallow church decisions and legislation. A result was that approximately one third of the ministers and congregations left the Church of Scotland and formed the Free Church of Scotland. Most of the Free Church of Scotland and the United Presbyterian Churches came together to constitute the United Free Church in 1900. Ultimately the various churches were reunited in 1929 after parliament had enacted the Church of Scotland Act 1921 to facilitate and permit the reunion. The 1921 Act is a remarkable document; the articles contain a statement of the separate jurisdiction of the church, marking her spiritual independence, and gave the church very considerable freedom in its government. The 1921 Act remains the major statement of the relationship between church and state in Scotland as far as the structure of Scotland is concerned, and it is worth noting that the monarch is not the head of the Church of Scotland though ties between both are maintained.

Article 4 of the 1921 Act is particularly important in terms of the autonomy of the church. It states that only Christ is its head, and the civil authority has no right to adjudicate in matters concerning doctrine, worship, government and discipline in the church. The effect of this article has been considered in three cases before the Scottish courts. The first is *Ballantyne Valentine v. Presbytery of Wigtown*,[43] where a local congregation opposed a merger and demanded the right to elect is own minister. The Court of Session held that this was an issue of government under Article 4 and refused to intervene. As Lord Murray put it, to order the election of a minister would be a clear interference by the state in the government of the church. In a second case, *Logan v. Presbytery of Dumbarton*,[44] a minister in a Church of Scotland parish sought judicial review of decisions of the presbytery which were of a disciplinary nature. The presbytery argued that the matters raised by the petitioner fell within the exclusive jurisdiction of the church and outside that of the civil courts by virtue of the 1921 Act. The court agreed with this latter view.

The most recent case was a decision of the Employment Appeal Tribunal in *Percy v Church of Scotland Board of National Mission*.[45] Helen Percy had been an associate minister in a Church of Scotland parish. Following allegations of misconduct when she had an affair with a married elder in the parish, she was suspended and a formal disciplinary hearing set up. Following mediation between the parties she resigned, but then initiated proceedings at an industrial tribunal in 1998 complaining of sexual discrimination, alleging that the church authorities had failed to take similar action against male ministers in similar circumstances. The employment tribunal dismissed the case because of a lack of jurisdiction, and an appeal followed in 2005. The church relied on article IV of the 1921 Act, believing the issue to fall under 'matters spiritual'. However the judgement of the House of Lords did not accept this, and overturned the Court of Session, Employment Appeal Tribunal and Employment Tribunal to hold that for the purposes of the Sex Discrimination Act 1975 a minister of religion was a 'worker'. Clearly, there appears to have been a shift in that the church may no longer enjoy the autonomy that it once did.

43 (1936) SC 625.

44 (1995) SLT 1228.

45 (2005) UKHL 73. See, on this whole topic, J Duddington, *The Church and Employment Law* (Routledge 2022).

The Lutheran Church[46]

Reformation

The Lutheran Church traces it interpretation of the doctrines and way of life of Christianity to the teachings of Martin Luther, and the movements that followed his reforms. It might be said that the starting point of what was subsequently called 'Lutheranism' began in 1517 when Martin Luther called attention to the teaching and practice of the Roman Catholic Church on 'indulgences', with the full or partial grant of the remission of the penalties of sin. His Ninety-Five Theses were propositions that he wished to debate, without the intention of breaking away from the Church itself. He was particularly incensed by the selling of indulgences by the Dominican preacher, Johannes Teztel, who had been authorised to do so by Pope Leo X in order to repay a loan and subsidise the rebuilding of St Peter's basilica in Rome. After defences written by Tetzel of the practice, the focus had shifted from the theology behind indulgences to the question of church authority. This fierce controversy resulted in the excommunication of Luther and his followers as they would not yield to the dictates of the Pope.

Traditionally thought to explicate Luther's teaching, the Augsburg Confession of 1530 gives an insight into how he saw relations between church and state. Article XVI states that 'lawful civil ordinances are good works of God' and so Christians were bound to obey their own governments and laws unless they were contrary to the law of God. This being the case, it was also right for Christians to hold civil office, and the Confession condemned the Anabaptists who forbade their following from holding such offices. Also, noting the tendency of popes and bishops to interfere in civil affairs to protect their interests, the Confession is clear that the power of the Church and civil power must not be confused:

> The power of the Church has its own commission: to teach the Gospel and administer the sacraments. Let it not interfere with the office of another; let it not transfer the kingdoms of this world; let it not abrogate the laws of civil rulers; let it not abolish lawful obedience; let it not interfere with judgments concerning civil ordinances and contracts; let it not prescribe laws to civil rulers concerning the form of the State.

Following the war between the Holy Roman Emperor, Charles V and the Schmalkaldic League (a military alliance of Lutheran princes), the eventual treaty that was signed, the Peace of Augsburg (1555) was significant in that one of the foundational principles (*cuius regio, eius religio*, 'whose realm, his

46 See, in general, John Witte Jr., *Law and Protestantism* (CUP 2002).

religion') allowed rulers to choose between Roman Catholicism and Lutheranism as the official religion of their state. So, the latter became formally established in various German principalities, followed by Sweden and other Scandinavian countries and eventually in North America.

However, though their legal existence was assured, and a clear division had been made in the Confession about secular and ecclesiastical power, the two aspects did not always remain completely separate. The theological controversies that dominated the Lutheran agenda between 1548 and 1577 began to divide Lutheran churches and theologians with increasing intensity, with most of these being on topics where Luther was not altogether clear or where he and his colleague, Philipp Melanchthon, had disagreed. Lutheran political authorities, notably Augustus the Elector of Saxony (1526–1586), with the help of theologians Jakob Andreae and Martin Chemnitz, forced compromises on the disputed points of theology. The resultant Book of Concord 1580, which contained the various Lutheran confessions of faith, was personally sponsored by Augustus, and signed by nearly 30 territories, states and cities in Germany.

Enlightenment

With the European Enlightenment embracing insights from the modern scientific revolution, traditional Christian assumptions were challenged, as was the harmony of reason and revelation. In contrast to medieval scholasticism, which advocated the use of reason but maintained the primacy of revelation, Lutheran theology declared reason to be the key to understanding the will of God and at the same time subordinated revelation. This idea dominated Lutheranism in the second half of the eighteenth century and led to divisions within it. It was against this background that the Prussian ruling house became involved in issues of worship. A Calvinist himself, while most of Prussia was Lutheran, King Frederick William III was convinced that no substantive theological differences separated the two churches and in 1817 directed that both churches should use an identical order of worship. In addition, as the Prussian government had become increasingly centralised, the king sought the same for both Reformed and Lutheran churches. Some accepted this while others fiercely opposed it and were either suppressed or persecuted, many eventually emigrating to the United States. Opposition continued in the reign of Frederick William IV and this led him to declare in 1852 that the union of Lutheran and Reformed churches was only administrative but not doctrinal.

Other monarchs also blurred the lines of the church-state separation. Lutheran ideas were introduced into Scandinavia. Gustav Eriksson Vasa, who had secured Swedish independence from Denmark in the sixteenth century and was eventually elected king of Sweden and Finland, sought to diminish the power of the Catholic Church in Sweden, supporting Lutheran preaching and publications. At his behest Church property was confiscated, and subsequent legislative measures at first curtailed and then ended Catholicism in Sweden. In 1528 Gustav Vasa helped secure the consecration of three Swedish bishops, among whom were two brothers with deep Protestant convictions and who popularised Lutheranism in Sweden. A significant political power in Europe by the seventeenth century, Lutheran's Sweden's king, Gustav II Adolf, entered the Thirty Years' War on the side of the struggling German Protestant states in 1630, and his military victories ensured that the war would not bring ruin to Protestantism. The Treaty of Westphalia (1648) appeared to give Catholic, Reformed and Lutheran Christians equal political and religious rights in the empire, though it has been noted that there were differences of opinion on the subject among historians as to how far this was actually achieved in the Holy Roman Empire afterwards.[47]

Modern Era

Until the end of the First World War, the administrative affairs of the Lutheran churches in Germany were handled by government offices, with the ruler exercising important power as 'presiding bishop'. However, at the end of the war, and with the new constitution of the Weimar Republic providing for the separation of church and state, the Lutheran Church was disestablished. At the same time, the constitution made modest provision of privileges both for the Roman Catholic and Lutheran Churches. Even so, dissatisfaction with the Weimar Republic, the political conservatism of many Lutheran leaders, and Luther's ideas on church and state appeared to facilitate the acceptance of many of the ideas of National Socialism when Adolf Hitler became German chancellor in January 1933. This totalitarian regime exposed a gap in Lutheran theology, where Luther had stressed, as a Christian duty, obedience to government, and had advocated resistance to a tyrannical government only if the preaching of the Gospel was in jeopardy. So when the Nazi government decreed discriminatory laws, many Lutheran theologians believed that it had the authority to do so. This led to a minority of Lutheran Church leaders and theologians to look again at the traditional Lutheran view. The result was the Theological Declaration of Barmen written to help Christians withstand the challenges of the Nazi party and the 'German Christians', a movement that did not see a conflict between Christianity and Nazi ideals.

Following the end of the Second World War, reorganisation took place within the Lutheran Church in Germany, but the division of Germany into East and West states brought its own challenges for the Church with the new East German republic. This society was hostile to Christianity and so Lutherans sought to avoid confrontation with the state even when the latter

47 RG Asch, 'Religious toleration, the Peace of Westphalia and the German territorial estates' (2000) 20(1) Parliaments, Estates and Representation 75–89. DOI: 10.1080/02606755.2000.9522099.

interfered in its spiritual matters (replacing confirmation with a 'youth consecration'). Rather than be confrontational with the state (in contrast with the Roman Catholic Church in communist Poland), East German Lutherans cooperated while affirming the need for the church to be the church. The slogan 'church within socialism' expressed this strategy, although by the late 1970s a rapprochement with the communist regime had begun. Nevertheless, membership of the Church declined significantly, as it did in Denmark, Norway, Sweden and Germany where the Lutheran Church enjoyed privileged status. By the middle of the twentieth century, a gradual process of autonomy from the state has taken place, with the Finnish Church becoming independent of state control in 1969 (though still supported by public funds), the Swedish Church ending its status as a state church in 2000, and a separation of the church from the state in 2017, where parliament previously had exercised a major voice in Church affairs.

Conclusion

In this chapter we have considered Catholic and Protestant approaches to church-state relations. From the earliest years of the Christian Church, we noted efforts to keep secular powers at a distance from the internal organisation of the Church. The boundaries were blurred though when the Pope himself became a temporal ruler in governing the papal states and, as we have seen, the Church itself has intervened in state affairs to protect its own interests. It has lamented at various stages those who have tried to side-line the Church (for example, in France), and has sought to secure its influence in negotiating concordats with various states. The most recent initiative has been to stress the role of papal legates in their mission to countries worldwide. The Church of England, on the other hand, was born of state power in the person of King Henry VIII and has remained allied with the state ever since. While it is involved in the parliamentary legislative process and though there have been calls for disestablishment, it sees itself as both having a degree of autonomy from the state, and in a position whereby it can minister to all, being a national Church. The Calvinist Church of Scotland, though established by parliamentary laws and historically having to struggle for autonomy, is in a position to deal with its own affairs, something which has been validated in recent court cases. Finally, the Lutheran Church, with its division between its ecclesiastical power, has faced its own challenges, not least in terms of how the Church critiques tyrannical civil authority.

In one sense, all of these Christian traditions have faced the same issues; how to relate to the civil authority while being true to the Gospel message they have received and carry forward, what role ought the state have in guaranteeing freedom of religion while not getting involved in spiritual matters, and how a 'state' church relates to or critiques civil society. That 'national' churches are gaining more autonomy from the state or disestablishing may be a sign of the increasing diversity of society to which they wish to respond.

It may also be a response to declining numbers which makes their position as a national church more tenuous, or to a belief that the idea of 'church' and 'state' is no longer plausible in an increasingly secularised society. Certainly, those from Catholic and Protestant perspectives would acknowledge this as a challenge.

Bibliography

Asch RG, 'Religious toleration, the Peace of Westphalia and the German Territorial Estates' (2000) 20(1) Parliaments, Estates and Representation 75–89, doi: 10.1080/02606755.2000.9522099

Connelly R, *Women of the Catholic Resistance in England 1540–1680* (Pentland Press 1997)

Costigane H, 'Catholic Adoption Agencies and "Gay Adopters"' (2008) 161 Law and Justice 98–110

Costigane H, 'Catholic Education in England—What Is to Be Taught?' (2009) 163 Law & Justice 103–9

Costigane H, 'A Protected Rite? Defending the Seal of Confession from Legal Challenge' (2013) 209(4) America 15

Coward B, 'Why Charles I was Executed in 1649' (1998) History Review 32

Croft P, 'The Gunpowder Plot: Pauline Croft Explains the Origins of Bonfire Night by Reconstructing Events 400 Years Ago' (2005) 52 History Review

Duddington J, *The Church and Employment Law* (Routledge 2022)

Gregory VII (Pope) 'Dictatus Papae' 1090 <https://sourcebooks.fordham.edu/source/g7-dictpap.asp>

Haigh C, *English Reformations: Religion, Politics, and Society under the Tudors* (Clarendon Press 1993)

Hastings A, *Church and State: The English Experience* (University of Exeter Press 1991)

Lacey A, *The Cult of King Charles the Martyr* (Boydell Press 2003)

Lunn D, *The Catholic Elizabethans* (Bath, Downside Abbey 1998)

McClain L, *Lest We Be Damned: Practical Innovation and Lived Experience Among Catholics in Protestant England 1559–1642* (Routledge 2004)

Meakin R, 'What are the Implications of Being a Church-Controlled Charity in the Church of England and the Roman Catholic Church?' (2016) 176 Law & Justice 18–38

Papal Encyclicals: Note: The text of encyclicals can be found on the Vatican website (www.vatican.va) and/or at Papal Encyclicals Online (https://papalencyclicals.net)

Affari Vos (1897)

Au Milieu Des Sollicitudes (1892)

Constanti Hungarorum (1893)

Diuturnum (1881)

Etsi Multa (1873)

Iamdudum (1911)

Incredibili (1863)

Meminisse Iuvat

Quod Numquam (1875)

Respicientes (1870)

Spesse Volta (1898)

Une Fois Encore (1907)

Vehementer Nos (1906)

Vix Dum a Nobis (1874)

Rowlands M, 'English Catholics in the Reign of Elizabeth' (2007) History Review 59

Schatz K, Papal Primacy: From its Origins to the Present, Collegeville, Minn (Liturgical Press, 1996)
Seel GE, *The Early Stuart Kings 1603–1642* (Routledge 2001)
Sirico LJ, 'The Trial of Charles I: A Sesquicentennial Reflection' (1999) 16(1) Constitutional Commentary 51
Strauss P, *In Hope of Heaven: English Recusant Prison Writing of the Sixteenth Century* (Peter Lang 1995)
Tanner N, *Decrees of the Ecumenical Councils* (Sheed & Ward 1990) 2 vols
'The Scots' Confession' Bratcher D (ed) (2018) <www.crivoice.org/creedscots.html>
Whateley CA, *Bought and Sold for English Gold? Explaining the Union of 1707* (Tuckwell Press 2001)
Williamson JA, *The Tudor Age* (D. McKay 1961)
Wingfield-Stratford E, *King Charles the Martyr* (Hollis & Carter 1950)
Witte J Jr., *Law and Protestantism* (CUP 2002)

Part Four

Catholic and Protestant Approaches to Particular Areas of Law

This part moves as it were from the general to the particular where the thrust of these chapters is to consider specific areas of law and to ask to what extent they were affected by the change in legal thought brought about by the Reformation. This is one area where the selection of topics for this book has been difficult, as it would have been possible to have included many other areas too and the final chapter, on charities and social welfare, could have been greatly expanded. As it stands it serves to some degree as a conclusion to the book in which various themes that appeared earlier are brought together.

Readers will also note changes in treatment in different chapters. Chapter 9, on marriage and education law, is mainly focused on post-Reformation developments, given that the impact of the Reformation on medieval marriage law is dealt with in Chapters 2 and 4. The introduction to this chapter is also valuable in giving an account of 'subtraction stories' being accounts of things that the historical churches used to do where their impact has been reduced over time. Chapter 10, on equity and conscience, is mainly focused on how equity developed pre-Reformation, as of course this is the significant period, and should also be read in conjunction with Chapter 7 where Calvinist thought on conscience is explored. Chapter 11 traces in fascinating detail the train of Christian engagement with human rights, with the concentration being on the post-Reformation period but beginning with some thoughts on what went on before. Chapter 12, on criminal law, highlights the way in which the Reformation affected, or did not affect, legal thought on criminal law and procedure and then we conclude with charities and social welfare as noted earlier.

DOI: 10.4324/9780429264115-12

9 Marriage Law and Education Law

Russell Sandberg

From 'Subtraction Stories' to Confounding Realities

When law and religion writers comment on marriage law and education law in England and Wales they typically recount how these laws still show evidence of their Christian past but point out that, although the Christian fingerprints are still visible on the law, they have somewhat faded. The account given is typically an example of what Charles Taylor has called 'subtraction stories':[1] accounts of things that the historical churches used to do where their impact has been reduced over time. In most of these subtraction stories, no distinction is made between the different branches of Christianity. Rather, the perceived declining social and legal power of the established Church of England is considered to be synonymous with the perceived decline of Christianity. And the underlying assumption if not argument is that the Christian hold on such laws will and should weaken further.

These subtraction stories fit in with the dominant narrative of post-Enlightenment secularisation. They are part of the prevalent background assumptions that Robert Gordon referred to as 'evolutionary functionalism'. Evolutionary functionalism lives up to its name. It describes the acceptance of two interlocking ideas. The first is the acceptance of the evolutionary idea that all societies follow 'an objective, determine progressive social evolutionary path' in a way that is 'natural (in the sense that some version of it will happen in every society unless "artificial" constraints force a deviation)'.[2] Although 'different generations have described this evolutionary processes somewhat differently',[3] the narrative employed is that of evolutionary progress.[4] The

1 C Taylor, *A Secular Age* (Harvard UP 2007) 22.

2 RW Gordon, *Taming the Past: Essays on Law in History and History in Law* (CUP 2017) 225.

3 Later Gordon noted that: 'Nobody ever thought this modal form was universal: some societies have deviated into fascism, others into communism; still others reverted to theocracy or virulent ethnic nationalism, and many have simply stagnated in traditional or primitive phases': RW Gordon, '"Critical Legal Histories Revisited": A Response' (2012) 37 Law & Social Inquiry 200, 200–1.

4 On which see further, P Stein, *Legal Evolution: The Story of An Idea* (CUP 1980).

DOI: 10.4324/9780429264115-13

second idea is the acceptance of the Durkheimian functionalist understanding of societies as having universal and specific needs which 'operate both as pressures and constraints' and of being functionally differentiated into different social institutions which seek to perform and manage these needs. Gordon's argument is that this pervasive evolutionary functionalism has turned both 'law' and 'society' into 'ahistorical, universal types'.[5] He noted that while lawyers 'once played a moderately important role in actually writing these histories', now legal writing 'is more likely just to assume that some objective, generally understood process of development has been working away in the background, and to leave the actual details of the process to vague implication'.[6] This narrative of progress is not only implicitly accepted, it is also not questioned. Evolutionary functionalism is so entrenched that it is almost unnoticeable.

In my recent work, I have developed Gordon's work further to suggest that the common law is actually characterised by 'entropic complexity' rather than evolutionary functionalism.[7] Developing ideas from social entropy theory, chaos theory and complexity theory,[8] 'entropic complexity' also does what it says on the tin. The concept of entropy denotes the gradual decline into disorder. The concept dates back to the second law of thermodynamics and the development of modern thermodynamics in the nineteenth century.[9] It underscores how a lack of order and predictability is the norm. An approach based upon entropy would see chaos—uncertainty, nuance and flexibility—as normal. This reverses the usual approach to the common law which

> assumes that although the law may appear to be irrational, chaotic and particularistic, if one digs deep enough and knows that one is looking for, then it will soon become evident that the law is an internally coherent and unified system of rules.[10]

Complexity theory underscores this by showing that entropy and chaos is the direction of travel. The effect of entropy and chaos is the development of

5 LF Edwards, 'The History in "Critical Legal Studies"' (2012) 37 Law & Social Inquiry 187.
6 Gordon (n 2) 227.
7 R Sandberg, *Subversive Legal History: A Manifesto for the Future of Legal Education* (Routledge 2021) 123–35.
8 For examples of work applying these theories to law see respectively D Collins, 'The Chaos Machine: The WTO in a Social Entropy Model of the World Trading System' (2014) 34(2) Oxford Journal of Legal Studies 353; RE Scott, 'Chaos Theory and the Justice Paradox' (1993) 35 William & Mary Law Review 329; and the essays in JTEW Murray and S Wheatley (eds), *Complexity Theory and Law: Mapping an Emergent Jurisprudence* (Routledge 2019) together with the response by R Nobles and D Schiff, 'Taking the Complexity of Complex Systems Seriously' (2020) 83(3) Modern Law Review 661.
9 KD Bailey, *Social Entropy Theory* (University of New York Press 1990) 52.
10 D Sugarman, 'Legal Theory, the Common Law Mind and the Making of the Textbook Tradition' in William Twinning (ed), *Legal Theory and the Common Law* (Blackwell 1986) 26.

complex systems. As Jamie Murray, Thomas E Webb and Steven Wheatley have commented:

> Complexity theory understands law as an emergent, self-organising system in which an interactive network of many parts—actors, institutions and 'systems' operate with no overall guiding hand, giving rise to complex collective behaviours that can be observed in patterns of law communications.[11]

Law, like any other complex system, hides its own chaos behind an image of stability. The role of the legal scholar is, therefore, to uncover the chaotic and unpredictable behaviour that is otherwise hidden. 'Entropic complexity' can be placed in opposition to the progress narrative provided by evolutionary functionalism since complexity theory 'is opposed to final destinations and only provides descriptions and analysis suitable for the moment'.[12] This raises the question of what the English and Welsh law on marriage and education would look like if the base assumptions of evolutionary functionalism were replaced by those of entropic complexity. This chapter argues that this would reveal a more nuanced and contradictory picture of the history of the law which would subvert common assumptions about the current law and our expectations of the future. Exploring the development of these areas of law over time, with particular reference to their interactions with the Christian churches, debunks any linear account of a secular 'progress'. In place of the usual subtraction stories, that highlight the perceived decline of influence of the churches, the following presents a confounding reality whereby legal change is often the result of pragmatic and unpredictable compromise and whereby the letter of the law often exists in different reality than the social practice.

The following adopts a chronological periodisation only to question it and to show the dissonance between the actual changes in education and marriage law and the prevalent secularisation narrative. It simultaneously maps the main developments in relation to both marriage and education law. This is itself innovative in that these two areas of law are often considered separately or as part of the broader history of church-state relations.[13] In so doing, it demonstrates that the direction of travel has been far from linear, definitely not inevitable and absolutely not irreversible. It presents the current law not as a stump of a once magnificent tree that has been chopped away at over time but rather as the product of historical quirk based on grubby compromises

11 Ibid 3.

12 Ibid 5. See also R Nobles and D Schiff, 'Taking the Complexity of Complex Systems Seriously' (2020) 83(3) Modern Law Review 66. The debate between the two accounts is discussed in R Sandberg, *Subversive Legal History: A Manifesto for the Future of Legal Education* (Routledge 2021) 130–33.

13 See Chapter 8 for a detailed exploration of this.

and an unwillingness if not downright refusal to consider comprehensive reform. This in itself recasts the debate as to reform. Seeing the present law as being the often accidental consequence of tweaks that were politically possible at particular times, rather than as some received wisdom passed down and 'improved' as societies advanced, makes the need for reform not only more compelling but also means that such reform could and should be more radical. Such a recasting highlights the benefits of a historical approach to law provided that such an approach rejects and challenges prevalent evolutionary functionalist thinking. This subversive use of legal history actually reflects the purpose of the historical study of law as purported by Frederic Maitland in a letter to Dicey in which he wrote:

> The only direct utility of legal history . . . lies in the lesson that each generation has an enormous power of shaping its own law. I don't think that the study of legal history would make men fatalists; I doubt that it would make them conservatives. I am sure that it would free them from superstitions and teach them that they have free hands.[14]

The Sixteenth Century

In *Law and Religion*, I suggested that the relationship between law and religion in England had developed through four broad overlapping but conceptually distinct phases: first, the temporal-spiritual partnership which followed the Norman Conquest; second, the era of discrimination and intolerance which resulted from the Reformation of the sixteenth century; third, the epoch of toleration which followed from Glorious Revolution of 1688–1689; and fourth, the current age of positive religious freedom which may be dated back to the Human Rights Act 1998.[15] There, and indeed generally, the English Reformation is considered to be a watershed moment in the history of the regulation of religion.[16] As Elton has commented, England 'wore her Reformation with a difference':[17] the divorce from Rome in the 1530s under Henry VIII was not a religious upheaval that required political and constitutional reconstruction, it was a political and constitutional act that led in time to religious upheaval. The effects of the sixteenth century and the ousting of the Roman Catholic Church

14 Frederic W Maitland, 'Maitland to AV Dicey, c. July 1896' quoted in CHS Fifoot, *Frederic William Maitland* (Harvard UP 1971) 143.

15 R Sandberg, *Law and Religion* (CUP 2011) Ch. 2. This drew on N Doe, 'National Identity, the Constitutional Tradition and the Structures of Law on Religion in the United Kingdom' in *Religions in European Union Law* (Proceedings of the European Consortium of Church and State Research, Luxembourg 1997) 93, 109–10.

16 And in the development of English law generally see R Sandberg, *A Historical Introduction to English Law: Genesis of the Common Law* (CUP 2023) chapter 7.

17 GR Elton, 'The Reformation in England' in G R Elton (ed), *The New Cambridge Modern History, vol 2: The Reformation, 1520–1559* (2nd edn, CUP 1990) 262.

with its authority in Rome and its replacement with the Anglican Church of England continues to shape or at least underpin much of what I have called 'religion law'; that is the rules developed by the state that affects religious groups and individuals. The Reformation shaped the legal status (and later the religious persuasion) of the English Church: a flurry of Reformation statutes saw the King become recognised as 'the only supreme head in earth of the Church of England'.[18] And this meant that other forms of religion were now not only illegal but treasonous. However, contrary to the schema I presented in *Law and Religion*, the Reformation had little effect on the development of marriage or education law.[19]

Marriage

In relation to marriage, the church courts had exclusive jurisdiction from the mid-twelfth century over marriage and divorce, applying Roman Catholic canon law. Despite the divorce from Rome, the radical reform of marriage which occurred on the Continent was not replicated in England: the existing canon law of the Church continued to apply until it was replaced unless it was 'contrariant or repugnant to the King's prerogative royal, or the customs, laws and statutes of this realm'.[20] Although there were some minor amendments, chiefly through the enactment of the Canons Ecclesiastical 1603–1604, it was not until the Marriage Act 1753 that significant reform occurred. And, as we will see, it was that Act that consolidated the monopoly of the Anglican Church—the reformation statutes had little to do with it. Marriage had developed as something that the churches did. It was not really the concern of the state. The Reformation identified church with state more explicitly but did not change the practice. This was largely because the practice was, if not in the shadow of the law, at arm's length away from it.

Education

The same was true in relation to education. Primary and secondary education grew out of the work of the churches. Literacy was for centuries tied up with the church.[21] The earliest schools that we know of, dating back to the Anglo-Saxon period, were linked to the church as were the Universities at Oxford and Cambridge, which were established in the early medieval period. However, as Elwyn Jones and Wynne Roderick pointed out, 'it is mistaken to

18 Act of Supremacy 1534.

19 For discussion of how religion interacts with these two areas of law and the need for reform see respectively R Sandberg, *Religion and Marriage Law: The Need for Reform* (Bristol UP 2021) and R Sandberg, *Religion in Schools: Learning Lessons from Wales* (Anthem Press 2022). See also Chapters 2 and 4 which deal in more detail with marriage law and the Reformation.

20 Submission of the Clergy Act 1533.

21 GE Jones and GW Roderick, *A History of Education in Wales* (U of Wales P 2003) 5.

regard late medieval education as the province only of the monasteries and the church—there was sufficient demand to foster the creation of grammar schools'.[22] Some of these grammar schools were created independently of the church, sometimes being closely tied with a university or with a borough corporation. Again, the Reformation changed very little in terms of law—largely because law rarely if at all concerned itself with education. Education, like marriage, was something left to what we would today call the voluntary sector.

The Seventeenth and Eighteenth Centuries

In *Law and Religion*, I suggested that the Glorious Revolution of 1688–1689 could be regarded as the beginning of a new phase in the regulation of religion. It could be regarded as the starting point of limited and piecemeal toleration. I argued that over the course of the seventeenth, eighteenth, nineteenth and twentieth centuries, most of the legal disabilities against alternative religions were removed. I stressed, however, that process was slow, piecemeal, uneven and sometimes contradictory. Reference to the law on education and marriage law underlines my comments about the process being uneven and contradictory. Indeed, it suggests that toleration came much later than the seventeenth century in relation to education and marriage law. The experiences during the centuries following the Reformation were notably different in these two areas and neither saw a process of toleration.

Education

In terms of education, the fusion of church and state had not led to any form of monopoly on education by the state or the state church and so there was nothing to relax. Instead, the demand for education gradually grew in the centuries that followed but it remained within the voluntary sector. The churches played a crucial role in this but they did not monopolise it. From the very start, education took various different forms: from guilds that were developed in many trades, to dissenting academies which were unofficially set up following the Reformation to Sunday Schools and later on to developments that took place under the auspices of the Poor Law.[23] There were a variety of different types of schools. While the wealthy educated their children at home, grammar schools catered for the sons of the middle classes. For the majority, however, there was no formal education with children typically working alongside their parents in agriculture or factories. There were some attempts to provide for elementary education (often now referred to as primary education).

22 Ibid 13.
23 About three quarters of all working class children were registered in Sunday Schools run by both the Church of England and other churches: W Cornish et al., *Law and Society in England 1750–1950* (2nd edn, Hart 2019) 420.

These ranged from 'dame' or 'private venture' schools staffed by women to charity schools founded by the Society for Promoting Christian Knowledge to voluntary day schools established on both faith and non-denominational bases.[24] The motivation for the provision of education 'remained religious, a matter for philanthropy rather than the state'.[25] The bulk of educational provision that had been built up before the nineteenth century, then, 'had been built up by charitable endeavour and private initiative'.[26] By contrast, 'central and local government played no significant role in the running of schools'.

Marriage

By contrast, in marriage law, the centuries following the Reformation saw the exact opposite of toleration. The Marriage Act 1753 gave the established Church a monopoly. It provided the foundations of the modern law on marriage. It imposed the canon law requirements upon all weddings except for Jews and Quakers: all marriages were to take the form of a public ceremony in the parish church at which a clergyman would officiate according to authorised rites and it required that the marriage be preceded by banns or licence. Breach of any of these requirements, which had previously made a marriage irregular, would now render it void. Although it was not the first attempt to regularise the performance and registration of marriage, the Marriage Act 1753 is often regarded to be a pivotal moment providing certainty as to who was married and stopping marriages taking place in ways that the state was unaware of. This was problematic because marital status bestowed certain legal rights and social attitudes at the time saw children born out of wedlock as being illegitimate. Although it has now been questioned whether the Act largely reinforced existing social conventions rather than stamping out a serious and prevalent problem of marriages being conducted in various and unusual ways,[27] nevertheless, the effect of the legislation was clear. The emphasis upon marriage taking place in a religious building open to the public continues to underscore the current law. The Act imposed uniformity: everyone had to marry according to the rites of the Church of England except Quakers and Jews to whom the Act did not apply but whose weddings were subsequently held to be valid by the courts. The monopolisation of the Church of England over marriage, therefore, was not the result of the Reformation but was only formally consolidated by the 1753 Act, though it is likely that this reinforced common social practices.

24 Ibid 411.
25 GE Jones and GW Roderick, *A History of Education in Wales* (U of Wales P 2003) 27.
26 Cornish et al. (n 23) 411.
27 R Probert, *Marriage Law and Practice in the Long Eighteenth Century* (CUP 2009).

The Nineteenth Century

Significant reforms to both areas of the law took place in the nineteenth century. Again, these changes fail to completely observe and therefore question the general template of ongoing toleration. In *Law and Religion*, I described how the ad hoc recognition of alternative religion led by the nineteenth century to some evidence of a distancing between church and state and the Church of England developing a greater level of autonomy as a result.

Marriage

On the face of it, there is some evidence of marriage law following this toleration template referred to earlier. The Marriage Act 1836 made provision for 'civil marriage' permitting marriages to take place in register offices following a civil ceremony in the presence of a registrar and witnesses. That Act also provided that buildings registered as a place of religious worship could be registered for solemnising marriages therein. This was a key component of the piecemeal toleration of other forms of religion. The foundations of the modern law of marriage were now fully laid out and the law had been built around the historic framework of Church of England weddings without any thought of principle.

Yet, the picture is more complex than that as the research of Rebecca Probert has underlined. Her work argues that how the 1836 Act is 'viewed may differ depending on whether it is seen against the backdrop of the earlier restrictions or the diversity of England and Wales today'.[28] For Probert, there is a need to question the common perceptions about the 1836 Act whereby it is 'seen as an important liberalizing measure' and the 'story told about it has generally been a positive one in that it has been recognised the religious (and irreligious) diversity of nineteenth-century England and Wales'. Probert notes that there is 'a tendency in at least some of the scholarship to exaggerate the extent to which the 1836 Act liberalised the law' in that many 'imply that it allowed couples to be married in any chapel and by any minister of religion'. As she noted, 'the exacting criteria for places of worship to be registered for weddings meant that many were not'. The Act required a separate building for all but Catholics and 20 householders had to certify that it was their usual place or worship. Furthermore, it was not until the Marriage Act 1898 that registered places of worship were permitted to appoint their own 'authorised person' in place of a registrar. And even today 'many registered places of worship have not appointed their own authorised person and remain dependent on a registrar attending and registering any weddings that take place there'. She noted that, above all else, how any given couple could marry depended very much on local factors.

28 R Probert, *Tying the Knot: The Formation of Marriage 1836–2020* (CUP 2021) Ch. 1.

Probert's work has also nuanced other aspects of the common understanding of the 1836 Act. She argues that our 'conception of the 1836 Act has to be understood against the background of the various proposals for reform that were put forward between 1819 and 1835'. She suggests that the complaints of Protestant dissenters before the Act focused on the 'compulsory conformity' to the rites of the Church of England. Rather than wanting the right to solemnise marriages themselves, they originally just wanted to omit part of the liturgy. This was reflected in the Act itself, which said nothing about who could conduct ceremonies (what was required was the presence of the registrar) and included prescribed words which made the ceremonies structurally similar to Church of England services. In practice, dissenters could marry in places of worship of other denominations. Probert further argued that the category of civil marriage has been misunderstood. The term 'civil' was not defined in the Act and the register office weddings were not envisaged as being the default. Rather, the 'option of getting married in a register office was intended for that small subcategory of dissenters who regarded marriage as a civil contract'. Moreover, civil was not originally synonymous with being secular. It was not until the Marriage and Registration Act 1856 that religious content became prohibited in civil ceremonies.

Notwithstanding Probert's work, the Marriage Act 1836 remains a watershed moment albeit one that needs to be placed within its context. The 1836 Act consolidated state control on marriage. This is shown in the way that rather than being exempt, Quaker and Jewish weddings were now incorporated into the legal framework. However, the Act did not sever the monopolistic assumptions that had previously been consolidated by the 1753 Act. Indeed, the legal requirement in the 1753 Act that marriages were to occur in the parish church became understood as creating a legal right for parishioners—and nowadays those with a qualifying connection[29]—to marry in the Church of England parish church,[30] with Church of England clergy being afforded conscience clauses to refuse to solemnise marriages of parishioners in certain circumstances such as the former spouse is still living.[31] So entrenched and interlinked were the law of the church and the law of the state regarding marriage that when the Church of England was disestablished in Wales in 1920,[32] provision was made that this would not affect marriage law and that in relation to marriage law the term Church of England would still be understood to include reference to the Church in Wales.[33] And even when the Matrimonial Causes Act 1857 transferred jurisdiction over matrimonial causes from the church courts of the

29 Church of England Marriage Measure 2008. Similar provision has been made in relation to the Church in Wales: Marriage (Wales) Act 2010.

30 Cf. N Doe, *The Legal Framework of the Church of England: A Critical Study in a Comparative Context* (Clarendon Press 1996) 359–60.

31 Matrimonial Causes Act 1965 s 8(2).

32 Welsh Church Act 1914.

33 Welsh Church (Temporalities) Act 1919 s 6; Marriage Act 1949 s 78(2).

Church of England to the common law courts, section 22 of the Act stipulated that the common law courts should continue to apply the same principles as the church courts had done. It is true that differences between church law and state law on marriage have increased. Most notably, although the prohibited degrees of consanguinity (prohibited relationships by blood) and affinity (prohibited relationships by marriage) have a clear religious base, a divergence has arisen between those rules of the church and those of the state leading to the enactment of a conscience clause permitting clergy to refuse to solemnise the marriage of those whose marriage would have been void before the state law changed.[34] However, the use of such conscience clauses underlines how, in the words of Rivers, the law on marriage remains 'compatible with a recognisably Christian view' with the church remaining 'free to teach a higher ideal, to which Christians and others can aspire'.[35]

Education

The nineteenth century also saw significant change in relation to education with state involvement deepening throughout the period. Advances were often caused by religious rivalry. From 1833 grants to support the construction of school buildings were provided but applications had to be channelled through a religious society and had to have at least half the cost raised privately.[36] From 1839, these were supervised by a special Education Committee of the Privy Council which imposed school inspections as a precondition of funding. Government expenditure on education soared from £31,000 in 1841 to £813,000 by 1861 and around four-fifths of that money went to the Church of England. In the 1860s, in addition to building costs, payment was made to schools on the basis of 4 shillings per child who attended and 8 shillings more if the child passed certain examinations.[37] Such government funding now made the continued interplay between education and religion more controversial. Some dissenting groups did not seek state aid and by 1815 there were over 350 independent dissenter schools.[38] And the issue of what religion was to be taught in schools and whether parents could withdraw their children from religious instruction arose for the first time.

The Education Committee resisted the call for Church of England doctrine to be taught in all schools that had state funding but unsuccessfully attempted to impose a conscience clause for parents to withdraw their children from

34 Marriage Act 1949, s 5A (amended by the Marriage (Prohibited Degrees of Relationship) Act 1986, s 3); Marriage Act 1949 (Remedial) Order 2006.

35 J Rivers, 'Is English Law Christian?' in Nick Spencer (ed), *Religion and Law* (Theos 2012) 143, 149.

36 Cornish et al. (n 23) 413–14.

37 This was intended to incentivise teachers whose salaries would be dependent upon exam performance but in the short term Government expenditure fell as many failed the tests: ibid 421.

38 Ibid 415.

religious instruction. This matter led to litigation in the 1840s.[39] The result was that 'conscience clauses became usual in any case where the foundation document did not positively require the teaching of a particular dogma'.[40] The turning point came with the Elementary Education Act 1870, often known as the 'Forster Act' after William Edward Forster who was responsible for education in Gladstone's Government. The Act established local school boards in areas where there were insufficient voluntary schools. Their function was to build and manage schools to fill up the gaps in the system provided by the denominations and charities to ensure that education was provided up to the age of 13. The Forster Act, therefore, 'saw a move from state subsidiary of voluntary education to state supplementation of voluntary education'.[41] It proved contentious amongst religious groups: while the Church of England 'wished to preserve and even to extend its grip on education; the Non-conformists fiercely opposed any additional financial support for church schools'.[42] The question of religious teaching 'dominated' the passage of the Bill through Parliament.[43] Parliamentarians considered whether the Act should require compulsory religious instruction, whether it should 'not be used or directed in favour of or against the distinctive tenets of any religious denomination' and whether there should be a conscience clause allowing a right to withdraw from this.[44] In the end a compromise was reached by what became known as the 'Cowper-Temple clause' (named after the compromise put forward by Liberal MP William Cowper-Temple) that 'no religious catechism or religious formulary distinctive of any particular denomination' was to be taught in these new schools.[45] This proved contentious with Disraeli criticising the compromise on the basis that there should be 'freedom of religious teaching'.[46] The 'Cowper-Temple clause' limited how denominational religious instruction in the new schools could be but did not mean that schools could not teach their religious ethos. Forster himself noted that the objection to catechisms and formularies rested 'not so much on account of the actual words but because the putting them in the hands of children appeared to be like claiming those children as belonging to a particular Church'.[47]

39 *Attorney-General v Cullum* [1842] 62 ER 948; *Re The King's Grammar School, Warwick* [1845] 41 ER 747; *Re Ilminster Free School* [1858] 44 ER 109.

40 Cornish et al. (n 23) 418.

41 Ibid 422.

42 G Elwyn Jones and GW Roderick, *A History of Education in Wales* (U of Wales P 2003) 79.

43 Cornish et al. (n 23) 422.

44 See the House of Commons discussion at Committee stage: HC Hansard (30 June 1870) columns 1236–63.

45 Elementary Education Act 1870, section 14(2).

46 HC Hansard (30 June 1870) column 1262.

47 Quoted in J Murphy, *The Education Act 1870: Text and Commentary* (David & Charles 1973) 61.

Further safeguards were provided in the Act, allowing parents to withdraw their children from activities that fell outside the clause such as school prayers and scripture lessons.[48] Section 7 stated that for the new public elementary schools, it would not be a condition that the child attends or does not attend 'any Sunday School or any place of worship'. It would also not be a requirement that 'he shall attend any religious observance or any instruction in religious subjects in the school or elsewhere' and that he may be withdrawn from this observation or instruction by his parent. It was stated that the time or times of religious observance or instruction should 'be either at the beginning or at the end or at the beginning and the end' of the school day so that 'any scholar may be withdrawn by his parent from such observance or instruction without forfeiting any of the other benefits of the school'. Parents could also withdraw their children from attending the 'school on any day exclusively set apart for religious observance by the religious body to which his parent belongs'. Inspectors would not inquire into instruction on religious subjects.

The splits caused by these provisions had a significant political effect and were to be far-reaching. The situation was worsened by the fact that the Act only applied to the new elementary schools which were only built where there was no existing sufficient provision and by the fact that a grace period was provided to allow churches to set up new schools before the new system came into effect.[49] As Anthony Howard noted:

> The result, inevitably, was a typically British compromise—or more bluntly, muddle—in which some parents could choose between secular and denominational education while others, mainly in rural villages, had no choice but to send their children to schools in which the dogmas of the Established Church formed a specific part of the curriculum[50]

These nineteenth-century developments culminating in the Forster Act saw the state take an interest in education for the first time and attempt to bring it within the purview of state law. It can therefore be compared as the education equivalent of the reformation legislation or indeed the Marriage Act 1753. However, the Forster Act did not lead to anything like the monopolisation of the Church of England that occurred under those other two developments. It was also not an act of toleration or of secularisation. Rather, it was an example of the state working alongside the existing provision provided mostly by the churches. Yet, this pragmatic response was never completely stable. Both marriage and education law were the object of significant legislation in the mid-twentieth century but while the Marriage Act 1949 largely consolidated

48 GE Jones and GW Roderick, *A History of Education in Wales* (U of Wales P 2003) 79.
49 Cornish et al. (n 23) 422.
50 Anthony Howard, *RAB: The Life of R A Butler* (Jonathan Cape 1987) 111.

the existing law, the education legislation was to prove much more controversial. As Howard commented, following the Forster Act:

> The seeds for the last great battle fought on behalf of the historical forces of Dissent in Britain had been sown. So firmly were they planted that they defied the successive efforts of Governments of differing political complexions over the next seventy years to uproot them

The Twentieth Century

In *Law and Religion* I highlighted the twentieth century as being when the latest phase in the history of the English regulation of religion occurred, though I debated whether the change was attributable to the mid-century development of international human rights regimes or whether it originated from the domesticalisation of those rights, largely by dint of the Human Rights Act 1998. Regardless of precisely when it occurred, I identified a legal move towards recognising religious freedom as a human right and noted that this meant that legal recognition and regulation was based on the equal treatment of all forms of religion or belief rather than upon tolerating religions other than the established church. I noted that the movement to this stage was by no means complete but noted that the new religion law of the late twentieth and early twenty-first century mostly followed this template. The new laws on discrimination epitomised this by outlawing discrimination on grounds of religion or belief and providing exceptions to variously worded beneficiaries that were open to religious groups. This shift was also seen in criminal law when the old offence of blasphemy—tied up with the idea that the state identification with religion rendered blasphemy akin to treason—was superseded by offences of stirring up religious hatred. Although, as these two examples show, there remained a question as to whether protection was afforded to non-religious beliefs as clearly intended by human rights treaties that spoke of 'religion and belief', nevertheless it was notable that protection was now given to the right of religious freedom in a way that moved away from toleration. Once again, however, reference to marriage law and education law does not provide evidence of this shift; once again, the picture is much more muddied.

Marriage

In terms of marriage law, the twentieth century saw comparatively little change. The Marriage Act 1949 consolidated the much older law and did not readjust the legal framework on getting married. It differentiates between marriages solemnised according to the rites of the Church of England/Church in Wales and marriages otherwise solemnised. This second category of marriages otherwise solemnised includes (1) civil marriages in a register office or in approved premises; (2) marriages 'according to the usages of the Society of Friends'; (3) marriages 'between a man and a woman professing the Jewish religion according to the usages of the Jews'; and (4) marriages in any place of worship registered under the Places of Worship Registration Act 1855 and section 41 of the Marriage Act 1949. All religions, other than the three specifically named in the Act, fall under this last category. They can therefore conduct lawful marriages provided that their buildings are registered and there is a registrar or authorised person present. Under section 43 of the Marriage Act 1949, an authorised person (such as the minister) can be appointed by the governing body or trustees of the building provided that their details are then authorised to the registrar general and to the superintendent registrar of the registration district in which the building is situated.

The fact that three religious groups are specifically named in the legislation has led to some confusion.[51] However, there is no 'gap' in the Marriage Act 1949 for religious groups other than the three mentioned. The problem is not that other religious marriages cannot be legally recognised under the Act.[52] It is rather that the requirements required for such recognition indirectly discriminate against some religions: the requirements that the wedding must be inside a registered place of worship and that a prescribed choice of words must be used do not fit with some religious traditions. By contrast, there is a 'gap' in terms of non-religious beliefs. Weddings conducted by belief organisations cannot be legally binding in their own right. Couples who have such weddings are not married in the eyes of the law unless and until they also undergo a civil ceremony. The Marriage Act 1949, therefore, remains an example of a piece of legislation reflecting toleration. It begins from the assumption that Church of England weddings are the norm; an assumption that is false sociologically. While in 1900 religious ceremonies accounted for 85 percent of all marriages and were 49 percent of all marriages by the late 1970s, by 2017 only 22 percent of all marriages were religious ceremonies, the lowest percentage on record, with civil marriages having outnumbered religious marriages every year since 1992 when civil weddings in approved premises were legalised.

Education

By contrast, in terms of education law, the twentieth century saw significant reform but contrary to the 'subtraction stories' often told about the perceived secularisation of the law, education reform actually clarified, consolidated and then reinforced the hold of Christianity. There were three major reforms in the twentieth century: the Education Act 1902, the Education Act 1944 (often known as the Butler Act) and the Education Reform 1988. The Education Act 1902 is often overlooked but brought about significant structural change. It replaced the school boards with local education authorities (LEAs) and

51 Law Commission, *Getting Married: A Consultation Paper on Weddings Law* (Consultation Paper 247, 2020) para 5.25 et seq.

52 See further R Sandberg, *Religion and Marriage Law: The Need for Reform* (Bristol UP 2021).

brought the voluntary schools 'under the control of the LEAs'.[53] These were mainly church schools and mainly associated with the Church of England. Such schools were now supported by the rates and in return LEAs appointed a third of the managers/governors of the school.[54] This meant that 'in return for a modest surrender of independence they had acquired financial security'.[55] The 1902 Act therefore formally recognised the 'dual system' whereby 'denominational schools run (but no longer wholly paid for) by the Churches lived cheek-by-jowl with schools both administered and supervised by the State'.[56] The passage of the Act witnessed 'a great deal of Nonconformist antagonism' in a way that made clear that further reform would be politically controversial.[57] It also led to civil disobedience from some dissenters who refused to pay their rates knowing that they would fund the Church of England school.

The only concession was made in the legislation was the 'Kenyon-Slaney clause' (named after William Kenyon-Slaney MP): section 7(6) which provided that religious education in schools not provided by the state was to be in accordance with the trust deed and was to be under the control of the by the managers/governors of the school unless the trust deed specified differently. Section 4(2) provided a further conscience clause allowing withdrawal from religious instruction on a basis similar to under the Forster Act, though references to the beginning or end of the school day were omitted and instead it was stated that 'the times for religious worship or any lesson on a religious subject shall be conveniently arranged for the purpose of allowing the withdrawal of any scholar therefrom'. Section 4(1) of the Act provided that 'no pupil shall, on grounds of religious belief, be excluded or placed in an inferior position' but relaxed the Forster Act ban on the use of religious catechisms. The 1902 Act stated that it did

> not require that any particular form of religious instruction or worship or any religious catechism which is distinctive to any particular denomination shall or shall not be taught, used or practiced in any school, college or hostel aided but not provided by the council.

It then went on to say, however, that:

> no catechism or formulary distinctive of any particular religious denomination shall be taught in any school, college or hostel so provided except in cases where the council, at the request of parents of scholars, at such times and under such conditions as the council think desirable, allow

53 Ibid 450. Some funding had previously been provided under the Voluntary Schools Act 1897.

54 Education Act 1902, section 6(2).

55 Cornish et al. (n 23) 450.

56 Anthony Howard, *RAB: The Life of R A Butler* (Jonathan Cape 1987) 112.

57 Cornish et al. (n 23) 451.

> any religious instruction to be given in the school, college or hostel otherwise than at the cost of the council: Provided that, in the exercise of this power, no unfair preference shall be shown to any religious denomination

Further legislation followed, particularly the Education Act 1918 which raised the school leaving age further and removed all fees, but these did not affect the rules applying to religious instruction and worship. English law drew a pragmatic compromise whereby the material distinction was not between religious and non-religious schools but between those who were provided by the LEA and those that were not. Schools outside of local authority control were completely run by the churches and in some areas this remained the only school available. There was therefore a certain disconnect between the letter of the law and the social reality. Furthermore, the letter of the law was not precise. Parental choice was respected by means of a conscience clause but the nature of religious instruction remained undefined. Perhaps this reflected the ubiquity and dominance of Christianity in general and the Church of England as the Established Church in particular and so there was simply no need to explain what was meant by religion. However, the messiness of the position underlined a feeling of unfinished business. And so legislation on education in the 1940s sought to clarify and change the law to reflect the idea that society had changed. The effect, however, was similar to that in weddings law in that the 1940s legislation consolidated and entrenched the historical position of the churches.

The Education Act 1944 renamed the Board of Education to become the Ministry of Education and differentiated between primary, secondary and further education, making LEAs responsible for ensuring that secondary education would be free and universally provided. It ushered in the tripartite system of education of grammar, secondary modern and technical schools. The Act also revolutionised both the position of the voluntary church schools that existed alongside the state schools and the teaching of religion in both types of school. Prior to the Act, the ban on teaching by catechism only applied to those schools completely run by local authorities. As Butler himself noted in his autobiography, voluntary schools which were mostly run by the churches, 'gave the religious instruction of the Church to which they belonged, while local authority schools gave religious instruction unconnected with the formulary or beliefs of any particular Church'.[58] Moreover, many areas were what he called 'single-school' areas where the Church of England school was the only school available and 'non-conformists naturally regretted sending their children to a school which taught the catechism of the Church of England'. Yet, Butler's reforms would strengthen rather than weaken the position of the Church of England. It has been noted that under the Butler Act 'the role of

58 Lord Butler, *The Art of the Possible: The Memoirs of Lord Butler* (Revised edn, Penguin 1973) 98.

Anglicanism within education was not only secured but enlarged'.[59] Butler saw the 1902 Act as having damaged both the Conservative Party and the Church of England and so the Act that he would be remembered for was 'an attempt to bring Church and state back together and reverse the effects of 1870 and 1902 in keeping them apart'.[60]

Manoeuvres from religious leaders themselves were to prove influential. In February 1941 leaders of the Church of England and the Free Churches published a joint letter to *The Times* laying out their 'five points' for reform.[61] These were that: 'all children in all schools should receive a Christian education'; 'religious education should be a recognised optional subject in teaching colleges'; 'the statutory restriction that religion should be the first or last lesson in the day should be dropped'; 'religious teaching should be inspected'; and 'all schools should start the day with an act of worship'.[62] These demands were repeated at a session with the new President of the Board of Education on Friday 15 August 1941 which Howard described as 'a pretty formidable example of the Church Militant in action'.[63] They were further repeated in a House of Lords debate in February 1942. Howard noted that these five points did not prove particularly difficult to accept and 'they were, in fact, all included ultimately in the 1944 Education Act'.[64] Yet, they required legislation which was difficult to obtain during war- time.

As Butler noted in his memoirs, developments by religious leaders were already paving the way to possible compromises:

> An important development that met the wishes of the Non-conformists and of many Anglicans was the 'agreed syllabus'. In Cambridgeshire in 1924 a committee of Anglicans, Free Churchmen and teachers had met and had drawn up a syllabus of religious instruction for use in the county's schools. By 1942 the Cambridgeshire syllabus was in use in over 100 local education authorities. Because of this, many Anglican managers were willing to hand over their schools to the local authorities in return for Christian teachings on these lines.[65]

In meetings with church leaders, Butler seized upon this new potential willingness for LEAs to play a greater role in voluntary schools in return for guarantees about religious teaching. On 5th June 1942, at a meeting with the new Archbishop of Canterbury William Temple, and other representatives of the National Society (the Church of England's schools organisation), Butler

59 Cornish et al. (n 23) 454.
60 Ibid 455.
61 Anthony Howard, *RAB: The Life of R A Butler* (Jonathan Cape 1987) 113.
62 Michael Barner, *The Making of the 1944 Education Act* (Continuum 2000) 40.
63 Anthony Howard, *RAB: The Life of R A Butler* (Jonathan Cape 1987) 113.
64 Ibid 123.
65 Ibid 100.

stressed 'the financial challenge the Church of England would face if it sought to maintain its school system unimpaired' and also 'the scale of the educational disadvantages it would be inflicting upon the children in its care'.[66] Moreover, he presented what 'he had convinced himself was the only possible solution to the problem'.[67] This solution which he said he had 'reached after much patience and experimentation was to make an offer of two alternatives'.[68] The Butler solution was to create two categories of voluntary schools, voluntary controlled schools and voluntary aided schools with the difference between the two being dictated by control and financing. This built upon the existing category of voluntary schools but crucially brought all schools within the system. It was thought that the nonconformist and most Church of England schools would opt for the voluntary aided model with the additional funding outweighing the cost of loss of some control while Catholic schools would go for the aided model, retaining further control but at a cost of providing more finance themselves.

The Education Act 1944 followed the schema that Butler had set. In country schools and voluntary controlled schools the 'secular instruction to be given to the pupils' including the times at which the school day and term would begin and end would be under 'the control of the local education authority and the governors of the school'.[69] Section 25 stated that

> the school day in every county school and in every voluntary school shall begin with collective worship on the part of all pupils in attendance at the school, and the arrangements made thereof shall provide for a single act of worship attended by all such pupils unless . . . the school premises are such to make it impractical to assemble them, for that purpose.

It was further stated that 'religious instruction shall be given in every county school and in every voluntary school'. As Gary McCulloch noted, this was 'the first time that these had been made statutory obligations for schools'.[70] The remainder of section 25 then outlined the parental right to withdraw in a similar manner to the previous legislation. Section 26 stated that collective worship in county schools should not be 'distinctive of any particular religious denomination' and that the religious instruction given 'shall be in accordance with an agreed syllabus adopted for the school or for those pupils and shall not include any catechism or formulary that is distinctive of any particular religious denomination'.

66 Anthony Howard, *RAB: The Life of R A Butler* (Jonathan Cape 1987) 125.
67 Ibid 126.
68 Lord Butler, *The Art of the Possible: The Memoirs of Lord Butler* (Revised edn, Penguin 1973) 102.
69 Section 23.
70 G McCulloch, *Educational Reconstruction: The 1944 Education Act and the Twenty-First Century* (Woburn Press 1994) 39.

Section 27 stated that in voluntary controlled schools religious instruction would also be given in accordance with the agreed syllabus unless parents requested that their children receive religious instruction in accordance with the school's trust. Under section 28, the religious instruction given at a voluntary aided school was under the control of the managers or governors of the school and was to be in accordance with the school's trust deed or where provision was not made in the trust deed 'in accordance with the practice observed in the school'. However, arrangements were to be made for religious instruction in accordance with the agreed syllabus adopted by the LEA where this was requested by parents and where pupils cannot 'with reasonable convenience' attend a school where that syllabus is in use and unless there were 'special circumstances' that made it 'unreasonable' for this to be accommodated.

Section 29 and Schedule 5 of the Act dealt with the procedure for preparing the agreed syllabus. Section 29 provided that LEAs would have the power to 'constitute a standing authority council on religious education to advise the authority'.[71] Schedule 5 stated that a conference would be convened to prepare any agreed syllabus and this would consist of four committees: the first of these was to consist of the representatives of religious denominations that the LEA considered ought to be represented 'having regard to the circumstances of the area'; the second, in England, was a committee of representatives of the Church of England; the third was to be a committee of teachers; and the fourth of representatives of the local authority. The LEA was to have regard to any unanimous recommendations made to them.[72] These provisions further entrenched the position of the Church of England since it meant that the Church had its own committee that had a deciding vote.[73]

The Butler Act made no further comment as to the content of religious instruction or worship.

The matter had been raised by an amendment in the House of Lords by the Bishop of Chichester.[74] Lord Selborne responded that stating it was not necessary to explicitly state this because the Act's provisions on the composition of the Standing Authority Council on Religious Education (SACRE) meant that the SACRE

> have to agree unanimously on the syllabus, and that at any rate ensures that it will be a syllabus which the Church of England can accept, and the Church of England is not going to accept a syllabus which is not in accordance with the Christian faith.

71 Such bodies were optional under the Act and there is evidence of similar bodies existing before the act.

72 Education Act 1944, section 29.

73 Cornish et al. (n 23) 454–55.

74 House of Lords Hansard, 21 June 1944, vol 132, Column 362.

This issue was, however, raised during the passage of what was to become the Education Reform Act 1988.

The 1988 Act proved to be a watershed moment in the history of education presenting a raft of reforms including the introduction of the National Curriculum.[75] The focus of the Thatcher government was not especially upon religious matters. However, the Bishop of London successfully tabled amendments to amendments to ensure that as he saw it the Bill did not represent a move towards secularism or a move away from traditional Christian values. In the House of Lords debate, he stated that these amendments were based upon five main principles:

> We have sought to provide a framework for worship which, first, maintains the tradition of worship as part of the process of education, giving proper place to the Christian religion; secondly, maintains the contribution of the collective act of worship to the establishment of values within the school community; yet, thirdly, does not impose inappropriate forms of worship on certain groups of pupils; fourthly, does not break the school up into communities based on the various faiths of the parents, especially in that it makes some groups feel that they are not really part of the community being educated in the school; and, lastly, is realisable and workable in practical terms of school accommodation and organisation.[76]

The Act as amended by the House of Lords certainly reinforced the place of Christianity. It stated that daily collective worship, which could be 'a single act of worship for all pupils or separate acts of worship for pupils in different age groups or different school groups',[77] had in a county school to 'be wholly or mainly of a broadly Christian character' and this would be satisfied 'if it reflects the broad traditions of Christian belief without being distinctive of any particular Christian denomination'.[78] However, every act of collective worship did not need to comply with this provision 'provided that, taking the school term as a whole, most such acts that take place in the school do comply'. Powers were given to the Standing Advisory Council on Religious Education to determine whether it was not appropriate for the rule to 'apply in the case of a county school or in the case of any class of description of pupil's, at such a school'.[79] It was further specified that the agreed syllabus adopted under Schedule 5 of the

75 On the Act generally, see e.g. L Bash and D Coulby (eds), *The Education Reform Act: Competition and Control* (Cassell 1989); D Lawton (ed), *The Education Reform Act: Choice and Control* (Hodder & Stoughton 1989); M Flude and M Hammer (eds), *The Education Reform Act 1988: its Origins and Implications* (Falmer Press 1990).

76 House of Lords Hansard, 7th July 1988, Column 434.

77 Education Reform Act 1988, section 6.

78 Section 7.

79 SACRES were now compulsory.

1944 Act 'shall reflect the fact that the religious traditions in Great Britain are in the main Christian whilst taking account of the teaching and practices of the other principal religions represented in Great Britain'.[80] The rationale was to 'reinforce' the Butler Act.[81] However, the 1988 Act clearly went beyond the Butler Act.[82] At the very least, the Act made explicit what had previously been implicit—and what may have been implicit and taken for granted in the 1940s was no longer uncontroversial in Thatcher's Britain. This applied not only to the idea that Christianity in general and the Church of England in particular were the norm but also the notion that local areas were largely mono-creedal. The growth of religious diversity and pluralism rendered quaint the idea that each locality could determine their own unique and distinct religious makeup and so as with marriage law, the disconnect between the law and the social reality became a constant theme in the literature.

Conclusion

The current domestic law governing religious observance in schools in England can now be found in the Education Act 1996 and the School Standards and Framework Act 1998. These provisions continue to be broadly the same as the settlement reached in 1944, as amended by the 1988 Act. In terms of marriage law, the matter remains governed by the Marriage Act 1949. The law on education and marriage continues, therefore, to be governed by legislative principles forged in the 1940s. It is therefore unsurprising that both areas of law have come in for criticism in terms of not adequately reflecting today's society.[83] The argument is typically made that these are areas where secularisation and modernisation has not gone far enough. Yet, the account in this chapter has questioned any interpretation of these areas of law as straightforward if incomplete 'subtraction stories'. Marriage and education law also do not correspond with the four phases of development I identified in *Law and Religion*. Rather, what we have seen is a pragmatic and often chaotic approach whereby law slowly, inelegantly and often inadequately has tried to regulate aspects of an activity that previously was largely, if not completely, dealt with by the voluntary sector. The picture is not one of the voices of the churches declining but rather of the state attempting—not entirely successfully—to

80 Education Reform Act 1988, section 8.

81 House of Commons Hansard, 15 December 1987, vol 124, column 439W.

82 For a further analysis see E Cox and JM Cairns, *Reforming Religious Education: The Religious Clauses of the 1988 Education Reform Act* (Kogan Page 1989).

83 On marriage see R Sandberg, *Religion and Marriage Law: The Need for Reform* (Bristol UP 2021). On education, some reforms to the teaching of religion are due to be introduced in Wales under the Curriculum and Assessment (Wales) Act 2021 (see R Sandberg, *Religion in Schools: Learning Lessons from Wales* (Anthem Press 2022)) and reforms have long been proposed in England, see e.g. Commission on Religious Education, *Religion and Worldviews: The Way Forward. A National Plan for RE.* (RE Council 2018).

obtain a foothold. Throughout there has been—and still is—a certain disconnect between the letter of the law and the social reality. This will probably never completely disappear but has in different times been partially rectified through legal changes in which the churches have played their part. Given the age of the current laws and the growing calls for reform, there is clearly a need now for further legal change, and this chapter has shown that, like its predecessors, such reform would not need to satisfy a narrative of secular progress. We can therefore be more imaginative as to what can be achieved. And in achieving this, there is a need for the state to work together with the churches and others as it has done in the past to minimise but also to accept the inherent chaos of the common law.

Bibliography

Bailey KD, *Social Entropy Theory* (University of New York Press 1990) 52
Barner M, *The Making of the 1944 Education Act* (Continuum 2000)
Bash L and Coulby D (eds), *The Education Reform Act: Competition and Control* (Cassell 1989)
Butler Lord, *The Art of the Possible: The Memoirs of Lord Butler* (Revised edn, Penguin 1973)
Collins D, 'The Chaos Machine: The WTO in a Social Entropy Model of the World Trading System' (2014) 34(2) Oxford Journal of Legal Studies 353
Commission on Religious Education, *Religion and Worldviews: The Way Forward. A National Plan for RE* (RE Council 2018)
Cornish W et al., *Law and Society in England 1750–1950* (2nd edn, Hart 2019)
Cox E and Cairns JM, *Reforming Religious Education: The Religious Clauses of the 1988 Education Reform Act* (Kogan Page 1989)
Doe N, *The Legal Framework of the Church of England: A Critical Study in a Comparative Context* (Clarendon Press 1996)
Doe N 'National Identity, the Constitutional Tradition and the Structures of Law on Religion in the United Kingdom' in *Religions in European Union Law* (Proceedings of the European Consortium of Church and State Research, Luxembourg 1997) 93
Edwards LF, 'The History in "Critical Legal Studies"' (2012) 37 Law & Social Inquiry 187
Elton GR (ed), *The New Cambridge Modern History, vol 2: The Reformation, 1520–1559* (2nd edn, CUP 1990)
Elwyn Jones G and Roderick GW, *A History of Education in Wales* (U of Wales P 2003)
Fifoot CHS, *Frederic William Maitland* (Harvard UP 1971)
Flude M and Hammer M (eds), *The Education Reform Act 1988: Its Origins and Implications* (Falmer Press 1990)
Gordon RW, '"Critical Legal Histories Revisited": A Response' (2012) 37 Law & Social Inquiry 200
Gordon RW, *Taming the Past: Essays on Law in History and History in Law* (CUP 2017)
Howard A, *RAB: The Life of R A Butler* (Jonathan Cape 1987)
Law Commission, *Getting Married: A Consultation Paper on Weddings Law* (Consultation Paper 247, 2020)
Lawton D (ed), *The Education Reform Act: Choice and Control* (Hodder & Stoughton 1989)
McCulloch G, *Educational Reconstruction: The 1944 Education Act and the Twenty-First Century* (Woburn Press 1994)
Murphy J, *The Education Act 1870: Text and Commentary* (David & Charles 1973)

Murray J, Webb TE and Wheatley S (eds), *Complexity Theory and Law: Mapping an Emergent Jurisprudence* (Routledge 2019)
Nobles R and Schiff D, 'Taking the Complexity of Complex Systems Seriously' (2020) 83(3) Modern Law Review 661
Probert R, *Tying the Knot: The Formation of Marriage 1836–2020* (CUP 2021) Ch. 1
Rivers J, 'Is English Law Christian?' in Nick Spencer (ed), *Religion and Law* (Theos 2012) 143
Sandberg R, *Law and Religion* (CUP 2011)
Sandberg R, *Religion and Marriage Law: The Need for Reform* (Bristol University Press 2021)
Sandberg R, *Subversive Legal History: A Manifesto for the Future of Legal Education* (Routledge 2021)
Sandberg R, *Religion in Schools: Learning Lessons from Wales* (Anthem Press 2022)
Sandberg R, *A Historical Introduction to English Law: Genesis of the Common Law* (CUP 2023)
Scott RE, 'Chaos Theory and the Justice Paradox' (1993) 35 William. & Mary Law Review 329
Stein P, *Legal Evolution: The Story of An Idea* (CUP 1980)
Sugarman D, 'Legal Theory, the Common Law Mind and the Making of the Textbook Tradition' in William Twinning (ed), *Legal Theory and the Common Law* (Blackwell 1986) 26
Taylor C, *A Secular Age* (Harvard University Press 2007)

10 Equity and Conscience

Richard Hedlund

Introduction

The two main parts of English law are the 'common law' and 'equity', which are primarily judge-made, and sit alongside statute law enacted by Parliament. From around the thirteenth to fourteenth centuries and up to 1875, the common law and equity were developed in separate courts. From 1875, the Judicature Acts, having fundamentally overhauled the judicial system, allowed claimants to bring both legal and equitable claims before the same court, and the judge could award both legal and equitable remedies.[1] Whether or not the common law and equity also merged in a substantive sense has been the subject of considerable debate, but that discussion is of no relevance here.[2]

There were several different courts that administered equity, though the primary equity court was the Court of Chancery, headed up by the Lord Chancellor.[3] Any claimant seeking an equitable remedy could petition the Lord Chancellor, praying relief on the basis that the defendant had acted unconscionably. Even today, conscience remains the fundamental yardstick used to determine whether the defendant has acted inequitably and whether or not an equitable remedy should be awarded.[4]

The use of conscience, however, has long raised questions and, indeed, concerns. Mostly, what is conscience and how do we know if a defendant has acted unconscionably? These are wider questions and cannot be comprehensively answered here. The focus of this chapter is looking at equity's conscience at the time of the English Reformation. How was it is understood by the Lord

1 Judicature Acts 1873–1875.
2 Consider, for example, S Worthington, 'Integrating Equity and the Common Law' (2002) 55 Current Legal Problems 223–62; A Burrows, 'We do this at Common Law but that in Equity' (2002) 22 Oxford Journal of Legal Studies 1–16.
3 The other principal equity court was the Court of Exchequer.
4 *Westdeutsche Landesbank Girozentrale v Islington LBC* [1996] AC 669, 705 (Lord Browne-Wilkinson). See also the exploration of the notion of conscience in Calvinist thought contained in Chapter 7.

DOI: 10.4324/9780429264115-14

Chancellors at that time, and did the English Reformation bring in a change to the use of conscience in equity?

The Reformation did introduce some considerable changes to theological doctrine. However, that did not always extend to how theologians understood conscience, at least not in the Anglican tradition. In particular, the juridical use of conscience in Chancery remained much the same. As has been noted judicially, 'unconscionability is a legal term, not a colloquial expression' and that whilst in 'everyday speech, "unconscionable" may be merely an emphatic method of expressing disapproval of someone's behaviour . . . its legal meaning is considerably more precise'.[5] Whilst its origins as a juridical concept lies in medieval scholastic theology and canon law, equity's conscience became a distinct English juridical concept that withstood the external theological upheavals.

The Lord Chancellor and the Creation of English Equity

The title of Chancellor is Roman in origin and refers to a senior government official with various administrative and judicial roles.[6] In mediaeval England, the office of Lord Chancellor was quite broad.[7] They served as the King's Secretary and were also Chaplain to the King's Chapel.[8] Indeed, many would act as *de facto* prime minister. Acting through the Chancery, the early Lord Chancellors were also given various judicial functions relating to the administration of justice and the development of the common law.[9]

The early common law did not always work out for the litigants.[10] In particular, the rules of procedure were deemed ineffective, and could cause injustices due to technicalities rather than the merits of the dispute.[11] Those who

5 *Australian Competition and Consumer Commission v CG Berbatis Holdings Pty Ltd* [2003] HCA 18; 214 CLR 51, [7] (Gleeson CJ).

6 AH Marsh, *History of the Court of Chancery and of the Rise and Development of the Doctrines of Equity* (Carswell 1890) 13—for example, the term Chancellor is still used in various Germanic countries as the term for 'prime minister', and in the Church of England the office of Chancellor denotes the judge in each Bishop's consistory court.

7 The formal title given to this office is Lord High Chancellor, to differentiate this role from other Chancellorships still used in the UK, such as the Chancellor of the Exchequer.

8 DM Kerly, *An Historical Sketch of the Equitable Jurisdiction of the Court of Chancery* (CUP 1890) 23.

9 Marsh (n 6) 17.

10 W Baildon (ed), *Selden Society, vol 10, Select Cases in Chancery, 1364–1471* (Bernard Quaritch 1896), Case 143, page 146. The original text reads: 'as good feith & consciens requyren' and 'answer after the lawe of consciens, whiche ys lawe executory in this courte for defaute of remedy by cours of the common lawe'.

11 W Holdsworth, *A History of English Law*, vol 2 (4th edn, Methuen 1936, reprinted 1966) 346–47; Sir John Baker, 'Reflections on "Doing" Legal History' in A Musson and C Stebbings (eds), *Making Legal History: Approaches and Methodologies* (CUP 2012) 9; see e.g. *Singularis Holdings Ltd v PricewaterhouseCoopers* [2014] UKPC 36, [20] (Lord Sumption) (on rules of evidence); *Knuller (Publishing, Printing and Promotions) Ltd v DPP* [1973] AC 435,

had suffered some injustice at the hands of the common law had the right to petition the King for grace.[12] Kings and emperors had always reserved for themselves the personal right to settle legal disputes.[13] However, the mediaeval English Kings were busy, and over the course of the fourteenth century, the task of hearing the petitions for grace were given over to the Chancery.[14] During the reign of Edward III, in the middle of the fourteenth century, the Court of Chancery established itself in Westminster Hall, where it would remain for many centuries.[15]

The Court of Chancery was headed by the Lord Chancellor, aided by the Clerks in Chancery, the chief of whom was the Master of the Rolls. When the office was created in the Middle Ages, the Master of the Rolls was responsible for keeping the records (written on parchments that were rolled up for storage, hence the title), but over the centuries, the Master of the Rolls took on a judicial function, acting as Chancery judge in the Lord Chancellor's absence.[16] That was absolutely necessary given the wide portfolio of duties that the Lord Chancellor was expected to undertake. The Clerks, likewise, worked to maintain the records kept in the Chancery, but, at least in the early days, also assisted the litigants, effectively as counsel.

The Lord Chancellors needed this support staff, not just because of their other governmental and legal duties. Almost all of the Lord Chancellors during the Middle Ages were senior clerics in the Catholic Church. Some were bishops and archbishops, whilst others were canons, deans, deacons and provosts. Holt CJ referred to this in a judgement when he noted that 'until the time of Henry the Eighth clergy-men sat in Chancery' and they had 'power over men's consciences'.[17] It meant that the Lord Chancellors had a variety of religious functions to undertake, alongside their work in government and the Chancery.

There were many reasons why clerics were appointed as Lord Chancellor. They were perhaps deemed trustworthy by the Kings. Due to the rules of celibacy in the Catholic Church, they had no dynastic ambitions, having no legitimate children, and were perhaps more trusted with the keys to power compared to the noblemen, many of whom ruthlessly vied for power.[18]

---

476 (Lord Diplock) (the medieval common law gave no remedies for fraud, whether criminal or civil): G. Mousourakis, *Comparative Law and Legal Traditions* (Springer, 2019) 266.

12 John Baker Sir, *An Introduction to English Legal History* (5th edn, OUP 2019) 107; Kerly (n 8) 25.

13 Consider the famous 'judgment of Solomon', 1 Kings 3:16–28, as an early recorded example of judicial authority being vested in a Monarch.

14 Marsh (n 6) 23, 29; Kerly (n 8) 26.

15 Kerly (n 8) 30.

16 MR Sir John Donaldson, 'The Office of Master of the Rolls' (1984) 17 Bracton Law Journal 19, 19.

17 *Jones v Morley* (1702) 12 Modern 159, 162; 88 ER 1234, 1236 (Holt CJ).

18 There are many examples of the ambitious rises and dramatic falls of noble families at the time; most infamous is perhaps that of the Boleyn family.

Kerly rightly points out that the medieval Lord Chancellors were not always appointed (or replaced) because of any legal or ecclesiastical knowledge, but rather out of political expediency.[19] Most famous to that effect was Thomas Wolsey, Cardinal-Archbishop of York, who was ignominiously removed from the Chancellorship having failed to secure an annulment for Henry VIII in his marriage to Catherine of Aragon.

There were also many reasons why the specific duty to hear petitions for grace, which would grow into the equity jurisdiction, was given to the Lord Chancellors. The role of Chancellor was inherently judicial, given their various common law functions (such as issuing legal writs). As clerics, they had legal training in the canon law and may have had judicial experience in the ecclesiastical courts, which had far greater jurisdiction at the time. Finally, again as clerics, they were trusted to be able to make decisions on the fairness and justness of a complaint, not least since the Church trained its clergy in classical philosophy, including Greek and Roman philosophies of justice and equity.[20] As Samet has argued, the function of equity and its use of conscience has been to infuse 'morality into private law', and who better to do so than clerics trained in law and theology.[21]

It is for this reason that it is necessary to understand the theological conceptualisations of conscience. Whilst English equity is secular (and always was), the medieval Lord Chancellors drew on what they knew. There is a debate as to what extent English equity is based on medieval canon law, but it is undeniable that there was an influence and that conscience, as a theological and juridical concept, came from the Catholic Church.[22]

The English Reformation

English equity emerged in the late Middle Ages, whilst England was still a Catholic nation. Indeed, England had been in communion with Rome since at least the year 664, following the Synod of Whitby. In this chapter, Catholicism is used to refer to the theological principles that underpin the Western Catholic Church, headed up by the Pope as Bishop of Rome. Catholic theology is not as uniform as is sometimes believed; for example, there are various

19 Kerly (n 8), 94.

20 J Moser, 'The Secularization of Equity' (1997) 26 Capitol University Law Review 483, 492.

21 I Samet, 'On Trusts, Angels, Morality and Fusion: Reply to My Critics' (2020) 21 Jerusalem Review of Legal Studies 50, 54.

22 See variously, G Spence, *The Equitable Jurisdiction of the Court of Chancery*, vol 1 (Lea and Blanchard 1846) 410; M Amen, 'Canonical Equity Before the Code' (1973) 33 Jurist 256, 271; J Coughlin OFM, *Canon Law: A Comparative Study with Anglo-American Legal Theory* (OUP 2010) 45; KK Kagan, *Three Great Systems of Jurisprudence* (Stevens & Sons 1955) 14; G Dodd, 'Reason, Conscience and Equity: Bishops as the King's Judges in Later Medieval England' (2014) 99 History 213, 225; R Newman, 'Equity in Comparative Law' (1968) 17 International and Comparative Law Quarterly 807, 808; E Kemp, 'The Spirit of the Canon Law and its Application in England' (2012) 14 Ecclesiastical Law Journal 5, 7.

interpretations of conscience by Catholic theologians, though the Thomist version is perhaps favoured. Bossy has noted that in the Middle Ages, Christianity (Catholicism) was more a 'body of people', a community, rather than an '"ism" or body of belief', which it has come to be regarded as in more modern times.[23] However, what unifies Catholicism is the supremacy of the Pope, who will have the final word on any disputes and discrepancies. The theological, but also legal and administrative, centrality of the Pope helps distinguish Catholicism from other Christian faiths.

In the 1520s, Martin Luther helped initiate the Protestant Reformation in Western Europe. The term Protestant, however, is a rather vague one. Martin Luther helped form a Lutheran theology, that underpins Protestant churches in many parts of Northern Europe (including Germany). However, within the Protestant umbrella are a variety of other theologies, such as Calvinism/Puritanism and Methodism.

The English Reformation began in the late 1520s, with Henry VIII's so-called great matter, namely Henry seeking to annul his marriage to Catherine of Aragon (colloquially, but erroneously, often referred to as the King seeking a divorce). As a result, England split from communion with Rome in the early 1530s.

The English reformers were obviously Protestant (in the sense of rejecting the authority of the Pope) but a variety of theologies were argued for by different reformers. England was, for a time, a Protestant nation, but this should not be equated to it adhering to either Lutheran, Calvinist, or any other specific theology. Indeed, the 'ten articles' put forward by Henry VIII would, if anything, suggest a distinct Henrician Church (which, in many ways, was theologically Catholic but without the Pope). A more radical Protestantism did emerge during the short reign of Edward VI, but this was stopped in its tracks by the return to Catholicism during the brief reign of Mary I. However, the restoration of Catholicism was not really completed by the time she died unexpectedly in 1558.[24] Under Elizabeth I, the Church of England was formed, which was a deliberately broad church, encompassing both Catholic and Protestant theologies.

This brief historical sketch, which will no doubt be well-known to many readers, is necessary in discussing the impact the Reformation might have had on English equity. Despite the terminology being used, it is debatable to what extent England actually became a full-on Protestant nation. Yes, it severed ties with the Pope and people had different views on topics like transubstantiation, but that does not necessarily entail adopting more radical Lutheran and

23 J Bossy, *Christianity in the West, 1400–1700* (OUP 1985) 171; quoted in S Smith, 'Interrogating Thomas More: The Conundrums of Conscience' (2003–2004) 1 University of St Thomas Law Journal 580, 595.

24 Much has been written about this—a strong biography with a focus on the religious issues is J Edwards, *Mary I—England's Catholic Queen* (Yale UP 2011).

Calvinist views. Indeed, the genius of the Anglican Church is its charting a path down the middle, accommodating theologies that were both Catholic and Protestant. This, of course, did not please fully committed Catholics or Protestants (famously, for example, Puritans would soon set out aboard the fabled ship *Mayflower* to form Puritan colonies in North America), but it no doubt worked for the vast majority.

Throughout these changes to religious thought and practice, the English political and legal system carried on as normal. None of the Tudor monarchs reformed the political or legal system; they merely replaced the office-holders with people more sympathetic to their religious views.[25] The Civil War and Oliver Cromwell's Commonwealth would only happen a century later, but even that did not result in any real long-term change in the system itself (indeed, the monarchy was restored soon after Cromwell's death). Overall, given everything that happened in the sixteenth and seventeenth centuries, there was a remarkable continuity in the political and legal systems.[26] For this reason, it should not be surprising that equity's use of conscience continued and that the definition remained fundamentally scholastic in nature.

The Nature of Conscience in Christianity

This section will seek to understand what is meant by conscience and how conscience has been conceptualised in Catholic and Protestant thought. This is a very broad concept, and this chapter cannot do it justice; what follows will be an identification of some of the key ideas.[27]

However, before doing so, it is necessary to start with a great caveat. There is no agreed upon definition of conscience. The noted and, perhaps, controversial Anglican preacher Henry Sacheverell noted in a sermon in 1707 that 'nothing has brought greater calamities on the World' than conscience, being so misunderstood and misapplied by people for their own gain and benefit.[28] Indeed, Sacheverell criticises theologians before him (especially the scholastics) for making it unnecessarily complex; he argues that conscience is fundamentally the knowledge of the natural and divine law, and its application to specific acts.[29] For this reason it is difficult to talk of any distinct 'Catholic' or

25 Lord Chancellors came and went, including famous Tudor Chancellors such as Thomas Wolsey, Cardinal-Archbishop of York; Saint/Sir Thomas More (depending on your theological bent); Richard, Baron Rich; and Bishop Stephen Gardiner.

26 An exception was the abolition of the Star Chamber in 1641 by Charles I, though this was no doubt a positive development given the court's reputation.

27 For deeper analysis, consider works such as JB Hammond and HM Alvaré, *Christianity and the Laws of Conscience* (CUP 2021). See also Chapter 6 'Conscience and Natural Law: A Calvinist Perspective'.

28 H Sacheverell, *The Nature, Obligations, and Measures of Conscience—A Sermon preached at the Leicester Assizes* (The Booksellers of London and Westminster 1707) 4.

29 Sacheverell (n 28) 5.

'Protestant' conscience; rather, it is necessary to consider the view of various theologians to understand the different ways in which conscience has been conceptualised.

Conscience in Early Christian Theology

Christian theology as a whole broadly agrees that conscience is, in essence, an exercise in moral reasoning. Understandably, Christian theology traces the idea of conscience back to the New Testament. An oft-cited passage therein is found in St Paul's Letter to the Romans.

> Indeed, when Gentiles, who do not have the law, do by nature things required by the law, they are a law for themselves, even though they do not have the law. They show that the requirements of the law are written on their hearts, their consciences also bearing witness, and their thoughts sometimes accusing them and at other times even defending them.[30]

A law written on a person's heart points towards Christian natural law theology, the idea that some moral precepts are inborn in all people.[31] The passage also goes some way to explain conscience. It is knowledge of that natural law and the application of that law to specific acts, either acts already done or acts being contemplated. Our conscience will approve or rebuke us, depending on whether the act is in accordance with the natural law.

In the Greek language, the term used for conscience is *synderesis*. This term can be defined as referring to 'self-knowledge' or self-awareness and then using that knowledge to pass judgements on your actions.[32] This is generally how *synderesis* is used in the New Testament, in particular in the letters of St Paul.[33] Christianity later turned to Latin, as it became accepted as the Roman state religion. Here, the word used is *conscientia*. The Latin word bears the same meaning as *synderesis* in Greek. From this Latin root, we get a variety of English words, such as 'conscious' and 'consciousness', which, again, mean being self-aware. Where being conscious means being aware of certain knowledge, conscience means the application of that knowledge to specific acts.

The concept of conscience was developed by an early Church theologian, St Jerome. He decided to treat *synderesis* and *conscientia* as being two distinct

30 Romans 2:14–15 (New International Version).

31 See Chapters 6 and 7 in this book and also D VanDrunen, 'Conscience and Natural Law in Scripture' in Hammond and Alvaré (n 27) 51; consider Romans 2:14–15, and, more generally, the Wisdom Books of the Old Testament. Comparisons can be made to the collective unconscious, as defined by psychologist Carl Gustav Jung; see Carl Gustav Jung, *The Archetypes and the Collective Unconscious* (2nd edn, Routledge 1959, tenth printing 1991) 4.

32 W Willis, 'Conscience in the New Testament' in Hammond and Alvaré (n 27) 24–25.

33 Ibid 37; consider Acts 23:1.

ideas. St Jerome regarded *synderesis* as the 'spark of conscience' and conscience itself is the process that 'corrects' people 'when they go wrong'.[34] In this duality, *synderesis* is what prods a person to act and conscience is what selects the right decision or rebukes the wrong decision. However, as seen, the two terms are really Greek and Latin for the same idea, namely self-awareness. Whether St Jerome intended to draw this distinction and why he made it remains unclear.[35] Nonetheless, the scholastic theologians would make good use of that duality.

Conscience in Scholastic and Catholic Theology

Whilst the scholastics used this new distinction between *synderesis* and *conscientia*, there was some disagreement as to what each concept meant and did. The prevailing Thomist school, which underpins Catholic theology, saw the difference in this way. *Synderesis* was the knowledge and understanding of what is right and wrong. This knowledge was partially inborn and possessed by all people, not just Jews or Christians. Further, knowledge could be learnt, not least by studying Scripture. Conscience was the process of applying that knowledge to specific acts. This duality works because the rational mind is able to understand and apply the moral precepts.

Reason was a strong component of the scholastic theology. They divided the rational mind into two distinct parts, the first being 'the understanding' and the second being 'the will'; the understanding part of the rational mind was the 'power of apprehension' and the willing part of the rational mind was 'a power of motion'.[36] Over time, this led to two slightly different visions of conscience within the scholastic movement. The first version of conscience, to which St Bonaventure ascribed, was the voluntaristic school, which believed that conscience was in the willing part of the rational mind. The second version, to which St Thomas Aquinas ascribed, was the intellectual school, which believed that conscience was in the understanding part of the rational mind.

Early scholastics included Peter Abelard and Philip the Chancellor. Abelard saw conscience as a 'mental operation', making 'intellectual' and 'moral' judgements.[37] Further, Abelard regarded conscience as 'our power to recognize obvious truths' and that our conscience issued a 'command' in response to such truths as to how we should or should not act.[38] Philip the Chancellor

34 St Jerome, *Commentary on Ezekiel, 1.7*; cited in T Potts (ed and trans), *Conscience in Medieval Philosophy* (CUP 1980) 79.

35 R Greene, 'Synderesis, the Spark of Conscience, in the English Renaissance' (1991) 52 Journal of the History of Ideas 195, 195; A McGrade, J Kilcullen, and M Kempshall, *The Cambridge Translations of Medieval Philosophical Texts, vol II: Ethics and Political Philosophy* (CUP 2001) 169; see similarly Anthony Fisher, *Catholic Bioethics for a New Millennium* (CUP 2012) 44.

36 J Wilks, *The Idea of Conscience in Renaissance Tragedy* (Routledge 1990) 11.

37 J Marenbon, *The Philosophy of Peter Abelard* (CUP 1997) 273.

38 Marenbon (n 37) 274–75.

repeated the distinction between synderesis as the part that knows general moral precepts and conscientia, which applied moral precepts to specific acts.[39] Philip came down in the voluntaristic school, and he wrote that *synderesis* was 'the spark of *conscientia*' that 'affects free choice by telling us to do good and restraining it from evil'.[40] This particular view of *synderesis* was later adopted by St Bonaventure.

St Bonaventure adhered to the voluntaristic school. He wrote that synderesis 'resides in the affective' part of the mind and 'urges toward good'.[41] In the same vein as Philip, Bonaventure also posited that *synderesis* is the 'spark of conscience', which is necessary because 'conscience by itself can neither move nor string nor urge except by means of synderesis, which, as it were, urges and ignites'.[42] Since *conscientia* was in the rational mind, it would not by itself act; *synderesis* is there as the catalyst for action.

Turning to *conscientia*, Bonaventure divided it into two parts.[43] Douglas Langston has proposed that the two parts should be referred to as the 'potential conscience' and the 'applied conscience', which are convenient descriptors.[44] The 'potential conscience' knows general 'practical principles' in terms of what is right and wrong. The 'applied conscience' is the actual rational act of applying those principles to specific situations.

Bonaventure offered further thoughts on where the potential conscience obtained its moral precepts. In part, there is inherent reason and the natural law, which is God-given to all people.[45] Furthermore, people also learn and obtain moral knowledge by study and experience.[46] In this respect, Langston rightly says that Bonaventure's idea of conscience is 'dynamic', in that it develops and grows over time.[47]

St Thomas Aquinas, whose writings have perhaps had the most influence on Catholic theology over the centuries, adopted a view of conscience that falls into the intellectual school. As he placed both *synderesis* and *conscientia* in the understanding part of the rational mind, the catalyst for acting had to come

39 Philip the Chancellor, *Summa de Bono*; cited in Potts (n 34) 104.
40 Philip the Chancellor, *Summa de Bono*; cited in Potts (n 34) 101, 104.
41 St Bonaventure, *Commentaries on the Sentences of Peter Lombard, Book II, Distinction 39, Article 2, Question 1–2*; cited in McGrade, Kilcullen, and Kempshall (n 35) 190.
42 St Bonaventure, *Commentaries on the Sentences of Peter Lombard, Book II, Distinction 39, Article 2, Question 1–3*; cited in McGrade, Kilcullen, and Kempshall (n 35) 190.
43 St Bonaventure, *Commentary on Peter Lombard's 'Books of Judgments', Book II, Distinction 39, Article 1, Question 1–1*; cited in and translated by Potts (n 34) 111.
44 D Langston, 'The Spark of Conscience: Bonaventure's View of Conscience and Synderesis' (1993) 53 Franciscan Studies 79, 82.
45 Potts (n 34) 37–38.
46 St Bonaventure, *Commentaries on the Sentences of Peter Lombard, Book II, Distinction 39, Article 1, Question 2–2*; cited in McGrade, Kilcullen, and Kempshall (n 35) 179.
47 D Langston, *Conscience and Other Virtues: From Bonaventure to MacIntyre* (The Pennsylvania State University Press 2001) 29, 36.

from elsewhere. *Synderesis* is 'naturally inborn in us'.[48] It is the storehouse of innate moral knowledge, which Bonaventure instead placed in the potential conscience. To Aquinas, *synderesis* is our connection to the law of reason. The moral principles of *synderesis* are partly inborn but are also learnt and acquired over time.[49] *Conscientia*, 'also in the rational part, applies these first principles to particular situations'.[50] Aquinas writes that conscience is 'an activity, namely, the actual application of moral science to conduct'.[51] It is an act of 'judgement' or an act of 'practical reason' based on 'a person's innate knowledge of natural law'.[52] Conscience was the direct application of moral precepts.

Aquinas' view of conscience as the duality of *synderesis* and *conscientia* is fairly straightforward and it is perhaps not surprising it has been widely adopted in Catholic theology. Firstly, *synderesis* knows moral knowledge, partly inborn and partly acquired. On this point, St John Henry Newman explained that a child has 'latent instincts about good and evil, truth and falsehood' but does not have 'experience enough' in life 'to elicit into form and action those innate principles of conscience'.[53] This highlights the role for educating the conscience and allowing it to grow with time and experience. Secondly, *conscientia* applies that morality to our acts, either planned acts or acts already carried out, to render a moral judgement. Again, Newman explained that conscience is a 'judgment' on 'something to be done or not done', and it does not deal with 'abstract doctrine'.[54] It is moral reasoning about real events.

The scholastics took conscience very seriously. Through our rational minds, it was our direct link to God.[55] Indeed, Bonaventure held that the commands of conscience came not from 'itself' but 'from God, like a herald proclaiming the edict of a king'.[56] When conscience spoke, you had to listen; to disobey your conscience was to disobey God.[57] Being a rational exercise, the scholastics also emphasised the importance of education and training, to better

48 St Thomas Aquinas, *Summa Theologica, 1a. lxxix 12,* cited in Thomas Gilby, *St Thomas Aquinas—Philosophical Texts* (OUP 1951) 290–91.

49 St Thomas Aquinas, *Disputations, II de Malo, 4,* cited in Gilby (n 48) 281.

50 Langston (n 47) 39.

51 St Thomas Aquinas, *Summa Theologica, 1a. lxxix 13,* cited in Gilby (n 48) 291.

52 N Feldman, 'The Intellectual Origins of the Establishment Clause' (2002) 77 New York University Law Review 346, 356.

53 John Henry Newman, *Parochial and Plain Sermons*, vol 1 (Christian Classics, New Impression 1966) 102.

54 John Henry Newman, *Difficulties of Anglicans*, vol II (Christian Classics, New Impression 1969) 256.

55 St Bonaventure, *Commentaries on the Sentences of Peter Lombard, Book II, Distinction 39, Article 1, Question 3–4a*; cited in McGrade, Kilcullen, and Kempshall (n 35) 184.

56 St Bonaventure, *Commentaries on the Sentences of Peter Lombard, Book II, Distinction 39, Article 1, Question 3–4b*; cited in McGrade, Kilcullen, and Kempshall (n 35) 185; John Henry Newman, *Difficulties of Anglicans*, vol II (Christian Classics, New Impression 1969) 247.

57 St Thomas Aquinas, *Summa Theologica, 1a-2ae, xix 5,* cited in Gilby (n 48) 292; Langston (n 47) 27.

understand the moral precepts that should be applied by your conscience.[58] Both Bonaventure and Aquinas discussed that importance and also what culpability applied to an act done in ignorance of God's laws. Culpability definitely applied to someone who had been offered the opportunity to learn about God's law but had refused to do so.[59] However, genuine ignorance of God's laws did not always lead to culpability. All that was asked for was education and following your conscience. Bonaventure noted that 'it is always a sin to act *against* conscience, because it always shows contempt for God, yet to act *according* to conscience is not always good'.[60] Aquinas wrote that 'every judgment of conscience, be it right or wrong, be it about things evil in themselves or morally indifferent, is obligatory'.[61] It shows clearly that conscience must be obeyed, but your conscience can be wrong in the sense that it genuinely was unaware of God's law (remember that whilst some moral precepts are held to be inborn, others must be learnt).

The scholastic conception of conscience, a rational exercise in moral reasoning, has continued into modern Catholic theology. Araujo writes that there are two aspects to forming a Catholic conscience: '(1) human reason, and (2) the teachings of the Church that are constitutive of the well-formed conscience'.[62] He continues by saying that the human reason 'is one that seeks objective truth and does not fear the search for it'.[63] Church teaching remains focused on cultivating and applying moral and ethical thought, and sees conscience as an aspect of reason.[64] A Catholic's understanding of morality comes from a multitude of sources, not merely scriptures but also from the views of papal encyclicals, the works of theologians, the lives of saints, Church art, music and so forth.[65] As such, Catholic teaching is an objective teaching formed by the

58 St Bonaventure, *Commentaries on the Sentences of Peter Lombard, Book II, Distinction 39, Article 1, Question 3–5*; cited in McGrade, Kilcullen and Kempshall (n 35) 185.

59 St Thomas Aquinas, *Summa Theologica, la-2ae, xix 6*, cited in Gilby (n 48) 292.

60 St Bonaventure, *Commentaries on the Sentences of Peter Lombard, Book II, Distinction 39, Article 1, Question 3–4a*; cited in McGrade, Kilcullen, and Kempshall (n 35) 184.

61 St Thomas Aquinas, *III Quodlibet 27*, cited in Gilby (n 48) 291.

62 R Araujo SJ, 'Forming the Well-Formed Conscience' (2008) 47 Journal of Catholic Legal Studies 319, 324.

63 Araujo (n 62) 325; Anthony Lusvardi SJ, 'The Law of Conscience: Catholic Teaching on Conscience from Leo XIII to John Paul II' (2012) 15 Logos 13, 26.

64 John Henry Newman, *Difficulties of Anglicans*, vol II (256); (fn. 54) John Henry Newman, *Parochial and Plain Sermons*, vol 1 (fn. 53) 21; Paul IV, *Pastoral Constitution on the Church in the Modern World—Gaudium et Spes* (7 December 1965) [16]; *Catechism of the Catholic Church* (Burnes & Oates 2000, reprint 2012) Rules 1778–1785; Langston (fn 47) 109–10; see further John Paul II, *Varitatis Splendor* (Papal Encyclical, 6 August 1993); also Pope Francis, *The Joy of the Gospel (Apostolic Exhortation,* 24th November 2013) [64].

65 Robert Barron, *Catholicism: A Journey to the Heart of the Faith* (Image Books 2011) 3–4; Scott Idleman, 'Private Conscience, Public Duties: The Unavoidable Conflicts Facing a Catholic Justice' (2006–2007) 4 University of St Thomas Law Journal 312, 323; SS Richard Gula, *Reason Informed by Faith: Foundations of Catholic Morality* (Paulist Press 1989) 155.

Church.[66] The morality of the Church does develop and it is wrong to say that it has been absolute from inception, and indeed there is diversity within the Church.[67] The Church refers to itself as God's 'pilgrim Church on earth', clearly showing that the Church as a whole is on a journey. That notwithstanding, certain core precepts have remained the same, which, as noted, are often referred to as natural law, and give an objective reality to which Catholic consciences can connect. The last word will be given to St John Paul II, who wrote that

> whereas the natural law discloses the objective and universal demands of the moral good, conscience is the application of the law to a particular case; this application of the law thus becomes an inner dictate for the individual, a summons to do what is good in this particular situation.[68]

Conscience in Protestant Theology

The causes for the Protestant Reformation were many and varied. Some of it may come down to disagreements about theology but also it was about protesting corruption in Rome. There was nothing new about that; for example, Queen Isabella I of Castile and Leon was 'often outraged by the goings-on in Rome', which may be a surprise from someone given the title 'Catholic monarch'.[69] This shows that there was a long run-up to the start of the Reformation and that the main concerns were corruption, greed and decadence in Rome rather than any theological disagreements.

There was a theological difference between Catholicism and Protestant movements in the arena of salvation. The Catholic Church accepts original sin, which stems from the Fall, when Adam and Eve were expelled from the Garden of Eden. Within Catholicism, salvation comes from faith and good deeds, which, as Berman puts it, requires 'will and reason'.[70] Conscience, by judging acts, could inform a person of their sin, and the Church could, either through the confessional or by decrees from the Ecclesiastical Court, demand penance in the form of acts (which could range from saying prayers to, for

66 This teaching authority of the Church has been greatly debated and was one of the central issues during the Protestant Reformation. To the Catholic Church, the Church derives its authority to teach an objective morality from scripture, including Jesus's parting words in Matthew, where he commanded his disciples to go and 'make disciples of all the nations' and to teach 'them to observe all that I have commanded you'. Jesus finished by saying, 'I am with you always, to the end of the age'; see Matthew 28:16–20. This suggests that the popes, as successors to St Peter, have an authority to teach.

67 D Carson, 'Reflections on Salvation and Justification in the New Testament' (1997) 40 Journal of the Evangelical Theological Society 581, 582.

68 John Paul II, *Varitatis Splendor* (Encyclical, 6 August 1993).

69 C Tremlett, *Isabella of Castile: Europe's First Great Queen* (Bloomsbury 2017) 80.

70 H Berman, 'Conscience and Law: The Lutheran Reformation and the Western Legal Tradition' (1987) 5 Journal of Law and Religion 177, 178.

instance, providing restitution for losses caused). Through reason, by learning and understanding the moral precepts and realising when one has sinned (as told to you by your conscience) and performing penance, a person could find salvation. It provides the individual with a degree of agency and control over their destiny.

The Protestant movement took a different view on this. One of the hallmarks of the various protestant faiths, including Lutheranism, is salvation through faith alone.[71] A second hallmark of the Protestant movement is the primacy (and, to an extent at least, exclusivity) of Scripture. Scripture did not really provide for many of the things the Catholic Church did, including the system of canon law and doing penance as a result of a confessional or a decree of the ecclesiastical court. Nelson writes that the result of this was the disappearance of canon law courts in Protestant nations, and as a result the 'historical notions of a law of conscience' also went away.[72]

Conscience began to take on a new role, becoming in effect a faculty of its own, above reason, which had been corrupted by the Fall. John Calvin called it a 'medium between God and man', though that is perhaps not that different from the reverence of conscience propounded by St Bonaventure.[73] As much as the early and scholastic Catholics disagreed about the exact nature of conscience, so did the various Protestant theologians. At its core, it is seen as an independent faculty (above the will and reason), which guides the individual, aided by reason (which is still there, just sinful and corrupted by the Fall) and the Holy Spirit.[74]

Martin Luther argued that conscience judged the person, not just the individual acts the person planned or had done.[75] Conscience was 'the essential self' and was where the person 'felt either justified or condemned before God and humanity'.[76] It is based on faith alone, and Luther argued that faith and reason should be kept separate, 'for nothing fights more strongly against faith, than the law and reason'.[77] He seeks to draw a clearer distinction between civil society (where humans are bound by human laws) and faith, where the Gospel alone is the guide. Luther writes that conscience, 'being feared with the terror of the wrath and judgment of God, ought to know nothing of the law and sin, but

71 Wilks (n 36) 3.

72 Benjamin Nelson, 'Conscience and the Making of Early Modern Cultures: *The Protestant Ethic* Beyond Max Weber' (1969) 35 Social Research 5, 16.

73 John Calvin, *Institutes of the Christian Religion*, vol II (John Allen (trans), Philip H Nicklin and Hezekiah Howe 1816) 335. See also Ch. 6 on Calvin and conscience.

74 Consider William Perkins, *A Discourse of Conscience* (1596); cited in Camille Wells Slights, *The Casuistical Tradition in Shakespeare, Donne, Herbert, and Milton* (Princeton UP 1981) vii.

75 Michael Baylor, *Action and Person: Conscience in Late Scholasticism and the Young Luther* (E. J. Brill 1977) 202; Langston (n 47) 73.

76 R Rittgers, *The Reformation of the Keys: Confession, Conscience, and Authority in Sixteenth-Century Germany* (Harvard UP 2004) 206.

77 Martin Luther, *A Commentary on Saint Paul's Epistle to the Galatians* (B. Blake 1833) 83.

of Christ only'.[78] Unfortunately, since every person is a sinner with a corrupted reason and salvation could only ever come from faith alone, the verdict of conscience could only be one thing: you are a sinner.[79] A priest's 'central task was to assure troubled consciences that forgiveness was a gift'.[80] Shaping the conscience was important, and priests maintained a role in 'moving their parishioners to true penance', but this was done through sermons rather than confessions.[81]

It is important not to become polemic about Lutheranism, but it has at times been regarded as rather negative in outlook, since salvation through faith alone can be seen as removing some agency from the faithful; a Catholic can at least do penance to seek forgiveness and salvation, whereas a Lutheran can only pray and have faith that salvation will come. However, this was not necessarily a new idea created by Luther. Indeed, Wilks posits that 'Luther drew his pessimistic conclusions as to the utter depravity of man's nature' from the writings of the later scholastic theologian William of Ockham; with Luther holding firm that our reason 'is corrupted by pride' and is 'bent ineluctably to sin'.[82]

John Calvin argued along the same lines in terms of salvation and the role of conscience in judging a person. As with the scholastics, he regarded conscience as important, as it provides our 'apprehension' of God's will.[83] Calvin does suggest that people have some inherent understanding of morality, akin to synderesis in the scholastic tradition.[84] As a result of that, God can use our conscience to 'dictate' what is 'proper or useless to do', which seems to have scholastic undertones.[85] However, Calvin's conscience is a 'sense of God's judgment' rather than the outcome of 'our own moral self-judgment', which separates Calvin from the scholastics, though there are also similarities between them, such as seeing conscience as an 'intellectual faculty' that uses inherent morality to make moral decisions.[86]

Calvin wrote that man is governed by two set of rules, the spiritual dictated by conscience and the temporal dictated by Kings.[87] Conscience should stand above the law when seeking justification from God, on the basis that Christ 'exceeds all the perfection of the law'.[88] Once 'liberated from the law', the people should with 'alacrity and promptitude' serve God.[89] The liber-

78 Ibid 85.
79 Rittgers (n 76) 206.
80 Ibid.
81 Ibid 105.
82 Wilks (n 36) 25.
83 John Calvin, *Institutes of the Christian Religion*, vol III (John Allen (trans), Philip H Nicklin and Hezekiah Howe 1816) 190–91.
84 D VanDrunen, 'Conscience and Natural Law in Scripture' in Hammond and Alvaré (n 27) 41.
85 Calvin (n 83) *Institutes of the Christian Religion*, vol III, 275.
86 David VanDrunen, 'Conscience and Natural Law in Scripture' in Hammond and Alvaré (n 27) 41.
87 Calvin (n 73) *Institutes of the Christian Religion*, vol II, 334.
88 Ibid 321–22x.
89 Ibid 323.

ated conscience is also free from obligations which are not imposed by God (particularly, such religious obligations seemingly imposed by the Pope).[90] It highlights the ever-increasing role given to conscience. It is a guide for the whole person, with only the scriptures for a guide. Wilks noted that even Scripture is still only of 'partial sufficiency' to inform conscience because 'God's will', to an extent at least, 'remains forever partly hidden and mysterious'.[91] Because parts of God's plan are hidden from humanity, it is doubtful that any person could have a perfect conscience.

The Puritans, following Calvin, came to place great value on the individual and subjective conscience, where each had the 'onerous duty of verifying the morality of his own actions in light of biblical sanction, and by a corroborative search of his own conscience'.[92] The Puritan view is that conscience must be obeyed because it is the will of God and to disobey conscience is a sin. This is true even if the conscience is misinformed or deceived; the onus is placed on the individual to have a correctly informed conscience, through the study of scriptures and the Decalogue.[93]

William Perkins was an influential theologian in the Elizabethan era, who was a Puritan but largely conformed to the Anglican Church. Following in the scholastic tradition, he posits that the soul consists of the 'understanding' and the 'will'.[94] The understanding is a rational part of the soul, through which we understanding right and wrong. The will is the faculty that chooses to act or not to act. Perkins places conscience within the 'understanding'.[95] This argument is fundamentally Thomist in nature. However, he goes on to say that conscience is 'a part' of the understanding, but really transcends it into becoming its own faculty.[96] He also goes on to say that 'every particular man has his own particular conscience', which points towards the more subjective notion of conscience, a personal faculty and personal link to God.[97]

However, there are no truly fundamental differences in how conscience is conceptualised between Perkins and the scholastics (who, as noted, did not present a unified view on theology), though there are differences in matters of faith. Treatise such as this one can help demonstrate the overall scholastic continuity in English equity, not least since Perkins' work was dedicated to Sir William Peryam, the Lord Chief Baron of the Court of Exchequer, which was one of the courts administering equity at this time.

90 Ibid 327.
91 Wilks (n 36) 3.
92 Ibid 35.
93 Ibid 38.
94 W Perkins, *A Discourse of Conscience* (John Legate, Printer to the University of Cambridge 1596) 1.
95 Ibid.
96 Ibid 2.
97 Ibid 4.

Joseph Butler was a leading Anglican theologian and Bishop, although writing some two centuries after the Reformation. Nonetheless, he wrote extensively about conscience, which can provide useful insights into any distinct Anglican conception of conscience. It has been argued that Butler was 'the person most responsible for the modern view that conscience is a faculty'.[98] This clearly follows on from Luther and Calvin, who also promoted this view, and separates conscience from reason and places it above reason. Butler held that conscience was an 'unerring faculty that judges actions as well as the agent'.[99] Indeed, the 'authority of conscience' is 'absolute', because our conscience is 'assigned [to] us by the Author of our nature' and a 'failure to follow the direction of conscience is, in fact, a failure to follow one's own nature'.[100] He continued by arguing that every man is a law to himself, and it is every person's 'obligation' to 'obey this law': where 'your conscience approves of and attests to such a course of action, is itself alone an obligation'.[101] This is a step away from the scholastic views of conscience, which held that it had to be obeyed but accepted that conscience could be wrong. Now, instead, conscience is an absolute moral decision-maker, which is always going to be right because it is gifted to us from God.

Langston has argued that this change in how conscience has been regarded is an 'unfortunate turn'.[102] This is because conscience was moved out of reason to instead be regarded as its own faculty, that over time seems to have become regarded as infallible.[103] Langston explains further that the 'scholastic discussions emphasized that conscience plays a role in practical reason and is closely connected to the development of the virtues' but that 'under the influence of Butler and Kant, conscience is conceived of as an independent entity (a faculty) that is infallible, directive, and punitive, and the guarantor of morality'.[104] Within this is a shift from the objective natural law propounded by the mediaeval Catholic Church to a more subjective approach to morality, based on individual readings and interpretations of Scripture.[105]

Protestant theologians also had to make sense of all the ills in society. Sacheverell argued that conscience can be affected by other factors, such as prejudice and passion, which can lead us astray from a 'true conscience'.[106] As with the scholastics, Protestants also emphasise the need to train and educate the

98 Langston (n 47) 80.
99 Ibid 81.
100 Ibid; J Butler, *Five Sermons Preached at the Rolls Chapel and a Dissertation Upon the Nature of Virtue* (Hackett 1983) 16–17, 37, 41.
101 Ibid.
102 Langston (n 47) 77.
103 Wilks (n 36) 37.
104 Langston (n 47) 84.
105 D Robinson *Conscience and Jung's Moral Vision: From Id to Thou* (Paulist Press 2005) 12.
106 Sacheverell (n 28) 10, 12; also A Cade, *Conscience, It's Nature and Corruption, with Its Repairs and Means to Inform It Aright* (John Williams 1661) 15.

conscience; otherwise people will sin whilst insisting they acted according to their conscience.[107] Whilst conscience is a God-given faculty, which itself is perhaps always right, a person can mistake other calls to action as coming from their conscience, when in fact those calls were based on other factors, whether ignorance, prejudice (which in itself may be regarded as ignorance), passion or other instinctive emotions.

Sacheverell posits that true conscience is based on three laws: God's law, human laws (that are consistent with God's law), and the 'moral law', which stems from reason.[108] John Tillotson, Archbishop of Canterbury, argued that to keep a clear conscience, we must 'have the patience to examine things thoroughly and impartially', we must be 'humble' and 'willing to learn, and never too proud or stiff to be better informed'; further, we must seek to be free of 'prejudice and passion, from self-conceit and self-interest'.[109] Whilst that exhortation may sound like a modern self-help book, Tillotson said it in a sermon preached in 1691, addressed to Queen Mary II.

The subjectivity that arose out of Protestant theology later led to the Enlightenment and the political ideas of liberalism and individualism.[110] In England, it was no doubt further enhanced by the constant back-and-forth of state religions in the Tudor era, and with members of various religious movements being persecuted in turn depending on who was the Monarch; it led to an idea of conscience and morality as being subjective and allowing individuals to 'decide on a course of action in the light of a specific set of circumstances'.[111] For example, with reference to abortion, a court has noted that 'the issue of abortion has been regarded in this country as being one of conscience and has therefore been the subject of free votes in Parliament', where MPs are not bound by a party whip but can exercise independent judgement in how to vote.[112] This is evidence of a subjective conception of conscience, which stems from the Protestant theologies.

There are merits with this approach, such as allowing minority voices to be heard. In celebration of the Lutheran reformation, Hedge writes that 'conscience has to be new-born when a new dispensation is given to the world'; the scholastic conscience, being linked to established principles and traditions, gives inadequate room for development, and Luther was to be praised for rising above that.[113]

107 J Tillotson, *A Conscience Void of Offence, Towards God and Men* (4th edn, H. Hills 1709) 6.
108 Sacheverell (n 28) 14.
109 Tillotson (n 107) 16.
110 FH Hedge, *Martin Luther and Other Essays* (Roberts Brothers 1888) 2.
111 A Walsham, 'Ordeals of Conscience: Casuistry, Conformity and Confessional Identity in Post-Reformation England' in H Braun and Vallance (eds), *Contexts of Conscience in Early Modern Europe 1500–1700* (Palgrave 2004) 40.
112 *R (on the Application of Crowter) v Secretary of State for Health and Social Care* [2021] EWHC 2536 (Admin) [31] (Singh LJ and Lieven J).
113 Hedge (n 110) 9.

There can also be some issues with this approach. The reason it may be 'unfortunate', to use Langston's word, is that it may empower individuals to do as they please, claiming their own conscience as an ultimate justification. That can make it difficult to morally condemn certain acts, such as exploitation for personal gain, even if a majority disapproves. That tug-of-war between unconstrained individualism and social conformity (which, of course, often comes with negative connotations) cannot be debated in this chapter, but it is played out in the different conceptions of conscience presented by the scholastics and the Protestants. The question for this chapter is now to look at how these theological conceptions of conscience were utilised in the equity courts.

Equity and the Court of Chancery

Conscience in the Medieval Court of Chancery

The Chancery jurisdiction was developed in the thirteenth and fourteenth centuries, with the Lord Chancellor being given the responsibility to hear petitions for grace by applicants who have suffered an injustice of some form in the common law courts. As the scholastic conceptions of conscience were developed and began to be used in the canon law, the Lord Chancellors soon adopted conscience for equity as well.

As England was a religious country, with people engaging with religion (not least by attendance at Mass), both conscience and the moral precepts that the Catholic Church taught were widely understood.[114] As the earlier section showed, there were some disagreements amongst the scholastics about the precise nature of conscience (and the respective roles of *synderesis* and conscientia), but the fundamental idea was clear. Conscience was a rational process of understanding and applying moral precepts. The Church held that those precepts were partly inborn in all people and otherwise they were taught and developed through personal experiences, including attendance at the confessional.[115] For this reason, it will not have been a surprise to anyone that the Lord Chancellors adopted conscience in equity, nor would there have been any major disagreement as to what they were referring to when speaking of unconscionability.

It is regrettable, therefore, that mediaeval Chancery judgements were not, as a matter of course, recorded and published. The judgements were given *in personam*, which means the order applied to the parties only, and did not bind or affect anyone else. That is different from legal judgements which are given *in rem*, meaning they bind everyone. For example, a legal declaration

114 T Haskett, 'Conscience, Justice and Authority in the Late-Medieval English Court of Chancery' in Anthony Musson (ed), *Expectations of the Law in the Middle Ages* (The Boydell Press 2001) 159.

115 R Barron, *Catholicism: A Journey to the Heart of the Faith* (Image Books 2011) 3–4; S Idleman, 'Private Conscience, Public Duties: The Unavoidable Conflicts Facing a Catholic Justice' (2006–2007) 312, 323; Gula (n 65) 155.

that John Smith is a legal owner of a property binds everyone who has dealings with that property. However, a Chancery order declaring that John Smith has an equitable interest in the property only binds John Smith and whoever has legal title; it does not in principle affect anyone else. For this reason, whilst some judgements remain, most of what is held in the Chancery records are the actual petitions. Nonetheless, a review of some of these petitions do give an insight into how conscience was understood and used.[116]

Early mediaeval petitions emphasised the fact that the Lord Chancellors, with some exceptions, were senior clerics. A standard signoff in the petitions is seeking a remedy 'for God and Charity'.[117] Others refers to God and Christ.[118] Indeed, given the high degree of discretion given to the Lord Chancellors at the time, long before the modern rules of equity had been developed, many petitions did not reveal a clear cause of action, but simply petitioned for grace, seeking a remedy 'for God and Charity'.[119]

There are repeated reference to conscience in fourteenth-century petitions.[120] This became increasingly prevalent in the fifteenth century.[121] This is not particularly surprising. Both St Thomas Aquinas and St Bonaventure died in 1274 and the canon law was still in development. However, by the fifteenth century, a comprehensive and codified canon law was in place.

The scholastic conception of conscience placed it within reason. Hence, whilst petitions increasingly referred to conscience, many petitions equally made reference to reason, as well as God, charity, right and justice.[122] The natural law has also been referred to as the law of reason.[123] There is therefore a clear terminological link between right, reason and conscience, and they could be used interchangeably (e.g. acting unconscionably is no different than acting against reason, or acting against what is deemed right). This interchangeability is exactly what the petitions are demonstrating.

116 For a more comprehensive review of early Chancery cases, see T Haskett, 'The Medieval English Court of Chancery' (1996) 14 Law & History Review 245.

117 Baildon (n 10) Case 124, page 121; see also cases 126, 127, 130; in case 45 the reference is to 'holy charity'.

118 Baildon (n 10) Case 91, page 84.

119 Baildon (n 10) Case 8, page 9; Case 31, page 35; Case 36, page 40; see F Roughley, 'The Development of the Conscience of Equity' in JT Gleeson, JA Watson and RCA Higgins (eds), *Historical Foundations of Australian Law*, vol 1 (The Federation Press 2013) 142.

120 The earliest reference to conscience in chancery petitions date to 1324 (discovery.nationalarchives.gov.uk/details/r/C9062921 and discovery.nationalarchives.gov.uk/details/r/C9149280); examples of further petitions include one from 1350 (discovery.nationalarchives.gov.uk/details/r/C9061901) and one from 1385 (discovery.nationalarchives.gov.uk/details/r/C9335527); unrelated to equity, the earliest reference to conscience in the National Archives is in a letter dated to 1218–1221 (discovery.nationalarchives.gov.uk/details/r/C9151992) (accessed 19/11/2021).

121 Baildon (n 10) Case 121, page 119.

122 Baildon (n 10) Case 19, page 23; Case 25, page 30; Case 39, page 43; Case 63, page 64.

123 Thomas Aquinas, 'Summa Theologiae' in Timothy McDermott (ed), *Concise Translation* (Methuen 1989) 287.

As the fifteenth century continues, references to conscience become more and more common. The Chancery soon became known as a court of conscience, a term often still referred to today.[124] As such, fifteenth-century petitions seek redress because the defendant has acted against 'law, right and good conscience' and/or because a remedy is warranted as 'law and conscience demand'.[125] Other petitions make reference to 'as good faith and conscience requires' and 'as right and good conscience requires'.[126] Again, reason, right and conscience are being used interchangeably. Another petition expressly refers to the 'law of conscience', which is the 'law executed in this court'.[127]

The reference to the law of conscience clearly signals the link to the natural law, an objective statement of morality. In particular, conscience is not presented as a personal and unerring faculty that stands above a corrupted reason, as conscience would later be conceptualised as in some Protestant theology.

Conscience in the Tudor/Reformation Court of Chancery

The key question for this chapter is whether the Reformation led to any changes in equity and how it perceived of its conscience. As such, it is necessary to look at what transpired in during the sixteenth century.

Even though conscience was understood as a rational exercise, based on objective moral precepts, the Lord Chancellors had personal discretion on how to determine cases, looking at whether the parties had acted unconscionably. There were necessarily concerns about decisions being made based on subjective and arbitrary grounds. These concerns were amplified during the Chancellorships of Thomas Wolsey and Thomas More.[128] In particular with regards to Wolsey, the concern raised was that he was basing decisions on his own moral standards, rather than applying any objective precepts from the natural law and Church teachings.[129] This is a serious concern, as judicial decisions should be based on identifiable reasons, not merely the personal musings of whoever happened to be the judge. As a result, criticisms against the

124 Baildon (n 10) Case 123, page 121.
125 Ibid Case 121, page 119.
126 Ibid Case 144, page 151. The original text reads: 'as gude faith and conscens requyer'; Case 144, page 153. The original text reads: 'as right and good conscience requiren'.
127 Baildon (n 10) Case 143, page 146. The original text reads: 'as good feith & consciens requyren' and 'answer after the lawe of consciens, whiche ys lawe executory in this courte for defaute of remedy by cours of the common lawe'.
128 DR Klinck, 'Lord Nottingham and the Conscience of Equity' (2006) 67 Journal of the History of Ideas 123, 124.
129 T Endicott, 'The Conscience of the King: Christopher St German and Thomas More and the Development of English Equity' (1989) 47 University of Toronto Faculty Law Review 549, 556; Roughley (n 119) 148; JA Guy, 'Wolsey, the Council and the Council Courts' (1976) 91 English Historical Review 481, 487.

Chancery were raised around this time.[130] It is debatable to what extent this was linked to the Reformation. Rather, the concerns seem to stem from the fact that the common law was becoming more fixed and the juxtaposition of the discretionary justice handed down in the Chancery became increasingly marked and, at least to lawyers, more problematic.[131]

Indeed, at this time Selden made his well-known complaint that equity varied with the Chancellor's foot; conscience was applied based on the subjective views of each Lord Chancellor.[132] It is debatable whether this was a genuine complaint; Spence argues that it was said 'more perhaps in jest than in earnest' on the basis that there were many 'erroneous views as to the nature' of equity during the Tudor era.[133] Nonetheless, Selden's comment is the 'classic common-lawyer's complaint'.[134] It suggests that the Lord Chancellor has too much discretion, the rules and principles of equity are too flexible, and the whole notion of conscience is too vague to have any practical value. Elsewhere, Selden complains that conscience must be anchored in the law, or else people could do as they please and justify it based on their own conscience.[135]

However, Selden's complaint can be counteracted. Spence posits that the equity jurisdiction could 'never could have been established, if the conscience of the judge had been his only guide'.[136] Furthermore, Spence notes that

> nothing is recorded as having been delivered judicially from the bench which can warrant the supposition that the private opinion or conscience of the judge, or what is perhaps equivalent, his whim or caprice, independent of principle or precedent, was a legitimate ground of decision.[137]

Equity could not have developed unless there was an objective framework on which it was based. Nonetheless, that objective framework was rather broad, and in the Tudor era there was a need to formalise the equity jurisdiction.[138] That process began with the publication in 1523 of an important treatise called the *Doctor and Student* dialogue.

130 G Behrens, 'An Early Tudor Debate on the Relation between Law and Equity' (1998) 19 Journal of Legal History 143, 144.
131 Kerly (n 8) 95.
132 R Milward (ed), *Table-talk: The Discourses of John Selden* (J.M Dent and Co. 1689) 44; H Jefferson Powell, '"Cardozo's Foot": The Chancellor's Conscience and Constructive Trusts' (1993) 56 Law and Contemporary Problems 7, 8.
133 Spence (n 22) 413.
134 Powell (n 132) 7.
135 Milward (n 132) 34.
136 Spence (n 22) 414; see also *Muschinski v Dodds* [1985] HCA 78; (1985) 160 CLR 583, [9] (Deane J).
137 Spence (n 22) 415.
138 Roughley (n 119) 161.

The dialogue was published by Christopher St German. It is one of the oldest English treatises on equity, and it includes long discussions on the nature of conscience. The publication had a long-lasting impact on English law, not least on the Chancery jurisdiction, and has been cited as authority.[139] Inevitably, St German's understanding of conscience and how it was used in Chancery has played a major role in shaping how conscience has been used in English equity. It helped to anchor a scholastic conception of conscience in English equity, that survived the Reformation and the eventual creation of the Church of England. Equally, the appointment of Thomas More marked a shift away from clerical Lord Chancellors, which helped entrench established practices and perhaps insulated equity from the religious changes in society.[140]

The *Doctor and Student* dialogue was published in 1523. The Lutheran Reformation was still quite young, which would suggest that no major alternative conception of conscience had yet been presented. Unsurprisingly, therefore, St German posits an overall scholastic view of conscience. He writes that synderesis tells us to do 'good', our reason tells us what is 'good' and conscience is the decision-making process to identify a good act or rebuking us for a prior bad act.[141] St German explained that conscience is 'grounded upon the law of God, and the law of reason, and upon the law of the realm not contrary to the said laws of God nor to the law of reason'.[142] The text shows deep reverence for reason and the rational mind, which again is fundamentally scholastic in nature. As with St Bonaventure, St German argued that conscience must learn and develop with experience. For example, he writes that if human laws are changed, our conscience must change with it, with the caveat that human laws should only be binding as long as they are compatible with the law of reason.[143] Ultimately, conscience is not simply a subjective idea based on the Lord Chancellor's personal views; it has an objective basis.

Even though conscience was objective, the equity jurisdiction had, up to this point, been very flexible and there was no doubt a need for it to become

139 The work covered a great extent of English law and has been cited up to modern times; i.e. *Roberts v Swangrove Estates Ltd* [2008] Ch 439, [65] (Mummery LJ); *Williams v Linnitt* [1951] 1 KB 565, 585 (Denning LJ); in one case a legal principle had been identified by Coke and St German, with Page Wood VC saying it thus 'cannot now be disputed', *Rider v Wood* (1855) 1 Kay and Johnson 644, 652; 69 ER 618, 621.

140 Kerly (n 8) 96. Three bishops served as Lord Chancellors in the 1550s under Edward VI and Mary I John Williams was the last clerical Lord Chancellor, holding office between 1621–1625 whilst also Bishop of Lincoln (he later become Archbishop of York).

141 Christopher St German, *Doctor and Student* (TFT Plucknett and JL Barton (eds), Selden Society 1974) 81 (synderesis), 85 (reason), 89 (conscience).

142 Christopher St German, 'Little Treatise concerning Writs of Subpoena' printed in JA Guy, *Christopher St German on Chancery and Statute* (Selden Society 1985) 123.

143 St German (n 141) 111; see also Aquinas (n 123) 284.

more formalised.[144] St German's work was an important part of that process.[145] It helped ensure that equity developed clearer rules and principles, so claimants and defendants knew what to plead, what remedies to seek and what defences could be raised. As Roughley writes, the 'sustained influence' of St German meant that 'scholastic conscience remained a touchstone of the theories of equity and conscience' as England went through the Reformation.[146]

In Chancery petitions dating to the Chancellorship of the Reformer Lord Audley, who was Lord Chancellor 1533–1544, the petitions pray a remedy as the defendants have acted 'against all right equity and good conscience' and 'against right and good conscience'.[147] This is the same phrasing that had been in use for almost two centuries. It did not simply disappear after Henry VIII had pulled England out of communion with Rome. Indeed, whatever complaints were made about the Chancellor's subjectivity, the Chancery had well-established procedural rules, which did not change with the Reformation.[148]

In the later Tudor period, the Chancellors kept working on the process of formalising equity. By contrast to the clerical Chancellors, who heard the equity petitions alongside all their other duties, the later Tudor Chancellors were increasingly trained lawyers and judges, who could devote more of their time to the Chancery.[149] Formalisation continued through the seventeenth century, where notable Chancellors such as Lord Nottingham taxonomised equity into a system still recognisable today. The legacy of the medieval conscience lived on.

Conclusion

As noted earlier, there was remarkable continuity in the legal system during and after the Reformation. There was no great upheaval in the Chancery in terms of the equity jurisdiction, which continued on, and in the coming centuries would become increasingly formalised and better structured.

The lack of a complete overhaul can come down to various facts. There was the sustained influence of works such as the *Doctor and Student* dialogue, which provided a juridical basis to the equity jurisdiction, quite independent of the religious changes that took place in the decades after its publication.

144 That said, a reading of the Chancery petitions shows a great deal of consistency over the fourteenth to the sixteenth centuries in terms of how they are framed and presented as well as in the terminology used, which suggests that there was a great deal of consistency and continuity between different Lord Chancellors.

145 Endicott (n 129) 558; M Macnair, 'Equity and Conscience' (2007) 27 Oxford Journal of Legal Studies 659, 662.

146 Roughley (n 119) 160.

147 JS Purvis, *Monastic Chancery Proceedings* (The Yorkshire Archaeological Society 1934)—consider petitions on pages 1, 15, 155, etc.

148 Kerly (n 8) 61.

149 Ibid 97–98.

Furthermore, the English state religion changed back and forth quite a lot during the later Tutor era, as both Edward VI and Mary I died unexpectedly quite early into their respective reigns; Edward VI was unable to fully commit England to a more radical Protestantism, and Mary I was unable to fully bring England back into the Catholic fold. Elizabeth I formed the Anglican Church, which was a deliberately broad church, incorporating both Catholic and Protestant ideas. Indeed, Slights notes that many Anglicans have continued to see conscience as a 'rational faculty', broadly following the scholastic tradition.[150]

The Monarchy, Parliament and the Courts carried on, more or less unaffected by the changes. What differed were the people who held office. Both equity and the common law carried on as before the Reformation. Property law, in particular, can even today be traced back to mediaeval roots, and the same goes for many of the equitable rights and remedies in relation to property. The Reformation did not impact on these. Theologically, the Protestant vision of conscience is different from the Catholic vision. However, that did not carry over into equity.

Bibliography

Amen M, 'Canonical Equity before the Code' (1973) 33 Jurist 256

Aquinas T, 'Summa Theologiae' in Timothy McDermott (ed), *Concise Translation* (Methuen 1989)

Araujo RSJ, 'Forming the Well-Formed Conscience' (2008) 47 Journal of Catholic Legal Studies 319

Baildon W (ed), *Selden Society, vol 10, Select Cases in Chancery, 1364–1471* (Bernard Quaritch 1896)

Baker Sir John, *An Introduction to English Legal History* (5th edn, OUP 2019)

Barron R, *Catholicism: A Journey to the Heart of the Faith* (Image Books 2011) 3–4

Behrens G, 'An Early Tudor Debate on the Relation between Law and Equity' (1998) 19 Journal of Legal History 143

Berman H, 'Conscience and Law: The Lutheran Reformation and the Western Legal Tradition' (1987) 5 Journal of Law and Religion 177

Bossy J, *Christianity in the West, 1400–1700* (OUP 1985) 171; quoted in Smith S, 'Interrogating Thomas More: The Conundrums of Conscience' (2003–2004) 1 University of St Thomas Law Journal 580

Burrows A, 'We do this at Common Law but that in Equity' (2002) 22 Oxford Journal of Legal Studies

Butler J, *Five Sermons Preached at the Rolls Chapel and a Dissertation upon the Nature of Virtue* (Hackett 1983)

Cade A, *Conscience, It's Nature and Corruption, with Its Repairs and Means to Inform It Aright* (John Williams 1661)

Calvin J, *Institutes of the Christian Religion* (John Allen (trans) (Philip H Nicklin and Hezekiah Howe 1816) vol III

Carson D, 'Reflections on Salvation and Justification in the New Testament' (1997) 40 Journal of the Evangelical Theological Society 581

150 CW Slights, *The Casuistical Tradition in Shakespeare, Donne, Herbert, and Milton* (Princeton UP 1981) 11; Wilks (n 36) 4.

Catechism of the Catholic Church (Burnes & Oates 2000, reprint 2012), Rules 1778–1785
Coughlin JOFM, *Canon Law: A Comparative Study with Anglo-American Legal Theory* (OUP 2010) 45
Donaldson Sir John MR, 'The Office of Master of the Rolls' (1984) 17 Bracton Law Journal 19
Edwards J, *Mary I—England's Catholic Queen* (Yale University Press 2011)
Endicott T, 'The Conscience of the King: Christopher St German and Thomas More and the Development of English Equity' (1989) 47 University of Toronto Faculty Law Review 549
Feldman N, 'The Intellectual Origins of the Establishment Clause' (2002) 77 New York University Law Review 346
Fisher A, *Catholic Bioethics for a New Millennium* (CUP 2012)
Francis Pope, *The Joy of the Gospel (Apostolic Exhortation, 24th November 2013)*, [64]
Greene R, 'Synderesis, the Spark of Conscience, in the English Renaissance' (1991) 52 Journal of the History of Ideas 195
Gula R, *Reason Informed by Faith: Foundations of Catholic Morality* (Paulist Press 1989)
Guy JA, 'Wolsey, the Council and the Council Courts' (1976) 91 English Historical Review 481
Hammond JB and Alvaré HM, *Christianity and the Laws of Conscience* (CUP 2021)
Haskett T, 'Conscience, Justice and Authority in the Late-Medieval English Court of Chancery' in A Musson (ed), *Expectations of the Law in the Middle Ages* (The Boydell Press 2001) 159
Hedge FH, *Martin Luther and Other Essays* (Roberts Brothers 1888) 2
Holdsworth W, *A History of English Law* (4th edn, Methuen 1936, reprinted 1966) 346–47, vol 2; Sir John Baker, 'Reflections on "Doing" Legal History' in A Musson and C Stebbings (eds), *Making Legal History: Approaches and Methodologies* (CUP 2012) 9
Idleman S, 'Private Conscience, Public Duties: The Unavoidable Conflicts Facing a Catholic Justice' (2006–2007) 4 University of St Thomas Law Journal 312, 323
Jefferson Powell H, '"Cardozo's Foot": The Chancellor's Conscience and Constructive Trusts' (1993) 56 Law and Contemporary Problems 7,
Jerome St., *Commentary on Ezekiel, 1.7*; cited in Timothy Potts (ed and trans), *Conscience in Medieval Philosophy* (CUP 1980)
John Paul II, *Pope Veritatis Splendor* (CTS 1993)
Jung Carl Gustav, *The Archetypes and the Collective Unconscious* (2nd edn, Routledge 1959, tenth printing 1991)
Kagan KK, *Three Great Systems of Jurisprudence* (Stevens & Sons 1955) 14; Dodd G, 'Reason, Conscience and Equity: Bishops as the King's Judges in Later Medieval England' (2014) 99 History 213
Kemp E, 'The Spirit of the Canon Law and its Application in England' (2012) 14 Ecclesiastical Law Journal 5
Kerly DM, *An Historical Sketch of the Equitable Jurisdiction of the Court of Chancery* (CUP 1890)
Klinck DR, 'Lord Nottingham and the Conscience of Equity' (2006) 67 Journal of the History of Ideas 123
Langston D, 'The Spark of Conscience: Bonaventure's View of Conscience and Synderesis' (1993) 53 Franciscan Studies 79
Langston D, *Conscience and Other Virtues: From Bonaventure to MacIntyre* (The Pennsylvania State UP 2001)
Lusvardi ASJ, 'The Law of Conscience: Catholic Teaching on Conscience from Leo XIII to John Paul II' (2012) 15 Logos 13, 26
Luther Martin, *A Commentary on Saint Paul's Epistle to the Galatians* (B. Blake 1833)

Macnair M, 'Equity and Conscience' (2007) 27 Oxford Journal of Legal Studies 659
Marenbon J, *The Philosophy of Peter Abelard* (CUP 1997)
Marsh AH, *History of the Court of Chancery and of the Rise and Development of the Doctrines of Equity* (Carswell 1890)
McGrade A, Kilcullen J, and Kempshall M, *The Cambridge Translations of Medieval Philosophical Texts, vol II: Ethics and Political Philosophy* (CUP 2001) 169
Milward (ed), *Table-talk: the Discourses of John Selden* (J.M Dent and Co 1689) 44; H Jefferson Powell, '"Cardozo's Foot": The Chancellor's Conscience and Constructive Trusts' (1993) 56 Law and Contemporary Problems 7
Moser J, 'The Secularization of Equity' (1997) 26 Capitol University Law Review 483
Mousourakis, G. *Comparative Law and Legal Traditions* (Springer, 2019)
Newman JH, *Difficulties of Anglicans* (Christian Classics, New Impression 1969) 256, vol II
Newman JH, *Parochial and Plain Sermons* (Christian Classics, New Impression 1966) 21, vol 1
Newman R, 'Equity in Comparative Law' (1968) 17 International and Comparative Law Quarterly 807,
Paul IV, *Pastoral Constitution on the Church in the Modern World—Gaudium et Spes* (7 December 1965) 16
Perkins W, *A Discourse of Conscience* (John Legate, Printer to the University of Cambridge 1596)
Purvis JS, *Monastic Chancery Proceedings* (The Yorkshire Archaeological Society 1934
Rittgers R, *The Reformation of the Keys: Confession, Conscience, and Authority in Sixteenth-Century Germany* (Harvard UP 2004)
Robinson D, *Conscience and Jung's Moral Vision: From Id to Thou* (Paulist Press 2005)
Roughley F, 'The Development of the Conscience of Equity' in JT Gleeson, JA Watson, and RCA Higgins (eds), *Historical Foundations of Australian Law* (The Federation Press 2013) vol 1
Sacheverell H, *The Nature, Obligations, and Measures of Conscience—A Sermon preached at the Leicester Assizes* (The Booksellers of London and Westminster 1707)
Samet I, 'On Trusts, Angels, Morality and Fusion: Reply to My Critics' (2020) 21 Jerusalem Review of Legal Studies 50
Slights CW, *The Casuistical Tradition in Shakespeare, Donne, Herbert, and Milton* (Princeton UP 1981)
Spence G, *The Equitable Jurisdiction of the Court of Chancery* (Lea and Blanchard 1846) 410, vol 1
St German C, 'Little Treatise concerning Writs of Subpoena' printed in JA Guy (ed), *Christopher St German on Chancery and Statute* (Selden Society 1985)
St German C, *Doctor and Student*, TFT Plucknett and JL Barton (eds) (Selden Society 1974)
Tillotson J, *A Conscience Void of Offence, Towards God and Men* (4th edn, H. Hills 1709)
Tremlett C, *Isabella of Castile: Europe's First Great Queen* (Bloomsbury 2017) 80
VanDrunen D, 'Conscience and Natural Law in Scripture' in JB Hammond and HM Alvaré (eds), *Christianity and the Laws of Conscience* (CUP 2021) 51
Walsham A, 'Ordeals of Conscience: Casuistry, Conformity and Confessional Identity in Post-Reformation England' in H Braun and E Vallance (eds), *Contexts of Conscience in Early Modern Europe 1500–1700* (Palgrave 2004)
Wilks J, *The Idea of Conscience in Renaissance Tragedy* (Routledge 1990) 11
Worthington S, 'Integrating Equity and the Common Law' (2002) 55 Current Legal Problems 223–62

11 The Reformation and Human Rights

David McIlroy

Introduction

Human rights are entitlements human beings have which are antecedent to the positive laws imposed by rulers and which place restrictions on the content of those positive laws. If their origin is traced back to human nature, then they are natural rights. If the entitlements arising from our human nature are regarded as compossible or capable of being harmonised, then those natural rights form part of or are derived from natural law.[1]

All history is interpretation. After the Second World War, with Eastern Europe in the shadow of communism and the Iberian Peninsula under dictatorship, Protestants could claim that the Reformation had been key in bringing about not only religious freedom but also other political and social rights. Thus German Reformed theologian Professor Jürgen Moltmann argued that human rights have a Christian origin because 'Human rights and personal liberties, freedom of religion, freedom of belief and of conscience, democratic forms of government and liberal views of life: all these things grew up together with Protestantism'.[2] As popular morality has increasingly departed from the teachings of the churches, the relationship between Christianity and modernity has become more contested within Protestantism itself as well as by Catholic critics.[3]

The story of the Reformation and human rights is the story of two ideas: the idea of natural law and the idea of natural rights. With regard to natural

1 RP George, 'Natural Law and Human Rights: A Conversation' in E Bucar and B Barnett (eds), *Does Human Rights need God?* (Eerdmans 2005) 135–44. For a discussion of the continued debates by both Catholic and Reformed thinkers about whether human rights represent a legitimate development or a drastic departure from the natural law tradition, see D McIlroy, 'Catholic and Protestant Approaches to Human Rights' (2017) 179 Law & Justice 135–58.

2 J Moltmann, *God for a Secular Society: The Public Relevance of Theology* (Christian Kaiser 1997) tr. M Kohl (SCM 1999), 91.

3 BS Gregory, *The Unintended Reformation: How a Religious Revolution Secularized Society* (Harvard UP 2012).

DOI: 10.4324/9780429264115-15

law, the story is largely one of continuity. With regard to natural rights, the story is one of radical change.

Theological Prolegomena: Natural Law and Human Dignity in Christian Thought

Christianity claims that Jesus of Nazareth was the Son of God, that he was God incarnate, and that he died on a cross and was raised again to life by God the Father through the power of God the Holy Spirit. Christianity claims that in Jesus of Nazareth there was a hypostatic union between the Word of God through which the universe was made and a human person who fully expressed the image of God unaffected by sin.

From those theological claims, expressed in the Creeds of Church and in the Councils of Nicaea, Constantinople, Ephesus and Chalcedon, follow myriad implications. For present purposes, there are two in particular to highlight. First, because Christianity is a monotheistic religion, Christians believe that there is a unitary moral order in creation.[4] Christians expect to find continuity between the teaching of Jesus of Nazareth and the moral order which they believe can be discerned in nature because the Jesus is none other than the Word of God. Second, Christians believe that all human beings have an inherent dignity,[5] and that Jesus of Nazareth affirmed this by the lengths to which he went in order to associate himself with the slave, the leper, the prostitute, the refugee, the criminal and all the others who were likely to be regarded as outcasts or sub-human in the ancient world. Those Creeds, Councils and theological convictions, Catholic, Protestant and Orthodox Christians hold in common.

Human Rights in the Middle Ages

Thomas Aquinas provided the classical exposition of the natural law in the Western Church.[6] Natural law provided both a restraint on Christian rulers[7] and a basis for Christians dealing with Jews, Muslims and pagans living in or on the fringes of Christendom. The Western Church taught, and Thomas

4 By contrast, since Isaiah Berlin's essay, 'Two Concepts of Liberty' in *Four Essays on Liberty*, (OUP 1969), 118, 164–72, secular theorists have tended to see different goods as incommensurable and any ordering as based on subjective preferences.

5 Desmond M Tutu, 'The First Word: to Be Human Is to Be Free' (2015) 30 Journal of Law and Religion 386.

6 Natural law thinking can be found in both the pagan Greek and Roman philosophers and in the Hebrew prophets. Both the Western and Eastern Church Fathers synthesised these streams of thought and emphasised that the Decalogue was both revealed and natural law: SS Harakas, 'Eastern Orthodox Perspectives on Natural Law' (1979) 24 American Journal of Jurisprudence 86.

7 A MacIntyre, 'Natural Law as Subversive: The Case of Aquinas' in *Ethics and Politics: Selected Essays*, vol 2 (CUP 2006) 41.

Aquinas, Francis of Assisi and others practised, dialogue, debate and persuasion with those who were outside Christian society. However, on the grounds of the health of both the individual heretic and society, and with the authority of Augustine of Hippo's approach to the Donatists, the Western Church sought the co-operation of rulers in the suppression of heresy. Movements subject to such repression included the Waldensians, the Cathars, the Lollards and the Hussites.

The greatest canon lawyer ever to become pope, Innocent IV (1243–1254) asserted in his commentary on *Quod super his* that pagans had natural rights to property and that therefore they could not be deprived of their property simply because they were pagans. Despite this, the Teutonic Knights and others waged war against the pagans of Lithuania and other areas on the north-east fringes of Christendom. In 1386, the marriage of Jogaila, Grand Duke of Lithuania, to Jadwiga of Queen of Poland, brought the Lithuanian pagans within the jurisdiction of a country with Christian monarchs (Jogaila having converted to Christianity as a condition of the marriage).

Notwithstanding the personal union of the monarchs of Lithuania and Poland, at the Council of Constance in 1414 the Teutonic Knights asserted their continuing right to attack the pagans of Lithuania on the basis that because the pagans were not Christians, they had no rights. Poland's advocate at the Council of Constance, Pawel Wlodkowic argued persuasively that pagans enjoyed natural rights to build a family, possess property and live in a sovereign country, and that it was the duty of Christians to protect from aggression those pagans who live in peace. Pagans could only be attacked if they were in clear breach of natural law and that only the pope had authority to determine whether such there had been such breaches. The Council upheld Poland's position in all its essential points.

The position by the mid-fifteenth century was that the teaching of the Western Church was clear. Canon law and secular laws were undergirded by natural law. That natural law gave rights to all to family life, to a fair trial and to property. In terms of freedom of religion, those brought up outside Christian society enjoyed the freedom to choose whether or not to accept Christianity; those within it were obliged to follow the teaching of the Church and, if they did not do so, rulers could punish them for their own sake and for the sake of protecting the homogeneity of Christian society.[8]

Human Rights and the New World

The discovery, and subsequent colonisation, of the Americas and the Reconquista of Spain brought a renewed focus on those natural law principles. On the one hand, Popes Nicholas V and Alexander VI gave Portugal and Spain

8 The Council of Constance's decision in favour of the Lithuanian pagans contrasts with its condemnation of Jan Hus, who was arrested on its arrival and subsequently burnt at the stake.

respectively licences to conquer lands owned by 'Saracens, pagans and other enemies of Christ wherever they may be found'.[9] On the other hand, Spanish priests and the theologians at the School of Salamanca argued that natural law protected the rights of the American Indians and that only breaches of natural law could justify military interventions by the European powers.

Dominican friar Antonio de Montesinos in 1511 preached to the Spanish settlers of Hispaniola,

> [Y]ou are in mortal sin, and live and die therein by reason of the cruelty and tyranny that you practice on these innocent people. Tell me, by what right do you hold these Indians in such cruel and horrible slavery?[10]

Bartolomé de Las Casas (1484–1566), who went to Hispaniola as part of the conquering Spanish army, came to recognise the oppression of the American Indians. Giving up his plantation, he became a Dominican priest, arguing in defence of the human dignity of the American Indians and their rights under natural law to retain their property, not to be reduced to slavery or *encomienda*, and to be converted to Christianity not by force but only by persuasion.[11]

Furthermore, although there is fierce debate about whether Pope Alexander VI endorsed the Spanish practice of *encomienda*, both before him (Pope Eugene IV, *Sicut Dudum* (1435)) and after him, the Popes condemned slavery. The papal bull *Sublimis Dei*, promulgated by Paul III in 1537, declared that 'the Indians . . . may and should, freely and legitimately, enjoy their liberty and the possession of their property; nor should they be in any way enslaved'.

Francisco de Vitoria (1483–1546) applied the Thomistic notion of the common good to the relations between the states of Europe and the peoples of the New World. Because American Indians were made in the image of God, they were entitled to ownership of their lands, to equality and to sovereignty, and had the right to engage in just war to defend them.[12] He specifically denied that the papal authority given to Spain to invade had any legitimacy.

In his key lecture, 'On the American Indians', Vitoria dismissed the suggestion that the American Indians were insufficiently rational to govern themselves (Question 1 Article 1, Question 3 Article 8) or that their failure to accept Christianity would deprive them of their rights (Question 1 Article 2). Military intervention would only be justified if (1) the American Indians had

9 Nicholas V, *Dum Diversas* (1452). See also Nicholas V, *Romanus Pontifex* (1455), Alexander VI, *Eximiae devotionis* (1493), *Inter caetera* (1493), *Dudum Siquidem* (1493).

10 OE González and JL González, *Nuestra Fe: A Latin American Church History Sourcebook* (Abingdon Press 2014) 1.

11 G Gutiérrez, *Las Casas: In Search of the Poor of Jesus Christ* (Orbis Books 1993); K Pennington, 'Bartolomé de Las Casas' in R Domingo and J Martínez-Torrón (eds), *Great Christian Jurists in Spanish History* (CUP 2018).

12 B Tierney, *The Idea of Natural Rights: Studies on Natural Rights, Natural Law and Church Law, 1150–1625* (Scholars Press 1997) 255, 272–87.

committed gross human rights violations such as cannibalism or human sacrifice, or (2) if the American Indians refused to act hospitably to Spanish travellers and traders, or (3) if the American Indians refused to allow Christian priests to carry out missionary activities.[13]

In a lurid example of the deference vice shows to virtue, the Kings of Spain and Portugal offered pretended breaches of natural law as justifications for the conquest of what was to become Latin America. The pretences were paper-thin.

Commanded by Emperor Charles V to stop writing or lecturing on the Indian question, Vitoria wrote in a letter to Miguel de Arcos that as the Peruvians had never injured the Spaniards, Pizarro's conquest amounted to the butchery of innocents and 'sheer robbery'.[14]

Human Rights and the Reformation

The magisterial reformers such as the Augustinian monk Martin Luther and the lawyer turned theologian John Calvin did not intend to found new churches; they sought to reform the Catholic Church. The magisterial reformers saw themselves as continuing and deepening the work of humanists such as Erasmus, in returning to the original Greek and to the teachings of the Church Fathers. Initially, it was only the radical reformers who sought a new understanding of the nature of the Church itself.

The Reformation Churches

Cataloguing the Protestant churches which emerged from the Reformation requires a taxonomy of their theology, ecclesiology and territoriality. At the risk of caricature, the Lutheran Church's theology emphasised grace in opposition to law. Martin Luther (1483–1546) sought to take the Church out of politics largely leaving law to secular rulers.[15] Lutheran ecclesiology retained bishops. The Lutheran Church became dominant in large parts of German-speaking or influenced Northern Europe, including the Nordic and Baltic countries.

In Western Europe, from Switzerland, through France, the Netherlands and Great Britain, the approach to reform which took hold is best described as 'Reformed' with a capital 'R'. This movement cannot be understood without reference to John Calvin (1509–1564). So-called Calvinism was, however, only one branch of this movement. The movement owed much to early

13 F de Vitoria, *Political Writings* (A Pagden and J Lawrance, eds) (CUP 1991); A Wagner, 'Francisco de Vitoria' in Rafael Domingo and Javier Martínez-Torrón (eds), *Great Christian Jurists in Spanish History* (CUP 2018).

14 G Cavallar, 'Vitoria, Grotius, Pufendorf, Wolff and Vattel: Accomplices of European Colonialism and Exploitation or True Cosmopolitans?' (2008) 10 Journal of the History of International Law 181.

15 J Witte, *Law and Protestantism: The Legal Teachings of the Lutheran Reformation* (CUP 2002).

reformers such as Ulrich Zwingli (1484–1531), Martin Bucer (1491–1551) and Theodore Beza (1519–1605), and subsequently splintered over disputes provoked by Jacobus Arminius's (1560–1609) teachings on the nature of grace and the extent of the atonement. Reformed churches differed in their ecclesiology. The Dutch Reformed Church was organised around the offices of pastor, elder, teacher and deacon. The Presbyterian Church of Scotland was governed by representative assemblies of elders. The Church of England and its counterparts in other parts of the United Kingdom were Episcopalian. Other Reformed churches held to a Congregationalist understanding of the Church.

Different in character from either the Lutheran or Reformed Reformations were the radical Reformations. The radical reformers had a distinctive ecclesiology. They believed that the church was a gathered congregation of the saints not an institution to which people belonged because of christening. The first wave of such radical reformers arose on the Swiss-German border and were known as the Anabaptists because of their practice of baptising those old enough to express personal belief in Christ rather than infants. Apart from the disastrous attempt to establish an Anabaptist Kingdom in Münster in 1534–35, continental Anabaptists were characterised by their extreme separation from the world and their refusal to participate in politics, government, law or the army, believing all use of 'the sword' to be incompatible with following Christ. An English-speaking Baptist movement started in 1609, which, while sharing the Anabaptist practices of believers' baptism and the gathered church, was more Reformed in its theology and willing to engage with and be involved in politics and secular legal institutions. Finally, in the mid-seventeenth century, the Quakers emerged as a movement emphasising personal inspiration from God, personal piety and a refusal to take oaths, to participate in war, and in many cases to pay tithes or to be involved with the established church in any way.

These differences in the theology, ecclesiology and geographical penetration of Protestant churches were reflected in diverse approaches to questions of natural law and human rights.

The Magisterial Reformers and the Natural Law

Although the magisterial reformers, both Lutheran and Reformed, accused the medieval Western Church of having erroneously assumed that human reason was unaffected by the Fall, Protestant fallibilism affected only the epistemology and not the ontology of natural law. Lutheran theologians such as Philip Melanchthon[16] and Reformed theologians such as Theodore Beza[17]

16 Philip Melanchthon, 'Loci Communes Theologici (1521)' in W Pauck (ed), *Melanchthon and Bucer* (H.A.U.M. 1969).

17 T Beza, *Lex dei moralis, ceremonialis et civilis* (1577), *Concerning the Rights of Rulers Over Their Subjects and the Duties of Subjects Toward Their Rulers*, Henri-Louis Gonin (trans) (University of Notre Dame Press 1956).

were as convinced as their Catholic counterparts that natural law really existed. The difference Protestant theology made was that, theoretically at least, Protestants thought that discovering the natural law was more difficult than some Catholic thinkers had assumed.

Despite this difference in their approaches, Protestant thinkers saw themselves engaged in a common task with their Catholic counterparts of discerning the natural law.[18] This sense continued throughout the seventeenth century up to and including the Lutheran thinker Samuel Pufendorf (1632–1694). Modern readers find Hugo Grotius's heavy referencing of classical pagan sources, medieval writers and more recent Catholic and Protestant thinkers, a distraction from his own arguments, but for Grotius (1583–1645) it was essential to demonstrate the extent of the commonality between his ideas and those of the greatest sages of European civilisation. Drawing on the work of Vitoria, Grotius supported the rights of native peoples not to have religious conversion imposed on them or to be dispossessed of their natural or property rights through war.[19]

Despite the continued affirmation of the existence of natural law, there were significant developments in thinking about where authority for discerning and enforcing natural law lay. Calvin had argued that the 'lesser magistrates'[20] were under a duty to curb the tyranny of kings. The German Reformed jurist, Johannes Althusius (1557–1638) developed this into a full-blown theory of subsidiarity in *Politica Methodice Digesta* (1603). Althusius argued that families, guilds, towns and provinces each had their own purposes and natural laws which it was their authority to obey. To some extent these were conservative theological moves, emphasising the plurality of authority characteristic of the Middle Ages in resistance to the novel claims that kings had a divine right of absolute rule over centralised states.

The Radical Reformation and Natural Law

The Anabaptists' focus was on 'the perfection of Christ'. They had no place for natural law and no need for it, since they professed no aspirations to be involved in the government of anything other than their own communities.[21] Their contribution to human rights arose out of their requests for governments

18 A MacIntyre explores the continued influence of natural law in the Scotland after the Reformation in chapter XII of *Whose Justice? Which Rationality?* (1988). D VanDrunen offers a panoramic history of natural law within Reformed Christianity in *Natural Law and the Two Kingdoms: A Study in the Development of Reformed Social Thought* (Eerdmans 2010).

19 Hugo Grotius, *Commentary on the Law of Prize and Booty* [1603], tr. GL Williams, Clarendon Press 1950; reprint Oceana Publications 1964), 12.97, pp. 221f. See also ibid 12.99, 12.103f. and 12.104, pp. 226, 236 and 238.

20 J Calvin, *Institutes of Christian Religion*, IV.20.31–32.

21 NG Wright, *Disavowing Constantine: Mission, Church and the Social Order in the Theologies of John Howard Yoder and Jürgen Moltmann* (Paternoster 2000), 40.

to leave them alone to worship God in the way they sincerely thought was right and to form their own associations. From their calls for freedom of religion flowered a wide variety of civil rights.

Natural Law and the Rise of Natural Rights

The legacy of the Reformation and the colonisation of the New World was to increase appeals to natural law. Over time, the content of such appeals changed as both Catholic and Protestant thinkers increasingly made arguments framed in terms of natural rights. The next section of this chapter explores how natural rights could be conceived of as corollaries of freedom of religion or as species of property.

The Reformation and Freedom of Religion

In the aftermath of the Second World War, it was common for Protestants to advance a Whig view of history according to which freedom of religion and other human rights were a natural and inevitable fruit of the Reformation. More recent scholarship has tended to emphasise how toleration arose as a practical accommodation either because living side by side proved to be possible or because the costs of religious wars proved to be prohibitive. The true picture is a complex mixture of how theoretical arguments and practical experience led to experiments in toleration which waxed and waned until the nineteenth century.

The Persistence of the Assumption That It Is the Duty of Rulers to Co-Operate With the Church

The term 'Constantinianism' is a misnomer, used to describe the relationship between a government and an established church.[22] Such arrangements can be conceived in a number of different ways. The Gregorian Popes and the reformers John Calvin and John Knox expected that the Church would tell rulers what to do and rulers would obey the instructions given by the Church. The Orthodox Church regarded the ideal relationship between the church and the state as a harmonious one, described as *symphonia*.[23] The Lutheran reformers acknowledged that rulers had much greater freedom, and direct accountability to God, to do what was necessary in order to maintain law and order.

What Catholic, Lutheran and Reformed Churches all had in common was the assumption that there was one true version of Christianity, and that rulers

22 The establishment of Christianity as the state religion of the Roman Empire and the outlawing of pagan practices occurred during the reign of Theodosius I (379–395).

23 DT Koyzis, 'Imagining God and His Kingdom: Eastern Orthodoxy's Iconic Political Ethic' (1993) 55 Review of Politics 267.

were bound to promote this version and under a duty to suppress alternatives. In Lutheran countries, this assumption received its strongest expression in Denmark where, from 1660 until 1849, to be Danish was to be Lutheran (with only a very small number of Roman Catholic, Reformed and Jewish congregations permitted in prescribed locations).

Freedom of Religion as Pragmatic Policy

An early example of toleration arising pragmatically is the Polish-Lithuanian Commonwealth. Under the Warsaw Confederation Act of 1573, the Polish-Lithuanian Commonwealth offered freedom of religion to the Catholic, Orthodox, Reformed and Lutheran Christians and to the Jewish[24] and Sufi Muslim communities within its borders. Another example would be the Duchy of Transylvania, in which Catholic, Lutheran Reformed and Unitarian Churches enjoyed legal recognition and equal rights as a result of Diets between 1536 and 1563.

Toleration within one country introduced for pragmatic reasons was also the experience of France. Henry IV ended the French Wars of Religion by, on the one hand converting from Reformed Christianity to Catholicism and, on the other hand issuing the Edict of Nantes (1598) which granted Reformed Christians freedom of conscience, restoration of their civil rights and the opportunity to work in all fields including in government.

By contrast, the bloody and seemingly interminable conflicts of the Thirty Years' War within the Holy Roman Empire resulted in the Treaty of Westphalia (1648) whose terms allowed rulers to decide which versions of Christianity to promote and to tolerate in their territories.[25]

The Treaty of Westphalia brought an end to the idea that religious difference could be a ground for one polity to go to war with another. It did not establish freedom of religion within a state but instead created a situation in which those unwilling to live under the church established in their home territory could emigrate to another place within the patchwork of jurisdictions within lands under German-speaking influence.

Freedom of Religion as a Loser's Creed

For Reformed Christians who held to a Presbyterian ecclesiology, pleas for toleration can be regarded as a 'loser's creed', made where Reformed Christians were in a minority (as in France), while in places where Presbyterians were in

24 Jews already enjoyed extensive legal rights under the General Charter of Jewish Liberties known as the Statute of Kalisz issued on 8 September 1264.

25 The Peace of Augsburg 1555 had first introduced the principle of *cuius regio, eius religio* between Catholicism and Lutheranism. The Peace of Westphalia extended this principle to Reformed Christianity as well.

a majority (as in Scotland), the idea that the civil powers should support the Church in enforcing the reigning orthodoxy persisted.[26] Samuel Rutherford's influential 1644 work, *The Law and the Prince; A Dispute for the Just Prerogative of King and People*, though using the idea of the covenant to support limited government and the rule of law, was opposed to religious toleration.[27]

There emerged, however, from Reformed Christians' bitter and bloody experience of persecution, a new theological account of authority and of rights. Its direction was set by Theodore Beza's 1574 tract, on *The Rights of Rulers and the Duties of Subjects*, written in the shadow of the St Bartholomew's Day Massacre of 1572. Beza described political authority in terms of a covenant between the people and their rulers to uphold the laws of God and nature and the rights and liberties of citizens.[28] Beza hinted at, but did not fully develop, broader rights of freedom of education, freedom of church government, freedom of speech, assembly and petition, and freedom of contract.[29]

John Witte reads Beza as refuting the duty of princes to enforce the true religion in the name of the rights of citizen to liberty of conscience and free exercise of religion. John Coffey argues, however, that the approach of Beza, like that of Stephanus Brutus Junius's *Vindicae, Contra Tyrannos: Or Concerning the Legitimate Power of the Prince Over the People, and of the People Over the Prince* (1579) was founded on the rights of subjects to defend true religion by force of arms and to rebel against tyrannous and idolatrous kings rather than a principled account of religious liberty *per se*.[30] Toleration was, for most Reformed theologians, still a matter of necessity and expediency. Nonetheless, an important door had been opened by the affirmation that a ruler's right to rule is conditional upon respecting and protecting the rights and liberties of their subjects. All that remained was to develop a principled account of why the choice of what to believe and how to worship was one of those rights.

The Radical Reformation's Plea for Freedom of Religion

In contrast to pleas for toleration by other Reformed Christians, arguments by Baptists, Congregationalists and Quakers arose out of their ecclesiology. Those who held to an independent ecclesiology argued for toleration 'based on their understanding of how the visible church was conceived in relation to the Old and New Testaments and how the freedom of individual

26 J Rose, 'Dissent and the State: Persecution and Toleration' in J Coffey (ed), *The Oxford History of Protestant Dissenting Traditions*, vol 1 (OUP 2020) 313.

27 As the title of Rutherford's 1649 work, *A free disputation against pretended liberty of conscience* makes clear.

28 J Witte Jr., *The Reformation of Rights* (CUP 2007) 137.

29 Ibid 140.

30 J Coffey, 'The Language of Liberty in Calvinist Political Thought' in Q Skinner and M van Gelderen (eds), *Freedom and the Construction of Europe, vol. 1: Religious Freedom and Civil Liberty* (CUP 2013) 305.

congregations applied to the freedom of the individual'.[31] One of the earliest example is the English Baptist Thomas Helwys who, in 1612, made a direct appeal for toleration to King James I, arguing that the king had no power over his subject's consciences.[32]

The radical reformers made their case by reference to the practice of the early Church. Local congregations enjoyed, they asserted, both in the New Testament and for three centuries afterwards, the freedom and independence to discern God's calling and God's commands for themselves.[33] As a consequence, neither an established church hierarchy nor a secular ruler had any authority to interfere with that freedom. The Colony of Rhode Island, founded by Baptist Roger Williams, put this into practice, securing a Royal Charter from Charles II in 1663 which guaranteed freedom of religion.

This freedom of the local congregation became freedom of the individual with the consequent re-conceptualisation of local churches as gathered congregations of individuals who had a personal relationship with or revelation from God. From there it was but a short step to think of churches as voluntary societies, a paradigm for all sorts of free associations of persons with shared concerns. It was also easy to expand the circle of issues subject to individual discernment from the sacred to the secular.

As Polly Ha explains:

> Early independent thought, which rejected the idea of a national church, held radical implications for the freedom of the individual, which was not only ecclesiastical in nature, but could be conceived of as a basic civil liberty that extended beyond the godly.[34]

Locke on Freedom of Religion

Given that pleas for toleration arose as a loser's creed or on the radical edges of the Reformation, how did such an idea become so widely accepted? The central figure is John Locke.

Charles I's attempts to impose absolutist rule in Britain had been defeated by Parliament, whose Puritan supporters were split between those who favoured a Presbyterian ordering of the Church and those who embraced the idea of congregational self-government by the churches. The Westminster Assembly approved the adoption of Presbyterian government for the Church of England but although Parliament endorsed the idea, it was never put into practice.

31 P Ha, 'Religious Toleration and Ecclesiastical Independence in Revolutionary Britain, Bermuda, and the Bahamas' (2015) 84 Church History 826; John Coffey, 'Puritanism and Liberty' in *Persecution and Toleration in Protestant England, 1558–1689* (Longman 2000).

32 Joe Early, Jr. *The Life and Writings of Thomas Helwys* (Mercer UP 2009).

33 J Cann, *Syon's Prerogative Royal* (1641).

34 Ha (n 31) 822.

On Charles II's restoration, Episcopalian government in the Church of England was restored. Although the Church of Scotland was Presbyterian, the prospects of a Presbyterian Church of England were decisively destroyed by the Clarendon Code (comprising the Corporation Act 1661, the Act of Uniformity 1662, the Conventicle Act 1664 and the Five Mile Act 1665). More than 2,000 clergymen were ejected from their positions for refusing to comply with the terms of the Act of Uniformity. There was now a large nonconformist minority in England, subject to penalties which excluded them from public office, from teaching in schools, from attending the Universities of Oxford and Cambridge, and from meeting in groups of more than five people who were not members of the same household.

Catholics were subjected to similar penalties under the Test Act 1673. This required all civil and military officials to disavow the doctrine of transubstantiation and to denounce certain practices of the Catholic Church as superstitious and idolatrous. They were also required to receive the Eucharist in the Church of England. In February 1685, Charles II died and was replaced by his brother James. James' conversion to Catholicism had already been revealed by his resignation of the post of Lord High Admiral rather than taking the oath under the Test Act.

The United Kingdom was not alone in 1685 in feeling the aftershocks of the Reformation. Amsterdam, where John Locke was in exile, was full of campaigns against the persecution of Anabaptists in Switzerland. Louis XIV of France (Henry IV's grandson) revoked the Edict of Nantes in October 1685. He ordered the destruction of Reformed churches and the closure of Reformed schools. The revocation of the Edict of Nantes hastened the emigration of Reformed Christians which had already been triggered by Louis XIV's use of the dragoons to intimidate Reformed Christians since 1681.

Against that background of renewed religious conflict and intolerance, Locke wrote his famous *Letter of Toleration* in Amsterdam in the winter of 1685–1686. Locke argued that each human being was responsible for their own salvation, that true belief could not be forced, and that the church was a voluntary society.[35] As a consequence, a wide range of theistic beliefs could be, and should, for the sake of public peace, be tolerated.

One notable exception was Catholicism. Locke's objection to the toleration of Catholics was principally political rather than religious. The Protestant rulers of England were, in his view, justified in imposing legal penalties on Catholics because the Pope, to whom Catholics owed their ultimate allegiance, was the head of a hostile foreign state. Locke's position was based not on prejudice (as was largely the case when questions were asked about the policies J.F. Kennedy, the first Catholic president of the United States, would adopt) but on the memory of the papal bull *Regnans in Excelsis*, issued by Pope Pius V on 25

35 D McIlroy, 'Locke and Rawls on Religious Toleration and Public Reason' (2013) Oxford Journal of Law and Religion 1.

February 1570, which declared Elizabeth I 'the pretended Queen of England and the servant of crime', to be a heretic and releasing all her subjects from any allegiance to her, even when they had 'sworn oaths to her', and excommunicating any that obeyed her orders.[36]

Locke is both the moment at which arguments for toleration arising out of the Reformation receive their definitive statement and the point at which the door is opened for a very different understanding of human rights. Those reformers who appealed for toleration did so in the name of freedom of conscience. Freedom of conscience as they understood it was the freedom to respond sincerely to God's calling and to God's commands as one understands them. Locke vacillates between that account, which is fully compatible with traditional conceptions of natural law and demurs only on the question of authority, and an alternative account of freedom conceived as the opportunity to pursue pleasure and to avoid pain. In *An Essay Concerning Human Understanding*, Locke explores the thesis that all human beings desire to be happy. He acknowledges the reasonableness of a subjectivist approach to the good if this life is all there is. Because, however, of his convictions as a Christian, Locke argues that true happiness lies in aligning our desires with 'the true intrinsick good' in things (*Essay II.xxi.51*). This intrinsic good is part of a God-given natural law, capable of being discerned rationally,[37] and forms a major part of Locke's argument in *Two Treatises of Government* (1690).

There are, therefore, two different accounts of the good and consequently two different conceptions of freedom in Locke's thought. One account is a development of the tradition of theistic natural law. The intrinsic goodness of things is to be found in their God-given nature and ordering. Human beings are free when they are able to discern that intrinsic goodness and to conform their desires to respond appropriately to it. Viewed in this perspective, Locke's argument for toleration is an argument that governments do not have an epistemic privilege in discerning the ultimate good that is God. The other account is hedonistic. Locke defined property as 'that property which men have in their persons as well as goods'.[38] Human beings have ownership over their bodies and their possessions and therefore should be free to choose for themselves the things we they think will cause them pleasure and to avoid the things which they think will cause them pain.[39] Seen in this light, natural

36 Rose (n 26) 316.

37 J Locke, 'Essays on the Law of Nature' in Mark Goldie (ed), *Political Essays* (CUP 1997) 79–133; in *An Essay* IV.iii.18, Locke says that moral rules are knowable with the same degree of certainty as 'any Demonstration in Euclid'.

38 Locke, 'The Second Treatise of Government', paragraph 173.

39 Joan Lockwood O'Donovan, 'Natural Law and Perfect Community: Contributions of Christian Platonism to Political Theory' (1998) 14 Modern Theology 20; 'The Concept of Rights in Christian Moral Discourse' in M Cromartie (ed), *A Preserving Grace: Protestants, Catholics and Natural Law* (Eerdmans 1997) 143–56; M Koskenniemi, 'Empire and International Law: The Real Spanish Contribution' (2011) 61 University of Toronto Law Journal 1.

rights can therefore be secularised, with ownership of things becoming the dominant paradigm.

Lockean scholars disagree about whether the two accounts are incompatible or whether they can be reconciled (because Locke believes that we can derive happiness from knowing that we have done our duty and because sanctions can alter the balance of pleasure and pain).[40] Whatever the answer to the conundrum of Locke's own ethics, a century later, Jeremy Bentham's *An Introduction to the Principles of Morals and Legislation* (printed 1780, published 1789) reduced good and evil to pleasure and pain in his utilitarian, anti-natural rights, philosophy.

Human Rights and the English and American Revolutions

Locke's arguments in the *Two Treatises on Government* and in *A Letter on Toleration* formed the unofficial philosophy of the Glorious Revolution in the United Kingdom. Catholics and Non-Conformist Protestants were tolerated but remained second-class citizens. The slave trade, a subject on which Locke's legacy was ambiguous at best, continued.[41]

If Locke's arguments for toleration were influential in the United Kingdom, they were foundational in the United States of America (though the example of Rhode Island was also significant). The United States Declaration of Independence and the United States Constitution contained thoroughly Lockean affirmations of equality, human dignity, freedom of religion and other basic rights, but conceived of in terms which prioritised property and freedom of contract. In the United States, without the threat of Papal-sponsored invasion, freedom of religion was extended to Catholics.

Human Rights and the French Revolution

The United Kingdom and France took different paths at the turn of the seventeenth century. The relative toleration of the constitutional monarchy

40 P Sheridan, 'Locke's Moral Philosophy' (2016) *Stanford Encyclopedia of Philosophy* <https://plato.stanford.edu/entries/locke-moral/> accessed 9 June 2021.

41 In his writings, Locke permitted slavery only in the form of captivity and forced labour imposed by the winning side in a war, and he opposed hereditary slavery. Critics of Locke point to him owning stock in the Royal African Company and having drafted the constitution of the Carolinas which permitted its proprietors to own slaves. Defenders of Locke stress that it was Charles II who paid Locke in stock in the Royal African Company in 1682 and that Locke sold his stock in 1685 when he went into exile. They also assert that his work on the constitution of the Carolinas was on the instructions of the Lords Proprietors, and that he was doing no more than giving effect to *their* intentions as a lawyer drafting a will would do: William Uzgalis, 'John Locke, Racism, Slavery, and Indian Lands' in N Zack (ed), *The Oxford Handbook of Philosophy and Race* (2017). 'Slavery-Entangled Philosophy' <https://aeon.co/essays/does-lockes-entanglement-with-slavery-undermine-his-philosophy> accessed 9 June 2021.

established in the United Kingdom in 1689 (though with significant restrictions on English Catholics and non-conformists and even more on Catholics in Ireland) contrasted with the absolutism of Louis IX's 72-year reign.

Louis XIV's revocation of the Edict of Nantes was followed by a period in which the Catholic Church and the French monarchy were very closely associated. Although this Gallican establishment was strongly supported by the Church hierarchy, it was opposed by the Jansenists, a reform movement whose members included Blaise Pascal. On 24 March 1730, Louis XV of France passed a law which only recognised as a legally valid marriage one which had been conducted by a Catholic priest. The Jansenists (though themselves Catholics) argued that this was contrary to the natural law because it denied legal recognition to the stable heterosexual relationships of Protestants, Jews and atheists and therefore legitimacy to the children of such relationships (unless they or a Catholic priest were willing to go through the Catholic ceremony with their fingers crossed).[42]

Among the intellectual supporters of the French Revolution was the American deist Thomas Paine (1737–1809). Paine's support for the French Revolution was motivated by a deep sense of the injustice of the Ancien Régime. His criterion for measuring the just society was based on an imagined social contract, in which the contracting parties, by definition, had gained nothing from and owed no obligations to prior generations. In Paine's account, the only just regime is a government which respects the people's rights and represents the people's interests.[43] In a letter written to Thomas Jefferson in 1789, Paine explained his idea of rights: he talks about 20 people, who were strangers to each other, meeting in an empty country. 'Each would be a Sovereign in his own natural right. His will would be his law, but his power . . . inadequate to his right'.[44] Paine then describes how such people would trade freedom for protection but without giving up their basic pre-social rights. As Paine puts it in the *Rights of Man*, 'society grants [the citizen] nothing. Every man is a proprietor in society and draws on the capital as a matter of right'.[45]

The nature of freedom and the relation between citizens and government is thus conceived of by Thomas Paine in wholly different terms to Reformed accounts of rights. On Reformed accounts, the basic question is one of authority and responsibility: whose responsibility is it to obey God on this point? In terms of citizens' duties toward one another, government has a responsibility

42 DK Van Kley, *The Religious Origins of the French Revolution: From Calvin to the Civil Constitutions 1560–1791* (Yale UP 1996) 127.

43 Y Levin, *The Great Debate: Edmund Burke, Thomas Paine, and the Birth of Right and Left* (Bascic Books 2014).

44 Ibid 93.

45 Ibid 93–94.

to ensure that they are fulfilled; in terms of citizens' duties toward God alone, government does not. For Paine by contrast,

> The formation of society was itself a choice made by free individuals, so the natural rights that people bring with them into society are rights to act as one chooses, free of coercion. . . . Politics, in this view, is fundamentally an arena for the exercise of choice, and our only real political obligations are to respect the freedoms and choices of others.[46]

The Nineteenth Century

Natural Law in the Nineteenth Century

By the middle of the nineteenth century, there were at least six different approaches to questions of natural law and natural rights. The Catholic Church's position was that laws were to be oriented towards the common good. Secular rulers had no authority to stop the spread of Catholic truth and so acted beyond the scope of their God-given powers if they attempted to do so. By contrast, however, secular rulers were entitled to co-operate with the Catholic Church in recognising Catholicism as the established religion and restricting freedoms of religion and expression for other forms of belief and unbelief. The French Revolution was the expression of an anticlerical liberalism which affirmed the natural rights of man, derived from a state of nature and capable of overriding all forms of tradition and authority. Protestantism had, meanwhile, spawned three streams of thinking about natural law and natural rights. One, derived from the magisterial reformers coming to mature expression in Grotius, shared with Vitoria a grounding of international order in natural law. This stream emphasised that human beings deserved to be treated with dignity, even in arenas of violent conflict. Another, whose origins can be traced back to the radical reformers and to those defenders of the rights of Reformed Christians in areas where they were in the minority, established a series of natural rights built around the idea of freedom of religion as the first freedom. A new conception of natural rights had sprung from this latter stream in the thought of John Locke. Natural rights were now understood as a species of individually controlled property. If Grotius's ideas were suited to the situation of the Reformed burghers of Dutch and Huguenot cities; Locke's ideas were amenable to English landowners and to American colonists. The Grotian and Lockean streams could be combined, as they were in the work of Samuel Pufendorf, whose ideas of natural law and international law drew on Grotius but whose emphasis on property and on the state being the sum of individual wills that constitute it are distinctly Lockean in tone.[47]

46 Ibid 91.

47 Pufendorf formulated his views independently of Locke, but in reaction against the ideas of Thomas Hobbes. Locke, by contrast, read Pufendorf's work and recommended that he be included in law curricula.

Locke's relationship with the classical tradition of natural law was fatefully ambiguous; while he affirmed the existence of natural law, his account of rights could be developed in reliance on human autonomy rather than the common good, with the consequence that rights were based on the exercise of the human will rather than the application of human reason. The Lockean approach was rendered in anticlerical liberal form by Thomas Paine. An account of natural rights as a species of property could dispense with the need for God as a hypothesis. It could therefore become a theory of natural rights without an account of natural law.[48]

Whilst all rights-based approaches were based on human dignity, they conceptualised it differently. Unlike the others, anticlerical liberalism did not base its account of human dignity on human beings having been made in the image of God. They were, instead, to be valued in and of themselves.

The final approach, which was to dominate much of the nineteenth and the first half of the twentieth century, was the utilitarianism of Jeremy Bentham (1748–1832). Bentham dismissed the ideas of natural law and natural rights, holding that the greatest happiness for the greatest number was the only sound basis for governmental action.

Human Rights and the Nineteenth Century

The nineteenth century saw significant advances in human rights in Europe but continuing violations of them in the Colonies of the European empires. The century began with movements to abolish the slave trade and ended with both Catholics and Protestants seeking to articulate theological responses to the challenges of industrialisation and modernity.

Slavery

Despite its widespread use by European powers, slavery continued to be condemned by Popes: by Benedict XV in *Immensa Pastorium* (1741) and by Gregory XVI in *In Supremo Apostolatus* (1839). Amongst Protestants, it was those who were themselves disadvantaged in some respect who advocated most strongly for the abolition of slavery.[49] The closest calls for the abolition of slavery came to official Reformed theology was in *The Larger Catechism* of the Westminster Assembly (1647).[50] Richard Baxter, a prominent Puritan divine who had been ejected from the Church of England in 1662, denounced the slave trade and slave traders in his *Chapters From a Christian Directory*

48 Oliver O'Donovan, *The Desire of the Nations* (CUP 1996) 247–48.

49 GM Ditchfield, 'Abolitionism and the Social Conscience' in A Thompson (ed), *The Oxford History of Protestant Dissenting Traditions, vol II: The Long Eighteenth Century c. 1689–c. 1828* (OUP 2018) 284.

50 Questions 129 and 130 of the Larger Catechism impose obligations on those in authority incompatible with chattel slavery.

(1673). The Quakers were particularly distinctive in censuring involvement in the slave trade from the 1750s onwards and of demonstrating that businesses could be run profitably without resort to it.[51] Reformed campaigners like former slave Olaudah Equiano (c. 1745–1797), former slave-trader John Newton (1725–1807) and William Wilberforce MP (1759–1833) were influential in the rise of abolitionism within the Church of England. When the Methodist Church and the evangelical movement in the Church of England in their opposition to slavery joined the denominations formed by the radical reformation, then the climate of public opinion made the trade in slaves and the institution of slavery morally indefensible.[52]

Developments in Freedom of Religion in the Nineteenth Century

The nineteenth century saw a general improvement in freedom of religion in the United Kingdom and France. This was not, however, because of developments in the theology of the Christian Churches. In England it was largely a result of practical politics. In the United Kingdom, the Duke of Wellington as prime minister drove the Sacramental Test Act 1828 and the Roman Catholic Relief Act 1829 through Parliament, bringing to end the penal laws and almost all of the restrictions on Catholicism and on nonconformism.[53] In France, the Revolution introduced religious tolerance, but its seedbed was a reaction to the extensive privileges the Catholic Church had enjoyed in the last century of the French monarchy and its inspiration was Voltaire's *Traité sur la tolerance* (1763). The French Revolution was anything but an unqualified success. From 1789 to 1905, France went through rapid and repeated changes in its form of government and until around 1880 the Catholic Church could legitimately hope that its privileges as the Established Church could be restored.

In Germany, by contrast, as Prussian expansion slowly formed the German Empire, the Lutheran and Reformed churches were merged in 1817 and brought under tight governmental control. Catholics were tolerated but forbidden from fulfilling any official functions for the state. Tensions between the Prussian government and the Catholic Church came to a head in the *Kulturkampf* of 1872 to 1878. After Pius XI's death, Leo XIII had, by 1887, negotiated successfully with Bismarck for the removal of the *Kulturkampf* laws.

51 J Walvin, *The Quakers: Money & Morals* (John Murray 1997) 1228–40.

52 R Anstey, *The Atlantic Slave Trade and British Abolition 1760–1810, Part One* (Humanities Press) (1975).

53 Full participation in the Universities of Oxford, Cambridge and Durham was not possible for Catholics, nonconformist Protestants or non-Christians until the Universities Tests Act 1871. The Jewish Relief Act 1858 allowed Jews to sit as members of Parliament. Restrictions on admittance to Catholic religious orders and on public processions were not abolished until the Roman Catholic Relief Act 1926.

The Catholic Church and Human Rights

As well as the context of consolidation of nation-states in Germany and Italy, empire-building across the globe, industrialisation was a major change in European society in the nineteenth century. It called for a moral response.

In the Catholic Church, Leo XIII's 1891 encyclical *Rerum Novarum* was a key foundation of modern Catholic social teaching. *Rerum Novarum* emphasises the rights and duties of both capital and labour. The right to private property, the right of association (especially the right to form trade unions), the right to education and the right 'of procuring the things which sustain life' were all affirmed. *Rerum Novarum* highlighted the way for Catholic social teaching to develop a comprehensive account of human rights, founded in human dignity and the common good and dependent on the recognition of the duties of different social actors towards one another.

Protestants and Human Rights

The nineteenth century saw distinct theologies emerge within Protestant Churches. Evangelicalism was a movement in self-conscious continuity with the magisterial reformers but with a heavy emphasis on personal conversion and the importance of the congregation similar to that of the radical reformers. Liberal Protestantism was an attempt to render Christianity compatible with developments in Enlightenment thought. Within Anglicanism, an Anglo-Catholic theology, emphasising the Church of England's continuity with the Church Fathers and the apostolic succession of its bishops, arose in Oxford in 1833.

Evangelicals and Human Rights

British evangelicals were active in the nineteenth century in promoting the rights of workers. The most prominent evangelical Parliamentarian, Anthony Ashley Cooper, 7th Earl of Shaftesbury (1801–1885) was described by *The Times* newspaper as having 'changed the whole social condition of England'. He piloted through Parliament legislation reforming lunatic asylums, banning children from working in mines, limiting working hours in mills and factories, introducing clean water supplies for cities and many other reforms seeking to promote human dignity. Outside of Parliament, his Ragged Schools Union demonstrated the aspiration for, and set a blueprint for, universal education.

Liberal Protestants and Human Rights

Liberal Protestantism tended to be associated with nationalism in the nineteenth century. It was not until the end of the nineteenth century that the social gospel movement began to develop within Liberal Protestantism. The social gospel movement emphasised that the dignity of human beings needed to be reflected in their social and economic conditions. However, this movement had been pre-shadowed by Christian Socialism, established in 1848 by F.D. Maurice and Charles Kingsley, though Christian Socialism was distinctive in its emphasis on co-operatives rather than relying on changes in the law.

The Neo-Calvinists and Human Rights

An important, systematic, Reformed approach to human rights was developed by the Dutch Neo-Calvinist theologian and politician Abraham Kuyper (1837–1920). Kuyper sought a way forward for European countries, in which the contribution to public life of their Christian citizens was not swept away by the anticlericalism of the French Revolution.

Kuyper argued that God's sovereignty was not replicated on earth in one single authority but was diffused between different spheres of human activity, each of which had its own sphere sovereignty. Families, church, schools and universities, hospitals, businesses, journalism, science, the arts etc. each of these had their own distinct goals to pursue. Organisations pursuing these goals had their own rights, and the role of the state was to facilitate and co-ordinate the exercise of those rights. Though framed in reaction to the French Revolution, Kuyper's ideas were an emphatic rejection, before the event, of the total control over society exercised by Fascism and Communism.

Kuyper's exposition of a modern Reformed political theology achieved considerable influence beyond his native Netherlands as a result of his visit to Princeton Theological Seminary in 1898. Kuyper's *Lectures on Calvinism* (also referred to as the Stone Lectures)[54] described, in laudatory terms, how the American constitutional experiment was the contemporary expression of Calvinist understandings of natural law, liberty and human rights. Kuyper grounded human rights in conscience. Liberty of conscience was the source from which liberty of association, liberty of the press, liberty of public worship and liberty of thought flowed.

As a politician, and prime minister of the Netherlands from 1901–1905, Kuyper was able to put his theory into practice, developing a framework in which the Dutch state permitted and encouraged the creation of Protestant, Catholic and secular schools, universities, trade unions and other social organisations.

Human Rights and the Twentieth Century

The Universal Declaration of Human Rights

In the aftermath of the Second World War, with the disintegration of the European colonial empires on the horizon and the Stalinist USSR firmly sitting at the table, the need for governments to be subject to universally accepted

54 A Kuyper, *Lectures on Calvinism* (Eerdmans 1931).

norms was as pressing as ever. The Universal Declaration of Human Rights by the United Nations in 1948 was profoundly influenced by Christians, despite human rights not yet being accepted by the official teaching of the Catholic and Orthodox churches and being rejected by some conservative Protestants.

Liberal Protestants were influential in the development of the international human rights instruments. The American Lutheran, Otto Frederick Nolde, was one of the drafters of the Universal Declaration of Human Rights, an important lobbyist at the United Nations for the World Council of Churches, and a campaigner for the establishment of the United Nations Commission on Human Rights.

The World Council of Churches affirmed, at its inaugural assembly in 1948:

> We are profoundly concerned by evidence from many parts of the world of flagrant violations of human rights. Both individuals and groups are subjected to persecution and discrimination on grounds of race, color, religion, culture or political conviction. Against such actions, whether of governments, officials, or the general public, the churches must take a firm and vigorous stand, through local action, in cooperation with churches in other lands, and through international institutions of legal order. They must work for an ever wider and deeper understanding of what are the essential human rights if men are to be free to do the will of God.[55]

Despite being at odds with the official teaching of their church, Catholics were also significant in the drafting of the Universal Declaration. In a series of essays published from 1943 onwards (and further writings censored by the Vatican), American Jesuit priest and theologian, John Courtney Murray (1904–1967) had argued for religious freedom and a pluralist approach to the public square.[56] More directly involved was the French philosopher Jacques Maritain (1882–1973). Maritain was a key advisor to the drafters of the Universal Declaration of Human Rights. He based his account of human rights on natural law, as the title of his 1942 book, *The Rights of Man and Natural Law*, makes evident, and on human dignity. In respect of human dignity, he said: 'The worth of the person, his liberty, his rights arise from the order of the naturally sacred things. . . . A person possesses absolute dignity because he is in direct relationship with the absolute'.[57] Acknowledgement of this 'absolute dignity' demands the recognition of the 'inalienable rights of the human person' and a reconceptualisation of governments as 'vicars of the multitude' rather than

55 R Traer, *'Liberal Protestants' in Faith in Human Rights: Support in Religious Traditions for a Global Struggle* (Georgetown UP 1991).

56 John Courtney Murray's key essays were collected together in *We Hold These Truths: Catholic Reflections on the American Proposition* (Sheed & Ward 1960).

57 Jacques Maritain, *The Rights of Man and Natural Law* (The Centenary Press 1944) 6.

vicars of God.[58] Nonetheless, 'every right possessed by man is possessed by virtue of the right possessed by God, Who is pure Justice, to see the order of His Wisdom in beings respected, obeyed and loved by every intelligence'.[59]

It would be wrong, however, to overlook the contribution of a Lebanese Greek Orthodox politician in the drafting of the United Nations Declaration of Human Rights. Charles Malik[60] was key in ensuring that the Declaration included the right to change one's religion within its definition of freedom of religion. He also challenged Eleanor Roosevelt's emphasis on 'individual rights' by referring to the rights of 'persons'. In so doing, he was standing within the tradition of Christian Pre-Enlightenment thought which understood rights as grounded in natural law and free obedience to God's ordering rather than as expressions of radical autonomy and self-sufficiency.

Reformed Attitudes to Natural Law

Protestant support for the Universal Declaration of Human Rights was grounded in the need for a practical response to the horrors of Nazism and in a commitment to civil rights which had arisen as corollaries of freedom of religion. Appeals to natural law were, however, rare. German-speaking Liberal Protestantism had been shaken to its core by the defeat in the First World War. The Swiss Reformed theologians, Emil Brunner and Karl Barth sought to return to the historic Christian beliefs in Jesus Christ as God incarnate. Although Brunner emphasised Jesus's divine status and his unique role in salvation, his social ethic gave a large place to natural law, termed by Brunner the orders of creation, conceived of in conservative terms. Barth saw how such ideas could be twisted by the Nazis, with submission to Jesus Christ displaced by blind faith and obedience to the Führer. The result was a debate in 1934, whose title when published in English needs its own spoiler alert: *Natural Theology Comprising 'Nature and Grace' by Professor Dr Emil Brunner and the Reply 'No!' by Dr Karl Barth*.[61]

In the aftermath of the Second World War, liberal Protestants promoted human rights, especially the right to freedom of religion but also a wide range of other political, social and economic rights. Evangelical and other conservative Protestants were similarly committed to freedom of religion but were

58 Jacques Maritain, *The Twilight of Civilization* (Sheed and Ward 1946).

59 Jacques Maritain, *Man and the State* (University of Chicago Press 1951) 96.

60 AG Roeber, 'Orthodox Christians, Human Rights and the Dignity of the Person: Reflections on Charles Malik (1906–1987)' (2018) 70 Journal of Eastern Christian Studies 285.

61 K Barth and E Brunner, *Natural Theology comprising 'Nature and Grace' by Professor Dr Emil Brunner and the Reply 'No!' by Dr Karl Barth* (P Fraenkel, trans) (Geoffrey Bles 1946). Karl Barth is identified as 'the source of a strong antinaturalist [i.e. anti-natural law] and antirights tendency among many later Protestants' in J Witte Jr. and Frank S Alexander (eds), *The Teachings of Modern Roman Catholicism on Law, Politics and Human Nature* (Columbia UP 2007) xxvi.

suspicious of human rights talk. Liberal Protestants neglected natural law; as a result of Barth's influence, conservative Protestants rejected natural law.

It was not until the last quarter of the twentieth century that Reformed Christians rediscovered their common ground with Catholic moral teaching on many social issues,[62] the ways in which natural law formed part of the heritage of the reformers and their heirs at least into the eighteenth century, and the place of natural law within the Bible.[63]

Developments in Catholic Thinking Regarding Human Rights

The second half of the twentieth century saw the Catholic Church integrate natural rights in the guise of human rights into its approach to natural law. The reconciliation of the Catholic Church to human rights as a general philosophical approach and to freedom of religion in particular came with Vatican II. The stance taken by the Council had already been anticipated by Jacques Maritain and John Courtney Murray, and it was Murray who played a key role in persuading the Council to acknowledge the place of freedom of religion as an aspect of human dignity.

John XXIII's 1963 encyclical *Pacem in Terris* (published six months after the end of the Cuban missile crisis) affirmed the importance of the Universal Declaration of Human Rights but nonetheless insisted that our true human destiny is the fulfilment of our relationship with God rather than the development of an autonomous self.

In respect of human rights, as in so many other areas of the Catholic Church's life, Vatican II represented a turning point.[64] Under John Courtney Murray's influence, in *Dignitatis Humanae Personae* the Church recognised the importance of freedom of religion as an expression of human dignity.[65] Catholicism, like the Reformed Churches 400 years earlier, had discerned that although the Church has a legitimate role in evangelising and teaching, faith and its expression are matters of personal expression and responsibility before God. Two of the major wings of the Church had united in their commitment to religious freedom, a freedom which remains fragile and under threat in much of the world today.

62 F Schaeffer, *A Christian Manifesto* (Crossway 1981).

63 D McIlroy, *A Biblical View of Law and Justice* (Paternoster 2004), D McIlroy, 'What's at Stake in Natural Law?' (2008) 89 New Blackfriars 508–21. John Barton, *Ethics and the Old Testament* (2nd edn, SCM Press 2010), D VanDrunen, *A Biblical Case for Natural Law* (Acton Institute 2006), *Divine Covenants and Moral Order: A Biblical Theology of Natural Law* (Eerdmans 2014).

64 PG Carozza and D Philpott, 'The Catholic Church, Human Rights, and Democracy: Convergence and Conflict with the Modern State' (2012) 15 Logos, A.J. Catholic Thought & Culture.

65 Second Vatican Council, Dignitatis Humanae, available at www.vatican.va/archive/hist_councils/ii_vatican_council/documents/vat-ii_decl_19651207_dignitatis-humanae_en.html.

Subsequent popes have continued to affirm the importance of human rights, understood as derived from natural law, an objective moral order and the common good. John Paul II, in his speech to the General Assembly of the United Nations celebrating the 50th anniversary of the United Nations said: 'there are indeed universal human rights, rooted in the nature of the person, rights which reflect the objective and inviolable demands of a universal moral law'.[66]

In the same vein, Benedict XVI, in his address to the United Nations in April 2008 affirmed that human rights are 'measures of the common good' arising from the foundation of the natural law 'inscribed on human hearts and present in different culture and civilizations'.[67]

Developments in Reformed Thinking Regarding Human Rights

Decisive in the Protestant Churches' awakening to a broader understanding of human rights was the effectiveness of the non-violent civil rights movement in the United States led by Baptist pastor Martin Luther King Jr. King's campaign was emphatically founded on human dignity and natural law rather than human autonomy.[68] His aims were to end 'humiliating segregation, political domination, and economic exploitation'. He sought the freedom for black people to participate in the common good as respected and equal members of society. This included the freedoms to be able both in practice as well as in theory, to vote, peacefully assemble and enjoy public amenities such as buses, libraries and restaurants, but also to live in a decent house and to earn an adequate income.[69] These aims were reflected in the United Nations International Covenant on Civil and Political Rights 1966 and the International Covenant on Economic, Social, and Cultural Rights 1966.

Prospects for the Future

The late twentieth century saw considerable developments in both Catholic and Protestant thinking. The Catholic Church incorporated human rights and a commitment to freedom of religion into its understanding of natural law.

66 Pope John Paul II, Address to the Fiftieth General Assembly of the United Nations Organization www.vatican.va/content/john-paul-ii/en/speeches/1995/october/documents/hf_jp-ii_spe_05101995_address-to-uno.html.

67 Pope Benedict XVI, Address of the Holy Father to the General Assembly of the United Nations Organization in New York (April 18, 2008) <http://www.vatican.va/holy_father/benedict_xvi/speeches/2008/april/documents/hf_ben-xvi_spe_20080418_un-visit_en.html>.

68 Martin Luther King, 'Beyond Vietnam, Address Delivered to the Clergy and Laymen Concerned About Vietnam at Riverside Church in New York City' (Apr. 4 1967) in Clayborne Carson and Kris Shepard (eds), *A Call to Conscience: The Landmark Speeches of Dr Martin Luther King Jr* (Warner Books 2001) 139; HJ Richardson III, 'Dr Martin Luther King Jr as an International Human Rights Leader' (2007) 52 Villanova Law Review 471 at 476, 484.

69 TF Jackson, '"Bread of Freedom": Martin Luther King, Jr. and Human Rights' (April 2008) Organization of American Historians Magazine of History 14.

Reformed and Lutheran theologians recovered the idea of natural law as the necessary foundation and framework for rights. Dutch American Reformed philosopher Nicholas Wolterstorff put forward a radical Christian vision for rights, inspired by the principled pluralism of Abraham Kuyper,[70] and calling for the Christian Churches to continue to make the fight against injustice integral to their mission.[71]

The dominant understanding, in the early twenty-first century, of churches in the Catholic, Lutheran and Reformed traditions is therefore one in which human rights are affirmed as the outworking of human dignity and the demands of natural law. Despite this, in Western countries where respect for human rights is well-established, some significant theologians (both Catholic and Protestant) have questioned whether excessive reverence is given to individual human rights, distorting moral reasoning and damaging legitimate expressions of communal morality.[72]

Rather than being distracted by culture wars in which claims are made for new rights, the Churches have an important role to play in reminding the world that for so many billions of people in the world the basic rights to life, to a fair trial, to freedom of religion and to a decent education, among other things, remain desiderata.

Conclusion

I have attempted in this chapter to trace the ways in which the Reformation contributed to the modern idea of human rights. Given the 430-year gap between Luther posting his 95 theses and the publication of the Universal Declaration of Human Rights, the genealogy is a long and complex one.

For nearly 200 years after the Reformation, Catholic and Protestant thinkers across Europe were engaged in a common enterprise of debating and developing the idea of natural law. If anything, the religious controversies of the Reformation, along with the discovery of the New World, increased the appeals by all sides to natural law. There were significant Reformed theologians such as Richard Baxter as well as important Catholic thinkers like Francisco de Vitoria who condemned slavery and the expropriation of the Amerindians. Freedom of religion emerged as practical policy before its theological justification became widely accepted, even among Protestants. Once the concept had taken root, a series of related freedoms, of association, of conscience, of expression and of education began slowly to be explored.

70 N Wolterstorff, 'Christianity and Human Rights' in J Witte Jr. and M Christian Green (eds), *Religion & Human Rights: An Introduction* (OUP 2012).

71 N Wolterstorff, *Journey toward Justice* (Baker Academic 2013).

72 A MacIntyre, *After Virtue: A Study in Moral Theory* (University of Notre Dame Press 1984) 69–70; N Biggar, *What's Wrong With Rights?* (OUP 2020).

The path from the liberties of the Duchy of Transylvania, the Polish-Lithuanian Commonwealth, the Dutch Republic and the England of the Hanoverian Revolution to the human rights instruments of the mid-twentieth century is not a smooth one. Theocentric ideas of natural law and international law were displaced by anthropocentric Enlightenment conceptions. Regime changes across Europe put back the cause of human rights in many places. The British Empire was notable for its lack of consistency and for the contrast between the rights of its home citizens (notably excluding the majority in Ireland) and those of its subject peoples, not only in respect of religion but also in terms of other civil, social and economic rights. The very idea of rights themselves was repudiated by the modern philosophies of utilitarianism and communism.

Faced with the challenges of first industrialisation and then the two world wars, the Christian churches had a common heritage on which to draw. That heritage consisted of the theological conception of human dignity and the historical engagement with the idea of natural law. The legacy of the Reformation was to transform the understanding of human dignity and of natural law through an emphasis on the natural rights of first congregations and then individuals. Such a transformation had not been the intention of the magisterial reformers but was first promoted by the radical reformers. Although the development of the freedom of religion occurred unevenly and in response to the failures in many places to re-impose religious uniformity after the Reformation, it also represented a radicalisation of a mainstream and long-term theological position. Expansionist wars in the name of Christianity were fought in the Middle Ages on the basis of punishing violations of natural law or defending the rights of Christians. This was because the medieval church recognised that those outside Christendom were free to choose to accept or reject the Christian faith. What the Reformation and reform movements within both the Catholic Church and the Protestant Churches in the centuries afterwards emphasised was the need for inner conviction and conversion, and the importance of sincere worship. It follows that freedom of religion should be extended to all.

The debates within and between the different strands of Christianity which emerged from the Reformation were a key factor in the development of legislation in respect of freedom of religion, civil rights and human rights. The path was not a smooth one, but the influence of Christian theology on the history, formulation and content of human rights cannot be ignored. Julian Rivers, a Reformed thinker in the Church of England, is right in his judgement that the 'Christian natural law tradition arguably reached its fulfilment in the Universal Declaration of Human Rights and the mid-twentieth century human rights movement more generally'.[73]

73 J Rivers, 'Is English Law Christian?' in N Spencer (ed), *Religion and Law* (Theos 2012) 147.

Bibliography

Anstey R, *The Atlantic Slave Trade and British Abolition 1760–1810, Part One* (Humanities Press 1975)

Barth K and Brunner E, *Natural Theology comprising 'Nature and Grace' by Professor Dr Emil Brunner and the Reply 'No!' by Dr Karl Barth*, P. Fraenkel (trans) (Geoffrey Bles 1946)

Barton J, *Ethics and the Old Testament* (2nd edn, SCM Press 2010)

Berlin I, 'Two Concepts of Liberty' in *Four Essays on Liberty* (OUP 1969) 118

Beza T, *Lex dei moralis, ceremonialis et civilis* (1577), *Concerning the Rights of Rulers Over Their Subjects and the Duties of Subjects Toward Their Rulers*, Henri-Louis Gonin (trans) (H.A.U.M. 1956)

Biggar N, *What's Wrong With Rights?* (OUP 2020)

Cann J, *Syon's Prerogative Royal* (1641)

Carozza PG and Philpott D, 'The Catholic Church, Human Rights, and Democracy: Convergence and Conflict with the Modern State' (2012) 15 Logos A.J. Catholic Thought & Culture

Cavallar G, 'Vitoria, Grotius, Pufendorf, Wolff and Vattel: Accomplices of European Colonialism and Exploitation or True Cosmopolitans?' (2008) 10 Journal of the History of International Law 181

Coffey J, 'Puritanism and Liberty' in *Persecution and Toleration in Protestant England, 1558–1689* (Longman 2000)

Coffey J, 'The Language of Liberty in Calvinist Political Thought' in Q Skinner and M van Gelderen (eds), *Freedom and the Construction of Europe, vol 1: Religious Freedom and Civil Liberty* (CUP 2013)

de Vitoria F, *Political Writings*, A Pagden and J Lawrance (eds) (CUP 1991)

Dignitatis Humanae <www.vatican.va/archive/hist_councils/ii_vatican_council/documents/vat-ii_decl_19651207_ dignitatis-humanae_en.html>

Ditchfield GM, 'Abolitionism and the Social Conscience' in A Thompson (ed), *The Oxford History of Protestant Dissenting Traditions, vol II: The Long Eighteenth Century c.1689-c.1828* (OUP 2018)

Early J Jr., *The Life and Writings of Thomas Helwys* (Mercer UP 2009)

George RP, 'Natural Law and Human Rights: A Conversation' in Bucar E and Barnett B (eds), *Does Human Rights need God?* (Eerdmans 2005)

González OE and González JL, *Nuestra Fe: A Latin American Church History Sourcebook* (Abingdon Press 2014)

Gregory BS, *The Unintended Reformation: How a Religious Revolution Secularized Society* (Harvard UP 2012)

Grotius H, *Commentary on the Law of Prize and Booty* [1603], G L. Williams (trans) (Clarendon Press 1950; reprint Oceana Publications 1964)

Gutiérrez G, *Las Casas: In Search of the Poor of Jesus Christ* (Orbis Books 1993)

Ha P, 'Religious Toleration and Ecclesiastical Independence in Revolutionary Britain, Bermuda, and the Bahamas' (2015) 84 Church History 826

Harakas SS, 'Eastern Orthodox Perspectives on Natural Law' (1979) 24 American Journal of Jurisprudence 86

Jackson TF, '"Bread of Freedom": Martin Luther King, Jr. and Human Rights' (April 2008) Organization of American Historians Magazine of History 14

John Paul II, 'Pope Address to the Fiftieth General Assembly of the United Nations Organization' <www.vatican.va/content/john-paul-ii/en/speeches/1995/october/documents/hf_jp-ii_spe_05101995_address-to-uno.html>

King Martin Luther, 'Beyond Vietnam, Address Delivered to the Clergy and Laymen Concerned about Vietnam at Riverside Church in New York City (Apr. 4, 1967)' in C Carson and K Shepard (eds), *A Call to Conscience: The Landmark Speeches of Dr Martin Luther King Jr* (IPM/Warner Books 2001) 139

Koskenniemi M, 'Empire and International Law: The Real Spanish Contribution' (2011) 61 University of Toronto Law Journal 1
Koyzis DT, 'Imagining God and His Kingdom: Eastern Orthodoxy's Iconic Political Ethic' (1993) 55 Review of Politics 267
Kuyper A, *Lectures on Calvinism* (Eerdmans 1931)
Levin Y, *The Great Debate: Edmund Burke, Thomas Paine, and the Birth of Right and Left* (Basic Books 2014)
Locke J, 'Essays on the Law of Nature' in Mark Goldie (ed), *Political Essays* (CUP 1997)
MacIntyre A, *After Virtue: A Study in Moral Theory* (University of Notre Dame Press 1984)
MacIntyre A, *Whose Justice? Which Rationality?* (Duckworth 1988)
MacIntyre A, 'Natural Law as Subversive: The Case of Aquinas' in *Ethics and Politics: Selected Essays* (CUP 2006) 41, vol 2
Maritain Jacques, *The Rights of Man and Natural Law* (The Centenary Press 1944)
Maritain Jacques, *The Twilight of Civilization* (Sheed and Ward 1946)
Maritain Jacques, *Man and the State* (University of Chicago Press 1951)
McIlroy D, *A Biblical View of Law and Justice* (Paternoster 2004)
McIlroy D, 'What's at Stake in Natural Law?' (2008) 89 New Blackfriars 508–21
McIlroy D, 'Locke and Rawls on Religious Toleration and Public Reason' (2013) Oxford Journal of Law and Religion
McIlroy D, 'Catholic and Protestant approaches to Human Rights' (2017) 179 Law & Justice 135
Melanchthon Philip, 'Loci Communes Theologici (1521)' in W Pauck (ed), *Melanchthon and Bucer* (Westminster Press 1969)
Moltmann J, *God for a Secular Society: The Public Relevance of Theology* (Christian Kaiser 1997), M Kohl (trans) (SCM 1999) 91
Murray John, *Courtney We Hold These Truths: Catholic Reflections on the American Proposition* (Sheed & Ward 1960)
O'Donovan Oliver, *The Desire of the Nations* (CUP 1996)
O'Donovan Joan Lockwood, 'Natural Law and Perfect Community: Contributions of Christian Platonism to Political Theory' (1998) 14 Modern Theology 20; 'The Concept of Rights in Christian Moral Discourse' in M Cromartie (ed), *A Preserving Grace: Protestants, Catholics and Natural Law* (Westminster Press Eerdmans 1997) 143–56
Pennington K, 'Bartolomé de Las Casas' in R Domingo and J. Martínez-Torrón (eds), *Great Christian Jurists in Spanish History* (CUP 2018)
Pope Benedict XVI Pope Address of the Holy Father to the General Assembly of the United Nations Organization in New York (April 18, 2008) <http://www.vatican.va/holy_father/benedict_xvi/speeches/2008/april/documents/hf_ben-xvi_spe_20080418_un-visit_en.html>
Richardson H J III, 'Dr Martin Luther King Jr as an International Human Rights Leader' (2007) 52 Villanova Law Review 471
Rivers J, 'Is English law Christian?' in N Spencer (ed), *Religion and Law* (Theos 2012)
Roeber AG, 'Orthodox Christians, Human Rights and the Dignity of the Person: Reflections on Charles Malik (1906–1987)' (2018) 70 Journal of Eastern Christian Studies 285
Rose J, 'Dissent and the State: Persecution and Toleration' in J Coffey (ed), *The Oxford History of Protestant Dissenting Traditions* (OUP 2020)
Schaeffer F, *A Christian Manifesto* (Crossway 1981)
Sheridan P, 'Locke's Moral Philosophy' (2016) *Stanford Encyclopedia of Philosophy.* <https://plato.stanford.edu/entries/locke-moral/>
Tierney B, *The Idea of Natural Rights: Studies on Natural Rights, Natural Law and Church Law, 1150–1625* (Scholars Press 1997) 255
Traer R, *'Liberal Protestants' in Faith in Human Rights: Support in Religious Traditions for a Global Struggle* (Georgetown UP 1991)

Tutu Desmond, 'The First Word: to be Human is to be Free' (2015) 30 Journal of Law and Religion 386

Van Kley DK, *The Religious Origins of the French Revolution: From Calvin to the Civil Constitutions 1560–1791* (Yale UP 1996)

VanDrunen D, *Natural Law and the Two Kingdoms: A Study in the Development of Reformed Social Thought* (Eerdmans 2010)

VanDrunen D, *A Biblical Case for Natural Law* (Acton Institute 2006), *Divine Covenants and Moral Order: A Biblical Theology of Natural Law* (Eerdmans 2014)

Wagner A, 'Francisco de Vitoria' in Rafael Domingo and Javier Martínez-Torrón (eds), *Great Christian Jurists in Spanish History* (CUP 2018)

Walvin J, *The Quakers: Money & Morals* (John Murray 1997)

Witte J, *Law and Protestantism: The Legal Teachings of the Lutheran Reformation* (CUP 2002)

Witte J Jr., *The Reformation of Rights* (CUP 2007)

Witte J Jr. and Alexander FS (eds), *The Teachings of Modern Roman Catholicism on Law, Politics and Human Nature* (Columbia University Press 2007)

Wolterstorff N, 'Christianity and Human Rights' in Witte J Jr. and Christian Green M (eds), *Religion & Human Rights: An Introduction* (OUP 2012)

Wolterstorff N, *Journey toward Justice* (Baker Academic 2013)

Wright NG, *Disavowing Constantine: Mission, Church and the Social Order in the Theologies of John Howard Yoder and Jürgen Moltmann* (Paternoster 2000)

Zack N (ed), *The Oxford Handbook of Philosophy and Race* (2017). 'Slavery-entangled philosophy' <https://aeon.co/essays/does-lockes-entanglement-with-slavery-undermine-his-philosophy>

12 The Reformation and the Birth of Criminal Law

Mathias Schmoeckel

Introduction

Since ancient times some deeds have demanded public punishment. The Ten Commandments, for example, contain norms that pronounce clear prohibitions of transgressions and their punishments. The similarity of the gods to the ruler is illustrated, for example, by the Codex Hammurabi: the monarch enacted such laws for his kingdom and thus promised to dispense and enforce justice in his kingdom, just as the gods gave their order to the earth. The very first part of this codex was called the 'realization of law and justice in the land'.[1] Principal ideas for the use of criminal law, such as retribution, general and special preventions of criminal acts, are very old. Here the talion principle was used to prevent abuse of this order.[2] In ancient Greece and Rome there were even special courts for such crimes. This reflected the gravity of the crime and the desire for purification of the society.

'Poena' as a loan word indicates both a reception of Greek law[3] and the terminological separation of that area of law which threatens punishment: 'Poena est noxae vindicta [. . .] omnium delictorum coercitio' (D. 50,16,131 pr./1) (*Punishment is the revenge of crime. . . the punishment of all crimes*). Retaliation seems to have been the dominant objective of criminal prosecution in these times. But in ancient Rome, crimes could be dealt with in public courts or in private proceedings:[4] excluding the state and the public, the father of a family could for a long time even determine life and death of his children and wife.[5] There was no clear-cut separation between criminal and civil law; instead

1 G Pfeiffer, *Lex Hammurapi* (M Schmoeckel and S Stolte eds, Examinatorium Rechtsgeschichte 2008) 1–4.

2 H Petschow, 'Zur Systematik und Gesetzestechnik im Codex Hammurabi' (1967) 57 ZA 146–72, 149.

3 D Flach, *Die Gesetze der frühen römischen Republik* (Darmstadt 1994) 25.

4 H Gottlieb Heumann/E Seckel, Handlexikon zu den Quellen des römischen Rechts, Jena 1907, 435 sub 1b): 'Privatstrafe'.

5 T Mommsen, *Römisches Strafrecht, Leipzig 1899* (reprint Darmstadt 1961), 16f.

DOI: 10.4324/9780429264115-16

the law of the Roman citizens clearly incorporated the possibility to sentence many crimes.

However, they did not develop the notion of an independent criminal law as a distinct legal subject. The classical jurists began to specifically deal with this matter,[6] so that modern authors could write famous textbooks on 'Roman criminal law'.[7] Therefore, the Digests contained separate sections on criminal law in the 'libri terribiles' (D. 48–50), even if this separation was not always precise and included mainly procedural issues. Nevertheless, it must be noted that this separation and categorisation was not contemporary but was only later sharpened by scholarly reviews.

In the Jewish-Christian tradition, established by the Church Fathers, courts had to guarantee justice in litigation. Public peace and alliance with God had been violated by the wrong-doer and the detection of his wrongs and a just punishment, in proportion to his fault, required reconciliation with the Almighty.[8] Courts had to find the true facts of the offence and to determine the equitable punishment. Human courts were regarded as lower courts to God's Last Judgement, so that wrongs corrected in life could no longer be punished by God, taking duly convicted criminals directly to paradise. From this perspective, judges acted as doctors in giving bitter medicine to the souls in order to ameliorate the wrong-doers and to lead them to a better life.

The correct punishment was disputed. While the Old Testament tried to limit the verdicts to the actual damage and prevent further violence by the famous phrase 'an eye for an eye' (Exodus 21, 23–25) and not more, the Sermon on the Mount (Mt 5:38) contradicted this rule explicitly, so that revenge, retribution and retaliation were generally forbidden.[9] And yet legislation against crimes was hardly capable of correcting the criminals. The penitence of the old church requested them to abstain from the Eucharist for 40 years, to remain outside the church for ten years and to only gradually approach the altar again. This system was not suited to deal with multiple wrongs in a lifetime.

In the following centuries, in the Frankish realm, criminal prosecutions were less and less used due to the weak power of the king. Bloody feuds and individual prosecution of crimes became characteristics of the kingdom. Some

6 M Bretone, *Geschichte des römischen Rechts. Von den Anfängen bis zu Justinian* (1992) 194.

7 G Geib, *Geschichte des römischen Criminalprozesses bis zum Tode Konstantins* (Göttingen 1842) 411; B Santalucia, *Diritto e processo penale nell'antica Roma* (Milano 1989); more cautiously M Scognamiglio, *Nullum crimen sine lege. Origini storiche del divieto di analogia in materia criminale* (Salerno 2009) passim.

8 For these ideas cf. M Schmoeckel, *Die Jugend der Justitia* (Archäologie der Gerechtigkeit im Prozessrecht der Patristik 2013).

9 M Schmoeckel, 'Retaliation. Christian Reasons for Punishment: An Overview' in M Hill, N Doe, RH Helmholz, and J Witte (eds), *Christianity and Criminal Law (Law and Religion)* (Routledge 2020) 62–79.

even deduced from this that there had been no criminal law and no punishments at all in the Germanic kingdoms.[10] Royal litigation acted against major crimes only in rare cases. Contrary to popular conceptions, Hermann Nehlsen was able to show some time ago that the knowledge of a public right to punishment was by no means forgotten or unknown in the Germanic kingdoms.[11]

Correcting morals was left to the church. The monastic movement in late antiquity instituted a different way of reacting to human wrongdoing, which first conquered the British Isles, then the European continent. The monks accepted private confessions and determined individual penitence according to individual culpability.[12] Even though the monks, from a religious point of view, sought to comprehend the bad deeds of the population in the confessional conversation, this was not criminal law but the confessional procedure, which was not yet contrasted with the secular procedure as a 'forum internum'.[13] It was a religious procedure, although it resembled more and more criminal prosecution. Furthermore, Hiberno-Scottish penitentials resemble modern criminal codes, as they defined the sins and their penitence. But for centuries, *forum externum* and *internum* were clearly separated.

This system became more dominant in the course of the twelfth century, when famous texts were written summarising the practice of penance, for example book 19 of Burchard of Worms' Decretum, which was therefore called 'Corrector sive Medicus'.[14] Though these practices could influence official and public courts, the *forum externum*, these different types of criminal prosecution must not be mixed up.

The highest maxim of canon law on crimes was 'ne crimina remaneant impunita'.[15] This maxim does not want to belittle the crimes, it just states the necessity to re-establish justice in society. What had become known in public had to be answered by a public and appropriate verdict. Therefore, in theory,

10 V Achter, *Geburt der Strafe* (V. Klostermann 1951).

11 H Nehlsen, 'Entstehung des öffentlichen Strafrechts bei den germanischen Stämmen' in: *Freiburger Festkolloquium für Hans Thieme, Gerichtslauben-Vorträge* (1983) 3–16; the finding was confirmed in J Weitzel (ed), *Hoheitliches Strafen in der Spätantike und im frühen Mittelalter, Konflikt, Verbrechen und Sanktion in der Gesellschaft Alteuropas, Symposien und Synthesen 7* (2002).

12 For an overview on this topic cf. A Firey (ed), *A New History of Penance* (Brill 2008); A Larson, *Master of Penance: Gratian and the Development of Penitential Thought and Law in the Twelfth Century* (Studies in Medieval and Early Modern Canon Law, Band 11) (Catholic U of America Press 2014); J Goering 'The Internal Forum and the Literature of Penance and Confession' (2004) 59 Traditio 175–227.

13 Classical: HJ Schmitz, *Bußbücher und das kanonische Bußverfahren*, vol 1 (1883, Reprint Graz 1958).

14 F Gagnon Le Corrector sive Medicus de Murchard de Worms (1000–1025): présentation, traduction et commentaire éthno-historique, Mémoire présenté à l aFaculté des études supérieures en vue de l'obention du grade de Maitre ès arts (M.A.) en histoire, Université de Montréal 2010 (https://papyrus.bib.umontreal.ca/xmlui/handle/1866/4915, last visited 3.8.2022).

15 L L Kéry, *Gottesfurcht und irdische Strafen: Der Beitrag des mittelalterlichen Kirchenrechts zur Entstehung des öffentlichen Strafrechts* (Böhlau Verlag 2006) 675ff.

capital punishment was seen as the *poena ordinaria*. This still had an element of prevention, but in many cases the punishment mirrored the deed in reflecting the special atrocity of the crime. *Poena extraordinaria*, however, could be any punishment, which had not formerly been enacted by laws. In the same line, *crimina ordinaria* were enacted by law unlike *crimina extraordinaria*. This indicates that to some extent crime prevention could be stipulated by custom or jurisprudence alone.

In the thirteenth century, secular lords intensified their own criminal prosecutions in order to demonstrate and legitimise their power. This reopened an international debate on the use and the necessity of criminal prosecution.[16] However, this period did not yet know any 'criminal law' as a distinct legal subject nor an individual criminal procedure. The terms *delictum* and *crimen* were still confused. The decretals after Bernard of Pavia had a fifth book, which was commonly characterised by containing provisions dealing with crimes, but there were also many other subjects in these texts, such as norms on international questions.[17]

The 'Tractatus de criminibus' was written in the twelfth century.[18] It is considered to be the oldest manual on criminal law of Roman origin and the first 'Summa de maleficiis'.[19] The author is thought to be a 'magister G' who worked on it in the late 1150s or early 1160s,[20] or between 1162 and 1164.[21] The first part does not deal with (substantive) criminal law, but with the form of procedure preferred in the European tradition from late antiquity to the eighteenth century, namely the accusation procedure, which was therefore also called *processus ordinarius*. Offences are only dealt with according to this principle:[22]

> Criminum alia sunt publica, alia priuata, alia nec publica nec priuata. Item alia sunt ordinaria, alia extraordinaria.
> *Some crimes are public, some are private, and some are neither public nor private. Likewise, some are ordinary, others extraordinary.*

High treason and similar acts are considered by the author as public offences that go back to the imperial legislation. Extraordinary offences are those whose

16 W Naucke, 'Straftheorie, Strafzweck' in *HRG*, vol 5 (1st edn, HRG 1998) 1–6: 2.

17 For an overview, see M Schmoeckel, *Canon Law (Tübingen - Mohr Siebeck 2019)* (2019) 265ff.

18 G Minucci (ed), *Tractatus criminum Saeculi XII* (Archi. Per La Storia Diritto Med. E Mod. 1997).

19 H Kantorowicz Il 'Tractatus criminum' in: Per il cinquantenario della 'Rivista penale' fondata e diretta da Luigi Lucchini, Città di Castello 1925, 361–76 = *Rechtshistorische Schriften*, ed. by H Coing/G Immerl (Karlsruhe 1970) 273–85.

20 A Gouron, 'On the origins of criminal law: the first criminal law treatises' in: K Kroeschell (ed), Festschrift für H. Thieme zu seinem 80. Geburtstag, Sigmaringen 1986, 263–283 = Ders., Études sur la diffusion des doctrines juridiques médiévales, CStS 264, London 1987, 47–57.

21 G Minucci, Prolegomena, in: Ders., Tractatus, xci.

22 G Minucci, Tractatus, 11: De divisione criminum, tit. 2.

punishment the judge has to decide himself, because the law does not give him any specifications.[23]

Later, this chapter will deal with a number of offences, but also with procedural issues, which, like torture, could also be used in civil proceedings. In criminal offences (*crimina*) a distinction is still made between those that are capital and those that can be punished either with corporal punishment or fines only.[24] No text at that time or in the following centuries distinguished between the substantive criminal law and criminal procedure.[25]

A much shorter text on the criminal system focuses more on punishments, but also includes the procedural perspective.[26] Of course, this helped to separate the seriousness of the criminal cases from the rest of the trials, but in my view this does not establish criminal law as an independent subject.[27] It would have been quite possible for the jurists, in view of the known material, to distinguish between criminal law and civil law or the rest of the material in substantive and/or procedural respects; but there was obviously no compelling reason to do so. All law was conceived as a way of instructing and enlightening society and individuals as to God's will. Law in general was a way of coming to terms with God's idea for the world.[28]

Only in the writings of Bartolus and his followers was there a clear notion of 'culpa' (culpability) as the essence of any crime and the reason of punishment established.[29] The following generations of lawyers used this new category to establish the first rules of criminal law. This is also demonstrated by the highly learned Johannes Bertachinus (1448–1492), who showed with his treatise on customs how much potential for modern dogmatisation had been accumulated in recent centuries. In his last and ninth book of this treatise he treated criminal law in the context of customary law.[30] Bertachinus

23 G Minucci, Tractatus, 15: De divisione criminum, tit. 2.

24 G Minucci, Tractatus, 40: tit V: De quaestionibus, 44: tit VI: De criminibus.

25 This is still true of some later works, cf. e.g. F Casonus, *Quaestiones criminales* (Venice 1584) but it was actually concerned with procedural issues such as the mode of trial and means of evidence such as circumstantial evidence and torture.

26 'De criminalibus causis', edited by J F von Schulte (ed), *Festschrift zur Feier des 22. Dezember 1888*, an welchem vor 50 Jahren Geheimrat Prof. Dr. Bernhard Windscheid in Bonn zum Doctor iuris utriusque promoviert wurde (Bonn 1888) 7–15. Similarly Tancred's 'Summula de criminibus', cf. R Fraher, 'Tancred's Summa de criminibus' (1979) 9 BMCL 23–35.

27 P Landau, 'Ne crimina maneant impunita. Zur Entstehung des öffentlichen Strafanspruchs in der Rechtswissenschaft des 12. Jahrhunderts' in M Schmoeckel u.a. (Hg.), *Der Einfluss der Kanonistik auf die europäische Rechtskultur, Band 3: Straf- und Straprozessrecht* (Norm und Struktur, 37.3) (Böhlau Köln 2012) 23–35, 24.

28 A Padovani, *Perché chiedi il mio nome? Dio, natura e diritto nel secolo XII* (Giappichelli 1997).

29 R Sorice, *Vittime Colpevoli e colpevoli innocenti. Ricerche sulle responsabilità penali nell'età del diritto comune* (Diritto cultura società. Storia e probleme della giustizia criminale, 11) (Bononia UP 2018).

30 M Schmoeckel, 'J Bertachinus und die Entstehung des gelehrten Steuerstrafrechts' in B Kretschmer and B Benno Zabel (eds), *Studien zur Geschichte des Wirtschaftsstrafrechts. Methoden—Analysen—Kritik* (Baden-Baden 2018) 433–49.

wanted to distinguish—still without the modern vocabulary—between intent and negligence, known or unknown or unclear criminal law. Gradually, rules concerning punishment evolved.

Furthermore, there were still no special regulations for 'criminal procedure'. Though the authors did distinguish between a procedure in civil cases (*civiliter*) and criminal matters (*criminaliter*), the difference was not categorical.[31] Only with regard to the severity of the punishment should judges and parties be more careful, particularly in evaluating legal evidence, not to sentence innocents too rashly. In cases where life or bodily integrity was potentially at stake, the judge should be more cautious in ordering harsh measures against the accused. However, torture could also be ordered in monetary cases and against witnesses if the judge deemed it necessary.[32] But there was no clear-cut difference in procedures. Moreover, lesser offences, which would eventually be punished just by fines, were also dealt with 'civiliter'. In consequence, a proceeding 'criminaliter' did not apply in all cases of punishments and therefore had a different meaning. Of course, since ancient times there had been the idea of punishment being used to prevent and deter crime. Seneca can be cited with his wise rule: 'nemo prudens punit quia peccatum est sed ne peccetur'.[33] But public prosecution and legal reactions to crimes sought to undo the wrongs committed. Presenting the convicted criminal in front of the main church before execution in order to amend for his guilt became as important as the execution itself.

In contrast to this older system, the law of the sixteenth and eighteenth centuries was able to develop the new subject of 'criminal law'. It will be shown here when and how this new independent legal field was established and how this invention relates to the Protestant Reformation. In other words, since when has the criminal offence been distinguished from a civil case? What was the reason for the new concept of public punishment that led to the autonomy of this subject?

Reformation

Legislation

The old system changed around 1500. There are several factors responsible for this. As early as the fifteenth century, a movement arose to adapt the legal

31 M Schmoeckel, *Humanität und Staatsraison. Die Abschaffung der Folter in Europa und die Entwicklung des gemeinentlichen Strafprozeß- und Beweisrechts seit dem hohen Mittelalter, Norm und Struktur 14* (Böhlau 2000) 321.

32 Ibid 238f, 492f.

33 Seneca, De ira 1.19.7: *'Nemo prudens punit, quia peccatum est, sed ne peccetur'*, (the wise man does not punish because the action committed is a sin, but so that the sin is not committed again in the future). a quotation from Plato, Protagoras 324 a; cf. M Lausberg Seneca and Plato (Calcidius) in the Preface to the Saturnalia of Macrobius, in: RMP (1991) 167–91: 179 fn. 41; more substantively Schilling A Nemo prudens punit quia peccatum est sed ne peccetur—Strafen und Strafzwecke im römischen Strafrecht, in: ZAR 21 (2015) 159–75.

system to modern ideas by improving old laws, a process called 'reformation'.[34] At the same time, another movement arose to regulate individual areas with the help of special, often rather short laws. These are known as police ordinances, which were directed towards the observance of public order (*policey*).[35] The aim of these laws was to define good order, to demonstrate the ruler's orthodoxy and to instruct and educate the population in the right way of life.[36]

In most cases, these new laws brought a further orientation towards the *ius commune*, that is, the legal tradition of Roman and canon law. This was particularly true for Roman canon law, which increasingly served the rulers' desire to make their own legislation more effective by means of an upstream chain of courts. At the same time, this was intended to prevent interference from outside, for example by the papal finding that justice had been denied according to papal standards.

These developments culminated in the Imperial criminal ordinance, the 'Halsgerichtsordnung', also called 'Constitutio Criminalis Carolina' of 1532. In its predecessors, the Halsgerichtsordnungen of Bamberg (1507) and Tyrol (1499), this law also refers to a movement that had already emerged in the fifteenth century.[37] The Tyrolean Criminal code, enacted by Emperor Maximilian as Duke of Tyrol and therefore also known as the 'Maximilianische Halsgerichtsordnung' (Maximilian's Criminal Ordinance), is often regarded as the first modern penal code. In fact, these texts are rather a code of criminal procedure and also define the right level of punishment for the individual offences according to their severity, which is why the offences themselves are also mentioned, yet hardly defined. The judge's perspective is essential for applying this law. This ordinance begins with the conditions of arrest and the prerequisites of torture, establishes the right punishment, and finally explains the ways of sentencing and execution as well as rivalling competences. The code defines how judges should proceed and punish in cases where criminal offences have been committed. Apart from the blending of substantive and procedural law, this code certainly already resembles a modern penal code.

34 For an introduction: R Schulze Reformation (source of law), in: *HRG*, vol 4, 1990, 468–72; G Dilcher, Stadtrecht, in: *HRG*, vol 4, 1990, 1863–1873: 1870f.

35 For an introduction, see Schmelzeisen, Policeiordnungen, in: HRG Bd. 3, 1984, 1803–1808; M Stolleis (ed), *Policey im Europa der Frühen Neuzeit, Studien zur europäischen Rechtsgeschichte 83* (Klostermann 1996) on this, the series: K Härter and M Stolleis (eds), *Repertorium der Policeyordnungen der Frühen Neuzeit, Studien zur europäischen Rechtsgeschichte 84, vol 1: Deutsches Reich* (Klostermann 1996). The juridical dimension and the theological interpretation dependent on it are unfortunately overlooked by Irene Dingel, 'Gute Ordnung. Ordnungsmodelle der Reformation und ihre Wirkung' in W Kinzig and J Winnebeck (eds), *Glaube und Theologie. Reformatorische Grundeinsichten in der ökumenischen Diskussion, VWGTh 54* (Leipzig: Evangelische Verlagsanstalt 2019) 293–308.

36 T Simon, 'Erziehungsgedanke in den frühneuzeitlichen Polizeiordnungen' in Eva Schumann (ed), *Das erziehende Gesetz, AAWG 30* (De Gruyter 2013) 59–74.

37 J Kohler and W Scheel, *Die Carolina und ihre Vorgängerinnen. Text, Explanation, History*, 4 vols, Halle a.S. 1900/02 (reprint Aalen 1968).

This combination of procedural law and criminal provisions is also found in the famous 'Layenspiegel' by Ulrich Tenngler (1445–1521/22),[38] who first published his work in 1509. The third part of the 'Layenspiegel' contains an account of criminal law mixed with procedural issues. Its introduction clearly separates the civil matters of the first two parts from the following 'Peinlichen sachen' (penal matters).[39] Such cruel legal consequences were regularly demanded in a time, in which deterrence was more important than efficient prosecution.

Protestant Reformation

Another influence on the evolution of criminal law can be found in the teachings of Luther and his companions.[40] It has often been debated whether these writings triggered new debates or just intensified an older discussion often called the 'Reformation before the Reformation'. There were, however, two new influences, which were both consequences of humanism. The one insight combined with this new scientific approach was that law was dependent on regional and epochal influences. It was therefore problematic to assume the influence of antique laws. The second consequence was that new laws had to be enacted which were adapted to the necessities of their respective region and its inhabitants. In Saxony, the Protestant Theologians of Wittenberg developed a new veneration for the 'Sachsenspiegel', the description of the regional customary law. It was another device to turn away from Rome.[41]

The rejection of papal authority was connected with the idea that every human being was equally capable to find the truth, so that the Roman Church could no longer presume to be the sole authority on defining crimes such as heresy. Instead, criminal prosecution should be the task of the secular lords in order to establish law and order, but—most of all—peace among their subjects. Luther in particular emphasised the necessity of harsh punitive justice for the maintenance of public order; only in this way could harsher punishments from God be averted from society.[42]

Melanchthon argued in addition that legislation could help to determine God's will, so that it could serve as a means to educate the population and to

38 B Pahlmann U Tengler (c. 1447–1511) in G Kleinheyer and J Schröder (eds), *Deutsche und Europäische Juristen* (Tübingen 2017) 446–49.

39 U Tenngler Layenspiegel, Mainz 1536, here: Leyenspiegels Dritter Teyl, fol.Cr.

40 On the Protestant Reformation and its relevance for law cf. generally J Witte, Jr., *Christianity and Law: An Introduction* (CUP 2008); V Mäkinen (ed), *Lutheran Reformation and the Law* (Brill 2006).

41 On the following, cf. already M Schmoeckel, *Recht der Reformation* (Mohr Siebeck 2014) 207f. 237f.; idem, Fragen zur Konfession des Rechts im 16. Jahrhundert am Beispiel des Strafrechts, in: I Dingel and WF Schäufele (eds), *Kommunikation und Transfer im Christentum der Frühen Neuzeit, VIEG.B 74* (Verlag Mainz : Philipp von Zabern 2007) 157–91.

42 Layenspiegel, T C with the references to the need for harsh prosecution, C verso with reference to 'the new Evangelical doctrine'.

increase discipline, which in turn could be a way, although not a condition, to better the chances of justification and faith.

Originally, Lutheran territories did not abandon penance and confessionals, where private sins (*peccata*) were sentenced with penitence, while the secular authority only decided on crimes (*crimen*). However, it had to use legislation also in order to ameliorate wrongs in society. This attempt to correct social discipline became an important criterion to judge the achievements of the secular authority. While the princes' public claim to punishment prevailed,[43] confessions and penitence gradually lost their significance in Lutheran countries.

In contrast, in the Roman Catholic field, the Council of Trent intensified the dualism of *peccatum* and *crimen*, of (secular) criminal justice and confessional jurisprudence, as they interpreted private confessions (the *forum internum*) as true criminal prosecutions. For this reason, the *forum internum* needed procedure just like the *forum externum*. The authority of Roman law tried to influence both levels of courts.

In both denominations, however, criminal law was used to influence the behaviour of the population. Social discipline was the purpose of these courts and criminal legislation. But in Protestant countries, the prince was the principal responsible for the good conduct of the people and responded directly to God. In case of disobedience, God's ire could be terrible and devastate the country. Floods, wars or pandemics could be a sign of his discontent and be interpreted as his reaction to royal sins. For this reason, princes saw themselves vulnerable to public attack, because every evil affecting the community could be interpreted in this sense as divine criticism of the authorities and indicate the guilt of the authorities.[44]

A further turn was brought about by the theology of John Calvin, who rejected the necessity of confessions and private penitence altogether. Instead, he emphasised the chance of every individual to turn to God, even after the greatest crime. Everybody should use all means for an inner reorientation, the *metanoia* of his soul.[45] His followers, therefore, invented alternatives to capital punishment, because even culprits should hope for justification.

In this perspective, it became even easier to separate misbehaviour and crimes from other legal issues. Due to the concentration of public penal power on the secular authorities, criminal law was increasingly distinguished from civil law in the laws and in the literature as the law of and among citizens. Furthermore, in order to demonstrate their concern for and commitment to these issues, it became a necessity for the secular lords to draft new legislation

43 E.g. clear in J Althusius Dicaeologicae libri tres (Frankfurt a.M. 1649 (2nd reprint Aalen 1967)), I.98, n.25, 355.

44 Concurring in the result, H Maihold, 'The Grounding of Modern Criminal Law in Christian Theology' (2018) 39 Kansai University Review of Law and Politics 21–40, 29.

45 M Schmoeckel, 'Metanoia. Die Reformation und der Strafzweck der Besserung' in R Schulze (ed), *Strafzweck und Strafform zwischen religiöser und weltlicher Wertevermittlung, Symbolische Kommunikation und gesellschaftliche Wertesystem 25* (Rhema 2008) 29–58.

on crimes or misdeeds in order to ensure the public order and good comportment of their people. Criminal codes or public ordinances were established in order to correct comportment in public or in private spheres, such as the definition of appropriate clothing. Due to the theology of Melanchthon, crimes no longer provoked the necessity of public reactions and could be avoided by good legislation. General prevention by criminal codes informed the people of prohibited activities and their punishment. In this perspective, laws assumed the character of schoolbooks addressed to the citizenry. These Protestant theologians used legal texts as a code of good conduct just like the Bible.

André Tiraqueau

As with many French jurists, it is impossible to determine whether André Tiraqueau (1488–1558) was a Protestant. He himself avoided revealing his denomination. This was typical for many Protestants and Catholics at the time, who thought their sacrifice of a public statement on their religious convictions were necessary for the peace and the unity of the French kingdom. Educated in Poitiers, a centre of humanism, he was appointed to the Parlement de Paris in 1541. In any case, he had been friends with François Rabelais since university; he profited much from his law student friend and called him 'Le bon, le docte, le sage, le tant humain, tant débonnaire et équitable Tiraqueau'.[46] Théodore de Bèze also praised him highly.[47]

In 1559, Tiraqueau's son edited posthumously his father's most famous work 'De poenis temperandis'.[48] This is how it is structured:

A. Causes d'atténuation ou de suppression de la peine
    I. Faute volontaire, involontaire, erreur
    II. Modalités de l'acte coupable
    III. Mobiles
B. Causes de non-imputabilité
    I. Démence
    II. Contrainte
    III. Age et sexe
C. Faits justificatifs
D. Mesures de politique criminelles
E. Circonstances atténuantes diverses
F. Grâces diverses
G. Moyens de procédure tendant à la mitigation de la peine

46 In the prologue to the fourth book of 'Pantagruel'.

47 JL Halperin, 'Tiraqueau André' in P Arabeyre, J-L Halpérin and J Krynen (eds), *Dictionnaire historique des juristes français XIIe-XXe siècle* (PUF 2007) 742f.; J Brejon, *Un jurisconsulte de la Renaissance. André Tiraqueau (1488–1558)* (Recueil Sirey 1937).

48 A Tiraquellus, *De poenis Legum, ac Consuetudinum, Statutorumque temperandis, aut etiam remittendis, & id quibus quotque ex causis* (1559 (reprint [in excerpts] Generic 1986)).

This might be translated as:

A. Reasons for mitigation or suppression of punishment
   I. Voluntary wrongs, involuntary, error
   II. Modalities of the culpable act
   III. Motives
B. Reasons for not punishing
   I. Insanity
   II. Constraint
   III. Age and sex
C. Justificatory reasons
D. Criminal policy measures
E. Several mitigating circumstances
F. Different pardons
G. Procedural means tending to mitigate the penalty

The text first deals with some general questions of criminal law, such as intent, mistake, imputability, coercion, age. After that, reasons for an increase and/or reduction of sentences are dealt with, such as the political nature of the crime, mitigating circumstances, and clemency decisions.

Only in the last part does Tiraqueau deal with procedural questions, such as what should happen in the case of insufficient evidence or in the case of statutes of limitations, etc., as well as in the inquisition process and where the judge lacks jurisdiction. It seems that elements of procedural law are again mixed with substantive criminal law. The very first part of Tiraqueau's *De poenis temperandis* makes clear that everything is to be dealt with that may have an effect on sentences; in the same way that the accused is likely to be interested in being helped by procedural as well as factual arguments. In doing so, Tiraqueau may have started from the general observation that, despite the statutory determination of the punishment for an offence, it is nevertheless necessary to search for all exculpatory and aggravating elements in the individual case, so that, after all, it is ultimately the judge who must determine guilt and the level of punishment in all cases.[49] Thus, this work really concentrates for the first time on the determination of the right level and type of punishment, although not on the rules and principles of substantive criminal law. This does not provide a list of criminal offences; it is not meant to explain what people have to avoid. It is addressed rather to the judge explaining how to combine reasons for harsher or milder punishment. In this perspective, it describes the technique of rendering a just verdict.

49 B Carpzov, *Practica novae imperialiis saxonicae Rerum Criminalium* (1635) p. 3 q.150 n.7, 510: 'cum hodiè omnes poenae arbitrariae factae sint'.

Abraham Saur

Abraham Saur (1545–1516) was a Protestant from Hesse who had studied law in Wittenberg and Marburg. He was appointed imperial notary in 1568. After a period as tutor to the children of Count Wolrad of Waldeck, he was employed as a lawyer (advocat and procurator) by the supreme court of Hesse, the 'Samthofgericht' at Marburg. He is remembered above all as a writer, for he wrote several books of legal content, which were long remembered, probably because of the German language Saur used. He drew on scholarly writings as models as well as his own practical experience. But he also wrote poems.

In particular, his 'Strafbüchlein' was well received by his contemporaries, as it was printed at least in seven editions. In his introduction, he referred to Jeremiah 21:12 in order to explain the task of a judge: he had to condemn the wicked but should also appeal to conscience and tell what could be hoped and feared. The index explains the contents of the book:

> Von allerley Falsch—Straff allerhand Falsches [. . .]
> Straff derer/so gefängliche Item/wahnwitzige oder sinnlose Weibspersonen beschlaffen,
> Vom Ehebruch
>
> Straff deß Ehebruchs/und was eigentlich ein Ehebruch sey . . .
>
> Von eusserlichen Schäden
> Straff der verätherey Straff der Brenner
> Von Pfandungen/
>
> Von Tödtungen und innerlichen Schäden
> Straff derer/somit Gifft oder Venen heimlich vergeben . . .

Folgen etliche Auszüge deß Mortes/so entschuldigen in sich haben

1. Von Nothwehr inn gemein
2. Von ungefährlicher Entleibung in und ausserhalb der Nothwehr
3. Von Widerstand einem Beschädiger
4. So dem Todtschläger durch den Entleibten der Todt gebräuwer worden were
5. Die entleibung eines Diebs im Diebstal
6. Also auch die Entleibung inn Fechten undd Ritterspilen
7. Wann Kinder/Unsinnige/jemand entleiben
8. Ubelthat der gar Alten
9. So ein Entleibung veraltet ist
10. Entleibung auß billichem Zorn
11. Todtschlag oder Ubelthat auß Trunckenheit
12. Deß Sohns wird von deß Vaters wegen verschonet
13. So ein Todtschläger ander mehr Ubelthäter anzeigt

14. So ein Todtschläger gar künstlich were
15. Von Geistlichen Todtschlägern
16. Wann jemand verwundet wird und darnach sribet/und man zweiffelt/ oder an der Wundergestorben sey
17. Wann jemand verwundet und von einem andern gar entleibt wird
18. Won Entleibung in Rumoren
19. So die Diener der Oberkeit jemand entleibt hetten

Von Begnadigung der Todtschlägern

1. Wie die Ursach/so zu Entschüldigung bekanntlicher That vorgewendet
2. So deß Thäters gegebene Artickul nit schlessen.
3. Aber wen der Unkost inn obgemelter Ausführung gehen sol

So einer in der Mordacht were in Gefängnüßkeme/und sein unschuld außführen wollte
Von Ausführung beschüldigter peinlicher Ubelthat

Von Gewalt und Diebstal
Von Vergewaltigung/und was vorgewältigte Thaten

1. Von schlechtem/heimlichen Diebstal
2. Vom ersten öffentlichen Diebstal
3. Vom ersten gefährlichen Diebstal durch einsteigen und brechen
4. Vom ersten Diebstal
5. Vom andern und dritten Diebstal
6. Von mehr dann einerley beschwerung
7. Von jungen Diebn
8. So einer etwas heimlichs nimpt von Gott
9. Von stelen/so sich erwann begibt
10. Von stelen in Fewersnöthen
11. Wie mit denselben Dieben/so einem andern die Frücht auß dem Felde stelen
12. Von Holsstelen
13. Straff der Fischdiebe
14. Von Viehdieben
15. Diebstal heiliger dinge
16. Straff der jenigen/so den Zoll verfahren
17. Straff der untrew in hinderlegten Gütern
18. Von LeutVerkäuffern/ . . . die tote ausgraben

[. . .]
Form wie man die Straff aussprechen soll
Man soll und muß straffen
In Peinlichen Sachen soll man schleunig procedieren,

man soll in Peinlichen Sachen auff kein gemein Geschrey achten
Wann aber die Sache klar/und der beklagte nach der beweisung nit bekennen wollte Die straffe soll und muß allein auff die Schüldigen gehen
Von Execution und Vollziehung gesprochenen Urtheil inn Peinlichen Sachen
Von etlichen Fällen so sich vor unn nach der Execution und Vollziehung der End- urtheil zutragen und begeben
Von der verurtheilten Ubelthäer Haab und Gütern

This old text is not always completely clear and there was still no common German at least for legal matters, but a translation of these headings could read:

Of all the wrongs—Punishment all kinds of wrong [. . .]
Punishment of those who/seize imprisoned items/rape insane or senseless female persons,
Of adultery
Punishment of adultery/and what actually constitutes adultery . . .
Of external damage
Punishment of treason
Punishment of burnings
From pledges/
Of killings and internal damages
Punishment of those who use poison clandestinely . . .

Some excerpts follow on murder/and possible excuses

1. On self-defence in common
2. Of killing by negligence in and outside of the self-defence
3. Of resistance by a damaged person
4. So the killer was brought near death by the killed
5. The killing of a thief in the act of theft
6. Also killing in fencing and knight games
7. When children/the crazy/kill someone
8. Crimes of the very old
9. If the killing is time-barred
10. If the killing is out of justifiable wrath
11. Death or misdeed due to drunkenness
12. The son is spared on account of the father
13. So the killer reports other wrongdoers
14. When a killer is rather artificial
15. Of clerical killers
16. If any man is wounded, and dies thereafter/and one doubts/whether he dies because of the wounds
17. When a man is wounded and is even disembowelled by another

18. Rumours of disembodiment
19. If the servants of the lordship killed someone

Pardoning of killers

1. Regarding the cause/if presented to excuse the deed
2. In case the articles of the culprit disagree with one another
3. Who will have to pay for the prosecution

In case a suspected murderer is brought to prison/and wants to plead his innocence

Of the execution of culprits due to criminal offences
Of violence and theft
Of rape/and what was forewarned deeds

1. Of bad/clandestine theft
2. Of the first public theft
3. Of the first dangerous theft by entering and breaking
4. Of the first theft
5. Of the other and third theft
6. Of more than one complaint
7. Of young thieves
8. When one takes something secretly from God
9. Of thefts/in case they occur
10. Of thefts in great fires
11. How to deal with the same thieves who steal another man's fruit out of the field
12. Of stealing wood
13. Punishment of fish thieves
14. Of cattle thieves
15. Theft of sacred things
16. Punishment of those who violate customs duty
17. Punishment of one who violates his duties as depositee
18. Of criminals who sell people/or dig up the dead

[. . .]
Forms in which to pronounce the punishment
One should and must punish
In embarrassing matters one should proceed swiftly,
In criminal cases one should not listen to public clamour
But if the matter is clear/and the defendant does not want to confess after the proof
The punishment should and must go solely on the culprits.

Of Execution and realisation of Judgments pronounced in criminal cases
Of several cases/That occur and happen before or after the execution and realisation of the Final Judgment
Of the goods of condemned culprits

This long quotation shows that the 'Strafbüchlein' 'Little Book of Criminal Law' was in the end a compendium of criminal law. Here the offences were compiled very comprehensively, which Saur could get hold of in the literature. It lists a long collection of crimes, starting with adultery, continuing with burnings, seizures, killings, poisonings. A new section begins with murder and cases of justification and ends with pardons. It even explains what should happen if someone is innocent in jail. A new list deals with cases of violence and theft. It ends with rules on how to announce verdicts, and how to punish. In criminal matters, immediate procedure is seen as advisable. In criminal cases, no one should listen to public clamour.

Saur obviously begins his treatise with especially serious crimes. First of all, blasphemy is mentioned, perjury is certainly also considered a breach of a duty towards God and therefore serious, and special forms of apostasy from Christianity follow. However, with breaking of the original vow (i.e. the renunciation of violence after the trial) and then coin counterfeiting we see that rather secular offences are included in this group. It is not possible to present all the chapters here. It is sufficient to show that as criminal offences adulterations, a kind of fraud, adultery, and sexual crimes against women follow.

This work thus collects criminal offences from all perspectives and, almost like a modern legal order, these elements of crime are arranged according to legal interests. Only at the end of the compilation are some procedural questions included. In a less than elegant manner, residual questions are dealt with here, partly dealing with general principles of punishment, further consequences of punishment, for example confiscation of property or questions of execution. In this respect, this part is not a relapse into general procedural law, but rather concludes the work, which concentrates on criminal offences, with general rules of various kinds.

Some offence groups are only loosely linked by 'external damage' but, with homicides and another large chapter on murder cases and subsequent cases of sentence reduction, Saur also shows the ability to be systematic. This is followed by robbery and theft. Finally, procedural issues are raised that affect sentencing. Here, the justification of the necessity of punishment and speedy sentencing is not aimed at procedural issues. It concludes by once again dealing with general issues concerning criminal sentencing.

Saur himself referred to the *ius commune*, the Carolina (discussed earlier) and also the state laws, insofar as he found supra-locally applicable law in them, which he had evaluated for his compilation. But several shortcomings are obvious: the list demonstrates hardly any systemisation or any plan for weightier or lesser matters. The list comprises the forms of crimes, but not the rules and principles of criminal law. Here, *ius commune* had not been studied enough.

This work is less interested in defining the criteria for just punishment, as we found in the work of Tiraqueau. It is more interested in the collection of offences. The long list shows a wealth of heterogeneous offences and protected legal interests. It depicts a comprehensive, complex society concerned to keep up public morals.

Anton Matthaeus II

The Dutchman Anton Matthaeus II (1601–1654) is the second generation in a line of law professors with the same name. These three jurists are therefore always distinguished by numbers according to their generation.[50] Already the father, Anton Matthaeus I (1564–1637), had been a law professor in Marburg and Heidelberg. His son studied law in Marburg and Groningen and ended up as a professor in Utrecht. The grandson, Anton Matthaeus III, also became a professor of law at Leiden and Utrecht.

Anton Matthaeus II published a famous work 'De criminibus ad lib. XLVII et XLVIII Dig. Commentarius' in 1644. At first glance it is a classical commentary on one part of the Digests. But as it concentrates on the last books, as they were devoted to criminal law issues, for which reason Justinian called them the 'terribiles libri',[51] this work specialises in criminal prosecution. In a preface he introduced the concept of ***crimen*** in order to provide a parenthesis for the following texts. It becomes clear that Matthaeus, like Tiraqueau, wanted to give a coherent account of the legal issues of the ***crimen***. But this was not solely about criminal law. Even the introduction did not completely exclude civil law issues in this context. In this respect, Matthaeus II used an innovative approach, tying it into a conventional form, whereby the character as a special investigation of criminal law was lost.

Conclusion: The Age of Prevention

Looking at the important role of the 'Layenspiegel' and the 'Strafbüchlein' by Abraham Saur, the significant contribution of the unlearned or less learned literature of the early modern period becomes clear.[52] Was this due to the fact that these authors were not bound by convention, even in terms of book

50 Ritter von Eisenhart J A Art. Matthäus, Anton (1601 to 1654), in: ADB Bd. 20, 1884, 617–19.

51 Constitutio Tanta, c.8, in: T Mommsen and P Krüger (eds), *Corpus iuris civilis, volume primum: Institutiones et Digesta* (Weidmann 1920) 13f. 16.

52 R von Stintzing, *Geschichte der populären Literatur des römisch-kanonischen Rechts in Deutschland am Ende des fünfzehnten und im Anfang des sechszehnten Jahrhunderts* (Kessinger Publishing 1967); E Seckel, *Beiträge zur Geschichte beider Rechte im Mittelalter, vol 1: Zur Geschichte der populären Literatur des römisch-kanonischen Rechts* (Kessinger Publishing 1898 (reprint 1967)); R Feenstra, *Droit Savant au Moyen Age et sa Vulgarisation, Variorum* (Variorum Reprints 1986).

format, but presented a work that sought to explain legal issues in simple terms to an interested but not legally educated society? Their innovative impact was not so much the result of long effort but lies in the presentation of a current trend in the common vernacular. Indeed, Saur's expositions were very popular and saw numerous reprints. Nevertheless, he remained an isolated case. He could not find a new school, nor did other authors later choose to imitate him. In this respect, Saur was less paving the way than expressing a mood of his time.

The change occurred in the time of the Protestant Reformation not by chance. While from antiquity to the sixteenth century crimes were punished in order to re-establish justice, punishment was a sort of public response which was expected. In most cases this was not intended as vengeance because the Sermon on the Mount clearly interdicted such punishments. Nevertheless, punishment had to define a particular consequence for the convicted criminal. In the course of the Protestant Reformation, however, law was rather seen as a means to ameliorate men. It could be seen as a manual for the use of the people in order to learn what was prohibited and what kind of punishment it would ensue. In Calvin's theology, men could always hope for a chance of justification. Even the worst wrongdoer could be justified by God, so that nobody should lose his life after his criminal offence; instead penitentiaries should teach how to lead a better life. General prevention of crime became the main objective of criminal legislation and prosecution. The history of criminal law could be described in relation to the mix of prevailing purposes of criminal prosecution.

As a result, one did not have to wait for Feuerbach and the generation that preceded him to find textbooks of criminal law in Germany. Their presentation of their sources is not consistently honest. It is true that Feuerbach referred extensively to Roman, canonical and imperial law as sources of criminal law,[53] thus inscribing his subject in the tradition of *ius civile* and *ius canonicum*. But this obscures the existence of criminal law as an independent subject in his scheme. Likewise, the independence of the sources is thereby ignored.

However, the actual proliferation of criminal law literature before and again after 1800 means that it was not until the establishment of fundamental rights in the Declaration of the Rights of Man and of the Citizen in 1789 that penal law as a *lex certa* and *praevia* demanded its own dogmatics. As long as conventional doctrine could still be applied on criminal laws, there were few reasons for a separate dogmatic treatment of criminal law.

As a result, it can be confirmed that the differentiation of a substantive criminal law as a separate subject of law was the consequence of the Protestant Reformation and its associated idea of social disciplining. Although the works mentioned here are less direct sources of the Reformation, they reflect a new understanding of the use of punishments. Tengler and Saur were influenced

53 JAP Feuerbach, *Lehrbuch des gemeinen in Deutschland gültigen peinlichen Rechts* (Giessen 1808) Prolegomena, §1, 4.

by and rooted in the teachings of the Reformation, though not theologians themselves. Among French authors, one finds from the 1530s onward that one's denomination was not made known in order to safeguard the appearance of remaining in the Roman Catholic Church.[54] But on the whole, French Protestant theologians like Calvin and Guillaume Farel before them had a very strong influence on France during this time, which is reflected in a widespread desire to codify the French law. The 'Ordonnance de Villers-Cotterêt' of 1539 was an important step for the development of the new French criminal law. It also stated that only French should be used in laws and in court.[55] This comes close to Melanchthon's idea of laws as manuals.

When transferring theological thoughts to law, one must also bear in mind that each subject has its own tasks, forms of expression, methods and standards, as Melanchthon already taught. In the search for theological influences, therefore, literal repetitions may not be conclusive. We must rather find material connections, in which ideas were taken over and changed. Here, the shaping of substantive criminal law as a separate subject in order to dogmatise punishment was a reaction to ideas which can already be found in the works of Melanchthon and others. Furthermore, it followed originally Lutheran convictions on the duty of the prince as a sword over the land, to establish peace and order in the country, and to prescribe for individuals how each was to behave in his situation.[56] In this process, criminal law took over functions that had previously been performed by the church and that, in the Roman Catholic sphere, were to be increasingly performed by confessors after the Council of Trent. The train of secularisation and the soteriological function of state and law betray the influences of the Reformation.

Bibliography

Achter V, *Geburt der Strafe* (V. Klostermann 1951)

Althusius J, *Dicaeologicae libri tres* (1649 (2nd edn, reprint 1967))

Andrea Marchisello, '"Abréviation des process": Le strategie dell'Ordonnance di Villers-Cotterêts (1539) per la riforma dell'amministratzionde della giustizia' in G Rossi (ed), *Il rinascimento giuridico in Francia* (2008)

Brejon J, *Un jurisconsulte de la Renaissance. André Tiraqueau (1488–1558)* (1937)

Bretone M, *Geschichte des römischen Rechts. Von den Anfängen bis zu Justinian* (1992) 194

Carpzov B, *Practica novae imperialiis saxonicae Rerum Criminalium* (1635)

54 M Schmoeckel, 'La Réforme à la française: liberté religieuse et stabilité du royaume' in F Jankowiak et al. (eds), *Mélanges Brigitte Basdevant-Gaudemet* (Universite Paris-Saclay 2022).

55 A Esmein, *Histoire de la procédure criminelle en France* (Paris 1892 ND Frankfurt a.M. 1969) 139; E Dezza, 'Pour pourvoir au bien de notre justice. Legislazioni statali, processo penale e modulo inquisitorio nell'Europa des XVI secolo' (2002) 1 *Acta historicae* 7–38, 15; Andrea Marchisello, 'Abréviation des process': Le strategie dell'Ordonnance di Villers-Cotterêts (1539) per la riforma dell'amministratzionde della giustizia, in G Rossi (ed), *Il rinascimento giuridico in Francia* (2008) 179–200, 184f.

56 Schmoeckel (n 41) 149f.

Casonus F, *Quaestiones criminales* (1584)

Dezza E, 'Pour pourvoir au bien de notre justice. Legislazioni statali, processo penale e modulo inquisitorio nell'Europa des XVI secolo' (2002) 1 *Acta historicae* 7–38, 15

Dingel I and Schäufele WF (eds), *Kommunikation und Transfer im Christentum der Frühen Neuzeit, VIEG.B 74* (Verlag Mainz : Philipp von Zabern 2007) 157–91

Dingel I 'Gute Ordnung. Ordnungsmodelle der Reformation und ihre Wirkung' in W Kinzig and J Winnebeck (eds), *Glaube und Theologie. Reformatorische Grundeinsichten in der ökumenischen Diskussion, VWGTh 54 (Evangelische Verlagsanstalt* 2019) 293–308

Esmein A, *Histoire de la procédure criminelle en France* (1892 reprint 1969) 139

Feenstra R, *Droit Savant au Moyen Age et sa Vulgarisation, Variorum* (1986)

Feuerbach JAP, *Lehrbuch des gemeinen in Deutschland gültigen peinlichen Rechts* (1808)

Firey A (ed), *A New History of Penance* (2008); Larson A, *Master of Penance: Gratian and the Development of Penitential Thought and Law in the Twelfth Century* (Studies in Medieval and Early Modern Canon Law, Band 11) (Catholic University of America Press 2014)

Flach D, *Die Gesetze der frühen römischen Republik* (Wissenschaftliche Buchgesellschaft 1994)

Fraher R, 'Tancred's Summa de criminibus' (1979) 9 BMCL 23–35

Gagnon F, *Le Corrector sive Medicus de Murchard de Worms (1000–1025): Présentation, traduction et commentaire éthno-historique, Mémoire présenté à l aFaculté des études supérieures en vue de l'obention du grade de Maitre ès arts (M.A.) en histoire* (Université de Montréal 2010) <https://papyrus.bib.umontreal.ca/xmlui/handle/1866/4915> accessed 3 August 2022

Geib G, *Geschichte des römischen Criminalprozesses bis zum Tode Konstantins* (1842) 411; Santalucia B, *Diritto e processo penale nell'antica Roma* (1989); more cautiously Scognamiglio M, *Nullum crimen sine lege. Origini storiche del divieto di analogia in materia criminale* (2009) passim

Goering J, 'The Internal Forum and the Literature of Penance and Confession' (2004) 59 Traditio 175–227

Gottlieb Heumann and Erich Seckel H, *Handlexikon zu den Quellen des römischen Rechts*, Jena 91907, 435 sub 1b): 'Privatstrafe'

Gouron A, 'On the Origins of Criminal Law: The First Criminal Law Treatises' in K Kroeschell (ed), *Festschrift für H. Thieme zu seinem 80. Geburtstag* (1986)

Halperin J-L, 'Tiraqueau André' in Patrick Arabeyre, Jean-Louis Halpérin, and Jacques Krynen (eds), *Dictionnaire historique des juristes français XIIe-XXe siècle* (2007) 742f

Härter K and Stolleis M (eds), *Repertorium der Policeyordnungen der Frühen Neuzeit, Studien zur europäischen Rechtsgeschichte 84, vol 1: Deutsches Reich* (1996)

Irene Dingel, 'Gute Ordnung. Ordnungsmodelle der

Kantorowicz H Il, 'Tractatus criminum' in Helmut Coing and Gerhard Immerl (eds), *Per il cinquantenario della 'Rivista penale' fondata e diretta da Luigi Lucchini, Città di Castello 1925, 361–376 = Rechtshistorische Schriften* (1970) 273–85

Kinzig W and Winnebeck J (eds), *Glaube und Theologie. Reformatorische Grundeinsichten in der ökumenischen Diskussion, VWGTh 54* (2019) 293–308

Kohler J and Scheel W, *Die Carolina und ihre Vorgängerinnen. Text, Explanation, History, 4 volumes, Halle a.S. 1900/02* (reprint 1968)

Landau P, 'Ne crimina maneant impunita. Zur Entstehung des öffentlichen Strafanspruchs in der Rechtswissenschaft des 12. Jahrhunderts' in M Schmoeckel u.a. (Hg.), *Der Einfluss der Kanonistik auf die europäische Rechtskultur, Band 3: Straf- und Straprozessrecht* (Norm und Struktur, 37.3) (2012)

Lausberg M, 'Seneca and Plato (Calcidius) in the Preface to the Saturnalia of Macrobius' (1991) RMP 167–91

Lotte Kéry L, *Gottesfurcht und irdische Strafen: Der Beitrag des mittelalterlichen Kirchenrechts zur Entstehung des öffentlichen Strafrechts* (2006)

Maihold H, *The Grounding of Modern Criminal Law in Christian Theology* (Kansai University Review of Law and Politics 2018)

Mäkinen V (ed), *Lutheran Reformation and the Law* (Brill 2006)

Minucci G (ed), *Tractatus criminum Saeculi XII* (Archi. Per La Storia Diritto Med. E Mod. 1997)

Mommsen T, *Römisches Strafrecht* (Duncker 1899) (1899, reprint 1961)

Mommsen T and Krüger P (eds), *Corpus iuris civilis, volume primum: Institutiones et Digesta* (1920) 13f. 16

Naucke W, 'Straftheorie, Strafzweck' in *HRG* (1st edn, 1998) vol. 5

Nehlsen H, 'Entstehung des öffentlichen Strafrechts bei den germanischen Stämmen' in *Freiburger Festkolloquium für Hans Thieme, Gerichtslauben-Vorträge* (1983) 3–16

Padovani A, *Perché chiedi il mio nome? Dio, natura e diritto nel secolo XII* (Milan 1997)

Pahlmann B, 'Ulrich Tengler (c. 1447–1511)' in Gerd Kleinheyer and Jan Schröder (eds), *Deutsche und Europäische Juristen* (2017)

Petschow H, 'Zur Systematik und Gesetzestechnik im Codex Hammurabi' (1967) 57 ZA 146–72: 149

Pfeiffer G, 'Lex Hammurapi' in M Schmoeckel and Stolte (eds), *Examinatorium Rechtsgeschichte* (Vahlen 2008)

Reformation und ihre Wirkung' in W Kinzig and J Winnebeck (eds), *Glaube und Theologie. Reformatorische Grundeinsichten in der ökumenischen Diskussion, VWGTh 54 (Evangelische Verlagsanstalt 2019)* 293–308

Ritter von Eisenhart JA, 'Art. Matthäus, Anton (1601 to 1654)' in ADB (1884), Bd 20, 617–19

Schilling A, 'Nemo prudens punit quia peccatum est sed ne peccetur—Strafen und Strafzwecke im römischen Strafrecht' (2015) 21 ZAR

Schmelzeisen, G, 'Policeiordnungen' in *HRG* (1984), Bd. 3, 1803–1808; Stolleis M (ed), *Policey im Europa der Frühen Neuzeit, Studien zur europäischen Rechtsgeschichte 83* (Frankfurt am Main: Klostermann 1996)

Schmitz HJ, *Bußbücher und das kanonische Bußverfahren* (1883, reprint 1958) vol. 1

Schmoeckel M, *Humanität und Staatsraison. Die Abschaffung der Folter in Europa und die Entwicklung des gemeinentlichen Strafprozeß- und Beweisrechts seit dem hohen Mittelalter*, Norm und Struktur 14 (2000)

Schmoeckel M, 'Metanoia. Die Reformation und der Strafzweck der Besserung' in Schulze R u.a. (eds), *Strafzweck und Strafform zwischen religiöser und weltlicher Wertevermittlung, Symbolische Kommunikation und gesellschaftliche Wertesystem 25* (2008) 29–58

Schmoeckel M (ed), *Der Einfluss der Kanonistik auf die europäische Rechtskultur, Band 3: Straf- und Straprozessrecht* (Norm und Struktur, 37.3) (2012) 23–35

Schmoeckel M, *Die Jugend der Justitia (Archäologie der Gerechtigkeit im Prozessrecht der Patristik* (2013)

Schmoeckel M, *Recht der Reformation* (Mohr Siebeck 2014)

Schmoeckel M, 'Bertachinus J und die Entstehung des gelehrten Steuerstrafrechts'in Bernhard Kretschmer and Benno Zabel B (eds), *Studien zur Geschichte des Wirtschaftsstrafrechts. Methoden—Analysen—Kritik* (2018) 433–49

Schmoeckel M, *Canon Law* (Tübingen Mohr Siebeck 2019)

Schmoeckel M, 'Retaliation. Christian Reasons for Punishment: An Overview' in M Hill, N Doe, RH Helmholz, and J Witte (eds), *Christianity and Criminal Law (Law and Religion)* (Routledge 2020) 62–79

Schmoeckel M, 'La Réforme à la française: liberté religieuse et stabilité du royaume' in Fr. Jankowiak et al. (eds), *Mélanges Brigitte Basdevant-Gaudemet* (2022)
Schulze R, 'Reformation (Source of Law)' in *HRG* (1990) vol 4, 468–72; Gerhard Dilcher, Stadtrecht, in: *HRG* (1990) vol 4
Seckel E, *Beiträge zur Geschichte beider Rechte im Mittelalter, vol 1: Zur Geschichte der populären Literatur des römisch-kanonischen Rechts* (1898 (reprint 967))
Simon T, 'Erziehungsgedanke in den frühneuzeitlichen Polizeiordnungen' in Eva Schumann (ed), *Das erziehende Gesetz, AAWG 30* (Göttingen 2013) 59–74
Sorice R, *Vittime Colpevoli e colpevoli innocenti. Ricerche sulle responsabilità penali nell'età del diritto comune* (Diritto cultura società. Storia e probleme della giustizia criminale, 11) (Bononia University Press 2018)
Tiraquellus A, *De poenis Legum, ac Consuetudinum, Statutorumque temperandis, aut etiam remittendis, & id quibus quotque ex causis* (1559 (reprint [in excerpts] 1986))
Virpi Mäkinen V (ed), *Lutheran Reformation and the Law* (Brill 2006)
von Schulte JF (ed), *Festschrift zur Feier des 22. Dezember 1888, an welchem vor 50 Jahren Geheimrat Prof. Dr. Bernhard Windscheid in Bonn zum Doctor iuris utriusque promoviert wurde* (1888) 7–15
von Stintzing R, *Geschichte der populären Literatur des römisch-kanonischen Rechts in Deutschland am Ende des fünfzehnten und im Anfang des sechszehnten Jahrhunderts* (1967)
WeitzelJ (ed), *Hoheitliches Strafen in der Spätantike und im frühen Mittelalter, Konflikt, Verbrechen und Sanktion in der Gesellschaft Alteuropas, Symposien und Synthesen 7* (2002)
Witte J Jr., *Christianity and Law: An Introduction* (CUP 2008)

13 The Reformation and Its Impact on the Law of Charities and Social Welfare

John Duddington

Introduction: What Was Actually Entailed by Charity and Social Welfare?

Charity is exercised by organisations and individuals. So far as organisations are concerned a main although not exclusive pre-Reformation source was monasteries. Writing of the period immediately before their dissolution between 1535–1540, James Clark said that

> While their performance of spiritual services aroused some suspicion,[1] it was widely agreed that that the religious houses still made a vital contribution to the whole spectrum of social welfare, from hospitality to charity and health care.[2]

Clark notes 'a widespread perception of a growing welfare problem' in the early years of Henry VIII's reign which, if true, would have added to the importance of the charitable role of monasteries.

Moreover monasteries also provided education and monastic schools, in addition to providing education for the novices, and often educated children destined for a lay career. Not only monasteries provided schools, for as Clark says, 'By 1509 there was a grammar school within geographical reach of most of England's provincial population'.[3] Some of these schools were founded and run by the clergy but others appear to have been secular.[4] There was also a growing tendency in the thirteenth and fourteenth centuries towards some degree of secularisation in, for example, the hospital movement also. Lindberg points out that 'the process of rationalisation and laicisation is evident in the growing specialisation, administrative, research and therapeutic concerns of

1 The basis of this suspicion was the belief that in some cases there was a transactional element involved: benefactions made to monasteries resulted in spiritual benefits to the donor.

2 J Clark, *The Dissolution of the Monasteries: A New History* (Yale UP 2021) 135.

3 Ibid 59.

4 See the examples collected by Clark (n 2) 59.

DOI: 10.4324/9780429264115-17

the numerous hospitals founded before the mid-fifteenth century'.[5] Another instance of the growing secularisation of charitable activity lies in the inability of the church in the later Middle Ages to deal with the increase in what Lindberg calls 'the massive pauperism arising from the social, demographic, economic, political and natural consequences of the late Middle Ages'.[6]

Charity and the Law

The Law of Succession

The impact of secular law on charitable giving in England was felt largely through the law of wills and the developing law of charity, because individual gifts to charity were often made by will and, in order to facilitate these gifts, the law developed certain principles which became the law of charitable gifts.[7]

Helmholz observes that: 'Securing the enforcement of charitable bequests was the stated reason for canonical intervention in the law of succession'.[8] Thus the ecclesiastical courts intervened to uphold charitable bequests precisely because it was in their interests to do so, because the gift was, in most cases, made for ecclesiastical purposes and this led, by the time of Henry III (1216–1272), to the ecclesiastical courts claiming jurisdiction over the law of wills and intestacy and, because the church applied Roman law, the result was that principles of Roman law influenced the English law of succession.[9] It appears that this was initially less so on the Continent, where Brundage points out that in Germany the preference was for inheritance by rule rather than by disposition, although it appears that by the eleventh century the desire for more flexible inheritance practices led to an increasing use of disposition by will. At the Reformation the ecclesiastical courts continued to exercise testamentary jurisdiction[10] until this was transferred to the Court of Probate by the Court of Probate Act, 1857. In this respect we can say that the Reformation has had little effect on the law and instead we see continuity between pre- and post-Reformation practice.

It is worth noting that the Reformation did appear to have an effect, not on the law of wills itself, but on the form of bequests in wills. Dickens studied the religious phraseology of wills in two counties, Nottinghamshire and Yorkshire, in the middle decades of the sixteenth century, when Protestant thinking was

5 C Lindberg, *Beyond Charity: Reformation Initiatives for the Poor* (Fortress Press 1993) 58.

6 Ibid 66.

7 In addition, charitable gifts were often held under a trust, which in turn contributed to the development of the law of trusts and of the system of equity: see Ch. 10.

8 R Helmholz, *The Oxford History of the Laws of England Vol 1: The Canon Law and Ecclesiastical Jurisdiction from 597 to the 1640s* (OUP 2004) 417. See also Chapter 3 of this volume.

9 Although the common law did manage to claim jurisdiction over debt claims against the estate of the deceased.

10 Subject to a gap from the Civil War to the Restoration—1643–1661.

beginning to make itself felt. The traditional form of bequest was to bequeath one's soul not only to Christ but also to the Blessed Virgin and the saints. However, he noted that from 1537–1538 a small but growing minority 'do not merely omit the saints, but also use positively Protestant language, stressing salvation through the merits of Christ alone'.[11]

The Law on Charitable Gifts: General

If we turn to charitable gifts we see instances, not so much of continuity from Roman law but instead the development of legal principles that have survived the Reformation. A decretal of Pope Gregory IX (1227–1241) strongly urged the faithful to seek salvation by the bequest of their wealth to 'pious causes',[12] and this was one instance of continued exhortations by the medieval church to this effect. The result was a flow of bequests for the repair of religious houses, monasteries and churches, for vestments, candles and incense and for the saying of masses and the upkeep of chantries. Charitable gifts for pious causes were given very favourable treatment by the courts and the effect of this is seen today, especially in two important areas of charity law.

The first is in the rule that, unlike private trusts, a gift to be held on charity will not fail where the objects are indefinite and as Jones says: 'generous rules of construction were developed to cure the uncertainty'.[13] Thus a gift to 'the church' was deemed to be to the parish church and one 'to the poor' was held to go to the poor of the parish given that the testator was buried there.[14] Moreover, where there is a clear intention to set up a charitable trust, the courts will endeavour to construe any wording so that, where possible, the trust is upheld.[15] Furthermore by section 69(1) of the Charities Act 2011 the Charity Commission has concurrent jurisdiction with the High County to establish a scheme for the administration of a charity. This could be used where the gift is so vague as to be only 'for charitable purposes' as well as in other cases.[16]

The second is the rule that, where on the construction of the charitable gift, it is impossible to carry out the wishes of the testator lawfully then the gift can be applied for purposes *cy-près* (so near) to those intended by the testator. One example would be a gift to a school which had either never existed or had ceased to exist. The evidence is that canon lawyers, before the Reformation, applied property *cy-près* and indeed the principle was known to Roman law following which, as Jones says, 'by the beginning of the seventeenth century

11 AG Dickens, *The English Reformation* (2nd edn, Batsford 1969) 214–15.

12 G Jones, *History of the Law of Charity 1532–1827* (CUP 1969) 3.

13 Ibid 5.

14 Ibid.

15 See Hailsham LC in *IRC v McMullen* (1981) AC 1.14.

16 Another advantage of a charitable trust in that it is not subject to the rule against inalienability which is part of the rule against perpetuities. See esp. R Maudsley, *The Modern Law of Perpetuities* (Butterworths 1979) 178–83.

it is a sophisticated and mature doctrine'.[17] It still applies today with a recent example being *Knipe v British Racing Drivers Motor Sport Charity*.[18]

The Law on Charitable Gifts: Gifts for the Saying of Masses for the Dead and for the Upkeep of Chantries

The Seven Corporal Works of Mercy are followed in the Catholic tradition by the Seven Spiritual Works of Mercy of which the last is 'to pray for the living and the dead'.[19] Praying for the living caused no difference at the Reformation but what of praying for the dead? The constant teaching of the Catholic Church is that those who have died can benefit from the prayers of the living. The result was twofold: gifts were left by will for the saying of masses for departed souls, often the soul of the testator, and then, as McCulloch says 'the medieval West developed a legally founded and endowed institution intended to regularise the prayer of Masses in saving an individual, a family or a group of associates: this was the chantry'.[20] These chantries employed priests to say the masses and the founder gave the chantry an endowment of land or of income intended to last in perpetuity.[21]

Chantry chapels soon became a target of the Reformation. The first attack was as early as 1531 where a statute (23.Hen.8.Ch.10) forbad trusts of hereditaments[22] for the purpose of having 'obits' (annual masses) said for any period longer than 20 years. Trusts for longer periods were, however, not affected. The real attack came in the Dissolution of Colleges Act 1547[23] where the preamble made the position clear by referring to the 'doctrine and vain opinion' of Purgatory and Masses which was continued out of 'blindness and ignorance'. Thus all chantries were by this statute vested in the King. There are two peculiarities to this Act, which were for a time overlooked.[24] The first is that it did not forbid the creation of new chantries but only suppressed existing ones and second that it did not forbid gifts for the saying of masses. However, the preamble was expressed in such forceful terms that the courts treated it as forbidding both.[25] The conclusion can only be that 'it was the policy of the law to

17 Jones (n 12) 74. See pps. 72–91 for a full account of the development of this doctrine.
18 (2020) EWHC 2988 (Ch.).
19 In the *Catechism of Christian Doctrine* (Burns and Oates 1921) (the old 'penny' catechism) the Corporal Works are set out in Answer 321 and the Spiritual Works at Answer 322.
20 D McCulloch, *The Reformation Europe's House Divided 1490–1700* (Penguin Books 2003) 12. McCulloch points out that the word 'chantry' is from *cantaria*—a place for singing given that masses were generally sung.
21 See N Orme, *Going to Church in Medieval England* (Yale UP 2022) 51–52.
22 Property that can be inherited e.g. land.
23 1 Edward VI c.14. Often called the Abolition of Chantries Act.
24 I have derived great assistance in writing this whole section from WS Lilly and AP Wallis (eds), *A Manual of the Law Specially Affecting Catholics* (Wm. Clowes 1893).
25 A further Act of 1559 (1 Eliz. C.24) referred to gifts for masses and prayers for the souls of the departed but appears to be retrospective only.

enforce uniformity of religion according to the doctrines of the Reformation, and to repress all doctrines opposed to it'.[26]

Thus the matter rested until the series of statutes, beginning in 1778, which by gradual stages relaxed the penal laws and permitted Catholics to exercise their religion without legal penalty. At this point the question of the validity of bequests for the saying of masses was bound to arise and when it did two questions would require an answer: Was the gift valid at all and, if it was, was it charitable?

Under the Roman Catholic Charities Act, 1832 it was lawful for Roman Catholics to acquire and hold property necessary for religious education, worship and charitable purposes. Thus, a gift to build a Roman Catholic church would be valid. However, in *West v Shuttleworth*,[27] where the question first arose, it was made clear that this did not apply to gifts for masses. Pepys MR held that there had never been any express statutory prohibition of trusts of masses for the dead but this made no difference, as he observed that the Dissolution of Colleges Act 1547

> has been considered as establishing the illegality of certain gifts, and, amongst others, the giving of legacies to priests to pray for the soul of the donor has, in many cases . . . been decided to be within the superstitious uses intended to be suppressed by that statute.

There the matter rested until *Bourne v Keane*[28] finally recognised the actual effect of the Dissolution of Colleges Act 1547 and *West v Shuttleworth* was overruled. Here the testator made a bequest to Westminster Cathedral for masses and gave his residuary personal estate to 'the Jesuit Fathers, Farm Street', for masses. The court took the point that there was a logical inconsistency in holding that the Roman Catholic Charities Act, 1832 allowed a gift to, for instance, build a church and then to go and hold that a gift for the celebration of masses in that church was invalid.

This decision, welcome as it was, did not end the matter, as the final step had still to be taken of holding that these trusts could be charitable. Until then they were still imperilled by the twin threats of the rule against non-charitable purpose trusts and the rule against perpetuities.[29]

In *Re Caus*[30] Luxmoore J. held that trusts for masses were charitable but then the speech of Lord Simonds in *Gilmour* v. *Coats*[31] cast doubt on the

26 Lilly and Wallis (n 24) 143.

27 2 My and K. 684.

28 [1919] A.C. 815.

29 See Hanbury and Martin, *Modern Equity* (J Glister and J Lee, eds) (22nd edn, Sweet and Maxwell 2021) esp. Ch. 16.

30 [1934] Ch. 162.

31 [1949] A.C. 426.

whether the offering of prayer by itself could in fact be a charitable object.[32] However, in *Re Hetherington*[33] Browne-Wilkinson VC finally settled the question by holding that the gifts in wills for the celebration of masses were charitable. He accepted expert evidence[34] that '[t]here is no obligation to celebrate the Mass in public as a matter of canon law' but he held that:

> Where there is a gift for a religious purpose which could be carried out in a way which is beneficial to the public (i.e. by public Masses) but could also be carried out in a way which would not have sufficient element of public benefit (i.e. by private Masses) the gift is to be construed as a gift to be carried out only by the methods that are charitable, all non-charitable methods being excluded.[35]

Moreover the element of public benefit was also to be found in the endowment of the priesthood.

Charities After the Reformation

The fundamental Christian impulse to charitable giving remained altered by the Reformation but it underwent a change due to the growing secularisation of society. Moreover Protestantism had a different attitude from Catholicism as to what should constitute objects of charity. In addition the Reformation cannot be viewed as a religious movement *per se:* it was itself the product of movements in society which had been in progress long before as we saw earlier in relation to, for instance, hospitals and also schools where grammar schools were founded by both clergy and laity in the late Middle Ages.

Influence of Secularisation on Charitable Giving

The secularisation of education gathered impetus after the Reformation. McCulloch notes that in France, for instance, 'the evangelical message was encouraged . . . by a movement to establish colleges (town schools) independent of church control'[36] and this was typical of many countries. In England, as Jones puts it: 'The objects of charity were to become more secular as the majority of Englishmen reflected less on the fate of their souls and became

32 In this case it was the offering of prayer by enclosed nuns.

33 [1990] Ch. 1.

34 It is noteworthy how much use the courts made in this case and in *Re Caus* of the nature of the mass. Would the admission of such evidence have made any difference in *West v Shuttleworth*?

35 This is really an application of the principle stated by Lord Hailsham put it in *IRC v McMullen* and referred to earlier: 'where it can be claimed that there is an ambiguity, a benignant construction should be given if possible'.

36 McCulloch (n 20) 197.

more concerned with the worldly needs of their fellow men'.[37] However, it is still true that as Rivers says,[38] 'The dissolution of the monasteries by Henry VIII in the early 1530' removed at a stroke the central medieval institutions for the relief of the poor, the orphaned, the sick and the aged and other ways had to be found to relieve particular needs.

In England there was an increasing process of government control of charitable giving which culminated in the Statute of Charitable Uses of 1601, which remained in force until the Charities Act, 2006.[39] The preamble to the statute set out a comprehensive list of good, 'godly, and charitable uses', which remain influential to this day, and established county commissions to inquire into breaches of trust and other misuses of charitable funds.[40] The fact that the words of the statute were couched in essentially secular terms shows the effect of the move away from charity as something regulated by the church and the increasing secularisation of society.

Changing Ideas of Charity

Ideas of what exactly is charity were undoubtedly changing before the Reformation with, to take but one example, the distinction between those poor who are 'worthy' and those not appearing in the Nuremberg Begging Order of 1478.[41] Even so, the Reformation gave a theological underpinning to many pre-existing legislative and administrative developments and accelerated them. As John Witte says:

> The Lutheran reformers rejected traditional teachings of both the spiritual idealisation of poverty and the spiritual efficaciousness of charity. All persons were called to do the work of God in the world, they argued; they were not to be idle or impoverished.[42]

Richard Tawney reinforces this point by observing that: 'the idleness of the mendicant[43] was both a sin against God and a social evil; the enterprise of the tradesman was at once a Christian virtue and a benefit to the community'.[44] This belief that only the 'worthy poor' were worthy recipients of charity, which persisted until at least Victorian times in England, had a major effect on how

37 Jones (n 12) 10.
38 J Rivers, *The Law of Organised Religions* (OUP 2010) 268.
39 The legislation is now mainly in the Charities Act, 2911.
40 The background to the Statute and its later history is explained in Jones (n 12) 22–56.
41 See fn. 11.
42 J Witte, *Law and Protestantism: The Legal Teachings of the Protestant Reformation* (CUP 2002) 20.
43 The reference is presumably to the mendicant friars although the categorisation of them as idle would be strongly disputed.
44 RH Tawney, *Religion and the Rise of Capitalism* (Pelican Books 1926) 123.

the state dealt with poverty. Here we can see the influence of the Reformation on the use of local boards and individuals, such as local justices in England, rather than the Church, with a direction to only reward the 'worthy poor'.

Conclusion

The view of Nicholas Orme[45] that 'Church congregations in Tudor England still lived in the world that had come into being when the Roman Emperors became Christian in the fourth century' is true in a broad sense of the charitable activities of churches and their members. Nevertheless, as the preceding chapter has shown, there were considerable changes afoot which would increasingly manifest themselves in counties affected by the spread of Protestantism even though the fundamental Christian impulse of charity remained constant across all branches of what was now a divided Christendom.

Bibliography

Clark J, *The Dissolution of the Monasteries: A New History* (Yale UP 2021)
Dickens AG, *The English Reformation* (2nd edn, Batsford 1969)
Hanbury and Martin, *Modern Equity* (J. Glister and J. Lee, eds) (22nd edn, Sweet and Maxwell 2021)
Helmholz R, *The Oxford History of the Laws of England, vol One, the Canon Law and Ecclesiastical Jurisdiction from 1597 to the 1640's* (OUP 2004)
Jones G, *History of the Law of Charity'1532–1827* (CUP 1969)
Lilly WS and Wallis AP, *A Manual of the Law Specially Affecting Catholics* (Wm. Clowes 1893)
Lindberg C, *Beyond Charity: Reformation Initiatives for the Poor* (Fortress Press 1993)
McCulloch D, *The Reformation Europe's House Divided 1490–1700* (Penguin Books 2003)
Orme N, *Going to Church in Medieval England* (Yale UP 2022)
Tawney RH, *Religion and the Rise of Capitalism* (Pelican Books 1926)
Witte J. Jr., *Law and Protestantism: The Legal Teachings of the Protestant Reformation* (CUP 2002)

45 Orme (n 21) at p. 394.

Index

Made in the USA
Las Vegas, NV
19 September 2026

b2a5ddb0-f52c-4f97-8da8-c938116b679aR01